Biostatistical Applications in Health Research

For information address:

Stat-Aid, Inc.
525 Anderson Ave
Rockville, MD 20850
VOICE: 301-279-7839
FAX: 301-251-7868
stat-aid.com

ISBN (10 digit) 0-9641832-1-8
ISBN (13 digit) 978-0-9641832-1-6

Library of Congress Control Number: 2006905354

CONTENTS

NOTICES

The examples in this text are not intended to be a reflection of good clinical practice nor are they intended to provide information on use of medications. Most the examples use data that have been created or modified to illustrate statistical methods.

SAS is a registered trademark of the SAS Institute, Inc.

PART ONE

Basic Concepts

Statisticians are used to dealing with uncertainty. Even so, there is one fact of which even statisticians are certain. That is the fact that we, as health researchers and practitioners, are always interested in applying the results of a study to persons, places, and/or times that were not included in the study. Rather, our purpose is to interpret a study's observations as they relate to some larger group. In statistical terms, the larger group is called the **population** and the smaller group is called the **sample**. As we interpret health research data from a particular sample, it is always with the intention of using the sample's observation to draw some conclusion about the population from which that sample was taken.

Since we are always in the position of using a sample to understand the population, it is important that we take samples so that each one is representative of the population. Unfortunately, we do not know how to do that. To appreciate the problem, let us think about a population that we understand completely. For instance, suppose we were to think about a deck of 52 cards. In this "population" there are two characteristics of its members: suit and rank. These characteristics are distributed uniformly among the members of the population, so that there are 13 cards in each of four suits and each suit has 13 ranks from deuce to ace. Now, thinking of that well-defined population, which five cards would you use to communicate the structure of the population?

If you feel frustrated with that question it is because there is no completely correct answer. Any set of five cards fails to communicate precisely the structure of the deck. If we are unable to select a representative sample from such a well-defined population, imagine selecting a representative sample from a population that is really of interest to health researchers. It just cannot be done!

Even though we do not know how to make each sample representative of the population, we do know how to make a collection of samples representative of the population. We can do that with the deck of 52 cards by shuffling the deck and dealing several "samples" of five cards. In other words, we could let chance determine which members of the population are going to be included in each sample. Any particular hand of five cards might be distinctly unrepresentative of the deck, but if we continued to deal hands of five cards, in the long run those hands would represent the deck. We do the same thing when we take samples from populations as part of research. We let chance determine which members of the population end up in the sample.

It is this principle of **random sampling** that makes it necessary to understand this role of chance when we are interested in interpreting the results of health research. The primary purpose of statistics is to consider how chance influences that interpretation. To be interpreters of health research data, we need to recognize that the samples we examine might, just by chance, be substantially different from the rest of the population. To do that, we need to be comfortable interpreting the results of statistical analyses. It is the purpose of this text to help you develop that level of comfort.

To understand statistics, we need to understand how chance influences observations in a sample and how the role of chance can be taken into account. Thus, we begin this text by examining the characteristics of chance and how we can use the sample's observations to draw conclusions about the population. First, in Chapter 1 we will look at chance itself to understand how it works. Next, in Chapter 2 we will examine the characteristics of a population to discover how its data can be described. Finally, in Chapter 3 we will concentrate on the sample to see how the sample's observations can be used to describe the population. Once we understand these basic principles, we will be ready to take a look at statistical procedures that are commonly used in health research.

CHAPTER 1
Thinking about Chance

In the introduction to this first part of the text, we learned that chance is used to select samples from the population that are, in the long run, representative of the population from which they came (Figure 1-1). Before we can appreciate how chance influences the composition of those samples, however, we need to understand some things about chance itself. In this chapter, we will look at the basic properties of chance and see how the chances of individual events can be combined to address health issues.

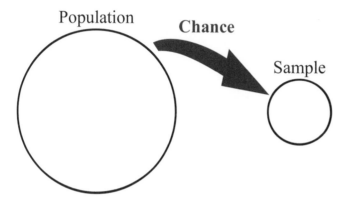

Figure 1-1 Chance determines which data values in the population end up in the sample.

To begin, we should point out that there are two terms that can be used interchangeably: **chance** and **probability**. In everyday language, probability (or chance) tells how many times something happens relative to the number of times it could happen. For example, we might think of the probability that a patient presenting with a sore throat has streptococcal pharyngitis. If we can expect 1 patient to actually have streptococcal pharyngitis out of every 10 patients seen with a sore throat, then the probability of having streptococcal pharyngitis is 0.10. Or equivalently, there is a 10% chance that a person selected at random from among persons with sore throats would have strep throat.

In statistical terminology, the number of times something happens is called its **frequency** and that "something" is called an **event**. The opportunities for an event to occur are called **observations**.[1] When using the concept of probability, we need to understand that there are two possible results for each observation: either the event occurs or the event does not occur. In the previous example, the event was streptococcal pharyngitis and the patients seen with a sore throat were the observations.

Every day language is often cumbersome when discussing issues in statistics. An alternative approach is to examine events and observations graphically. We do this by constructing a **Venn diagram**. In a Venn diagram, we use a rectangle to symbolize all of the observations and a circle to symbolize those observations in which the event occurs.

---

[1]Statisticians also refer to the opportunity for an event to occur as a **trial**. Since the term *trial* refers to a clinical experiment in health research, we will exclusively use the term *observation* to refer to the opportunity for an event to occur.

Figure 1-2 is a Venn diagram we could use to think about the probability that a patient with a sore throat has streptococcal pharyngitis.

Figure 1-2 An example of a Venn diagram. The rectangular area represents all observations. The circular area represents the observations in which the event occurs. The area within the rectangle but outside of the circle represents those observations in which the event did not occur.

There are some aspects of observations and events that are evident in a Venn diagram. For instance, we can see that the entire rectangle outside of the circle corresponds to observations in which the event does not occur. When an event does not occur, we say that the **complement** of the event occurs. In this case, the event is having strep throat and its complement is not having strep throat.

The way in which a Venn diagram tells us about the magnitude of the probability is by the area of the circle representing the event relative to the area of the entire rectangle. A way in which we can compare these areas is by creating a **Venn equation**. A Venn equation uses the parts of a Venn diagram in a mathematical equation that show how the probability of an event is calculated. For the probability that a patient with sore throat has streptococcal pharyngitis, the Venn equation would look like Figure 1-3.

Probability of strep throat =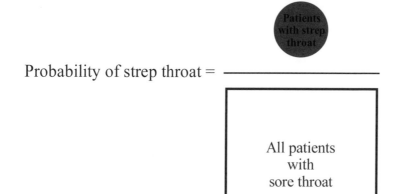

Figure 1-3 A Venn equation illustrating the probability that a patient with sore throat has streptococcal pharyngitis.

A Venn equation helps us to see another property of probabilities which is that probabilities have a distinct range of possible values. Since an event cannot exist without an observation, the circle can only be as big as the rectangle. In other words, the numerator must be a subset of the denominator. The result of this property is to make the largest possible value for a probability equal to one (or 100%). The value of one occurs when every observation in the denominator is also an event in the numerator. When the probability of an observation being an event has a value of one, it is **certain** that the event will occur.

The numerator of a probability contains the number of events. The largest value possible is equal to the number of observations. The smallest value possible is zero. If the numerator of a probability is equal to zero, this implies that none of the observations are events and, therefore, that the probability is equal to zero as well. A probability of zero indicates that it is **impossible** for an event to occur. A probability can be no smaller than zero and no larger than one.[2]

When we want to calculate a probability, it is easier to use some mathematical shorthand. To symbolize a probability, we use a lowercase "p" followed by a set of parentheses. Within those parentheses we identify the event addressed by the probability. Then, the equation looks like this:

$$p(\text{event}) = \frac{\text{number of events}}{\text{number of observations}} \qquad \{1.1\}$$

Next, let us take a look at an example that illustrates calculation of a probability and its interpretation.

Example 1-1 Suppose that we did throat cultures for 100 patients who complained of a sore throat and that 10 of those cultures were positive for streptococcus. What is the probability that a person picked at random would have a positive strep culture?

In this question, a positive strep test is the event and someone with sore throat is an observation. To calculate the probability of a person having a positive strep culture, we can use Equation{1.1}.

$$p(\text{event}) = \frac{\text{number of events}}{\text{number of observations}} = \frac{10}{100} = 0.1$$

Thus, there is a probability of 0.1 (or a 10% chance) that a person selected from the group of patients with a sore throat would be positive for streptococcus.

A part of the shorthand we use to show how probabilities are calculated concerns the complement of an event (i.e., an observation in which the event does not occur). Rather than insert the description of the complement of the event within the parentheses, we more often put a bar over the description of the event. So, $p(\overline{\text{event}})$ stands for the probability of the complement of the event occurring (i.e., the probability of the event not occurring). For the complement of having strep throat, we could use $p(\overline{\text{strep}})$. There are two properties of a

---

[2]This range of possible values between zero and one means that a probability is also a proportion.

collection of events that an event and its complement always demonstrate. The first is **mutual exclusion**. A collection of events is said to be mutually exclusive if it is impossible for two or more events to occur in a single observation. In this case, it is certainly impossible for a person both to have strep throat and to not have strep throat.

The second property of an event and its complement is that they are **collectively exhaustive**. A collection of events is said to be collectively exhaustive if every observation is certain to consist of at least one of the events. Here, that implies that every person with a sore throat either has or does not have strep throat. Clearly this is true.

For events that are both mutually exclusive and collectively exhaustive (like an event and its complement), there is a special relationship among the events: the sum of their probabilities is equal to one. In mathematical language, the relationship between the probability of an event occurring and the probability of the complement of the event occurring is shown in Equation{1.2}.

$$p(\text{event}) + p(\overline{\text{event}}) = 1 \qquad \{1.2\}$$

A little bit of algebra shows us that we can calculate the probability of the complement of an event by subtracting the probability of the event from one. This is shown in Equation{1.3}.

$$p(\overline{\text{event}}) = 1 - p(\text{event}) \qquad \{1.3\}$$

This relationship also can be described in graphic language as the in Venn equation in Figure 1-4.

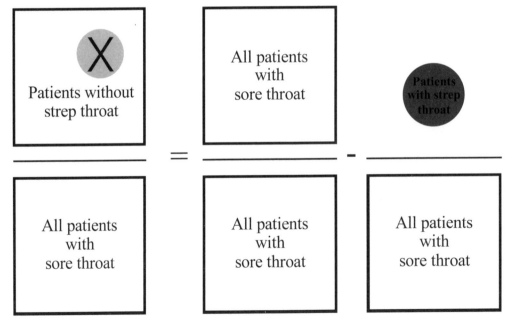

Figure 1-4 A Venn equation illustrating the relationship between the probability of the complement of the event (e.g., not having strep throat) and the probability of an event (e.g., having strep throat).

So far, we have seen how we can think about probabilities using everyday language, graphic language, and mathematic language. Each one of these ways of examining statistical issues has its own advantages. The sorts of things we have learned about probability include the fact that probabilities have a discrete range of possible values ranging from zero (indicating that the event cannot occur) to one (indicating that the event always occurs). Also, we have examined the relationship between an event and its complement. This relationship has two important properties of a collection of events. These properties are being mutually exclusive and collectively exhaustive. A collection of events is mutually exclusive if only one of the events can occur in a single observation. To be collectively exhaustive, the collection of events needs to encompass every possibility so that at least one of the events occurs in every observation. Next, we will take a look at other kinds of collections of events.

COMBINATIONS OF EVENTS

There are two ways in which we might be interested in how two or more events relate to each other. One way is that the events occur together in the same observation. We call this the intersection of events. Another way is that at least one event occurs in an observation. We call this the union of events.

Intersections

In health research and practice, we are often interested in situations in which more than one event occurs in a single observation. For instance, we might be interested in the relationship between a high-fat diet and development of atherosclerosis. The sorts of people in whom we would be most interested are those who have both of those events, since they are the ones for whom a high-fat diet could have contributed to the risk of disease.

In statistical terminology, we refer to the occurrence of two or more events in a single observation as the **intersection** of the events. Figure 1-5 illustrates the probabilities of a high-fat diet and atherosclerosis and the intersection of those two events. Their intersection is where the two circles overlap. These are the observations in which a person has both a high-fat diet and atherosclerosis.

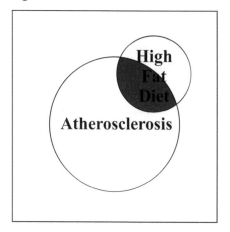

Figure 1-5 Venn diagram illustrating the relationship between a high-fat diet and development of atherosclerosis. The area in which the circles overlap represents those persons who have both a high-fat diet and atherosclerosis.

The probability of an observation including both events (i.e., the intersection of those events) considers the size of the overlap relative to all observations. Figure 1-6 shows a Venn equation representing the probability of the intersection of high-fat diet and atherosclerosis.

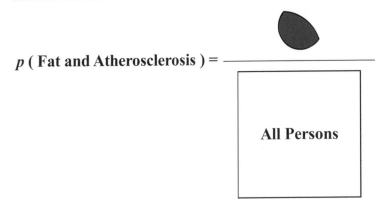

$$p\ (\textbf{ Fat and Atherosclerosis }) =$$

Figure 1-6 Venn equation for the probability that a person has both a high-fat diet (Fat) and has atherosclerosis. In the numerator is the area of overlap (intersection) of the two circles in the Venn diagram (Figure 1-5). The denominator represents everyone regardless of whether or not they have a high-fat diet or atherosclerosis (i.e, the entire rectangle).

If we want to calculate the probability of an intersection of events, we use what is called the **multiplication rule**. To see how the multiplication rule works, let us begin with a Venn equation (Figure 1-7).

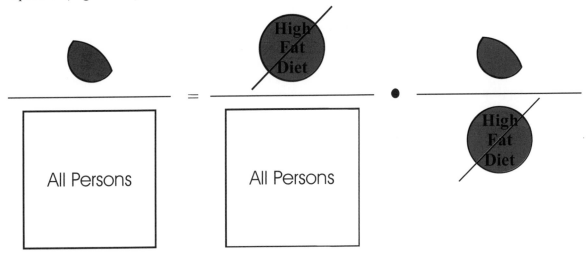

Figure 1-7 Venn equation of the multiplication rule used to calculate the intersection of high-fat diet and atherosclerosis.

To the left of the equals sign in the Venn equation in Figure 1-7 is the probability of the intersection of having a high-fat diet and developing atherosclerosis as shown in Figure 1-6. In the numerator of that probability are the persons who had both events. In the denominator are all persons regardless of diet or disease. Immediately to the right of the equals sign is the probability that someone has a high-fat diet. In the numerator of that probability are the persons with a high-fat diet and in the denominator are, as before, all persons regardless of diet or disease.

The second fraction to the right of the equals sign also is a probability[3], but it looks different from any probability we have encountered so far. Specifically, it does not include all the observations (represented by the rectangle in a Venn diagram) in its denominator. Rather, it includes only those persons with a high-fat diet in its denominator. This is an example of a very important kind of probability, called a **conditional probability**. A conditional probability tells us the probability of an event occurring given that another event has occurred. In this case, the conditional probability tells us the probability of a person having atherosclerosis given that the person has a high-fat diet.

In mathematical notation, a conditional probability also looks different from other probabilities we have encountered. Equation {1.4} illustrates the mathematical notation for the Venn equation in Figure 1-7.

$$p(A \text{ and } B) = p(A) \cdot p(B \mid A) \qquad \{1.4\}$$

where

$p(A \text{ and } B)$ =   probability that an observation will include both event A and event B (i.e., the probability of the intersection of A and B)[4]

$p(A)$ =   probability that an observation includes event A (i.e., the unconditional probability of event A)

$p(B \mid A)$ =   probability that an observation will include event B given that it includes event A (i.e., a conditional probability of event B)

Or, in terms of a high-fat diet and atherosclerosis:

$$p(\text{Fat and Atherosclerosis}) = p(\text{Fat}) \cdot p(\text{Atherosclerosis} | \text{Fat}) \qquad \{1.5\}$$

From a statistical point of view, it does not matter which event is addressed by the conditional probability.[5] Thus, the probability of the intersection of high-fat diet and atherosclerosis could also be calculated as:

---

[3]Recall from page 5 that, to be a probability, a fraction's numerator must be a subset of its denominator. This is the case here, because those persons with both a high cholesterol diet and atherosclerosis (the numerator) are all included in the circle representing persons with atherosclerosis (the denominator).

[4] In set notation this is $p(A \cap B)$.

[5]The way in which the probability of the intersection is calculated depends only on which probabilities are obtained as part of a particular health research study. If our information about the relationship between high-fat diet and atherosclerosis comes from a cohort study (a study in which the probability of disease is compared between exposed and unexposed persons), for example, the conditional probability we would measure is the probability of the disease given exposure status. In a case-control study (a study in which the odds of being exposed is compared between persons who have and do not have the disease), however, the conditional probability we measure is the probability of the exposure given disease status.

$$p(\text{Fat and Atherosclerosis}) = p(\text{Atherosclerosis}) \bullet p(\text{Fat} \mid \text{Atherosclerosis}) \qquad \{1.6\}$$

In Equations {1.5} and {1.6}, we can see that a vertical line is used to separate the two events in the parentheses of a conditional probability. The event to the left of the vertical line is called the **conditional event**. It is the conditional event that the probability addresses. In Equation{1.5}, the conditional event is having atherosclerosis, so this conditional probability tells us about the chance that someone has atherosclerosis. The event to the right of the vertical line is called the **conditioning event**. The conditioning event defines the circumstance in which we are interested in the probability of the conditional event. Here, having a high-fat diet is the conditioning event. Thus, Equation {1.5} tells us that we are interested the probability of having atherosclerosis given (i.e., under the condition) that someone has a high-fat diet.

The reason that conditional probabilities are so important in health research is the fact that they tell us about an important aspect of the relationship between events. Namely, conditional probabilities can be used to see if the occurrence of one event changes the probability of the occurrence of another event. If, for example, we are interested in whether or not there is this sort of relationship between a high-fat diet and having atherosclerosis, we could compare the conditional probability in Equation {1.5} to the probability that someone has atherosclerosis given that they do not have a high-fat diet ($p(\text{Atherosclerosis} \mid \overline{\text{Fat}})$). If those two conditional probabilities have the same value, then we can conclude that a high-fat diet does not influence the chance of having atherosclerosis. In that case, the three probabilities in Equation {1.7} are all equal to the same value.

$$p(\text{Atherosclerosis} \mid \text{Fat}) = p(\text{Atherosclerosis} \mid \overline{\text{Fat}}) = p(\text{Atherosclerosis}) \qquad \{1.7\}$$

Or, in more general terms:

$$p(B \mid A) = p(B \mid \overline{A}) = p(B) \qquad \{1.8\}$$

where

$p(B \mid \overline{A})$ = probability that an observation will include event B given that it does not include event A (i.e., another conditional probability of event B)

In statistical terminology, we say that two events are **statistically independent** when the probability of one of the events is not affected by occurrence of the other event.[6] In biologic

---

[6]The term "statistically independent" as statisticians use it can be confusing when we consider the everyday meaning of "independence." If we were to say, for example, that two persons are independent, we are likely to infer that there is no connection between them. This is not what the statistician is implying. Rather, the

terms, events that are statistically independent cannot have a causal relationship (or any other type of relationship).

To determine if events are statistically independent, we need only to compare two of the three probabilities in Equation{1.8}. If those two probabilities are equal to the same value, then all three probabilities are the same and the conditional and conditioning events are statistically independent. We will take a look at an example of this relationship shortly, but first let us see how conditional probabilities are calculated.

To calculate a conditional probability, we use Equation {1.4} algebraically rearranged as in Equation{1.9}.

$$p(B \mid A) = \frac{p(A \text{ and } B)}{p(A)} \qquad \{1.9\}$$

Or, in terms of a high-fat diet and having atherosclerosis:

$$p(\text{Atherosclerosis} \mid \text{Fat}) = \frac{p(\text{Fat and Atherosclerosis})}{p(\text{Fat})} \qquad \{1.10\}$$

This process of identifying statistical independence is illustrated in Example 1-2.

Example 1-2 Suppose that, in a particular valley of the Mojave Desert, there are 2,500 residents. Of those 2,500 residents, 625 work for ACME Borax, Inc., a company that recovers chemicals from the brine under a salt flat that covers most of the valley floor. Of the 2,500 residents of the valley, 500 have been diagnosed with leukemia. Of the 500 diagnosed with leukemia, 125 are persons who work for ACME Borax, Inc. Given that information, is working for ACME statistically independent of being diagnosed with leukemia?

First, let us consider the relationship between working for ACME and having leukemia. We are told that 625 persons work for ACME and, of those, 125 have leukemia. From that information, we can calculate the probability of having leukemia under the condition that a person works for ACME using Equation {1.9}:

$$p(\text{Leukemia} \mid \text{ACME}) = \frac{p(\text{Leukemia and ACME})}{p(\text{ACME})} = \frac{\dfrac{125}{2,500}}{\dfrac{625}{2,500}} = 0.2$$

To determine if working for ACME and having leukemia are statistically independent

---

statistician is saying that you do not need to consider whether or not one event has occurred when addressing the probability of another event. When a statistician implies that there no connection between events, the statistician says that they are "mutually exclusive" rather than "statistically independent."

events, we need to compare that conditional probability to either the probability of having leukemia given that a person does not work for ACME or to the overall (i.e., unconditional) probability of having leukemia. The later probability is:

$$p(\text{Leukemia}) = \frac{\text{Number with leukemia in valley}}{\text{Total number in valley}} = \frac{500}{2,500} = 0.2$$

Since these two probabilities are equal to the same value, we can conclude that working for ACME and having leukemia are statistically independent events. In other words, working for ACME does not change the probability of having leukemia.

_____

So far, we have seen that we can use the multiplication rule to calculate the probability of two events occurring in a single observation (i.e., the intersection of those events). To calculate the probability of the intersection of more than two events, we simply include each additional event in the multiplication of conditional probabilities. For each additional event, we include the conditional probability of the event with the conditioning events being all of the events listed previously in the equation. For example, we can calculate the intersection of three events as shown in Equation{1.11}.

$$p(A \text{ and } B \text{ and } C) = p(A) \cdot p(B \mid A) \cdot p(C \mid A \text{ and } B) \qquad \{1.11\}$$

where

$p(C \mid A \text{ and } B)$ = probability that an observation will include event C given that it includes events A and B (i.e., a conditional probability of event C)

If the events are statistically independent of each other, we can use a simplified version of the multiplication rule. This simplification is to multiply the unconditional probabilities of the events. Equation {1.12} shows the simplified version for the intersection of three events just examined in Equation{1.11}.

$$p(A \text{ and } B \text{ and } C) = p(A) \cdot p(B) \cdot p(C) \qquad \{1.12\}$$

The reason that we can use this simplified version of the multiplication rule is that, by definition, the conditional and unconditional probabilities are the same for statistically independent events (as shown in Equation{1.8}). If the three events are not statistically independent, however, we need to use Equation {1.11} to calculate the intersection of events.

Unions

When our interest is in the probability of any (i.e., one or more) of a collection of events occurring in the same observation, we say that we are interested in the **union** of those events. Suppose, for example, that we are considering two risk factors for atherosclerosis: high-fat diet and smoking. In that case, we might be interested in calculating the probability that a person has at least one of those risk factors (i.e., either high-fat diet or smoking or both high-fat diet and smoking). To illustrate this, let us add smoking to the Venn diagram in Figure 1-5. Then the Venn diagram of all three events will look something like the one in Figure 1-8.

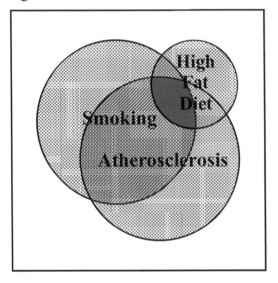

Figure 1-8 Venn diagram showing the relationship between high-fat diet, smoking, and atherosclerosis.

The union of the two risk factors is satisfied if a person either has a high-fat diet or smokes (or both). Thus, the numerator of the probability of the union of those two events includes the part of the Venn diagram covered by either circle.

Figure 1-9 shows the Venn equation for the union of smoking and high-fat diet.

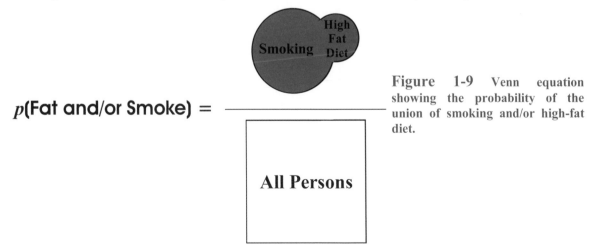

Figure 1-9 Venn equation showing the probability of the union of smoking and/or high-fat diet.

To calculate the probability of the union of two events, we use the **addition rule**. As the name implies, in the addition rule the probabilities of each of the event are added together.

Since adding the probabilities together includes the intersection of those events twice, the probability of the intersection of the events must be subtracted from the sum. This calculation for the union of smoking and a high-fat diet is illustrated by the Venn equation in Figure 1-10.

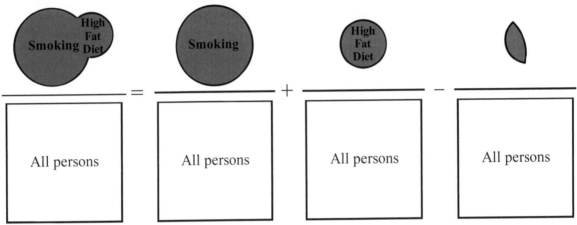

Figure 1- 10 Venn equation showing calculation of the union of smoking and a high-fat using the addition rule.

In mathematical terms, the calculation of the union of two events is performed as shown in Equation{1.13}.

$$p(A \text{ and/or } B) = p(A) + p(B) - P(A \text{ and } B) \qquad \{1.13\}$$

where

$p(A \text{ and/or } B)$ = probability that an observation will include event A and/or event B (i.e., the probability of the union of events A and B)[7]

Now, let us take a look at an example addressing the union of two events.

Example 1-3 Suppose that we are planning a clinical trial of a new live vaccine. In this study, we want to exclude persons who are either pregnant or immunocompromised. Suppose that we estimate that the population from which we are planning to take our sample includes 20% of the total number of persons who are pregnant and 10% of the total number who are immunocompromised. If being pregnant and being immunocompromised are statistically independent events, what proportion of our sample will excluded due to either of

---

[7] In set notation, this is $p(A \cup B)$.

these characteristics?

To calculate the probability of the union of two events, we use Equation{1.13}. For this application, Equation {1.13} looks like the following:

$$p(\text{Preg and/or Comp}) = p(\text{Preg}) + p(\text{Comp}) - p(\text{Preg and Comp})$$

We know the probability that a person selected at random from the population will be pregnant ($p(\text{Preg}) = 0.2$) and the probability that a person selected at random from the population will be immunocompromised ($p(\text{Comp}) = 0.1$). We are not given the probability of the intersection of these two events (i.e., the probability that a person will be both pregnant and immunocompromised). We are told, however, that these two events are statistically independent. That tells us that we can use the simplified version of the multiplication rule illustrated for three statistically independent events in Equation {1.12}. For the two events of being pregnant and being immunocompromised, their intersection can be calculated as follows:

$$p(\text{Preg and Comp}) = p(\text{Preg}) \cdot p(\text{Comp}) = 0.2 \cdot 0.1 = 0.02$$

Now that we have the probability of the intersection of the two events, we are ready to calculate their union.

$$p(\text{Preg and/or Comp}) = p(\text{Preg}) + p(\text{Comp}) - p(\text{Preg and Comp})$$
$$= 0.2 + 0.1 - 0.02 = 0.28$$

Thus, we can expect that 28% of the persons we select from the population will be excluded from the study because they are either pregnant or immunocompromised (or both).

As with the multiplication rule we used to calculate the probability of the intersection of events, the addition rule for calculation of the probability of the union of events has a simplified version that can be used under a special condition. For the addition rule, that condition is that the events are mutually exclusive. If so, the probability of the union of events can be calculated by simply adding together the probabilities of the events. The intersections of the events do not need to be subtracted from that sum because, by definition, the probability of the intersection of two mutually exclusive events is equal to zero.

Bayes' Theorem

Earlier, we learned that there are two types of events in a conditional probability: the conditional event(s) and the conditioning event(s). We also learned that these types of events have very different roles in a conditional probability. The conditional event is the event for which the probability is calculated (i.e., conditional probabilities tell us the chance of the conditional event occurring). All of the characteristics of unconditional probabilities (those discussed at the beginning of this chapter) apply to the conditional event. For instance, the probability of the complement of the conditional event is found by subtracting the conditional probability from one (see Equation{1.3}). Equation {1.14} shows that relationship for conditional probabilities.

$$p(\overline{A}\,|\,B) = 1 - p(A\,|\,B) \qquad \{1.14\}$$

The conditioning event defines the condition under which we are interested in the probability of the conditional event. None of the characteristics of unconditional probabilities discussed at the beginning of this chapter apply to the conditioning event. For example, we cannot find the probability of the conditional event given that the conditioning event does not occur by subtracting from one the conditional probability given that the conditioning event occurs. Equation {1.15} shows this inequality in mathematical notation.

$$p(A\,|\,\overline{B}) \neq 1 - p(A\,|\,B) \qquad \{1.15\}$$

So, there are important differences in the way in which conditional and conditioning events affect interpretation of conditional probabilities. Under most circumstances, we need only keep these differences in mind. Under some circumstances, however, the conditional probabilities we know something about have the conditional and conditioning events reversed relative to our interest. Examples of such "backward" conditional probabilities are the sensitivity and specificity of a diagnostic test. Sensitivity tells us the probability that a person with a particular disease (D) will have a positive test result (T). Specificity tells us the probability that a person without that disease ($\overline{D}$) will have a negative test result ($\overline{T}$). In mathematic notation, Equations {1.16} and {1.17} describe the sensitivity and specificity of a diagnostic test.

$$\text{Sensitivity} = p(T\,|\,D) \qquad \{1.16\}$$

$$\text{Specificity} = p(\overline{T}\,|\,\overline{D}) \qquad \{1.17\}$$

Since the conditioning event is having the disease, sensitivity can only be interpreted for those persons known to have the disease. Likewise, specificity can only be interpreted for those persons known not to have the disease. When a diagnostic test is used, however, it is not known whether or not the person has the disease. What is known is whether the test has a positive or negative result. To interpret a diagnostic test, we need to interchange the conditional and conditioning events in sensitivity and specificity.[8] The way in which we do this is by using Bayes' Theorem. Equation {1.18} shows Bayes' Theorem in general terms.[9]

$$P(B \mid A) = \frac{p(B) \cdot p(A \mid B)}{[p(B) \cdot p(A \mid B)] + [p(\overline{B}) \cdot p(A \mid \overline{B})]}$$ {1.18}

where

$p(B \mid A)$ = probability of event B occurring given that event A has occurred

$p(B)$ = unconditional probability of event B occurring

$p(A \mid B)$ = probability of event A occurring given that event B has occurred

$p(\overline{B})$ = unconditional probability of event B not occurring

$p(A \mid \overline{B})$ = probability of event A occurring given that event B has not occurred

Example 1-4 applies Bayes' Theorem to sensitivity and specificity.

Example 1-4 Suppose that we are screening a particular population for cervical cancer. In that population, 1 out of 1,000 women has cervical cancer. The diagnostic test we use for screening has a sensitivity of 0.9 and a specificity of 0.7. What is the probability that a person with a positive test result really has cervical cancer?

To begin, let us take a look at the information we have. Knowing that 1 out of 1,000 women in the population have cervical cancer tells us that the probability that any particular woman has cervical cancer is 0.001. A sensitivity of 0.9 implies that a person with cervical cancer has a 90% chance of having a positive test result and a specificity of 0.7 implies that a person without cervical cancer has a 70% chance of having a negative test result. In mathematic notation, we know that:

---

[8]Since sensitivity and specificity are "backwards" conditional probabilities, you might wonder why we use them to address the performance of a diagnostic test. The reason is the way in which studies examine diagnostic tests. In one study, the test is used on persons with the disease. That study estimates sensitivity. In another study, the test is used on persons without the disease. That study estimates specificity.

[9] This looks complicated, but it is relatively easy to derive. Bayes understood that the intersection of two events can be expressed in two different ways, so that $p(A \text{ and } B) = p(A) \cdot p(B \mid A) = p(B) \cdot p(A \mid B)$. Solving that equation for $p(B \mid A)$ and recognizing that:
$p(A) = p([A \text{ and } B] \text{ or } [A \text{ and } \overline{B}]) = [p(B) \cdot p(A \mid B)] + [p(\overline{B}) \cdot p(A \mid \overline{B})]$, we get Equation{1.18}.

$$p(D) = 0.001$$
$$p(T \mid D) = 0.9$$
$$p(\overline{T} \mid \overline{D}) = 0.7$$

Our interest is in the probability that a person with a positive test result has cervical cancer. At first this sounds like the sensitivity, but it is not the same thing. In sensitivity, our interest is confined to people who have the disease. To interpret a positive test result however, we need to confine our interest to persons with a positive result. Thus, our interest is in the same events that make up sensitivity, but with the conditional and conditioning events transposed (i.e., $p(D \mid T)$). We can transpose conditional and conditioning events by using Bayes' Theorem (from Equation {1.18}).

$$p(D \mid T) = \frac{p(D) \cdot p(T \mid D)}{[p(D) \cdot p(T \mid D)] + [p(\overline{D}) \cdot p(T \mid \overline{D})]}$$
$$= \frac{0.001 \cdot 0.9}{[0.001 \cdot 0.9] + [\{1 - 0.001\} \cdot \{1 - 0.7\}]} = 0.003$$

So, the probability that a woman with a positive test result has cervical cancer is 0.003. You might be surprised that this probability is so low. The principle reason it is so low is the fact that cervical cancer occurs in only 1 out of 1,000 women. Among women with positive test result this changes to 3 out of 1,000. So, the chance of cervical cancer is 3 times as great among women with a positive test result, but it is still a low probability (i.e., 0.003). Bayes' theorem has helped us to appreciate the meaning of a positive test result when the diagnostic test is used for screening this population.

_____

Now that we have an understanding of probabilities, we are ready to apply what we have learned to the process of taking samples from populations. In the next chapter, we will begin doing that by focusing on populations.

CHAPTER 2

Describing Populations

The purpose of research is to describe a population. In a very general sense, what we want to do is to describe the **distribution** of data in the population (Figure 2-1). A distribution of data tells us not only which data values exist in a population, but also how frequently each value occurs. In this chapter, we will take a look at the distribution of data in the population and see how we can use knowledge of that distribution to take chance into account.

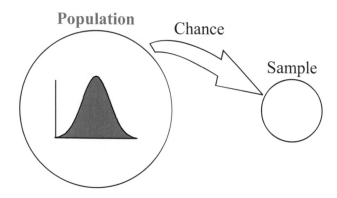

Figure 2-1 **Our purpose in research is to describe the distribution of data in a population**

TYPES OF DATA

One of the things that determine the distribution of data in the population is the type of data it describes. For our purpose there are three types of data: continuous, ordinal, and nominal. An important part of understanding statistical methods is being able to distinguish these three types of data, so we will begin thinking about distributions by describing those three types of data.

Continuous data have a large number of possible values,[1] which are evenly spaced. By "evenly spaced" we mean that a change in value of one unit is the same regardless of where in the range of possible values that the change occurs. Examples of continuous data include age, weight, blood pressure, and pH.

Ordinal data have values that can be ordered,[2] but the values are not considered to be evenly spaced. In fact, any intrinsic spacing between values is ignored when we consider the data to be ordinal. Examples of ordinal data include the number of persons in a household, patient satisfaction scores, and stage of disease.

Nominal data differ from ordinal data in that they cannot be ordered in any relevant way. Also included as nominal data are any data that have only two possible values. Examples of nominal data include gender, race, disease status (e.g., active vs. in remission),

---

[1]The formal definition of continuous data states that these data have an infinite number of possible values. In practice, however, we are able to measure only a finite number of possible values. Recognition of this fact allows us to analyze data that do not really have an infinite number of possible values (like the number of hairs on your head) as though they were continuous.

[2]For a statistician to consider a set of data to be ordered, the data must consist of a minimum of three different values. As a result, data with only two possible values are considered to be nominal data.

and country of origin.

There are two ways in which we can describe the distribution of data in a population. One way is to describe that distribution graphically. The other is to describe them mathematically.[3] We will begin with the graphical approach.

DESCRIBING DISTRIBUTIONS GRAPHICALLY

The types of graphs we use can be separated into two groups. One group is for **continuous data**. The other is for either ordinal or nominal data, both of which are considered to be **discrete data**. First we will look at graphing discrete data, since the options for discrete data are more limited than the options for continuous data.

Graphing Discrete Data

For discrete data, we usually describe the distribution graphically by using a **bar graph**. In a bar graph, data values are listed on the horizontal axis and how frequently each value occurs is indicated by the vertical axis. Figure 2-2 illustrates a distribution of ordinal data arranged in a bar graph.

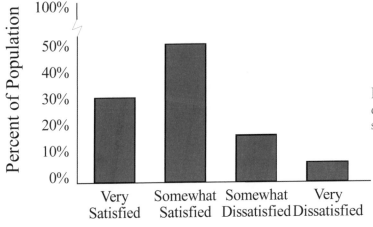

Figure 2-2 A bar graph of the distribution of patient satisfaction scores.

Next, let us take a look at an example (Example 2-1) that illustrates how a bar graph is constructed to describe discrete data graphically.

Example 2-1 In the United States, the ABO blood group phenotypes occur with percentages approximately equal to the values in the following table:

---

[3] A third way in which we might try to describe distributions is in literary language. For example, we could say that a distribution is a symmetric bell-shaped curve.

Phenotype	Percentage
O	45%
A	40%
B	10%
AB	5%

Let us describe those data graphically as a bar graph.

___

These are nominal data, because they describe categories that cannot be ordered in any relevant way. When drawing a graph of nominal data, there is no prescribed order for the bars. The table lists the phenotypes in order of decreasing percentages. The following bar graph is organized in the same way.

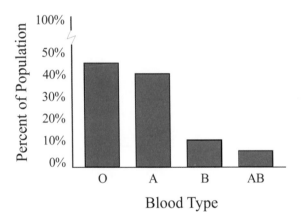

Graphing Continuous Data

If we were to use a bar graph to display continuous data, we would need to have a very large number of bars if each bar represented a single data value.[4] Instead, we use a **histogram** to display the distribution of continuous data. In a histogram, each bar represents an interval of data values rather than a single value. Also, we remind ourselves that the bars in a histogram represent a continuum of data, rather than discrete values, by drawing the bars so that they touch each other. Figure 2-3 illustrates a distribution of continuous data displayed in a histogram.

___

[4]Theoretically, there are an infinite number of possible values for continuous data. This implies that we would need to have an infinite number of bars if each bar represented a single data value.

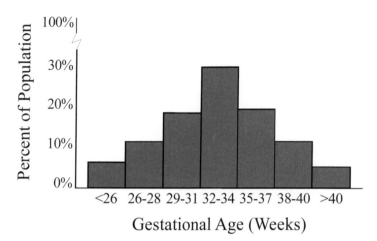

Figure2-3 Histogram illustrating the distribution of gestational ages in a population.

In the next example, we will see how a histogram is constructed from continuous data values.

Example 2-2 Suppose that we were to measure changes in serum cholesterol levels before and after one month on a low-fat diet for 11 patients newly diagnosed with hypercholesterolemia. Imagine that the following are the values we observe when the serum cholesterol levels after the diet are subtracted from the serum cholesterol levels before the diet: 10, 42, 5, 9,-2, 0, 16, 28, 4, -5, and 3 mg/dL. Let us graphically describe those data as a histogram.

To construct a histogram, we need to define the intervals of values that will correspond to each bar. There are two aspects of these intervals that we need to consider. First, we need to decide how wide the intervals will be. The fewer the data values we will graph, the larger the intervals need to be to give an impression of the shape of the distribution (otherwise many bars would be missing since the interval includes no observations). Next, we need to decide where to begin the first interval. This choice also can change the appearance of the histogram, especially if there few data values.

For this histogram, let us use 10 mg/dL for the width of the intervals. That will give us five bars representing these 11 data values. If we were to start the first interval at -10 mg/dL, we would get the following histogram:

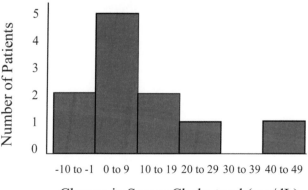

Change in Serum Cholesterol (mg/dL)

On the other hand, if we were to start the first interval at -5 mg/dL, we would get the following histogram:

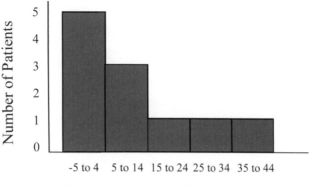

Change in Serum Cholesterol (mg/dL)

Both of these histograms are correct. Even so, they give a somewhat different impression about the shape of the distribution. As the number of bars in the histogram increases, the choice of where to begin the first interval has less effect on the histogram's shape.

There are many other ways in which continuous data can be described graphically. One that has been commonly used in statistical analysis software is the **stem-and-leaf plot**.[5] The stem-and-leaf plot is similar to a histogram, but with two differences. The first difference is that the data values are listed vertically, instead of horizontally as in a histogram. The second difference is that a stem-and-leaf plot displays all of the data values in addition to the frequency of data in specified intervals as in a histogram. Thus, the stem-and-leaf plot provides more information about the data than does the histogram.

The first step in constructing a stem-and-leaf plot is to define the intervals of data that will be used. To define those intervals, we consider all but the right-most digit in each data value. For example, a data value of 2.5 will be assigned to the interval that includes values from 2.0 to 2.9.[6] These groups make up the "stem" of a stem-and-leaf plot. This is the same process that we use to begin construction of a histogram, but a stem-and-leaf plot represents groups as separate rows in a table instead of bars in a graph. The next step in developing a stem-and-leaf plot is to represent each data value in a particular row according to the value of the right-most digit (these are the "leaves").

This sounds confusing, but it will be clearer when we look at an example of a stem-and-leaf plot (Example 2-3).

---

[5] The reason that the stem-and-leaf plot is a popular choice in statistical analysis software has its origin in the days in which computer output was limited to typing ASCII characters. These are the only characters needed to produce a stem-and-leaf plot.

[6] If there are more than a few data values to be plotted, intervals can represent a smaller range of values. For instance, one interval might include values from 2.0 to 2.4 and another interval might include values from 2.5 to 2.9.

Example 2-3 In Example 2-2, we constructed a histogram to describe changes in serum cholesterol levels before and after one month on a low-fat diet for 11 patients newly diagnosed with hypercholesterolemia. The differences in serum cholesterol levels were: 10, 42, 5, 9,-2, 0, 16, 28, 4, -5, and 3 mg/dL. Let us graphically describe those data using a stem-and-leaf plot.

To begin, let us sort the data by decreasing numeric magnitude and then, separate the right-most digits from the other digits. If there is only one digit in a data value, the other digit is represented by 0 (or -0 when the data are negative).

Data Value	Other Digits	Right-most Digit
42	4	2
28	2	8
16	1	6
10	1	0
9	0	9
5	0	5
4	0	4
3	0	3
0	0	0
-2	-0	2
-5	-0	5

Next, we create groups according to the value of the "other" digits. Each possible value for those "other" digits is included, even if there are no data values observed in that interval.

Other Digits (stem)	Right-most Digit (leaves)
4	2
3	
2	8
1	06
0	03459
-0	25

That is a stem-and leaf plot for the data in Example 2-2. The number of right-most digits in each group tells us how frequently data values occur in that group. This is the same information that we get when we use a histogram to describe continuous data graphically. With a stem-and-leaf plot, however, the "bars" extend horizontally instead of vertically (compare this plot to the first histogram in Example 2-2). In addition, the value of the right-most digit is listed in a stem-and-leaf plot, telling us the actual numeric data value.

Another way to describe a distribution of continuous data graphically is by using a line instead of bars to represent the frequency with which data values occur. This type of graph is called a **frequency polygon**. To begin thinking about a frequency polygon, we can think about a histogram with a line connecting the middle of the upper extreme of each bar. Each one of the bars in a histogram represents an interval of continuous data. If we have lots of data values (as in a population), we can make each bar represent a narrower interval of values. The result will be that the number of bars in the histogram will increase and the width of each bar will decrease. Also as the number of bars increase, the line representing those bars becomes smoother. Figure 2-4 shows that process.

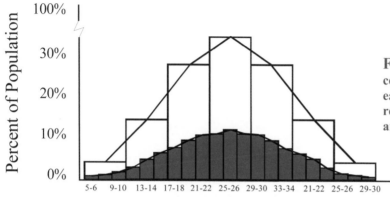

Figure 2-4 Smoothing of the line connecting the upper midpoints of each bar as the interval represented by each bar decreases and the number of bars increases.

Now, if we were to imagine making each of the bars represent a single data value, the histogram would consist of an infinite number of infinitely narrow bars. When that happens, the bars in the histogram disappear, leaving just the line that traces the tops of all of the bars, creating a **frequency polygon**. Figure 2-5 illustrates a frequency polygon.

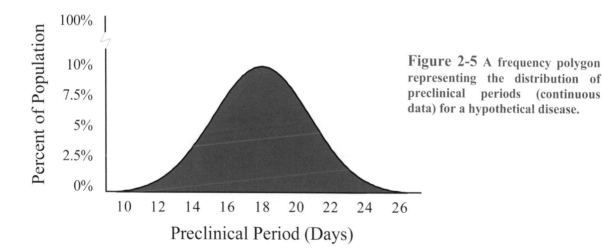

Figure 2-5 A frequency polygon representing the distribution of preclinical periods (continuous data) for a hypothetical disease.

So, one of the ways in which we can think about distributions of data in the population is graphically. Next, we will see how those distributions can be represented mathematically.

DESCRIBING DISTRIBUTIONS MATHEMATICALLY

An advantage of a frequency polygon is that the line can be described mathematically as well as graphically. We will not be looking at the actual mathematical formulas for distributions. Instead, we will identify a distribution by naming it and by providing the detail needed so that our particular distribution is described.

In Figure 2-5 we see a symmetric bell-shaped curve that is very commonly used by statisticians to take chance into account. This is a **Gaussian distribution**.[7] When we name our distribution a Gaussian distribution, the statistician thinks of a mathematical equation that can be used to calculate probabilities of getting various data values from the population.

Naming the distribution a Gaussian distribution, however, is not enough to allow the statistician to calculate probabilities. The problem is that there are lots of different Gaussian distributions. These distributions differ according to where they are centered on the continuum of data values and according to how spread out they are around that center. If we specify these two characteristics, we can describe our unique Gaussian distribution completely.

The characteristics that mathematically describe a particular distribution are called the **parameters** of the distribution. A Gaussian distribution has two parameters. One is a parameter of **location** that tells where the distribution is centered. The other is a parameter of **dispersion** that tells how spread out are the data values. If we want to describe a particular Gaussian distribution, we need to provide numeric values for those two parameters.

Parameter of Location

The parameter that tells us where a Gaussian distribution is centered on the continuum of possible values is the **mean**. Figure 2-6 shows Gaussian distributions that have different means.

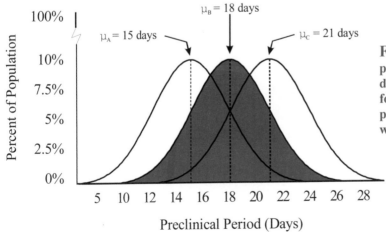

Figure 2-6 Three frequency polygons representing the distributions of preclinical periods for a hypothetical disease in three populations (A, B, and C), each of which has a different mean.

---

[7]The Gaussian distribution is also called the **normal distribution**.

The mean is probably the most often used and best understood value that we calculate from a distribution of data. Even so, if asked to define a mean of a population, you probably would rely on a mathematical definition. Specifically, you would (most likely) suggest that a population's mean is the sum of all data values divided by the number of data values in the population. In mathematical language, the mean of the population's distribution of data is represented as shown in Equation{2.1}:

$$\mu = \frac{\sum Y_i}{N} \qquad \{2.1\}$$

where

μ　　=　mean of the distribution of data in the population (symbolized with the Greek letter "mu").

$\sum Y_i$　=　sum ($\sum$) of the individual data values (Y_i) in the population.

N　　=　number of data values in the population.

Another way to understand the mean of a distribution of data, however, is by imagining the distribution to be a 3-dimensional object instead of a 2-dimensional one. Then the mean can be thought of as the center of gravity of the distribution. In other words, the mean is the point in a distribution at which the distribution "balances" (there is an equal "weight" of data above and below the mean). Adding data values just above the mean will cause the mean to shift slightly to the right, whereas adding data far above the mean will cause the mean to shift substantially to the right. This conceptualization of the mean is illustrated in Figure 2-7.

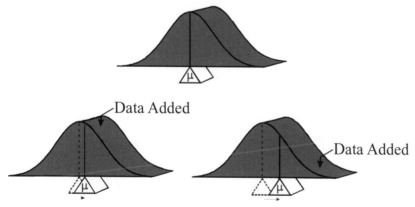

Figure 2-7 Illustration of the mean being the center of gravity of a distribution of data. Like a physical center of gravity, the position of the mean is affected more by data added farther from it than it is by data added closer to it.

Although the mean of a distribution of continuous data is the parameter of location that is used in the mathematical description of the Gaussian distribution, there are other ways in which the location of a distribution can be represented. The most commonly used alternative to the mean is the **median**. The median is the physical center (rather than the center of gravity) of a distribution. That is to say, the median is selected so that half of the data values are greater the median and half are less than the median. Extreme observations cause the median to move in the direction of the observation, but, unlike the mean, the amount that the median moves is the same regardless of whether the observations added are close to or far from the median. Thus, the median is less affected by the addition of extreme data values than is the mean.

For a symmetric distribution (e.g., a Gaussian distribution) the mean and the median are equal. When a distribution is asymmetric (i.e., **skewed**), the mean will be closer to the extreme data values than will the median. This is illustrated in Figure 2-8.

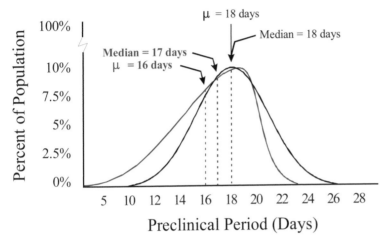

Figure 2-8 Relationship between the mean and the median. For a symmetric distribution (in black), the mean and the median are equal to the same value. For a skewed distribution (in color), the mean is closer to the most extreme values than is the median.

Another measure of location is the **mode**. The mode is the most frequently occurring data value. An advantage of the mode is that it can be determined for nominal data. It is not used in health research as a measure of location for distributions of continuous or ordinal data, because it communicates so little information about the location of a distribution of data.

Now, let us take a look at an example (Example 2-4) in which we will calculate and compare the mean and median of a skewed distribution.

Example 2-4 In Examples 2-2 and 2-3, we looked at the change in serum cholesterol levels for 11 persons on a low-fat diet. Now, let us use these same data to calculate the mean and the median change in serum cholesterol as if those persons made up the entire population.

To calculate the mean, we use Equation {2.1}:

$$\mu = \frac{\sum Y_i}{N} = \frac{10 + 42 + 5 + \dots + 4 - 5 + 3}{11} = \frac{110}{11} = 10\,\text{mg/dL}$$

To find the median, we begin by arranging the observations in order of numeric magnitude:

Order	1	2	3	4	5	6	7	8	9	10	11
Value	-5	-2	0	3	4	5	9	10	16	28	42

When there are an odd number of data values, the median is the middle value.[8] Here, we have 11 data values, so the median is the sixth largest value. This is the median since there are 5 values above it and 5 values below it. In this case, the median of the changes in serum cholesterol levels is equal to 5 mg/dL (in color).

In this example, the mean (10 mg/dL) is considerably larger than the median (5 mg/dL). This implies that the distribution of data values is asymmetric with a few extreme (in this case, higher) data values that affect the mean more than the median. In Example 2-2 we constructed a histogram for these data. From the histogram, it is clear that the distribution has that kind of asymmetry.

Here, we have an odd number of data values, so the median is the number in the middle. When there is an even number of data values, we usually say that the median is equal to the mean of the two numbers in the middle. For instance, suppose that we have data from a 12th person and that person's change in serum cholesterol is greater than 9 mg/dL (for the median, it does not matter how much greater). Then, the median would be the mean of 5 mg/dL and 9 mg/dL as follows:

$$\text{Median} = \frac{5+9}{2} = 7\,\text{mg/dL}$$

Both the mean and the median are measures of location, but it is the mean that is used to describe the location of a Gaussian distribution. Next we will take a look at ways in which we can describe the dispersion of a distribution of continuous data.

Parameter of Dispersion

For data from a Gaussian distribution, even after the location of the distribution has been specified using the mean, there are still an infinite number of possible distributions with that same mean. These distributions differ in how much the data vary from the mean. Figure 2-9 illustrates Gaussian distributions with the same mean, but with different dispersions around the mean.

---

[8] The median is easiest to calculate for an odd number of data values for which there is one, and only one middle value. That is to say, when there are no other values equal to the middle value. For instance, suppose that 5th largest data value in Example 2-4 were also equal to 5 mg/dL. If that were the case, 5 mg/dL is not really the median value, since there are 4 values below it and 5 values above it. Unfortunately, statisticians do not agree as to what should be done to find the median in this case. Fortunately, the different methods for determining the median in this circumstance give us values for that are usually close to each other in numeric magnitude.

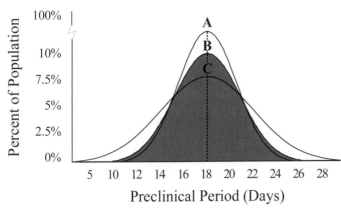

Figure 2-9 Gaussian distributions of the length of the preclinical period for a hypothetical disease in each of three populations. All three populations in this figure have the same mean, but they have different dispersions of preclinical periods. Preclinical periods in population A are the least dispersed and preclinical periods in population C are the most dispersed.

Graphically, we can see that data values in a distribution are, on the average, farther from the mean of the distribution the more dispersed it is. To describe the average distance between data values and the mean, we might use Equation {2.1}, substituting differences between the data values and the mean for the data values in the numerator of that equation. Then, we could calculate the mean distance between the data values and the mean. This modification of Equation {2.1} is shown in Equation {2.2}:

$$\text{Mean differences from the mean} = \frac{\sum (Y_i - \mu)}{N} \qquad \{2.2\}$$

One surprising feature of Equation {2.2} is that it is always equal to zero, regardless of how dispersed the data values are! This is because the mean is the "center of gravity" of a distribution, and thus there is an equal "weight" of data on either side of the mean. In other words, the sum of the positive differences from the mean will always be exactly equal to the sum of the negative differences.[9] To make Equation {2.2} useful as a measure of the amount of dispersion in a distribution of continuous data, we need to keep the negative differences from canceling the positive differences. The way statisticians do this is by squaring the differences between each data value and the mean before adding them up.[10] Equation {2.3} illustrates that calculation:

$$\sigma^2 = \frac{\sum (Y_i - \mu)^2}{N} \qquad \{2.3\}$$

where

σ^2 = variance of the distribution of data in the population (symbolized by the Greek letter "sigma" squared)

---

[9]This is true regardless of the whether or not the distribution is symmetrical.

[10]Statisticians often use this solution of squaring to get rid of negative values. We will encounter this several times in the remaining chapters of this text.

$$Y_i \quad = \quad \text{a data value}$$

$$\mu \quad = \quad \text{mean of the distribution of data in the population}$$

$$N \quad = \quad \text{number of data values in the population}$$

The value calculated in Equation {2.3} is the parameter of dispersion for the Gaussian distribution. It is called the **variance** of the distribution and we symbolize it using the Greek letter sigma squared (σ^2). The reason that we use a squared sigma is to remind us that the units of measurement for the variance are the square of the units for the data. Thus, the variances of the distributions in Figure 2-9 have days^2 as their units of measurement.

To express the dispersion of a distribution in the same units in which the data are measured, we often take the square root of the variance as the value that describes the dispersion of a distribution of continuous data. The square root of the variance is called the **standard deviation**. The relationship between the variance and the standard deviation is illustrated in Equation {2.4}:

$$\sigma = \sqrt{\sigma^2} = \sqrt{\frac{\sum (Y_i - \mu)^2}{N}} \qquad \qquad \{2.4\}$$

where

$$\sigma \quad = \quad \text{the standard deviation of the distribution of data in the population (symbolized with the Greek letter "sigma").}$$

$$\sigma^2 \quad = \quad \text{the variance of the distribution of data in the population}$$

$$Y_i \quad = \quad \text{a data value}$$

$$\mu \quad = \quad \text{the mean of the distribution of data in the population}$$

$$N \quad = \quad \text{the number of data values in the population}$$

Other than the fact that the variance has squared units of measure and the standard deviation has the same units of measure as do the data, there is no difference between the two. When asked "What is the measure of dispersion of a Gaussian distribution?" we can respond with either the variance or the standard deviation. Both are correct.[11]

Now, let us take a look at an example (Example 2-5) in which we determine the variance and the standard deviation of a distribution of data.

---

[11] In fact, both the variance and the standard deviation appear in the mathematical formula for the Gaussian distribution.

Example 2-5 In Examples 2-2 through 2-4, we looked at the change in serum cholesterol levels for 11 persons on a low-fat diet. In Example 2-4, we found that the mean change in serum cholesterol is equal to 10 mg/dL. Now, let us use those same data to calculate the variance and standard deviation of change in serum cholesterol for that group of 11 patients as if those persons made up the entire population.

To calculate the variance, we use Equation{2.3}. To prepare for that calculation, it is easier to keep track of things if we arrange the data in a table. Also, it is helpful to use the table to calculate the values we will use in the numerator of Equation{2.3}.

Patient	Y_i	$Y_i - \mu$	$(Y_i - \mu)^2$
TY	10	0	0
HT	42	32	1,024
IO	5	-5	25
SO	9	-1	1
IM	-2	-12	144
SU	0	-10	100
RC	16	6	36
EH	28	18	324
AF	4	-6	36
LU	-5	-15	225
LN	3	-7	49
Total	110	0	1,964

Notice that one of the columns we have included in the table gives the differences between each data value and the mean of all of the data. As implied by Equation {2.2}, this adds up to zero. Including this column in our calculations can help us check for calculation errors.

Now, let us calculate the variance of those data using Equation{2.3}.

$$\sigma^2 = \frac{\sum (Y_i - \mu)^2}{N} = \frac{1,964}{11} = 178.5 \, \text{mg/dL}^2$$

And, we can use Equation {2.4} to calculate the standard deviation of changes in serum cholesterol among these 11 patients:

$$\sigma = \sqrt{\sigma^2} = 13.4 \, \text{mg/dL}$$

Thus, we can say that the average squared difference between all of the data values and the mean is equal to 178.5 mg/dL^2, or we could express the dispersion of changes in serum cholesterol in mg/dL by saying that the standard deviation is equal to 13.4 mg/dL.

The variance (or the standard deviation) is the parameter of dispersion for the Gaussian distribution. There are other ways in which we might express dispersion, however, even if they are not parameters of the Gaussian distribution. One example is the **range**. The range is the difference between the lowest and the highest data values. The range, however, has limits as a measure of dispersion of the distribution of data in the population. The primary reason for this is that the range uses a very limited amount of information about the distribution; it reflects the relationship between only two data values (i.e., the lowest and the highest values). The dispersion of all of the remaining data values does not affect the value of the range. This feature makes the range incapable of reflecting other aspects of dispersion. For example, Figure 2-10 illustrates how two distributions can have the same range, but be substantially different in their amount of dispersion.

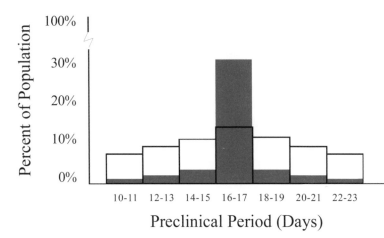

Figure 2-10 Histograms of two distributions with the same range, but different variances. The distribution represented by the colored bars has very little dispersion, since most of the persons have a preclinical period between 16 and 17 days. The distribution represented by unfilled bars, however, has quite a bit of dispersion, since there are a substantial number of persons with preclinical periods throughout the entire range of values.

Another characteristic of the range that diminishes its usefulness as a measure of dispersion is the fact that it is influenced by the number of data values in the distribution.[12] The reason for this is the fact that the most extreme data values are usually the most infrequently occurring values. As the number of data values in a distribution increases, it becomes more likely that the distribution will include those extreme values. Thus, we can expect to see the value of the range increase as the number of data values increase, even if there is no change in the variance and standard deviation of the distribution.

There is another measure of dispersion that is related to the range, but that is not influenced by the number of data values in the distribution. This measure of dispersion is the **interquartile range**. A quartile consists of one-quarter of the data values. To calculate the interquartile range, the distribution is first divided in half by determining the median. Then, the median of each half is used to separate the entire distribution into four equal parts.

---

[12] We usually think of populations as having a very large number of data values (i.e., N is a very large number). In large populations, this is not an important problem. In smaller populations and especially in samples from populations, this can seriously affect the usefulness of the range as a measure of dispersion.

The interquartile range is the distance between the extremes of the middle two quartiles (thus, delineating the middle half of the distribution).

We will see how to calculate an interquartile range shortly, but first let us consider how to interpret it. Probably the easiest way to interpret the interquartile range is to relate it to the standard deviation. If we were to multiply the interquartile range from a Gaussian distribution by 2/3, it would be equal to the standard deviation of that distribution.[13]   For distributions that are not Gaussian, 2/3 of the interquartile range will be somewhat smaller than the standard deviation of the distribution. Calculation of the standard deviation is illustrated in Equation{2.5}.

$$\sigma = \frac{2}{3} \cdot IQR \qquad\qquad \{2.5\}$$

where

σ =   standard deviation of a Gaussian distribution.

IQR =   interquartile range of a Gaussian distribution.

So, when we are comfortable with the concept of a standard deviation, it is only a small step to become comfortable with the interquartile range. The next example (Example 2-6) illustrates calculation and interpretation of an interquartile range.

Example 2-6 In Examples 2-2 through 2-5, we looked at changes in serum cholesterol levels before and after one month on a low-fat diet for eleven patients newly diagnosed with hypercholesterolemia. The following are the changes in serum cholesterol levels when serum cholesterol after the diet is subtracted from serum cholesterol before the diet: 10, 42, 5, 9,-2, 0, 16, 28, 4, -5, and 3 mg/dL. Now, let us determine the interquartile range of the changes in serum cholesterol for that group of 11 patients.

To begin, we need to arrange the data in order of numeric magnitude and determine the median, just as we did in Example 2-4:

Order	1	2	3	4	5	6	7	8	9	10	11
Value	-5	-2	0	3	4	5	9	10	16	28	42

To find the interquartile range, we find the median of each half of the distribution separated by the median of the entire distribution.

---

[13]This comes from considering that, in a Gaussian distribution, an interval of one standard deviation beyond the mean accounts for 1/3 of the data values (we will see this later in this chapter) and that the interquartile range accounts for 1/2 of the data values. Thus, the interquartile range is equal to 1/2 divided by 1/3 standard deviations.

Lower Half					Median	Upper Half				
-5	-2	**0**	3	4	5	9	10	**16**	28	42

So, the median of the lower half is equal to zero and the median of the upper half is equal to 16. We have now divided the distribution of data into four equal parts (i.e., having the same number of data values).

Q1		Q2		Q3		Q4	
-5 -2	0 3	4 5	9	10 16	28	42	

IQR

The interquartile range is the difference between the data values that separate the two extreme quartiles (i.e., Q1 and Q4). In this case that difference is equal to 16-0=16.
   To interpret the interquartile range, we can calculate the corresponding standard deviation by using Equation{2.5}.

$$\sigma = \frac{2}{3} \cdot IQR = \frac{2}{3} \cdot 16 = 10.7 \, \text{mg/dL}$$

For a Gaussian distribution, the standard deviation calculated using the interquartile range will be equal to the standard deviation calculated using Equation{2.4}. In this case, the standard deviation calculated from the interquartile range (10.7 mg/dL) is smaller than the value we calculated using Equation {2.4} in Example 2-5 (13.4 mg/dL). The reason for this is that the distribution of these data is not really a Gaussian distribution. In fact, it is asymmetric. This can be seen in the histograms in Example 2-2.

The relationship between the standard deviation and the interquartile range is similar to the relationship between the mean and the median. Both the mean and the standard deviation are influenced by how far away data values are. The interquartile range is like the median in that it is influenced only by the direction of data values relative to the measurement and not by how extreme those data values are. Thus, two-thirds of the interquartile range is a better estimate of the standard deviation when the data include extreme values that might not be part of the same distribution. We will consider this further in Chapter 3 when we are thinking about estimating the standard deviation of the distribution of the data in the population from the sample's observations.

TAKING CHANCE INTO ACCOUNT

Once we are able to describe the distribution of data, we can calculate probabilities that certain data values in the population will be selected to be part of the sample. The way in which we do this is very similar to the way in which probabilities are calculated from a Venn diagram. Namely, the probability of certain data values being selected is equal to the part of the distribution that corresponds to those data values divided by the entire distribution. Figure 2-11 illustrates this process.

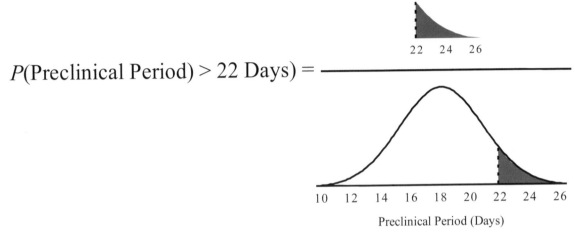

Figure 2-11 Venn equation illustrating the probability of selecting a person with a preclinical period equal to or greater than 22 days; this equation compares the part of the distribution that corresponds to 22 days or more to the entire distribution.

In Figure 2-11, an interval of values (i.e., 22 days or more), rather than a single data value (e.g., 22 days) is addressed in the probability. This will always be the case when we are thinking about distributions of continuous data. The reason for this is that there are so many possible values for continuous data (theoretically, an infinite number) that the probability of any single value is virtually zero.

The mathematic method for calculating areas in sections of curves involves calculus (namely, integration of the mathematical equation describing the distribution). Fortunately, we do not need to do this calculus ourselves! Instead, we use a statistical table that tells us the result of integrating a Gaussian distribution. Our only task is to change our distribution so that it is on the same scale as the distribution described in the table.

Standard Normal Distribution

There are several standard distributions that we will encounter as we examine various statistical procedures. The first of these is the **standard normal distribution**. The standard normal distribution is a Gaussian distribution that has a mean equal to zero and a standard deviation equal to one. When data values are converted to that scale (i.e., $\mu = 0$ and $\sigma = 1$), we call those converted data values **standard normal deviates** and symbolize them with the letter z (instead of Y). Figure 2-12 shows the standard normal distribution.

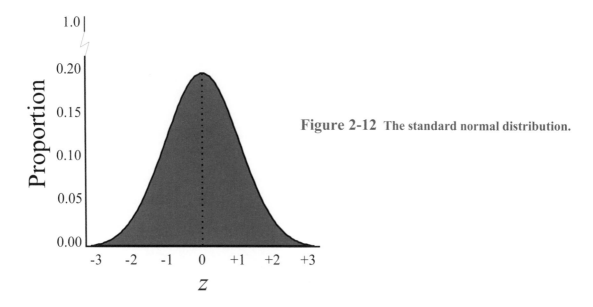

Figure 2-12 The standard normal distribution.

To use the standard normal distribution, we need to convert our data from their original scale to the standard normal scale. As it turns out, this conversion is rather straightforward. To change the scale so that it has a mean of zero, we subtract the mean from each of the data values. To change the scale so that it has a standard deviation of one, we divide by the standard deviation of the data measured on the original scale. Equation {2.6} shows how we can convert a particular data value from its original scale to the standard normal scale.

$$z = \frac{Y_i - \mu}{\sigma} \qquad \{2.6\}$$

where

z = standard normal deviate (**z-value**) that represents the data value Y_i.

Y_i = data value on the original scale.

μ = mean of the distribution of Y_i.

σ = standard deviation of the distribution of Y_i.

This process of converting a value from its original scale to the standard normal scale is illustrated graphically in Figure 2-13.

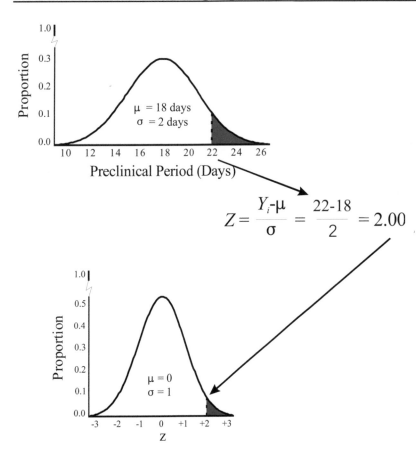

$$Z = \frac{Y_i - \mu}{\sigma} = \frac{22 - 18}{2} = 2.00$$

Figure 2-13 Conversion of a preclinical period of 22 days on the data's original scale (i.e., days) to a value of 2.00 on the standard normal scale involves subtraction of the mean from the original distribution and division by the standard deviation of that same distribution.

Now, let us take a look at an example of how we can convert data values from their original scale to the standard normal scale.

Example 2-7 Imagine that the incubation period for salmonella-induced gastroenteritis has a Gaussian distribution with a mean of 25 hours and a standard deviation of 6 hours. Suppose we are interested in examining students in a university 35 hours after they were exposed to salmonella. If we are interested in the probability of selecting an infected person with a incubation period greater than 35 hours (i.e., they will be asymptomatic at 35 hours), we can use the standard normal distribution to calculate that probability. In preparation, let us determine what value on the standard normal scale would correspond to 35 hours on the original scale.

In this problem, we are provided with the following information summarized using the corresponding mathematic symbols:

$$\mu = 25\,\text{hours} \qquad \sigma = 6\,\text{hours} \qquad Y_i = 35\,\text{hours}$$

To convert 35 hours to the standard normal scale, we use Equation{2.6}:

$$z = \frac{Y_i - \mu}{\sigma} = \frac{35 - 25}{6} = 1.67$$

So, 35 hours on a scale that has a mean of 25 hours and a standard deviation of 6 hours is equal to 1.67 on the standard normal scale.

___

The purpose of converting data to the standard normal scale is so that we can use a table to determine the probability of selecting certain intervals of data values. Table B.1 (in Appendix B) gives us probabilities for standard normal deviates. The values on the margins of that table are the standard normal deviates. Units and tenths of a standard normal deviate are listed on the left margin and hundredths are listed on the top margin. In the body of the table are the probabilities. Specifically, these are the probabilities of selecting by chance the corresponding standard normal deviate or a larger standard normal deviate.[14] Since our data value is represented by that standard normal deviate, the probability of selecting by chance the standard normal deviate or a larger value is the same as the probability of selecting by chance the data value or a larger value. This principle is illustrated graphically in Figure 2-14,

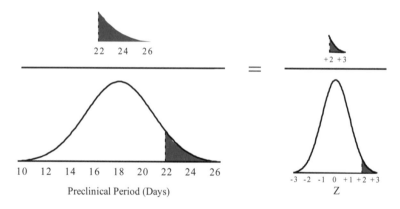

Figure 2-14 The probability of selecting a preclinical period equal to or greater than 22 days is the same as the probability of selecting corresponding standard normal deviates from the standard normal distribution (a standard normal deviate equal to or greater than 2.00).

and mathematically in Equation {2.7}.

$$p(\text{Preclinical period} \geq 22\,\text{days}) = p(z \geq 2.00) \qquad \{2.7\}$$

Now, let us take a look at an example of using the standard normal table (Table B.1) to find a probability for an interval of data values.

___

[14] These are also interpreted as the probability of selecting a larger standard normal deviate (i.e., excluding the specific standard normal deviate). The reason that the same probability is used regardless of whether or not the specific value is included is because the probability of selecting any single value from a distribution of continuous values is virtually zero.

Example 2-8 In Example 2-7, we considered a Gaussian distribution of incubation periods with a mean of 25 hours and a standard deviation of 6 hours. In that example we were interested in the probability of selecting someone from the population with an incubation period equal to or greater than 35 hours. To prepare to calculate that probability, we determined that a standard normal deviate of 1.67 on the standard normal scale corresponds to 35 hours on the original scale. Now, let us determine the probability associated with those values.

Turn to Table B.1 and find the row that corresponds to the units and tenths of the standard normal deviate (1.6) and the column that corresponds to the hundredths of the standard normal deviate (7). Where that row and column intersect is the probability of selecting, by chance, a standard normal deviate equal to or greater than 1.67. That probability is equal to 0.0475. This process can be illustrated graphically as follows:

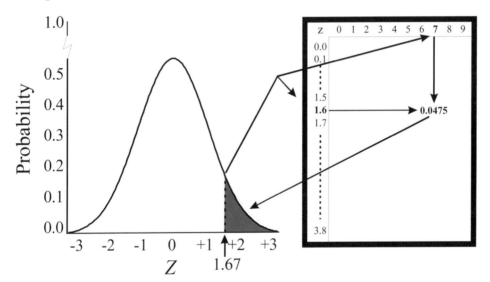

Now, we use the principle illustrated in Figure 2-4 and Equation {2.7} to determine the probability of an exposed person having an incubation period greater than 35 hours. Since 1.67 on the standard normal scale is the same as 35 hours on the original scale, we can conclude that the probability of selecting someone with a incubation period greater than 35 hours also is equal to 0.0475.

$$p(\text{Incubation Period} > 35 \text{ hours}) = p(z > 1.67) = 0.0475$$

This tells us that almost 5% of the persons in this population who are infected with salmonella will be asymptomatic 35 days post-infection.

Table B.1 consists of probabilities of selecting a standard normal deviate equal to or greater than values that range from 0 to 3.89. All of these values are positive. If the data value that we want to convert to the standard normal scale is smaller than the mean on the original scale, Equation {2.6} will result in a negative standard normal deviate. This is not a problem, since the standard normal distribution is symmetric around its mean of zero. Instead, we can find the probability of obtaining the absolute value[15] of the standard normal deviate and interpret that probability as the chance of obtaining the negative standard normal deviate or less. The next example illustrates how this is done.

Example 2-9 In Examples 2-7 and 2-8, we considered that the incubation period for salmonella-induced gastroenteritis has a Gaussian distribution with a mean of 25 hours and a standard deviation of 6 hours. In those examples, we were interested in selecting a person with an incubation period greater than 35 hours. Now, let us determine the chance of selecting a person with an incubation period of less than 12 hours.

The information provided in this example is the same as information provided in Example 2-7, except for the data value we need to convert to a standard normal deviate. Thus, we can use Equation {2.6} as we did in that previous example, substituting 12 hours for 35 hours.

$$z = \frac{Y_i - \mu}{\sigma} = \frac{12 - 25}{6} = -2.17$$

To find the probability associated with -2.17, we look for the absolute value of -2.17 (i.e., 2.17), since negative values do not appear in Table B.1. From the table, we learn that the chance of selecting a standard normal deviate of 2.17 or more is equal to 0.0150. Since the standard normal distribution is symmetric around zero, we can conclude that the probability of selecting a standard normal deviate equal to -2.17 or less also is equal to 0.0150.

Often, we are interested in the probability of obtaining a data value either equal to or greater than a particular value or equal to or less than another particular value.[16] Such a probability is called a **two-tailed** probability. This term comes from our reference to extreme values in a distribution as being in the "tail" of that distribution.[17] To calculate a two-tailed probability, we just need to recall from Chapter 1 how to calculate the probability of the

---

[15]In other words, we change negative values to positive values.

[16] For example, we might be interested in a clinical measurement that has abnormal values both above and below the range of normal results. Blood pressure is such a measurement. If someone has a blood pressure within the range of normal, we say that they are "normotensive." A person who has a blood pressure below the range of normal is "hypotensive" and a person who has a blood pressure above the range of normal is "hypertensive." Then, we might be interested in the probability that someone selected at random from the population would be either hypotensive or hypertensive.

[17]Consequentially, the probability of data values in a single interval in either tail of a distribution is called a **one-tailed** probability

union of two events. We do that by using the addition rule.[18] Figure 2-15 shows this calculation as a Venn equation,

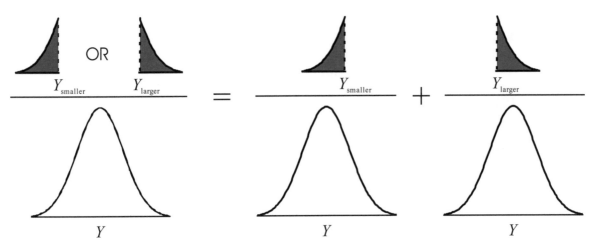

Figure 2-15 A Venn equation showing how the addition rule is used to calculate a two-tailed probability.

and Equation {2.8} shows it in mathematic language.

$$p(Y \leq Y_{smaller} \text{ and/or } Y \geq Y_{larger}) = p(Y \leq Y_{smaller}) + p(Y \geq Y_{larger}) \qquad \{2.8\}$$

where

$p(Y \leq Y_{smaller} \text{ and/or } Y \geq Y_{larger})$ = probability of getting a data value either less than or equal to one particular value ($Y_{smaller}$) or greater than or equal to another particular value (Y_{larger}). This is a two-tailed probability.

$p(Y \leq Y_{smaller})$ = probability of getting a data value equal to or less than a particular value ($Y_{smaller}$). This is a one-tailed probability.

$p(Y \geq Y_{larger})$ = probability of getting a data value equal to or greater than a particular value (Y_{larger}). This is a one-tailed probability.

$Y_{smaller}$ = smaller of two particular data values.

Y_{larger} = larger of two particular data values.

Another probability in which we are often interested is the probability of getting a data value between two particular values (i.e., in the middle of the distribution). To determine this probability, we begin by calculating the probability of getting a data value in the tails of the

---

[18]We use the simplified version of the addition rule for this calculation since the probability of getting a value in one tail is mutually exclusive of the probability getting a value in the other tail.

distribution (i.e., those values that are excluded from the part for which we want to calculate a probability). Those tails are the complement of the values in the middle in which we are interested. In Chapter 1, we learned that we can calculate the probability of the complement by subtracting the probability of the event from one (see Equation 1.3). Figure 2-16 shows this principle applied to a distribution of data,

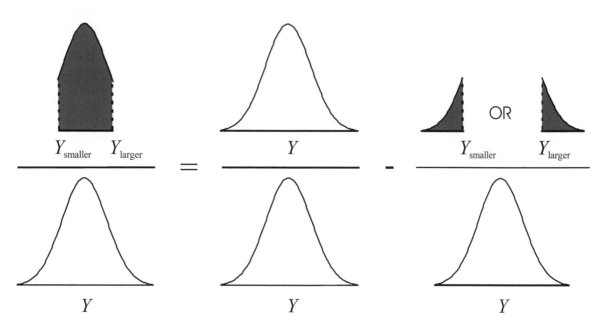

Figure 2-16 Venn equation showing how to calculate the probability of getting a data value from an interval in the center of the distribution.

and Equation {2.9} shows it in mathematic language.

$$p(Y_{\text{samller}} \leq Y \leq Y_{\text{larger}}) = 1 - p(Y \leq Y_{\text{smaller}} \text{ and/or } Y \geq Y_{\text{larger}}) \qquad \{2.9\}$$

where

$p(Y_{\text{samller}} \leq Y \leq Y_{\text{larger}})$ = probability of getting a data value between two particular values (Y_{smaller} and Y_{larger})

Now, let us take a look at an example that shows how to calculate these probabilities.

Example 2-10   In the previous examples, we have been considering that the preclinical period for salmonella-induced gastroenteritis has a Gaussian distribution with a mean of 25 hours and a standard deviation of 6 hours. In Example 2-8, we calculated the probability selecting a person with a incubation period equal to or greater than 35 hours. That probability is equal to 0.0475. In Example 2-9, we calculated the probability of selecting a person with an incubation period equal to or less than 12 hours. That probability is equal to 0.0150. Now, let us determine the chance of selecting a person with a incubation period between 12 hours and 35 hours.

This example asks us to calculate the probability of getting a data value in the middle of the distribution. To calculate this probability, we begin by calculating the probability of its complement: the probability of getting a value from either tail of the distribution. To find that probability, we use Equation {2.8}:

$$p(Y \leq Y_{smaller} \text{ and/or } Y \geq Y_{larger}) = p(Y \leq Y_{smaller}) + p(Y \geq Y_{larger}) = 0.0475 + 0.0150 = 0.0625$$

Next, we calculate the probability of the complement of getting a value from either tail of the distribution as shown in Equation 2.9:

$$p(12\,days \leq Y \leq 35\,days) = 1 - p(Y \leq 12\,days \text{ and/or } Y \geq 35\,days) = 1 - 0.0625 = 0.9375$$

Thus, there is a probability of 0.9375 that a person selected at random from the population would have an incubation period between 12 hours and 35 hours.

Table B.1 can be used to determine the probability associated with any standard normal deviate between the values of zero and 3.89,[19] but there are a few values that are helpful to emphasize. The numeric magnitude of a standard normal deviate tells us how many multiples of the standard deviation a data value is away from the mean. Understanding this fact allows us to interpret means and standard deviations reported in the health research literature. For instance, if the distribution of data is a Gaussian distribution, the mean ± one standard deviation includes about two-thirds of all the data values in the distribution.[20] Likewise, the mean ± two standard deviations include about 95% of the data values in the distribution.[21] This relationship between the standard deviation and the proportion of data values in a Gaussian distribution[22] is illustrated in Figures 2-17 and 2-18.

---

[19] The probability associated with higher z-values is very small, so they are included in Table B.1.

[20] From Table B.1, we find that a standard normal deviate of one corresponds to a probability of 0.1587 in one tail of the distribution. Thus, the mean ± one standard deviation includes 1 - (0.1587 + 0.1587) = 0.6826 or 68.26% of all the data values in the distribution.

[21] More precisely, the mean ± two standard deviations includes 95.44% of the data values in the distribution.

[22] If the distribution of data is not a Gaussian distribution, these proportions will be smaller. The lower limits of these proportions are 0% for the mean ± one standard deviation and 75% for the mean ± two standard deviations regardless of the type of distribution.

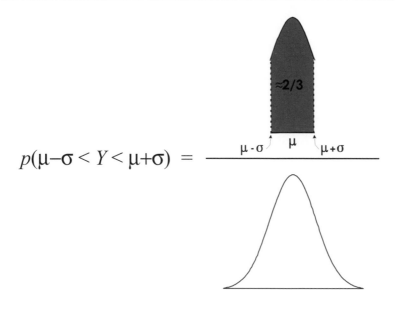

$$p(\mu-\sigma < Y < \mu+\sigma) = $$

Figure 2-17   Approximately two-thirds of all data values in a Gaussian distribution are in the interval specified by the mean ± one standard deviation.

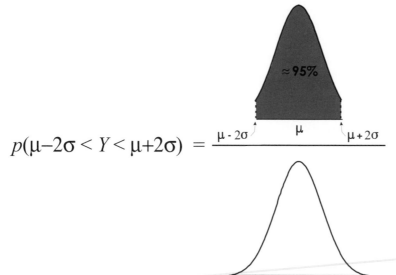

$$p(\mu-2\sigma < Y < \mu+2\sigma) = $$

Figure 2-18   Approximately 95% of all data values in a Gaussian distribution are in the interval specified by the mean ± two standard deviations.

Now, let us take a look at an example of how we can use these relationships to interpret the results of health research.

Example 2-11   In a research article reporting the result of a study of determinants of gestational age at birth (*N Engl J Med* 1998;339:1434-9) the following means and standard deviations appear in a table:

Number of Infants	Gestational Age (Weeks)
Singleton	39.2 (±1.9)[1]
Twins	35.8 (±3.2)
Higher order	32.2 (±3.3)

[1]Mean ± SD

Based on that information, compare the distributions of gestational age in the population for each of these three groups.

From the means and standard deviations of gestational age, we can specify an interval of data values that will include a given percentage of all data values in a Gaussian distribution. To include two-thirds of all births, we take the mean gestational age and add and subtract the standard deviation. To include 95% of all births, we take the mean and add and subtract two standard deviations. The following table summarizes these calculations:

Number of Infants	Gestational Age (Weeks)	2/3 of All Births	95% of All Births
Singleton	39.2 (±1.9)	37.3 to 41.1	35.4 to 43.0
Twins	35.8 (±3.2)	32.6 to 39.0	29.4 to 42.2
Higher order	32.2 (±3.3)	28.9 to 35.5	25.6 to 38.8

From those intervals, we can get an idea of how the distributions would appear. For instance, we can see that the mean of gestational age for each of the groups is outside the intervals of values that represent about two-thirds of the data values for the other two groups. Those means are included, however, in the intervals that represent about 95% of the data values in the other two groups.

Use of integers as multiples of the standard deviation to specify a certain proportion of the population's data is an approximation. This approach is useful when we want to calculate an interval of data values in our head. If we want to be more precise, however, we can use the table of standard normal deviates (Table B.1) to find the exact multiple of the standard deviation that specifies a certain proportion of a Gaussian distribution. To do this, we look for one-half of the complement of the proportion of data values in the body of the table. For instance, if we were interested in the central 95% of the data values in a Gaussian distribution, we would look in Table B.1 to find the standard normal deviate that corresponds to a probability of 0.0250 [= (1-0.95)/2]. That standard normal deviate is equal to 1.96. So, a more precise interval of data values corresponds to the mean ± 1.96 times the standard deviation. For the gestational ages of singleton births in Example 2-11, the precise interval that includes 95% of the data values goes from 35.5 weeks to 42.9 weeks. This exact interval is just slightly narrower than the approximate interval determined in Example 2-11 (35.4 weeks to 43.0 weeks).

In this chapter we have looked at the distribution of data in the population and we have seen how understanding that distribution allows us to determine the effect of chance on selecting individuals from the population. In the next chapter, we will examine the ways in which we can use the sample's observations to describe the distribution of data in the population.

CHAPTER 3
Examining Samples

Any sample consists of a subset of the data in a population. Our task is to examine the observations in the sample and, as a result of that examination, draw conclusions about the distribution of data in the population. We do this by using two approaches (Figure 3-1). One approach is to use the data in the sample to come up with a good guess about the numeric value of a parameter of the distribution of data in the population. This approach is called **estimation**. Another is to use the data in the sample to test a hypothesis about a parameter of the distribution of data in a population. This approach is called **hypothesis testing**. In this chapter, we will see how those two approaches allow us to draw conclusions about a population by examining a sample.

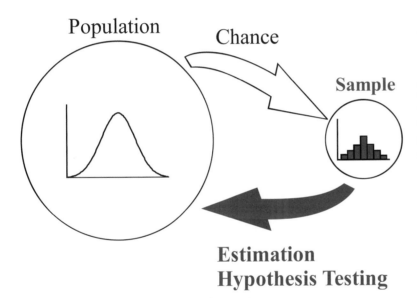

Figure 3-1 The sample's observations are used to make estimates or test hypotheses about the distribution of data in a population.

As we prepare to make a transition from thinking about a population to examining a sample, it is important that we make the distinction between the population and the sample clear. Conceptually, the population is the group about which we would like to draw a conclusion, but which we can never actually examine.[1] The sample, on the other hand, is the group that we examine, but we are not satisfied simply describing the results of that examination. Instead, we are interested in applying the results of examining the sample to our understanding about the population.

    This distinction between the population and the sample is sufficiently meaningful that statisticians have a number of conventions they use when referring to each of these groups. Those conventions are summarized in Table 3-1.

---

[1] In health research, the population has three dimensions: person, place, and time. It is the dimension of time that makes it impossible to examine the entire population. The other dimensions make it highly unlikely, but not impossible.

Table 3-1 Conventions used to distinguish between the population and the sample.

POPULATION	SAMPLE
Data are the values in the population.	**Observations** are those data values selected to be included in the sample.
Parameters are the numeric values that mathematically define the distribution of data in the population (e.g., mean and variance). We never know the actual value of a parameter.	**Estimates** are the values calculated from the sample's observations that are used to guess at the value of the population's parameters.
Greek letters are used to symbolize the population's parameters in mathematic equations.	**English letters** are used to symbolize the sample's estimates in mathematic equations.
N symbolizes the number of data values in the population.	n symbolizes the number of observations in the sample.

Now that the distinction between the population and the sample is clearer, we are ready to discover how the sample's observations can be used to draw conclusions about the population.

ESTIMATION

The purpose of estimation is to make a good guess at the value of a parameter in the population. There are two kinds of estimates that we can make from the sample's observations. A **point estimate** is the single best guess about the value of the population's parameter. The trouble with point estimates is that they have a low probability of being exactly equal in value to the population's parameter.[2] To make an estimate that has a good chance of being equal to the population's parameter, we need to use an interval of values, rather than a single value.[3] Such an estimate is called an **interval estimate** or a **confidence interval**.

Point Estimates

In Chapter 2 we learned that we need two parameters to mathematically describe a distribution of continuous data.[4] These are the mean and the variance (or standard deviation). In developing point estimates, we use the sample's observations to calculate the

---

[2]Recall from Chapter 2 that the probability of any particular value from a continuum is virtually zero because of the large number of possible values in the denominator of that probability.

[3]It was this principle that led us to calculate probabilities for intervals of data values, instead of for specific data values, in Chapter 2.

[4]In the introductory chapters of this text, we are confining our interest to distributions of continuous data. Later, we will see how these principles apply to distributions of other types of data.

most likely values for those parameters in the population. One feature that these estimates must have is that they must be equal, on the average, to the parameter that they estimate. This implies that, if we took lots of samples from the population, the mean of all of the estimates made from all of those samples would be equal to the population's parameter.[5] Such an estimate is said to be **unbiased**. Every estimate we calculate from the sample's observations must be an unbiased estimate of the population's parameter, or it is not an accurate reflection of the parameter, even on the average.

The first method of calculating an estimate we consider when searching for an unbiased estimate is one in which the same calculations are performed on the sample's observations as would be performed to calculate the population's parameter. For instance, Equation {2.1} illustrates how the mean of the population's data would be calculated if we knew the values of all of those data. Equation {3.1} shows that same calculation performed on the sample's observations.

$$\overline{Y} = \frac{\sum Y_i}{n} \qquad \{3.1\}$$

where

$$\overline{Y} \quad = \quad \text{mean of the observations in the sample (called "Y bar")}$$

$$\sum Y_i \quad = \quad \text{sum of the individual data values in the sample}$$

$$n \quad = \quad \text{number of observations in the sample}$$

Before we go further, we need to make a distinction between equations for the population's data and equations for the sample's observations. To do this, we need to confess that we can never know all of the data in the population. If we cannot know all the data in the population, we cannot calculate the population's parameters. Thus, Equation {2.1} describes a concept, not a calculation. On the other hand, we do know all the observations in the sample. So, we can do the calculation described in Equation {3.1}.

The value calculated in Equation {3.1} is the mean of the sample's observations. More important, it is an unbiased estimate of the mean of the population's data. In other words, the mean of the sample's observations is, on the average, equal to the mean of the population's data. Equation {3.2} shows this important relationship in mathematical notation.

$$\mu \stackrel{\wedge}{=} \overline{Y} = \frac{\sum Y_i}{n} \qquad \{3.2\}$$

---

[5]This requirement stems from the use of chance to select the members of the population who will be part of the sample. This strategy results in samples that are representative of the population only on the average. Any particular sample's estimate, however, is unlikely to be exactly equal to the population's parameter.

where

μ = mean of the data in the population

$\triangleq$ = "is estimated by"

$\overline{Y}$ = mean of the observations in the sample (called "Y bar")

Estimating the variance of the distribution of data in the population is a little more complicated than estimating the mean. If we were to use the same calculations on the sample's observations that we used to define the population's variance (Equation {2.3}), we would get a biased estimate of the population's variance. This is because the variance of the sample's observations is systematically smaller than the population's variance.

The reason for this bias is that the most extreme data values (i.e., those that are farthest from the mean) occur very infrequently in the population. As a result, it is very unlikely that these extreme data values will be included among the sample's observations. These extreme data values, however, have the greatest impact on the numeric magnitude of the variance. Since samples systematically exclude these influential values, the sample's variance systematically underestimates the population's variance.[6] This bias is illustrated in Equation {3.3}.

$$\sigma^2 > \frac{\sum (Y_i - \overline{Y})^2}{n} \qquad \{3.3\}$$

where

$>$ = "is greater than"

σ^2 = variance of the distribution of data in the population.

To calculate an unbiased estimate of the population's variance, we need to make a change in Equation {3.3} that will increase the numeric value of the sample's estimate of the population's variance. Also, we want that change to have more impact on the estimate of the variance from smaller samples than from larger samples. The reason for this is that as the size of the sample increases, the probability of including extreme values in the sample also increases. Thus, the larger the sample, the less biased is the estimate shown in Equation {3.3}. To accomplish both of these goals, we subtract one from the number of observations in the sample in the denominator of Equation {3.3} to provide an unbiased estimate of the population's variance. Equation {3.4} illustrates that unbiased estimate of the population's variance.

---

[6]This bias does not affect the sample's estimate of the mean since missing extreme data values above and below the population mean are balanced and, thus, cancel each other. In the variance, however, squaring the differences between the data values and the mean prevents canceling of negative and positive effects.

$$\sigma^2 \triangleq s^2 = \frac{\sum (Y_i - \bar{Y})^2}{n-1} \qquad \{3.4\}$$

where

σ^2 = population's variance of distribution of data

s^2 = sample's estimate of the population's variance.

At first, the choice to subtract one from the number of observations in the sample in calculation of the variance's estimate might seem arbitrary, but it is not. Instead, n-1 reflects the amount of information available in the sample for estimation of the variance (called the "**degrees of freedom**"). Since we need at least two observations to observe dispersion, the amount of information in the sample present to estimate the variance is equal to n-1 instead of n.

Now, let us take a look at an example of point estimation.

Example 3-1 Suppose that we are interested in the efficacy of a new topical treatment for glaucoma. To investigate this efficacy, we identify nine persons with elevated intraocular pressure. Each of those persons is randomly assigned to use the new treatment in one eye and the standard treatment in the other eye. After one week of treatment, the difference in intraocular pressure between the two eyes (ΔIOP) is measured for each person (mmHg). Suppose that we observed the following results:

PATIENT	ΔIOP
TH	3
IS	0
MA	3
KE	2
SM	-3
ES	11
OH	1
AP	6
PY	4
Total	27

From those observations, let us calculate unbiased estimates of the population's parameters.

To begin, we need to estimate the mean difference in intraocular pressure. To calculate that estimate, we use Equation{3.2}.

$$\mu \triangleq \bar{Y} = \frac{\sum Y_i}{n} = \frac{27}{9} = 3 \text{ mmHg}$$

Thus, our best guess of the mean of the distribution of data in the population is 3 mmHg.

Next, we will use Equation {3.4} to calculate an estimate of the population's variance. In preparation for that calculation, we need to calculate the squared differences between each of the observations and the estimated mean. The following table shows those calculations.

PATIENT	ΔIOP	$Y_i - \bar{Y}$	$(Y_i - \bar{Y})^2$
TH	3	0	0
IS	0	-3	9
MA	3	0	0
KE	2	-1	1
SM	-3	-6	36
ES	11	8	64
OH	1	-2	4
AP	6	3	9
PY	4	1	1
Total	27	0	124

Now, we are ready to use Equation {3.4} to calculate the sample's estimate of the population's variance.

$$\sigma^2 \triangleq s^2 = \frac{\sum (Y_i - \bar{Y})^2}{n-1} = \frac{124}{9-1} = 15.5 \text{ mmHg}^2$$

So, an unbiased estimate of the population's variance is equal to 15.5 mmHg^2. If we prefer, we can estimate the standard deviation by taking the square root of the variance estimate:

$$s = \sqrt{s^2} = \sqrt{15.5 \text{ mmHg}^2} = 3.94 \text{ mmHg}$$

_____

If we had used Equation {3.3} instead of Equation {3.4} to calculate the variance estimate in Example 3-1, we would have gotten (124 /9 =) 13.8 mmHg^2 for the variance, which corresponds to a standard deviation of 3.71 mmHg. These values are both less than those we calculated (15.5 mmHg2 and 3.94 mmHg, respectively). Since they underestimate the population's parameters, they are biased estimates. The degree of bias observed for that sample of 9 patients is equal to 0.23 mmHg (3.94-3.71) for the standard deviation. If the sample were bigger, the degree of this bias would be smaller.

Example 3-1 illustrates how the mean, variance, and standard deviation of the population's distribution can be estimated from the sample's observations by showing the calculations we would use if we were to derive those estimates by hand. Doing that is a good way to understand these estimates but, in practice, we will be using computer programs to calculate these estimates. In Chapter 4, we will look at these same estimates as we would encounter them from a statistical analysis program.

Even though these point estimates are equal to the population's parameters on the average, any particular point estimate (i.e., from a particular sample) is probably not exactly equal to its corresponding parameter. The problem is that we use chance to determine the composition of a sample and point estimates do not take that role of chance into account. Interval estimates, on the other hand, reflect this role of chance. We will see how to calculate interval estimates later in this chapter, but first we need to think some more about how chance affects a sample's estimate.

The Sampling Distribution

In Chapter 2, we looked at the distribution of data in the population and used that distribution to address the probability that certain members of the population would be selected for inclusion in the sample. Thus, we were interested in the role of chance as it affects individuals. Now, we have a different focus. Instead of the effect of chance on individuals, we are interested in the effect of chance on estimates.

Although these two roles of chance are related, it makes it easier for us to understand statistical procedures if we think of a different distribution for each. To take chance into account for individuals in the population, we use the distribution of data. To take chance into account for estimates of the population's parameters, we use a distribution called the **sampling distribution**. In a sampling distribution, we look at the frequency of different estimates that we could obtain if we were to take all possible samples with n observations from the population. Figure 3-2 illustrates the origin of the sampling distribution for estimates of the mean from a distribution of continuous data.

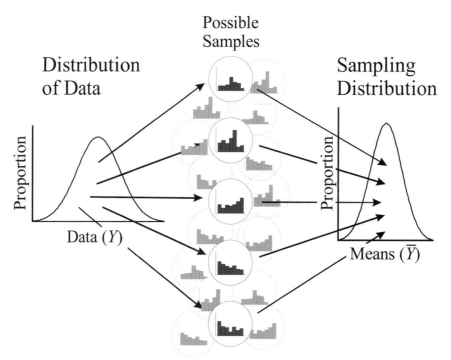

Figure 3-2 The sampling distribution shows estimates of the mean from all possible samples with n observations.

It is the sampling distribution that tells us about the role of chance in getting particular estimates of a population's parameter. Clearly, this is an important distribution to understand. Unfortunately, the sampling distribution has a characteristic that sometimes acts as an impediment to understanding. That is that the sampling distribution does not really exist, except as a mathematical construct of the distribution of data. For the sampling distribution to be an entity in and of itself, we would have to take all possible samples of a given size from the population and estimate the mean from the observations in each sample. In truth, we take only a single sample from which we calculate a single estimate of the mean. Even so, the sampling distribution represents the mathematical effect of chance on estimates (e.g., of the mean) and, thus, allows us to think of that role of chance graphically, instead of mathematically.

In Figure 3-2, both the distribution of data and the sampling distribution are represented as Gaussian distributions. To use the standard normal distribution to calculate the probability of obtaining a particular data value (via the distribution of data) or a particular estimate of the mean (via the sampling distribution) we need to assume that the corresponding distribution is a Gaussian distribution. For the distribution of data, this is an uncomfortable assumption. Most distributions of biologic and physical data are asymmetric and, therefore, not Gaussian distributions.[7] This fact limits the usefulness of the methods described in Chapter 2, at least when applied to distributions of data.

This same limitation does not apply to sampling distributions, however. This is because sampling distributions (for estimates of a parameter of location like the mean) tend to be Gaussian, even if the data from which the sample was taken is not Gaussian. This tendency of sampling distributions to be Gaussian is addressed by what is called the "**central limit theorem**."

According to the central limit theorem, the distributions of estimates of a parameter of location (e.g., the mean) will always be Gaussian if the data themselves have a Gaussian distribution. The central limit theorem goes on to state that sampling distributions, regardless of the distribution of data, tend to be Gaussian with that tendency increasing as the size of the samples increase. By the time we consider samples with about 30 observations or more, the sampling distribution will be Gaussian regardless of the shape of the distribution of data. Figure 3-3 illustrates the central limit theorem by showing the results of a computer simulation of the sampling process with various sample's sizes.

---

[7]The most common distribution of natural data is called the log-normal distribution. The log-normal distribution has a Gaussian distribution of the logarithms of the data values. This is the reason that we often analyze data on a log scale.

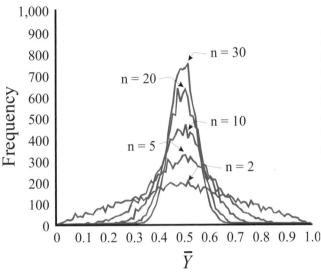

Figure 3-3 Computer simulation of sampling from a uniform distribution of data (i.e., a distribution in which all data values occur with the same frequency) to illustrate the tendency of the sampling distribution for estimates of the mean to be Gaussian, with that tendency increasing as the size of the sample increases.

If the sampling distribution is a Gaussian distribution, then we need to provide estimates for its mean and variance (or standard deviation) if we want to calculate probabilities of obtaining certain estimates of the mean. Of these two, the mean of the sampling distribution is the easier to determine. To see how the mean of a sampling distribution is determined, recall that the definition of an unbiased estimate states that unbiased estimates are equal to the population's parameter, on the average. This is reflected in the sampling distribution by the mean of that distribution being equal to the population's parameter being estimated. Thus, the mean of the sampling distribution of estimates of the mean in the population is equal to the population's mean. This is illustrated in Equation{3.5}.

$$\mu_{\bar{Y}} = \mu \stackrel{\wedge}{=} \bar{Y} \qquad \qquad \{3.5\}$$

where

$\mu_{\bar{Y}}$ = mean of the distribution of estimates of the mean (i.e., the sampling distribution)

μ = mean of the distribution of data

$\bar{Y}$ = sample's estimate of the mean of the distribution of data

The variance of the sampling distribution is only a little more complicated to understand than the mean of that distribution. There are two things that affect the variability of estimates. One of those is the variability of the data. The greater the dispersion of the data values, the more variability we expect to see among estimates of the mean. The other is the size of the sample. The larger the sample, the less variability we expect to see among estimates of the mean.

To understand why the size of the samples affects the variability among estimates of the mean, imagine what happens to the estimate of the mean when an extreme data value is included in the sample. If the sample consists of few other observations, the extreme value will result in an estimate of the mean that is far from the actual mean in the population. If the sample consists of many observations however, the influence of that extreme data value will be diminished by less extreme values and even some extreme observations in the opposite direction.[8]

Thus, there are two things that influence the dispersion of the sampling distribution: the variance of the distribution of data and the number of observations in the sample. Equation {3.6} shows that relationship in mathematical language.

$$\sigma_{\bar{Y}}^2 = \frac{\sigma^2}{n} \stackrel{\wedge}{=} \frac{s^2}{n} \qquad \{3.6\}$$

where

$\sigma_{\bar{Y}}^2$ = variance of the distribution of estimates of the mean (i.e., the sampling distribution)

σ^2 = variance of the distribution of data in the population

s^2 = sample's estimate of the variance of the distribution of data

n = sample's size

If we were to take the square root of the variance of the sampling distribution, the result would be the standard deviation of that distribution. To help us keep the sampling distribution and the distribution of data distinct, however, we give a special name to the standard deviation of the sampling distribution. It is called the **standard error**. Equation {3.7} shows the standard error in the population and how its estimate is calculated from the sample's observations.

$$\sigma_{\bar{Y}} = \sqrt{\frac{\sigma^2}{n}} \stackrel{\wedge}{=} s_{\bar{Y}} = \sqrt{\frac{s^2}{n}} \text{ or } \frac{s}{\sqrt{n}} \qquad \{3.7\}$$

where

$\sigma_{\bar{Y}}$ = standard error (i.e., the standard deviation of the sampling distribution) in the population

$s_{\bar{Y}}$ = sample's estimate of the standard error

s^2 = sample's estimate of the variance of the distribution of data

---

[8]A way to think about this process of estimating a mean is to imagine it as a process of "buffering" data values. In this analogy, we can think of the observations close to the mean as reducing the impact of extreme observations in the sample.

$$n \quad = \quad \text{sample's size}$$

The next example illustrates the way in which the standard error is estimated from the sample's observations.

Example 3-2 In Example 3-1 we looked at study of the efficacy of a new topical treatment for glaucoma and observed the difference in intraocular pressure between the two eyes for each of 9 persons. From those observations, we calculated estimates of the parameters of the population's distribution of data. In that example, we estimated the mean to be equal to 3 mmHg and estimated the variance to be equal to 15.5 mmHg^2. Now, let us use these same data to estimate the parameters of the sampling distribution

---

As stated in Equation {3.5}, the mean of the sampling distribution is the same as the mean of the distribution of data. Thus, the sample's estimate of the mean of the sampling distribution is equal to the sample's estimate of the mean of the distribution of data. In Example 3-1, we calculated that estimate and found it to be equal to 3 mmHg.

To calculate the estimate of the standard error, we use Equation {3.7}:

$$\sigma_{\bar{Y}} \triangleq \sqrt{\frac{s^2}{n}} = \sqrt{\frac{15.5}{9}} = 1.31 \text{ mmHg}$$

Thus, the estimates of the parameters of the sampling distribution are 3 mmHg for the mean and 1.31 mmHg for the standard error.

Now that we are aware of the sampling distribution and familiar with its parameters, we are ready to address the influence of chance on estimates of the population's mean.

Interval Estimates

The idea behind interval estimation is to calculate an interval of values to estimate the population's parameter with a specified level of confidence that the population's parameter is included within the interval. The interval we calculate is usually centered on the point estimate, our best single-value guess at the value of the parameter. The result is called a **two-sided confidence interval**.[9]

How wide we make the confidence interval depends on two things. First, the width of the interval reflects our desired level of confidence that the population's parameter is

---

[9]If we were to allow one of the limits of the interval estimate to be equal to infinity, we would create a **one-sided** confidence interval. A one-sided confidence interval is not centered on the point estimate, making it more difficult to interpret. We will not consider one-sided confidence intervals in this text.

included in the interval. To have a higher level of confidence, a wider interval is required.[10]

Second, the width of the interval is affected by the precision with which we can estimate the population's parameter from the sample's observations. That precision is reflected by the standard error. As the standard error decreases, so does the width of the interval estimate. The standard error can be decreased in two ways. One way is by decreasing the variance of the distribution of data (σ^2). That is to say, the more precisely the data are measured, the more precisely the mean is estimated. The other way is by increasing the size of the sample. The larger the sample, the more precise is the estimate of the mean from that sample's observations.

Calculation of the limits of the interval estimate is similar to calculation of the interval of data values that corresponds to a given percentage of a Gaussian distribution we discussed at the end of Chapter 2 (for instance, see Example 2-11). There is an important difference between limits of the interval estimate and the limits of the interval that corresponds to a given proportion of the distribution of data. This is that the limits of the interval estimate are calculated from the sampling distribution, while the interval of data values is calculated from the distribution of data. There are two implications of that difference. First, we use the standard error instead of the standard deviation when calculating an interval estimate. Second, we are assured by the central limit theorem that it is appropriate to use methods based on Gaussian distributions as long as the size of the sample is not too small.

In Chapter 2, we looked at both an approximate method and an exact method for calculating the interval of data values. The approximate method presented looks at interval multipliers of the standard deviation to determine the data interval that corresponds to a particular proportion of all of the data values. This approximate method is useful when interpreting means and standard deviations tabulated in a research article. That application was demonstrated in Example 2-11.

We can use a similar method to calculate an approximate interval estimate. When calculating an interval for means, rather than for data, it is multiples of the standard error we use, instead of the standard deviation, since the interval for means is calculated from the sampling distribution instead of the distribution of data. The next example shows how this can be done for tabulated means and standard errors from a research article.

Example 3-3 In a study of 53 patients with renal disease (*N Engl J Med* 1998; 339:1364-70), the mean blood pressure during the winter months was reported as "153 (±3)" mmHg for systolic pressure and "82 (±2)" mmHg for diastolic pressure. The text of this report tells us that the numbers in parentheses are the corresponding standard errors. Let us use the approximate method to interpret these results.

---

[10] The extremes for the level of confidence are 0% and 100%. At a 0% level of confidence, we are certain that the population's parameter is not included in the interval. A 0% interval is equal to the point estimate. At a 100% level of confidence, we are certain that the population's parameter is included in the interval. A 100% interval includes all possible values for the parameter (e.g., -∞ to +∞).

When we used the approximate method to interpret standard deviations in Example 2.10, we calculated intervals centered on the mean and having limits of either one standard deviation or two standard deviations on either side of the mean. Those intervals encompass about 2/3

and about 95% of the data in a Gaussian distribution of data, respectively. If we were to calculate those same intervals, but with multiples of the standard error instead of the standard deviation, the intervals would include about 2/3 and about 95% of the possible estimates of the mean in a Gaussian sampling distribution. The following table shows those approximate confidence intervals we obtain using the information provided in this research article:

MEASUREMENT	MEAN	SE	±1SE	±2SE
Systolic Blood Pressure	153 mmHg	3 mmHg	150 to 156 mmHg	147 to 159 mmHg
Diastolic Blood Pressure	82 mmHg	2 mmHg	80 to 84 mmHg	78 to 86 mmHg

These intervals give us an idea of how different the means would be if we were to take several samples from the population. For systolic blood pressure, about 95% of the means would be in the 12 mmHg interval between 147 and 159 mmHg. Similarly, 95% of mean diastolic blood pressure values would be in the 8 mmHg interval between 78 and 86 mmHg. These intervals reflect the precision with which we are able to estimate the means.

_____

The approximate method of calculating an interval estimate is appropriate when we are performing an informal interpretation of health research data. If we are using interval estimates in a formal interpretation (i.e., in writing a research article or making a presentation) however, we should use the exact method to calculate interval estimates. The exact method involves a standard normal deviate that corresponds to one-half of the complement of the level of confidence we desire. For a 95% confidence interval, the standard normal deviate would correspond to 2.5% (or a proportion of 0.025). Equation {3.8} illustrates how that exact method is used to calculate an interval centered on the point estimate of the mean.

$$\mu \triangleq \bar{Y} \pm (z_{\alpha/2} \cdot \sigma_{\bar{Y}}) \qquad \{3.8\}$$

where

μ = population's mean

$\bar{Y}$ = sample's estimate of the population's mean

α = complement of the degree of confidence desired (e.g., if we want a 95% confidence level, $\alpha=1-0.95=0.05$)

$z_{\alpha/2}$ = a standard normal deviate that corresponds to a probability of one half the complement of the degree of confidence we desire in one tail of the standard normal distribution

$\sigma_{\bar{Y}}$ = standard error (i.e., the standard deviation of the sampling distribution) in the population

Now, let us take a look at an example using this method to calculate an interval estimate.

Example 3-4 In Example 3-3, we calculated approximate interval estimates for mean systolic and diastolic blood pressure during the winter months among 53 persons with renal disease. Now, we will use the exact method to calculate 95% two-sided interval estimates for those means.

To calculate an exact interval estimate, we use Equation{3.8}. In this equation, we need a standard normal deviate that corresponds to one-half of the complement of the degree of confidence we desire. In this case, we are going to calculate a 95% confidence interval, so α is equal to 1-0.95=0.05. Since this will be a two-sided interval estimate, we need to find a standard normal deviate that corresponds to half of α (0.05/2=0.025) in the upper tail of the standard normal distribution. From Table B.1, we find that standard normal deviate by finding a probability of 0.0250 in the body of the table. That probability corresponds to the row headed by "1.9" and the column headed by "6." So, the standard normal deviate that corresponds to a probability of 0.025 is equal to 1.96. With that value and the estimates of the standard errors from Example 3-3, we obtain the following 95%, two-sided confidence intervals for the results reported in this research article.

MEASUREMENT	MEAN	SE	±1.96SE
Systolic Blood Pressure	153 mmHg	3 mmHg	147.1 to 158.9 mmHg
Diastolic Blood Pressure	82 mmHg	2 mmHg	78.1 to 85.9 mmHg

These confidence intervals are close to the approximate intervals using two standard errors on either side of the mean. Even so, we should use this exact method to calculate intervals we intend to publish.

Interval estimation is one way that we can take into account the role of chance in determining the composition of our sample. In this approach, we calculate an interval centered on the sample's estimate of the population's parameter. The width of this interval determines the level of confidence we can have that the population's parameter is, in fact, included in the interval. Also influencing the width of the interval is the precision of the estimate. Another way in which we can take the role of chance into account in determining the composition of our sample is through the process of hypothesis testing. This is the next topic we will consider in this chapter.

HYPOTHESIS TESTING

There are four steps in the process of statistical hypothesis testing. The first step is the formulation of the hypothesis about the nature of the population that will be tested. Next, we take a sample from the population. Then, we calculate the probability of getting that sample if the hypothesis were true. In the final step, we reject the hypothesis as a description of the population if the probability of getting that sample if the hypothesis were true is sufficiently small. These steps are illustrated in Figure 3-4.

(1) Formulate hypothesis

$$\text{Hyp: } \mu_0 = 0$$

(2) Take sample from
     population

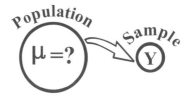

(3) Calculate probability of getting
     an estimate as far from the
     hypothesized value as the sample's
     estimate if the hypothesis were true

$$P(\text{estimate} \geq \overline{Y} \mid \mu = 0)$$

(4) If probability is small,
     reject hypothesis

$$\text{Hyp:} \cancel{\mu = 0}$$

Figure 3-4 Steps in testing a statistical hypothesis.

The first step in statistical hypothesis testing is to formulate the hypothesis to be tested. At this point, no data have been collected from the population. Thus, the hypothesis to be tested is not in any way influenced by the sample's observations. Instead, the hypothesis is a tentative description of the population that might be changed after the data are collected and analyzed.

The hypothesis to be tested has to satisfy two requirements. First, the hypothesis has to describe a condition that is interesting to test. Second, the hypothesis must make a specific statement about the population. For instance, if the hypothesis addresses the population's mean, the hypothesis must suggest a single numeric value for that mean. The types of hypotheses that satisfy both of these requirements are usually statements about the population that suggest that there are no relationships between measurements. In that circumstance, differences are equal to zero, ratios are equal to one, and nothing changes in relation to anything else. Because of that characteristic, the hypothesis that we test is called the **null hypothesis** and is identified by the symbol H_0. The next example illustrates how the null hypothesis is formulated.

Example 3-5 In Example 3-1 we were interested in the efficacy of a new topical medication that is intended to lower intraocular pressure. The study that was performed involved 9 patients with ocular hypertension. Each of those patients was randomly assigned to use the new medication in one eye and the standard treatment in the other eye. After one week of treatment, the difference in intraocular pressure between the two eyes was measured. Now, let us develop the null hypothesis that we could test in this study that would address the efficacy of the new medication.

The reason that we are doing this study is because we think that there will be a difference between the intraocular pressures in each person's eyes. That is the hypothesis that motivated us to perform the study, but it cannot be used as the null hypothesis. The reason is that this hypothesis does not make a specific statement about the population (i.e., it does not provide a single numeric value for the mean difference in intraocular pressure). For a hypothesis to be testable, it must make a specific statement about the population.

Instead of testing the hypothesis that motivated the study, we can use its denial (i.e., the complement of that hypothesis) since it provides a specific value for the population's mean; namely zero. Thus, the null hypothesis that we will test is that the mean difference in intraocular pressure between each person's eyes is equal to zero in the population. In mathematical shorthand, we can represent that null hypothesis as,

$$H_0 : \mu_0 = 0$$

where μ_0 is the value of the population's mean difference according to the null hypothesis.

Quite a bit of what we do when analyzing data is to accomplish the third step of hypothesis testing. In that step, we calculate the probability of getting an estimate (e.g., of the mean) at least as far from the hypothesized value as the sample's estimate if the null hypothesis were true. This probability is called the **P-value**. The P-value is a conditional probability in which the conditional event is obtaining an estimate at least as extreme as the sample's estimate and the conditioning event is the null hypothesis being true.[11] Equation {3.9} illustrates the P-value in mathematic language (we will also look at the P-value graphically in a moment).

$$P\text{-value} = p(\text{estimate} \geq \overline{Y} \mid H_0 \text{ true}) \qquad \{3.9\}$$

Calculation of a P-value is similar to calculation of the probability of selecting persons from

---

[11]It is the need to calculate the P-value that requires a null hypothesis to make a specific statement about the population. It would be extremely complicated, if possible at all in practice, to calculate a P-value for a null hypothesis that includes more than one value.

the population within an interval of data values, as we did in Chapter 2 (Equation {2.7}). There are three differences, however, between calculation of the probability of obtaining an interval of data values and calculation of a P-value. One difference is that, in hypothesis testing, the population's mean is taken to be equal to the specific value stated in the null hypothesis, rather than the population's actual value. Thus, we think of the sampling distribution defined by the null hypothesis, instead of the actual sampling distribution. The sampling distribution representing the null hypothesis being true is called the **null distribution**. Figure 3-5 illustrates the null distribution when the null hypothesis states that the mean is equal to zero.

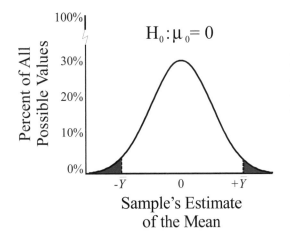

Figure 3-5 The sampling distribution as defined by the null hypothesis (i.e., the "null distribution"). $\overline{Y}$ is the absolute value of the point estimate obtained in the sample.

The second difference is that calculation of a P-value involves the sampling distribution, rather than the distribution of data. Thus, the standard deviation used in calculation of a P-value is the standard deviation of the sampling distribution (i.e., the standard error). Equation {3.10} illustrates how a standard normal deviate can be calculated as part of the process of determining a P-value.

$$z = \frac{\overline{Y} - \mu_0}{\sigma_{\overline{Y}}}$$ {3.10}

where

z	=	standard normal deviate that corresponds to the sample's estimate of the population's mean
$\overline{Y}$	=	sample's estimate of the population's mean
μ_0	=	value of the population's mean stated in the null hypothesis
$\sigma_{\overline{Y}}$	=	standard deviation of the sampling distribution (i.e., the standard error)

The third difference is that the P-value is almost always calculated by considering both tails of the sampling distribution. This implies that the P-value is the probability of getting a sample with an estimate at least as far from the value in the null hypothesis, without specifying on which side of that value the sample's estimate ($\overline{Y}$) occurs. We will consider this issue further, but first let us take a look at Figure 3-6 which illustrates the *P*-value in graphic language.

$$P\text{-value} = \frac{\text{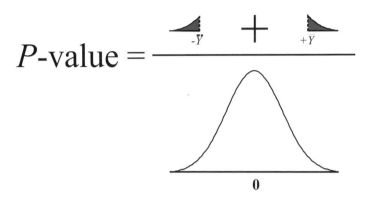}}{}$$

Figure 3-6 Calculation of a *P*-value from the null distribution. $\overline{Y}$ is the absolute value of the point estimate obtained in the sample.

Now, let us take a look at an example of how to calculate the *P*-value.

Example 3-6 In Example 3-5, we were interested in the efficacy of a new topical treatment for ocular hypertension. In that example, we considered the null hypothesis that the mean difference in intraocular pressure between a person's eyes is equal to zero in the population. In Example 3-1, we found that the mean difference in intraocular pressure is equal to 3 mmHg for these 9 patients. In Example 3-2, we calculated the standard error for the mean difference in intraocular pressure and found it to be equal to 1.31 mmHg. Now, let us assume that the population's standard error is equal to our estimate and calculate the *P*-value that we can use to test the null hypothesis that the mean difference in intraocular pressures between each person's eyes is equal to zero in the population.

P-values are determined from the sampling distribution, so we will use Equation {3.10} to calculate the standard normal deviate that will represent the observed mean difference on the standard normal distribution:

$$z = \frac{\overline{Y} - \mu_0}{\sigma_{\overline{Y}}} = \frac{3 - 0}{1.31} = 2.29$$

So, a standard normal deviate of 2.29 corresponds to a sample's mean of 3 mmHg if the mean difference in the population is really equal to zero (i.e., if the null hypothesis were true). In Table B.1, we find that a standard normal deviate of 2.29 or greater corresponds to a probability of 0.0110. If we confine our interest to means above zero, the *P*-value would be equal to 0.0110. If we were interested in means that are at least as far away from zero as 3 mmHg in either direction, the *P*-value would be equal to 0.0110 for means greater than zero plus 0.0110 for means less than zero. In that case, the *P*-value is equal to 0.0220.

The following is a graphic illustration of how this *P*-value is calculated. First, the sample's estimate of the mean change in intraocular pressure is converted from its original scale:

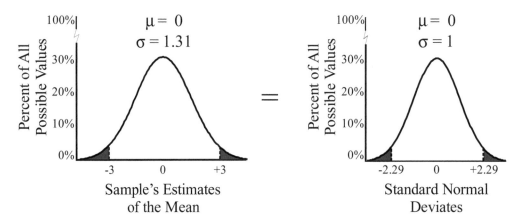

Then, the probability of obtaining the corresponding standard normal deviate (2.29) or a larger value is determined by looking up 2.29 in Table B.1. That probability is equal to 0.0110. Finally, the *P*-value is calculated as follows:

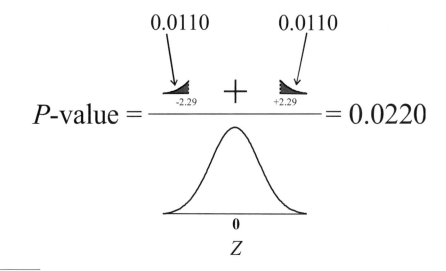

The final step in testing a statistical hypothesis is to stop believing in (i.e., to reject) the null hypothesis if the *P*-value is small enough. This is called "rejecting" the null hypothesis. When we reject the null hypothesis, we say that the result is **statistically significant**.

    To reject the null hypothesis, we need to decide how small the *P*-value needs to be to cause us to doubt its veracity. Usually, we consider a *P*-value equal to or less than 0.05 to be small enough to reject the null hypothesis. Thus, in Example 3-6, the conclusion we would draw having gotten a *P*-value of 0.0220 is that the null hypothesis is not true. That is to say, we would reject the null hypothesis.

    When we reject the null hypothesis, something else happens automatically: we believe that a second hypothesis is true. This second hypothesis is called the **alternative hypothesis**. Since our belief in the alternative hypothesis occurs only by the process of eliminating the null hypothesis, the alternative hypothesis must include all possibilities for the population that are not included in the null hypothesis.[12] So, if the null hypothesis states that the population's mean is equal to zero, the alternative hypothesis is that the population's mean is not equal to zero.

An alternative hypothesis that includes values on both sides of the value in the null hypothesis is called a **two-sided** alternative hypothesis. It is when we have a two-sided alternative hypothesis that the *P*-value is calculated from both tails of the sampling distribution. A **one-sided** alternative hypothesis, however, includes values on only one side of the value in the null hypothesis and the corresponding *P*-value is calculated only from the single tail of the sampling distribution on that same side of the value in the null hypothesis.

Virtually all alternative hypotheses should be two-sided. To use a one-sided alternative hypothesis, it must be impossible for the population's value to occur on the other side of the null value.[13] This is rarely true, so all of the alternative hypotheses we will consider in this text are two-sided.

At the final step in the process of hypothesis testing we can reject the null hypothesis if the *P*-value is sufficiently small (i.e., $P \leq 0.05$). If the *P*-value is not small enough to reject the null hypothesis (i.e., $P > 0.05$), however, we do not accept the null hypothesis as being true. Instead, we avoid drawing a conclusion about the null hypothesis when it cannot be rejected. The statistical terminology we use when the *P*-value is too large to reject the null hypothesis is to say that we "fail to reject" the null hypothesis.

To understand why we "fail to reject" rather than "accept" the null hypothesis, we need to consider the potential errors that we might make when we are testing a null hypothesis. There are two types of errors possible. A **type I error** occurs when the null hypothesis is true, but we mistakenly reject it. A **type II error** occurs when the null hypothesis is false, but we wrongly accept it. Those errors are illustrated in Table 3-2.

Table 3-2 **There are four possible results in the process of hypothesis testing. In two of those four possible results, our conclusion is incorrect.**

CONCLUSION

		Accept H_0	Reject H_0
TRUTH	H_0 True	Correct	Type I Error
	H_0 False	Type II Error	Correct

---

[12] In statistical terms, the null hypothesis and the alternative hypothesis are a collectively exhaustive set.

[13] The reason that it must be <u>impossible</u> for the population's value to occur on the other side of the value in the null hypothesis to use a one-sided alternative hypothesis is because the alternative hypothesis is embraced through the process of elimination once the null hypothesis is rejected. For a one-sided alternative hypothesis to be appropriate, values on the other side of the null value must be eliminated by a process other than rejection of the null hypothesis.

The probability of making a type I error is symbolized by the Greek letter α (alpha). Equation {3.11} illustrates α in mathematical language,

$$\alpha = p(type\ I\ error) = p(\text{reject } H_0 \mid H_0 \text{ true}) \qquad \{3.11\}$$

and Figure 3-7 illustrates α graphically.

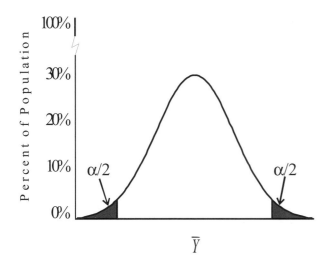

Figure 3-7 The value of α is split between the two tails of the sampling distribution corresponding to the null hypothesis when the alternative hypothesis is two-sided.

The value of α is chosen when we decide how small a P-value must be before we reject the null hypothesis. If we use the conventional value of 0.05, the probability of making a type I error is then also equal to 0.05 (i.e., α =0.05). Thus, the probability of making a type I error is known and it is considered to be sufficiently small to justify rejection of the null hypothesis when the P-value is equal to or less than α. When the alternative hypothesis is two-sided, the value of α is evenly divided between both tails of the sampling distribution as defined in the null hypothesis. Figure 3-7 illustrates α when the alternative hypothesis is two-sided.

The next example shows how we use the value of α to draw a conclusion about the null hypothesis.

Example 3-7 In Example 3-6, we calculated a P-value of 0.0220 when testing the null hypothesis that the mean difference in intraocular pressures between the two eyes of each patient (one treated with new medication) is equal to zero in the population. If we are willing to take a risk of 0.05 of making a type I error, what is the best conclusion to draw?

By saying that we are willing to take a 0.05 risk of making a type I error, we are saying that the value of α is 0.05. If the P-value is equal to or less than the value of α, we can reject the null hypothesis. Since the P-value is less than 0.05, we can reject the null hypothesis that the mean difference in intraocular pressures is equal to zero in the population. Then, through the process of elimination, we can accept the alternative hypothesis. The two-sided alternative hypothesis is that the mean difference in intraocular pressures is not equal to zero in the population. The biologic interpretation is that the new medication makes a difference in intraocular pressure.

The probability of making a type II error is symbolized by the Greek letter β (beta). Equation {3.12} illustrates β in mathematical language.

$$\beta = p(\text{type II error}) = p(\text{accept } H_0 \mid H_0 \text{ false}) \qquad \{3.12\}$$

The probability of making a type II error is based on the assumption that the null hypothesis is false and, therefore, that the alternative hypothesis is true. Since the alternative hypothesis does not provide a specific value for the population's parameter, it is essentially impossible to calculate the probability of making a type II error. This inability to determine the probability of making a type II error makes statisticians uneasy. We do not mind taking a chance of being wrong, as long as we know the magnitude of the risk, but we do not know the risk of making a type II error.

One way to avoid the risk of making a type II error is to never conclude that the null hypothesis is true. Illustrated in Table 3-.3, that strategy eliminates the left-hand column of the table, including the situation in which we can make a type II error. When we say that we "fail to reject" the null hypothesis, what we are really saying is that we refuse to draw a conclusion about the null hypothesis, since to do so would involve the risk of making a type II error.

Table 3- 3 Avoiding a type II error by not accepting the null hypothesis as true when it cannot be rejected.

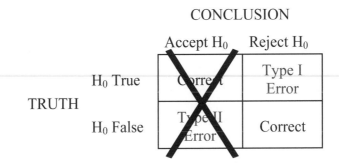

Relationship Between Interval Estimation and Hypothesis Testing

In this chapter, we have described two methods that take the role of chance into account in selecting the sample from the population: interval estimation and hypothesis testing. Since it is the same role of chance that these two methods take into account, you might expect the methods to be related to each other. In fact, the method of calculating a confidence interval and the method of testing a hypothesis that we have considered are algebraically identical.[14] From a mathematical point of view, it does not really matter which approach we use. We can calculate a confidence interval if we know the *P*-value of the sample's estimate or we can test a hypothesis if we know the limits of the confidence interval. The latter is the easier of the two. To test a null hypothesis using a confidence interval, we decide whether or not the value in the null hypothesis is included within the confidence interval. To be included in the interval, the null value must be greater than the lower limit and less than the upper limit. If the null value is included in the confidence interval, we would fail to reject the null hypothesis with α equal to the complement of the degree of confidence that the interval reflects (i.e., $\alpha = 0.05$ for a 95% confidence interval). If, on the other hand, the value in the null hypothesis is either equal to or less than the lower limit or it is equal to or greater than the upper limit, we can reject the null hypothesis with that same value of α. This method of interpreting a confidence interval is illustrated in the next example.

Example 3-8 In Example 3-7, we tested the null hypothesis that the mean difference in intraocular pressures between a patient's two eyes was equal to zero for a group of 9 patients when the two eyes were treated with different topical medications. Now, let us suppose that we were to take chance into account by calculating a 95% confidence interval. What conclusion could we draw about the null hypothesis by examining the confidence interval?

Using Equation {3.8} and the standard error of 1.31 mmHg calculated in Example 3-2, we get the following 95%, two-sided confidence interval for the mean difference in intraocular pressure:

$$\mu = \overline{Y} \pm (z_{\alpha/2} \cdot \sigma_{\overline{Y}}) = 3 \pm (1.96 \cdot 1.31) = 0.4 \text{ to } 5.6 \, \text{mmHg}$$

96Now, we can test the null hypothesis that the mean difference in intraocular pressures is equal to zero in the population by determining whether or not zero is included in the confidence interval. Since zero is less than the lower limit of the confidence interval, we can reject the null hypothesis that the mean difference is equal to zero. Biologically, the new medication makes a difference in intraocular pressure. This is the same conclusion we drew in Example 3-7.

In these first three chapters, we have examined the logical basis for what we do and say about statistical analysis of health research data. For the next 9 chapters, we will discover the methods themselves, when they should be used, and how to interpret the results.

---

[14]This is true for all methods we will discuss for continuous data. It is almost true for the methods we will discuss for nominal data. We will consider this distinction in Chapter 6.

PART TWO

Univariable Analyses

In Part One, we examined three basic principles of statistics. First, we found out how chance works. Next, we considered different ways in which a population's data can be described. Finally, we learned how a sample's observations can be used to describe the population's data. Now that we understand these basic principles, we are ready to learn about the actual methods that are used to analyze data encountered in health research.

The organization of the remainder of this text is designed to reflect how a statistician selects an appropriate method to analyze a particular set of data. There are two reasons that the text is organized in this way. First, this organization helps us to see how different statistical methods fit together. As you read the remaining chapters, you should get the impression that statistical methods share the same logical framework. Second, this organization will assist you when using this text as a reference. When you are ready to analyze your own data or interpret the results of someone else's analysis, you can use the flowchart presented below (Flowchart 1) to find the chapter that discusses the statistical procedure that is most commonly used to analyze a particular set of data. Before we talk about specific statistical methods however, we need to take a look at how a statistician thinks when faced with data to analyze.

As part of the process of research, the researcher records data. These data, however, are not necessarily used in statistical analyses in the same form that they are recorded. Statisticians think of the collection of data to be used in a statistical procedure a little bit differently than the collection of data that are recorded by the researcher. Rather than data, statisticians think about **variables**. Variables represent the researcher's data in the mathematics of statistical methods.

Variables have two characteristics. The first of these characteristics is determined by the type of data the variable represents. For continuous or ordinal data, corresponding variables represent those data just as they were observed. Thus, there is a one-to-one correspondence between continuous or ordinal data recorded by the researcher and continuous or ordinal variables analyzed by the statistician.

Nominal data, however, are a little bit different. In statistical procedures, nominal variables are limited to a dichotomous (yes/no) classification that indicates presence or absence of a condition. Nominal data with only two categories, such as gender, can be expressed by one nominal variable. Here, we might use a nominal variable indicating the presence or absence of, say, being female. For nominal data consisting of more than two categories, on the other hand, more than one nominal variable is needed to represent those data. It is important to appreciate this relationship, since different statistical methods are designed to analyze different numbers of variables.

As an example of the relationship between nominal data and nominal variables, let us consider race as a characteristic that we might measure with four categories: black, Asian, white, and other. In this case, we need to create three nominal variables to indicate a person's race. The first variable might indicate the presence or absence of being black, the second variable might indicate the presence or absence of being Asian, and the third variable might indicate the presence or absence of being white. Notice that we do not need a fourth variable to indicate the presence or absence of being a member of a race included in the category called "other," for anyone who is not black, Asian, or white <u>must</u> be a member of one of the other races. In general, if nominal data contain k categories, then k-1 nominal variables will be used in statistical procedures to represent those k categories.

The second characteristic of variables is determined by their function in the statistical analysis. A variable can serve either of two functions. The first function is to represent the data of primary interest to the researcher. This is the variable for which estimates are to be made or hypotheses are to be tested. We call the variable that represents the data of primary interest the **dependent variable**. For illustration, let us say that we are interested in the effect of some intervention on serum lipid levels. Here, it is of primary interest to make estimates or test hypotheses about serum lipid levels; therefore, the dependent variable should represent some measure of the lipid level.

Most often in health research, a single statistical analysis will involve only one dependent variable. If a set of research observations includes more than one collection of data for which an estimate will be made or a hypothesis will be tested, the usual approach is to conduct more than one analysis, each involving one of the variables of primary interest as the dependent variable. For instance, if we have several different measurements of serum lipids (e.g., HDL, LDL, total cholesterol), the usual approach to analyze these observations would be to examine each of the serum lipid measurements in a separate statistical analysis.[1]

The second function of variables in statistical analysis is to specify conditions under which estimates will be made or a hypothesis will be tested for the dependent variable. Variables that serve this function are known as **independent variables**. In our example of a study of an intervention to affect serum lipid levels, an independent variable would tell us whether or not a particular patient received the intervention. In other words, we are interested in comparing serum lipid levels between persons who received and persons who did not receive the intervention. Therefore, the independent variable indicating the presence or absence of the intervention defines the conditions under which we wish to examine the dependent variable. Other independent variables we might have included in this example are age and gender. Our reason for including age and gender in our analysis is probably because we would like to take into account (or control for) their effect on serum lipid levels. The way in which we can control for characteristics when analyzing data is to include the variables representing those characteristics in the analysis. Another role of independent variables is to control for their effect.

A key to understanding how statisticians think is by understanding variables. Once we are comfortable with variables, we are ready to see the way in which a statistician begins to select a statistical method to analyze a particular set of data. The following flowchart illustrates that process:

---

[1]Procedures for analyzing a single dependent variable are collectively called **univariate** methods. Statistical procedures that involve more than one dependent variable are collectively called **multivariate** methods. Multivariate methods are rarely encountered in the health research literature except those areas of research that overlap social or behavioral sciences. Multivariate methods will not be discussed in this text.

Flowchart 1 The process a statistician uses to begin selecting a statistical method and how that process relates to the structure of this textbook.

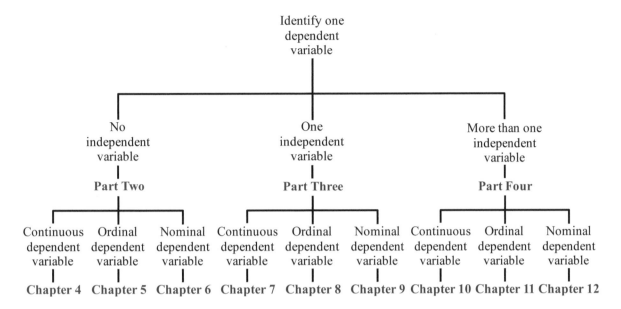

Flowchart 1 not only summarizes the way in which a statistician begins to select an appropriate statistical method, but it also outlines the organization of the next nine chapters of this text. Inspection of this flowchart reveals that the next three parts of the text are characterized by the number of independent variables involved in the analysis. Thus, in Part II we will be interested in analyzing a dependent variable without any independent variables. Methods used to examine sets of observations containing a dependent variable and no independent variables are known as **univariable** methods, hence the name of Part Two is "Univariable Analyses." Having no independent variables in an analysis implies that there are no special conditions under which we are interested in making an estimate or testing a hypothesis about the dependent variable. Instead, we are interested in the dependent variable in general.

In Part Three, we will discuss **bivariable** methods in which we have one dependent variable and one independent variable. In bivariable analysis, there are special conditions under which we are interested examining the dependent variable. In Part Four, the conditions under which we are interested in the dependent variable can be rather complex due to **multivariable** statistical methods that are used to analyze the dependent variable and more than one independent variable.[2]

As you examine the chapters within the next three parts of this text, you will notice that

---

[2]Notice a subtle distinction in terminology here. Multi**variable** methods are appropriate for three or more variables while multi**variate** methods are appropriate for more than one dependent variable. The root "variable" refers to the number of variables without regard to their function. The root "variate" refers only to the number of dependent variables. A very common mistake and source of confusion in statistical terminology that you will find in the health research literature is a reference to a statistical procedure that examines one dependent variable and more than one independent variable as a multivariate rather than a multivariable procedure.

each part contains three chapters that correspond to the three types of data that can be represented by the dependent variable. In selecting an analytic approach, the statistician determines the number of variables, identifies dependent and independent variables, and classifies the type of data contained in the dependent variable.

Each chapter in the remaining parts also begins with another component of the flowchart. These flowcharts are extensions of one we have just examined. The flowcharts at the beginning of those chapters will help us choose a particular method of analysis for a set of data. They will summarize the issues we have to consider in choosing a statistical procedure. In each chapter, you will find a discussion of how to evaluate those issues.

Following any branch of the flowchart to its end will reveal the name of a standard distribution or statistical approach that is appropriate for either interval estimation or statistical hypothesis testing on the corresponding data set. In Chapter 3, we learned that estimation and hypothesis testing are closely related processes. In this text, we will discuss these procedures mostly from the point of view of statistical hypothesis testing. By that choice, we do not mean to imply that hypothesis testing is the only, or even the better, way to evaluate a data set. It is however, the more commonly encountered approach in the health research literature.

CHAPTER 4
Univariable Analysis of a Continuous Dependent Variable

In this chapter we will take a look at the appropriate way in which to analyze a continuous dependent variable with no independent variables. That approach is summarized in Flowchart 2, which is a continuation of Flowchart 1.

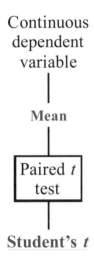

Continuous
dependent
variable

Mean

Paired t test

Student's t

Flowchart 2 Flowchart showing univariable analysis of a continuous dependent variable. The point estimate that is most often used to describe the dependent variable (the mean) is in color. The common name of the statistical test (paired t test) is enclosed in a box. The standard distribution that is used to test hypotheses and calculate confidence intervals (Student's t) is in color and underlined.

In Chapter 2, we learned that continuous data are most often assumed to come from a distribution that can be described, at least in part, by two parameters: the mean (μ) and the variance (σ^2).[1] Although estimation and hypothesis testing for continuous data can focus on either parameter, we are almost always concerned with estimating or testing a hypothesis about the mean.[2] In Chapter 3, we examined procedures for estimation and hypothesis testing for the mean when we have a single dependent variable and no independent variables. Specifically, those procedures involved conversion of the sample's estimate of the population's mean to the standard normal scale by subtracting the hypothesized population's mean (μ_0) from the sample's mean ($\overline{Y}$) and dividing by the standard error ($\sigma_{\overline{Y}}$). This is a relatively straightforward procedure. Unfortunately, it is a little bit too simple to be entirely appropriate when analyzing real data.

To understand why the method described in Chapter 3 is not the method we should use to analyze a continuous dependent variable, let us take a moment to review what it is that we are doing when we perform statistical procedures on a mean observed in a sample. The sample that we have observed is only one of many possible samples that we could have obtained from the population. Therefore, the mean that we have calculated from our sample

---

[1]This is not the same as assuming that the distribution of data is a Gaussian distribution, or any other particular type of distribution. Rather, this only assumes that the mean and variance help to characterize the distribution.

[2]In Chapter 2, we found out that the mean is a parameter of location of a distribution of continuous data. Most statistical methods used to analyze health research data address measures of location.

is only one of many possible means. We assume that chance, and only chance, determines which of all of the possible means we have actually observed in our sample. Regardless of whether we are interested in estimation or hypothesis testing, the purpose of the statistical procedure that we apply to our sample's observations is to take this influence of chance into account.

The method of converting a sample's mean to the standard normal scale appropriately reflects the influence of chance on estimation of the population's mean, but it overlooks another effect of chance. To see this other effect, let us reexamine the method we used to convert the sample's mean to the standard normal scale in Chapter 3 (Equation {3.10}).

$$z = \frac{\overline{Y} - \mu_0}{\sigma_{\overline{Y}}} \qquad \{4.1\}$$

where

z = a standard normal deviate (i.e., a value from the standard normal distribution)

$\overline{Y}$ = the sample's estimate of the mean of the distribution of data

μ_0 = the value of the population's mean according to the null hypothesis (H$_0$)

$\sigma_{\overline{Y}}$ = the population's value of the standard error of the mean ($\sigma_{\overline{Y}} = \sqrt{\dfrac{\sigma^2}{n}}$)

Notice that the denominator of Equation {4.1} consists of the population's standard error. To include the population's standard error in that calculation, we need to assume that we know the variance of the distribution of data in the population (σ^2). Since we cannot observe the entire population, we cannot know the population's variance exactly. Rather, we estimate the population's variance from the sample's observations. To reflect that estimation, the right-hand part of Equation {4.1} becomes:

$$\frac{\overline{Y} - \mu_0}{s_{\overline{Y}}} \qquad \{4.2\}$$

where

$s_{\overline{Y}}$ = the sample's estimate of the standard error of the mean ($s_{\overline{Y}} = \sqrt{\dfrac{s^2}{n}}$)

Now that we are being realistic about what we know and what we have to estimate, we realize that there are two parameters that we are estimating from the sample's observations: both the mean and the variance. Conversion of the sample's mean to the standard normal scale allows us to take into account the effect of chance in estimating the population's mean.

It does not, however, allow us to take into account the way in which chance influences our estimate of the population's variance as well. To take into account the influence of chance in estimating the population's variance, we need to use a different standard distribution. The distribution that allows us to take into account the independent roles of chance in estimating both the mean and the variance is **Student's *t* distribution**.

Student's *t* Distribution

Student's *t* distribution is a **standard distribution**. By that we imply that values from Student's *t* distribution and their associated probabilities appear in a table that we can use to convert observed values to take into account the role of chance in selecting the sample. Unlike when we used the standard normal distribution, however, we do not assume that the population's distribution of means from all possible samples of a certain size (i.e., the sampling distribution for the mean) is shaped like Student's *t* distribution, differing only in the value of its mean and variance. Rather, we continue to assume that the population's distribution of all possible estimates of the mean is a Gaussian distribution.[3]

In Chapter 3, we converted the sample's mean to the standard normal scale to avoid having to use calculus to calculate probabilities. This is also an advantage of converting to Student's *t* scale. Conversion to Student's *t* scale provides an additional advantage that we will examine in a moment. First, let us see how to convert observed values to *t*-values.

Recall that the standard normal distribution is a Gaussian distribution with a mean equal to zero and a variance equal to one. Student's *t* distribution also has a mean equal to zero and a variance equal to one. Therefore, conversion of the sample's mean to a value in Student's *t* distribution is accomplished in exactly the same way as is conversion to the standard normal distribution. Specifically, we subtract the population's mean from the sample's mean and divide by the standard error. This is illustrated in Equation{4.3}.

$$t = \frac{\overline{Y} - \mu_0}{s_{\overline{Y}}} \qquad \{4.3\}$$

where

t = Student's *t*-value that corresponds to the sample's mean

The calculation to the right of the equals sign in Equation {4.3} is identical to the calculation of a standard normal deviate in Equation{4.2}. Student's *t* distribution is not, however, the same as the standard normal distribution. What distinguishes them from each other is that Student's *t* distribution has three, rather than two, parameters. That is to say, three summary measures are needed to fully characterize Student's *t* distribution mathematically. In addition to a mean and variance (as with the standard normal

---

[3]Because of the central limit theorem (Chapter 3), we are comfortable making this assumption for the distribution of estimates of the mean, as long as the sample's size is not too small.

distribution), Student's *t* distribution has a third parameter called **degrees of freedom**.

As we said previously, our interest in Student's *t* distribution is to take into account the fact that we are estimating the population's variance, as well as the population's mean, from our sample's observations. Degrees of freedom reflect the amount of information a sample contains for estimation of the population's variance. At first, we might suppose that the amount of information in a sample to estimate the population's variance is the same as the number of observations in that sample. This is almost correct. Actually, the amount of information in a sample that can be used to estimate the population's variance is equal to the number of observations in the sample minus one. A way to think about degrees of freedom is that they are equal to one when we have the smallest possible sample that allows the variance to be estimated. We cannot estimate the variance from a single observation, since the variation for a single observation is always equal to zero. Thus, the smallest sample that will allow estimation of the variance has two observations.

Figure 4-1 shows Student's *t* distribution for a few different values of degrees of freedom. Notice that the distribution becomes less dispersed or spread out as the degrees of freedom increase. Since degrees of freedom reflect how much information a sample contains to estimate the population's variance, degrees of freedom reflect the influence of chance in estimating the variance. The larger a sample's size, the more degrees of freedom it contains. As the degrees of freedom increase there is less influence of chance on a variance estimate. Degrees of freedom in Student's *t* distribution cause us to "penalize" ourselves for our uncertainty in estimation of the population's variance: The larger our sample's size, the less the penalty.

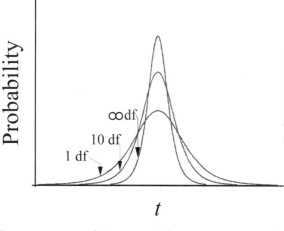

Figure 4-1 Student's *t* distribution. The dispersion of Student's *t* distribution decreases as the degrees of freedom increase. When the degrees of freedom are equal to infinity, Student's *t* distribution is the same as the standard normal distribution.

For a moment, let us consider an extreme value for degrees of freedom. Suppose we had an infinitely large sample. Then, we would have infinite degrees of freedom and, thus, an infinite amount of information to estimate the variance. Student's *t* distribution with an infinite number of degrees of freedom is exactly the same as the standard normal distribution. When we think about it, that makes good sense. If we have an infinitely large sample, then we have, in fact, observed the entire population. If we observe the entire population, we are certain that our estimate of the population's variance is exactly equal to the population's variance. Therefore, we need not penalize ourselves and we can use the standard normal distribution. In practice, this is never the case. With large samples, however, the penalty for uncertainty in estimation of the variance is very small.[4]

Student's *t* distribution is the first of several distributions that we will encounter in this text that are related to the standard normal distribution. These distributions are members of the **Gaussian family** of distributions. This and other members of the Gaussian family and their relationships to each other appear in Appendix C. One characteristic that we will discover about all members of the Gaussian family except the standard normal distribution is that degrees of freedom is one of their parameters. In each case, degrees of freedom will be used to reflect the amount of information in a sample. Thus, understanding degrees of freedom is an important step in understanding many statistical procedures.

Table B.2 presents values from Student's *t* distribution and their corresponding probabilities. This table has a format that is substantially different from the format of the table presenting values from the standard normal distribution (Table B.1). In Table B.2, the probabilities associated with different Student's *t*-values appear in the top row. In that row are two lines of probabilities. The top line of probabilities (labeled "α(2)"), tells us the probability split evenly between the two tails of Student's *t* distribution. The bottom line of probabilities (labeled "α(1)"), tells us the probability in the upper tail of Student's *t* distribution. This bottom line of probabilities is similar to the probabilities associated with standard normal deviates in Table B.1.

In the body of Table B.2 are Student's *t*-values that correspond to the probabilities in the top row of the table. In the left-most column of Table B.2 are the degrees of freedom. Notice that the degrees of freedom in the left-most column go up to infinity (∞). When the sample has infinite degrees of freedom, we are certain that we have estimated the variance correctly. Now, take a look at the *t*-values in that last row. The value that corresponds to infinite degrees of freedom and an α of 0.05 split between the two tails of Student's *t* distribution is equal to 1.96. If that number sounds familiar, it is because 1.96 is the standard normal deviate that corresponds to an α of 0.05 split between the two tails of the standard normal distribution!

Interval Estimation

We can use Student's *t* distribution in hypothesis testing or interval estimation for a mean from a univariable sample of continuous data. Let us first consider interval estimation. We calculate a two-sided confidence interval for the population's mean in the same way that we did using the standard normal distribution (see Equation {3.8}). Now, however, we recognize that we should use a *t*-value with n-1 degrees of freedom rather than a standard normal deviate. Equation {4.4} shows how a two-sided confidence interval is calculated using Student's *t* distribution.

---

[4]When the degrees of freedom are equal to 60 (corresponding to a sample size of 61 in the current application) the *t*-value is equal to 2.00 which is quite close to 1.96.

$$\mu \stackrel{\triangle}{=} \overline{Y} \pm (t_{\alpha/2} \cdot s_{\overline{Y}})$$ {4.4}

where

$t_{\alpha/2}$ = *t*-value that corresponds to α split between the two tails of Student's *t* distribution

Now, let us take a look at an example that compares confidence intervals calculated with a standard normal deviate to confidence intervals calculated with a *t*-value.

Example 4-1 In Example 3.4, we calculated 95% two-sided confidence intervals for the mean systolic and diastolic blood pressures during the winter months among 53 patients with renal disease. In that example, we used a standard normal deviate to represent the level of confidence. That approach assumes that we know the value of the population's variance. Now, let us recalculate those confidence intervals recognizing that the variances have been estimated from the sample's observations.

In Example 3.4, the confidence interval for mean systolic blood pressure ranged from 147.1 to 158.9 mmHg and the confidence interval for mean diastolic blood pressure ranged from 78.1 to 85.9 mmHg. Those calculations used a standard normal deviate of 1.96 to represent the role of chance in deriving those estimates. Now, we will recalculate those confidence intervals, recognizing that the variances have been estimated from the sample's observations and taking into account the independent roles of chance in estimating the means and the variances of blood pressure values. For both intervals, the *t*-value we will use to represent 95% confidence is found from Table B.2 by selecting the column that corresponds to an α of 0.05 split between the two tails of Student's *t* distribution and the row that corresponds to 53 - 1 = 52 degrees of freedom. Since 52 degrees of freedom is not listed in Table B.2, we can use the next lower number of degrees of freedom that is listed.[5] That value is 50 degrees of freedom.

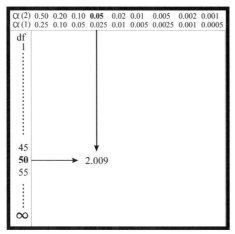

---

[5] This is a "conservative" approach in that it overestimates the role of chance in selecting the sample.

Thus, the *t*-value we will use in our calculations is equal to 2.009. With that information, we are ready to use Equation {4.4} to calculate confidence intervals for systolic and diastolic blood pressures.

$$\mu_{SBP} = \overline{Y} \pm (t_{\alpha/2} \cdot s_{\overline{Y}}) = 153 \pm (2.009 \cdot 3) = 147.0 \text{ to } 159.0 \text{ mmHg}$$

$$\mu_{DBP} = \overline{Y} \pm (t_{\alpha/2} \cdot s_{\overline{Y}}) = 82 \pm (2.009 \cdot 2) = 78.0 \text{ to } 86.0 \text{ mmHg}$$

Notice that both of these confidence intervals are slightly wider than the confidence intervals we calculated in Example 3.4 (147.1 to 158.9 mmHg for SBP and 78.1 to 85.9 mmHg for DBP). The reason for this is that we are now taking the additional role of chance in estimating the variance into account. Since these intervals reflect a greater role of chance, they have to be wider to represent the same level of confidence that they include the population's means. With 50 degrees of freedom, the increase in the width of the confidence intervals is small. If we had fewer observations and, therefore, fewer degrees of freedom, there would be a larger increase in the width of the confidence intervals to reflect the greater role of chance in estimating the variance.

Hypothesis Testing

Recall from Chapter 3 that statistical hypothesis testing involves testing a specific condition for the population's parameter described in the null hypothesis. For most univariable samples, it is difficult to imagine what value we should hypothesize for the population. For instance, consider Example 4-1. In that example, we examined systolic and diastolic blood pressure measurements made on patients with renal disease. Our objective was to calculate an interval estimate for the mean systolic and diastolic blood pressure values in the population from which those patients were selected for observation. That is a logical way in which to take chance into account for those data. It is difficult to imagine, however, what hypothesis might be tested using those same observations. To perform statistical hypothesis testing, we need to state a specific value for the population's mean. Often, with univariable samples, there is no hypothetical value that has biologic relevance. For this reason, interval estimation is more commonly used than hypothesis testing for univariable samples.

There is, nevertheless, one kind of univariable sample in which hypothesis testing makes sense. This is when we have a **paired sample**. The most common type of paired sample is when we make two measurements of the same characteristic under different conditions for each subject.[6] Example 3.5 illustrates such a paired sample for a continuous dependent variable. There, each patient's intraocular pressure was measured twice: once in the eye receiving the new treatment and once in the other eye receiving the conventional

------

[6]Less commonly, we might see paired samples in which similar, but not identical, individuals are compared one to each other. For example, a paired sample might consist of individuals compared to their siblings.

treatment. The dependent variable that is examined using statistical hypothesis testing in that case is the <u>difference</u> in intraocular pressure measurements taken for these two eyes. Since each patient has only one difference, this is a univariable sample.[7] The sensible null hypothesis for such a paired sample is that the mean difference is equal to zero, indicating that the measurements are the same under the two conditions.

To perform statistical hypothesis testing on the mean from a univariable sample, we convert the sample's mean to a Student's t statistic using the method in Equation{4.3}. The next example illustrates such a hypothesis test.

Example 4-2 In Example 3.1, we considered the mean difference in intraocular pressure in a group of 9 patients who received a new medication in one eye and the standard treatment in the other eye. In Example 3.6, we tested the null hypothesis that the mean difference in intraocular pressure is equal to zero in the population by using the standard normal distribution to determine the P-value. Now, let us recognize that the variance of differences in intraocular pressure is unknown and, thus, must be estimated from the sample's observations. What effect does this additional role of chance have on the results of testing that null hypothesis?

In Example 3.1, the sample's estimate of the population's variance in intraocular pressure was 15.5 mmHg and the standard error was found to be equal to 1.31 mmHg. Recognizing that this standard error was calculated from an estimate of the standard deviation, rather than from the actual standard deviation does not change the value of the standard error. Therefore, we use that same standard error in Equation {4.3} to calculate the t-value that corresponds to a mean change in the difference in intraocular pressure of 3 mmHg.

$$ t = \frac{\overline{Y} - \mu_0}{s_{\overline{Y}}} = \frac{3-0}{1.31} = 2.29 $$

Thus, a t-value of 2.29 corresponds to a mean difference in intraocular pressure of 3 mmHg. This is the same as the standard normal deviate calculated in Example 3.6. Recognizing that the variance is estimated from the sample's observations does not change the result of the calculation. Instead, it is the interpretation of that result that changes. In Example 3.6, we used Table B.1 to get a P-value of 0.0220. Now, we need to use Table B.2 to find the P-value that reflects the independent roles of chance in estimating the variance as well as the mean. To find that P-value, we look for 2.29 in the row of the table that corresponds to 9 - 1 = 8 degrees of freedom.

When we go to Table B.2 to find a t-value of 2.29 in the row that corresponds to 8 degrees of freedom, we find that a t-value of 1.860 corresponds to a probability of 0.10 split

---

[7]A legitimate paired sample will allow a particular individual to be compared to one, and only one, other individual. Groups that are balanced according to some characteristic, but in which individual members of every pair cannot be identified are called **group** (or **frequency**) matched samples. It is not appropriate to use univariable methods to compare group-matched samples.

between the two tails of Student's t distribution and a t-value of 2.306 corresponds to a probability of 0.05 split between the two tails of that distribution.

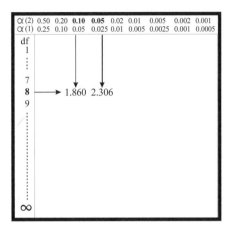

Since 2.29 occurs between these two probabilities, we can express the P-value as being less than 0.10, but greater than 0.05. In mathematical shorthand, that P-value is:

$$0.10 > P > 0.05$$

Even though we do not know the exact value of the P-value, we do know that it is greater than 0.05. Thus, we cannot reject the null hypothesis that the mean change in intraocular pressure is equal to zero in the population. Instead, we fail to reject that null hypothesis.

The effect of recognizing the additional role of chance in estimating the variance of changes in intraocular pressure has altered our conclusion about the null hypothesis, since the P-value is now greater than 0.05. It will not always be the case that the conclusion we can draw will be different using these two approaches, but recognizing the additional role of chance in estimating the variance of dependent variable values will always result in a higher P-value.

Example 4-2 showed how we could perform the paired t test by hand. Going through those calculations can be helpful in understanding this statistical method, but when we are analyzing real data, we will probably use a computer program to do the calculations for us. In SAS,[8] the paired t test is part of the information that is automatically provided by the UNIVARIATE procedure[9] is used to analyze a univariable sample with a continuous dependent variable. That procedure provides us with a lot of information about our sample, including the results of a paired t test. In the next example, we will interpret output from the UNIVARIATE procedure.

---

[8] SAS is the most frequently used statistical software for analyzing health research data, thus we have selected it to demonstrate the type of information provided by such software.

[9] This is a misnomer. The "UNIVARIABLE" procedure would have been a better name for a program that analyzes one dependent variable and no independent variables.

Example 4-3 In Example 4-2, we performed a paired t-test on a set of data from a study in which we looked at the difference between intraocular pressure in both eyes for a sample of 9 persons. Let us now examine output from SAS's UNIVARIATE procedure and see what information it provides to us about a univariable sample with a continuous dependent variable.

The following output is the result of analyzing these data using SAS:

```
                        The UNIVARIATE Procedure
                          Variable:  IOP

                              Moments

   N                       9      Sum Weights              9
   Mean                    3      Sum Observations        27
   Std Deviation    3.93700394    Variance              15.5
   Skewness         0.75848924    Kurtosis         1.6408503
   Uncorrected SS        205      Corrected SS           124
   Coeff Variation  131.233465    Std Error Mean   1.31233465

                   Basic Statistical Measures

           Location                    Variability
     Mean      3.000000     Std Deviation        3.93700
     Median    3.000000     Variance            15.50000
     Mode      3.000000     Range               14.00000
                            Interquartile Range  3.00000

                  Tests for Location: Mu0=0

      Test            -Statistic-      -----p Value------
      Student's t    t  2.286002     Pr > |t|      0.0516
      Sign           M         3     Pr >= |M|     0.0703
      Signed Rank    S        14     Pr >= |S|     0.0547

                    Quantiles (Definition 5)

                    Quantile      Estimate
                    100% Max         11
                    99%              11
                    95%              11
                    90%              11
                    75% Q3            4
                    50% Median        3
                    25% Q1            1
                    10%              -3
                    5%               -3
```

```
                    1%                    -3
                    0% Min                -3

                    Extreme Observations

        ----Lowest----              ----Highest---
        Value       Obs             Value      Obs
         -3          5                3         1
          0          2                3         3
          1          7                4         9
          2          4                6         8
          3          3               11         6

    Stem Leaf                         #          Boxplot
      10 0                            1             0
       8
       6 0                .           1             |
       4 0                            1         +-----+
       2 000                          3         *--+--*
       0 00                           2         +-----+
      -0                                            |
      -2 0                            1             |
         ----+----+----+----+
```

Quite a bit of information is provided by SAS when we use the UNIVARIATE procedure to analyze our data. From a statistical programmer's point of view, it is better to provide too much information than not enough. That leaves us with the task of focusing on the information we need and ignoring the rest. Our purpose in using the UNIVARIATE procedure to analyze these data is to estimate the parameters of location and dispersion and to perform a paired-t test. That information appears in color (provided by us, not by SAS).

The results of performing a paired-t test appear under the heading, "Tests for Location: Mu0=0." The t-value is equal to 2.286002, which, when rounded, is consistent with the t-value we obtained in Example 4-2 (2.29). More importantly, SAS provides us with the P-value associated with that t-value, so we do not have to look it up in table. That P-value is equal to 0.0516. To test the null hypothesis that the mean difference in intraocular pressure is equal to zero in the population, we compare the P-value to α (0.05). Since the P-value is greater than α, we fail to reject that null hypothesis.

In addition to this information, there are other pieces of information that are familiar to us after reading Chapters 2 and 3 in this text. Among these is a stem and leaf plot that can give us an overall impression about the distribution of data in the sample. We have put that plot in color also.

Now, we are ready to go on to the next chapter, which examines univariable analysis of an ordinal dependent variable.

CHAPTER 5
Univariable Analysis of an Ordinal Dependent Variable

We learned in Chapter 2 that ordinal data can differ from continuous data in either (or both) of two ways. One way is that ordinal data might include a small number of potential values. The other way is that ordinal data are not necessarily evenly spaced. There are some types of information in health research that are naturally measured on an ordinal scale. For example, the Bethesda system for cervical cytology includes four stages of epithelial cell abnormalities on a Pap smear. These are: ASCUS (atypical squamous cells of undetermined significance), LSIL (low-grade squamous intraepithelial lesion), HSIL (high-grade squamous intraepithelial lesion), and squamous cell carcinoma. These data have both characteristics of ordinal data. They have a small number of possible values (i.e., four) and we are unable to say that the spacing between each stage is the same (i.e., the "distance" between ASCUS and LSIL is not necessarily the same as the "distance" between LSIL and HSIL).

Statistical methods for ordinal dependent variables can be used to analyze data that naturally occur on an ordinal scale, but this is not the most common use of these methods. Rather, these statistical procedures are used more often to analyze continuous data that have been converted to an ordinal scale. When these methods are used in that way, we refer to them as **nonparametric** methods.

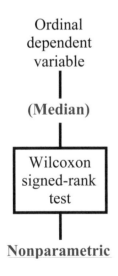

Flowchart 3   **Flowchart showing univariable analysis of an ordinal dependent variable. The point estimate that is most often used to describe the dependent variable (the median) is in color. The common name of the statistical test (Wilcoxon signed-rank test) is enclosed in a box. The general procedure that is used to test hypotheses and calculate confidence intervals (nonparametric) is in color and underlined.**

Nonparametric methods are an alternative to statistical methods designed for continuous data. Thus, the statistical procedures we will encounter in chapters addressing ordinal dependent variables will have parallel procedures for continuous dependent variables. In Chapter 4, we discussed the paired t test. In this chapter, we will discuss the **Wilcoxon signed-rank test** (Flowchart 3). The Wilcoxon signed-rank test is the nonparametric parallel to the paired t test.

Given the relationship between statistical methods for continuous and ordinal dependent variables, we need to think about which of the two approaches is the more appropriate one under a specific set of conditions. The distinction is based on assumptions made about the sampling distribution. When we analyze continuous data represented by a continuous dependent variable, we take the effect of chance on the estimate of the mean into account by considering the sampling distribution for the mean. Statistical methods for continuous dependent variables assume that the sampling distribution is a Gaussian distribution. We learned in Chapter 3 that the sampling distribution for the mean tends to be a Gaussian distribution with that tendency increasing as the size of the samples increases. We know that this is true from the central limit theorem.

When a sample of continuous data contains few observations, the sampling distribution for the mean depends on the distribution of data to be a Gaussian distribution. If the distribution of data in such a small sample does not appear to be a Gaussian distribution, we become concerned about the assumption that the sampling distribution is a Gaussian distribution. One solution to this problem is to represent those continuous data with an ordinal dependent variable instead of with a continuous dependent variable. Distributions of ordinal data do not have parameters like distributions of continuous data do (i.e., the mean and variance). Without a parameter to estimate, there is no sampling distribution to take into account the role of chance. Without a sampling distribution, there is no assumption that the distribution is a Gaussian distribution. Thus, statistical methods designed for ordinal dependent variables can be used to analyze continuous data converted to an ordinal scale to avoid this assumption of a Gaussian sampling distribution.

The first step in using a nonparametric test on continuous data involves conversion of the data to an ordinal scale. This conversion is accomplished by representing the continuous data by their relative ranks. What ranking accomplishes is to maintain the order of numeric magnitude without the information about how far apart data values are from one another. The particular rules for ranking differ somewhat depending on the particular test that will be performed, but there are two rules that are consistent for all nonparametric tests. The first rule is that the rank of one is assigned to the smallest data value and that the ranks increase as the numeric magnitude of the data increases. The second rule tells us how to assign ranks to data that are of the same numeric magnitude on the continuous scale. In this case, we give all of those data values the same rank and that rank is equal to the mean of the ranks they would have been assigned if they were of different numeric magnitudes. This sounds a bit complicated, but it is easier to see how this works by examining an example.

Example 5-1 In Example 3-1 we examined data from 9 persons with elevated intraocular pressure. Each of those persons was randomly assigned to use a new topical treatment for glaucoma in one eye and a standard topical treatment in the other eye. After one week of treatment, the difference in intraocular pressure (ΔIOP) between the two eyes was measured for each person. The following results were observed:

PATIENT	ΔIOP
TH	3
IS	0
MA	3
KE	2
SM	-3
ES	11
OH	1
AP	6
PY	4

Now, let us convert those continuous data to an ordinal scale by ranking.

The smallest data value is a difference in intraocular pressure of -3 mmHg for patient SM, so we will give this data value a rank of one. Then we assign the next higher rank to the next higher data value. In this set of data, two patients had a difference in intraocular pressure of 3 mmHg. If they had different numeric magnitudes, they would be assigned the ranks of 5 and 6. Because they are equal to the same value, we assign the average of those ranks to both data values:

PATIENT	ΔIOP	RANK
TH	3	5.5
IS	0	2
MA	3	5.5
KE	2	4
SM	-3	1
ES	11	9
OH	1	3
AP	6	8
PY	4	7

Thus, we might want to analyze continuous data by converting these continuous data to an ordinal scale. When continuous data are converted to an ordinal scale, we do not have to make the assumption that the estimates from all possible samples have a Gaussian distribution (i.e., that the sampling distribution is Gaussian). It is important to remember, however, that nonparametric methods are not completely free of assumptions. Regardless of the statistical method we use, we always assume that, at the minimum, dependent variable values were obtained by a random sample of the population of interest (as discussed in Chapter 2).

Estimation

Unlike distributions of continuous (or nominal) data, distributions of ordinal data do not have parameters that mathematically describe them. Even so, there are numbers we can use to summarize data on an ordinal scale. To be appropriate for data on an ordinal scale, summary values must not be influenced by how far apart data values are.

Recall from Chapter 2 that the mean is the parameter of location we use for data on a continuous scale. That mean is the "center of gravity" of the distribution. By calling the mean the center of gravity of the distribution, we recognize that the mean is affected by the numeric distance between data values. Thus, the mean would not be an appropriate way to summarize ordinal data.

In that same chapter, we encountered another measure of location of a distribution: the median. The median is the "physical center" of a distribution of data rather than its center of gravity. By physical center, we imply that half of the data values occur on either side of the median. How far away those data values are from each other does not change the median. Thus, the median is an appropriate measure to summarize the location of a distribution of ordinal data.

In addition to the point estimate of the median, it is also possible for us to take chance into account by calculating an interval estimate for the median. This is not something that SAS provides us, so it must be calculated by hand. The way this is done is by calculating the ranks of the limits of the confidence interval. The ranks associated with 90%, 95%, and 99% confidence intervals for samples with 7 to 40 observations are given in Table B.11. The next example demonstrates how this table is used to determine a confidence interval for a median.

Example 5-2 In Example 2-2, we looked at the change in serum cholesterol levels for 11 persons on a low-fat diet. Those data values are: 10, 42, 5, 9, -2, 0, 16, 28, 4, -5, and 3 mg/dL. In Example 2-4 we calculated the median of those data and found it to be equal to 5 mg/dL. Now, let us determine a 95% confidence interval for that estimate of the median.

First we need to rank these data. This was done in Example 2-4 to prepare to calculate the median. These ranks are:

Rank	1	2	3	4	5	6	7	8	9	10	11
Value	-5	-2	0	3	4	5	9	10	16	28	42

Next, we look at Table B.11 and determine which ranks correspond to the limits of a 95% confidence interval when we have a sample of 11 observations. To do this, we find 11 in the left-most column and 95% in the top row. Where those intersect, we find that the lower limit has a rank of 2 and the upper limit has a rank of 10. The data value with a rank of 2 is equal to -2 mg/dL. The data value with a rank of 10 is equal to 28 mg/dL. Thus, the 95% confidence interval for the estimate of the median is equal to -2 to 28 mg/dL.

Hypothesis testing

We learned in Chapter 3 that the first step in statistical hypothesis testing is to formulate the hypothesis to be tested (i.e., the null hypothesis). So far in this text, all of the null hypotheses we have encountered have made specific statements about the population's parameter. Since a distribution of ordinal data has no parameters, we need to think about a different sort of null hypothesis. In Chapter 4, the null hypothesis addressed by the paired t test was that the mean difference is equal to zero in the population. The Wilcoxon signed-rank test is the nonparametric equivalent to the paired t test. The null hypothesis tested in the Wilcoxon signed-rank test is that a balance exists between positive and negative differences. This nonparametric null hypothesis makes a specific statement about the distribution of ordinal data, but it does that without referring to a parameter.

The first step in all nonparametric procedures is to assign relative ranks to each of the data values. Each nonparametric procedure has its own particular way in which this ranking is done. In the Wilcoxon signed-rank test we rank the **absolute value** of the differences rather than the differences themselves. Also, data values of zero are not ranked at all.[1] The next example shows how this method of ranking data is performed.

Example 5-3 In Example 5-1 we examined data taken from 9 persons with elevated intraocular pressure. In that example we ranked these data so that the negative data values had the lowest ranks. Now, let us rank the absolute value of these data in preparation for performing the Wilcoxon signed-rank test.

First, we record the absolute value for each data value and then, we rank those absolute values. That process is summarized in the following table:

-----

[1] The purpose of the Wilcoxon signed-rank test is to compare positive differences with negative differences. Data of zero provide no information about this balance.

PATIENT	ΔIOP	|ΔIOP|	RANK
TH	3	3	4
IS	0	-	-
MA	3	3	4
KE	2	2	2
SM	-3	3	4
ES	11	11	8
OH	1	1	1
AP	6	6	7
PY	4	4	6

After ranks have been assigned, we then separate those ranks according to the original sign of the data on the continuous scale. Then, we add up the ranks that correspond to positive data values (T+) and add up the ranks that correspond to negative data values (T-). These two sums of ranks are the results of the Wilcoxon signed-rank test (Equations {5.1} and {5.2}).

$$T_+ = \sum \text{Ranks of positive differences} \qquad \{5.1\}$$

$$T_- = \sum \text{Ranks of negative differences} \qquad \{5.2\}$$

Which data values are negative and which are positive is entirely arbitrary. In the example we have been discussing, the sign of a difference in IOP depends on whether the pressure in the eye that received the new treatment is subtracted from the pressure in the eye that received the standard treatment or vice versa. We only need to select one of the two sums of ranks to compare to values in a table of Wilcoxon signed-rank test statistics. For a two-sided alternative hypothesis, we choose the sum of the ranks that is the smaller of the two.[2]

The table we use to test the null hypothesis in the Wilcoxon signed-rank test is Table B.3. If we take a look at Table B.3, we find a structure somewhat like the structure of the table for the paired *t* test (Table B.2). Across the top of Table B.3 we see one- and two-sided values of α similar to those in Table B.2. Down the left-most column of Table B.3 is the number of observations in the sample. This is not too different from the degrees of freedom in the left-most column of Table B.2. There is, however, one important difference between these two tables. In Table B.2, Student's *t* values get bigger as the value of α (and, therefore, the *P*-value) gets smaller, but in Table B.3 the opposite is true. Table B.3 is the only table we will use in which α and the *P*-value get smaller as the test statistic gets smaller. This is something we need to keep in mind when using Table B.3.

---

[2]If we are interested in a one-tailed test, the choice of which of the two statistics to compare to a value in the table (Table B.3) is determined by which of the two statistics the alternative hypothesis implies will be the smaller.

Now, let us take a look at an example of how the Wilcoxon signed-rank test statistic is calculated and compared to values in the corresponding table.

Example 5-4 In Example 5-3 we ranked data taken from 9 persons with elevated intraocular pressure using the method of ranking required by the Wilcoxon signed-rank test. Now, let us calculate the Wilcoxon signed-rank test statistic for these data and draw a conclusion about the null hypothesis that there is a balance of negative and positive differences in IOP in the population. To draw that conclusion, let us use $\alpha = 0.05$.

Only one of the differences in IOP is negative. That is the difference for patient SM. All the rest of the (non-zero) differences are positive. Thus, we find the following sums of ranks using Equations {5.1} and {5.2}:

$$T_+ = \sum \text{Ranks of positive differences} = 4+4+2+8+1+7+6 = 32$$

$$T_- = \sum \text{Ranks of negative differences} = 4$$

Since the sum of the negative difference ranks (4) is smaller than the sum of the positive difference ranks (32), it is the former that we compare to values in Table B.3. In the left-most column of Table B.3, we need to find the number of observations in the sample. This number of observations only includes those without differences equal to zero. In this sample, therefore, the number of non-zero observations is eight. If we look in that row of the table, we find that our calculated value of 4 occurs between the values of 3 (corresponding to an α of 0.05) and 5 (corresponding to an α of 0.1). Thus, the P-value is less than 0.1 and greater than 0.05. Since these are greater than α of 0.05, we fail to reject the null hypothesis.

Example 5-4 shows how the Wilcoxon signed-rank test can be performed by hand. This test, like other nonparametric tests, is relatively easy to calculate by hand. Even so, it is likely that we will use a computer to perform the Wilcoxon signed-rank test when we are analyzing data from a health study. If we use SAS to perform the Wilcoxon signed-rank test, we would use the UNIVARIATE procedure, just as we did for the paired t test in Chapter 4 The next example highlights the parts of the output from the UNIVARIATE procedure that relate to an ordinal dependent variable.

Example 5-5 In Example 4-3 we looked at output from SAS's UNIVARIATE procedure used to analyze data from a study in which we looked at the difference between intraocular pressure in both eyes for a sample of 9 persons. Let us now find the parts of that output that are relevant to a univariable sample with an ordinal dependent variable.

The following output is the result of analyzing these data using SAS:

```
                        The SAS System
                    The UNIVARIATE Procedure
                        Variable:  IOP

                          Moments

N                        9      Sum Weights              9
Mean                     3      Sum Observations        27
Std Deviation    3.93700394     Variance              15.5
Skewness         0.75848924     Kurtosis         1.6408503
Uncorrected SS         205      Corrected SS           124
Coeff Variation  131.233465     Std Error Mean    1.31233465

                 Basic Statistical Measures

          Location                   Variability
   Mean      3.000000     Std Deviation        3.93700
   Median    3.000000     Variance            15.50000
   Mode      3.000000     Range               14.00000
                          Interquartile Range  3.00000

                 Tests for Location: Mu0=0

      Test            -Statistic-      -----p Value------
      Student's t    t  2.286002       Pr > |t|    0.0516
      Sign           M         3       Pr >= |M|   0.0703
      Signed Rank    S        14       Pr >= |S|   0.0547

                 Quantiles (Definition 5)

                 Quantile      Estimate
                 100% Max          11
                 99%               11
                 95%               11
                 90%               11
                 75% Q3             4
                 50% Median         3
                 25% Q1             1
                 10%               -3
                 5%                -3
                 1%                -3
                 0% Min            -3
```

The items in this output that are relevant to an ordinal dependent variable are in color. They include the median and the result of the Wilcoxon signed-rank test. The median is equal to 3 mmHg and the P-value for the Wilcoxon signed-rank test is equal to 0.0547. Since this P-

value is greater than α (0.05), we fail to reject the null hypothesis that there is a balance of positive and negative difference in intraocular pressure between each person's two eyes. This is the same as the conclusion we drew as a result of performing the Wilcoxon signed-rank test by hand (Example 5-4).

Statistical Power of Nonparametric Tests

We have learned in this chapter that continuous data can be converted to an ordinal scale to circumvent some of the assumptions required for the analysis of continuous dependent variables. We also learned that information about the distance between data values is lost when continuous data are converted to an ordinal scale. We gain flexibility by performing such a conversion, but we must pay a price. The resultant loss of information can mean a loss of statistical power which, in turn, implies a greater chance of failing to reject a false null hypothesis.

Loss of power occurs when the assumptions required by a statistical procedure for a continuous dependent variable are satisfied, but instead we choose to convert our continuous data to an ordinal scale for analysis. In other words, it occurs when it would have been appropriate to use a statistical procedure designed for a continuous dependent variable, but we used a nonparametric procedure instead.

The decision of whether or not to convert data to another scale is a common one in analysis of health research data. Unfortunately, it is not often an easy decision to make. In this text we will look only at the loss of power that can occur when we make an incorrect decision. One way to examine power is by considering P-values. The greater the power of a statistical procedure, the smaller the P-value will be.[3] To examine this loss of power for the intraocular pressure data we have been using in our examples, let us look at the P-values: the P-value for the Wilcoxon signed-rank test is 0.0547 (from Example 5-5) whereas the P-value for the paired t test is 0.0516 (from Example 4-3). Since the nonparametric test has a higher P-value, a larger difference in intraocular pressures would be required to reject the null hypothesis. Using either P-value we fail to reject the null hypothesis. Here, as well as in most instances, the loss of statistical power due to use of a nonparametric test will be small[4] and will not affect the conclusion we draw in statistical hypothesis testing.

In the next chapter, we will encounter the last univariable statistical methods: those designed to analyze a nominal dependent variable.

---

[3]We can think of the P-value as the minimum value of that we could have used in an analysis and still have rejected the null hypothesis.

[4]Some nonparametric tests are associated with a substantial loss of power, but they are not commonly used (for the very reason that they have low statistical power). The nonparametric tests that we describe in this text are among the most powerful nonparametric tests available.

CHAPTER 6
Univariable Analysis of a Nominal Dependent Variable

Much of the data that we encounter in health research are measured on a nominal scale.[1] We learned in the introduction to Part Two that a nominal variable consists of dichotomous (yes/no) information. For an individual, a nominal variable indicates either the presence or absence of some characteristic (e.g., gender) or the occurrence or nonoccurrence of some event (e.g., death). When information is combined for several individuals, however, nominal dependent variables are often summarized as probabilities or rates. In this chapter, we will see how to estimate probabilities and rates and how we can take into account the role of chance on those estimates.

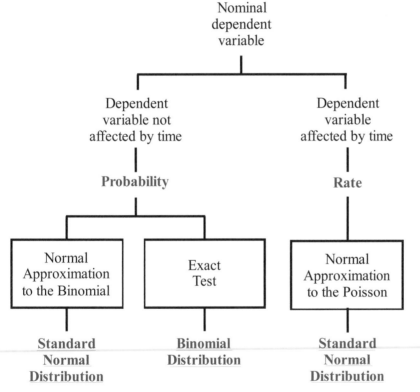

Flowchart 4 Flowchart showing univariable analysis of a nominal dependent variable. The point estimates that are most often used to describe the dependent variable (either a probability or a rate) are in color. The common names of statistical tests are enclosed in boxes. The standard distributions that are used to test hypotheses and calculate confidence intervals are in color and underlined.

Distributions of Nominal Data

A distribution of nominal data that are represented by a single nominal variable (i.e., having two possible values) can be represented graphically as shown in Figure 6-1. To completely

---

[1] Continuous or ordinal data can also be converted to a nominal scale. If this is done, information is lost and the chance of making a type II error increases.

describe this distribution of data, we need only a single parameter. The most commonly used parameter is the probability of the event or characteristic. That probability is considered to reflect the location of the distribution of nominal data. There is no need for a second parameter (like variance for a distribution of continuous data). Once you know the probability of the event, you know everything you need to describe or draw the distribution of nominal data. For the distribution in Figure 6-1, the probability of the event or characteristic is equal to 0.4. We know that is the case since 40% of the population has the event or characteristic and 60% do not have the event or characteristic.

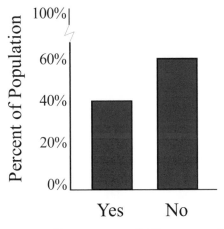

Figure 6-1 Distribution of nominal data with two possible conditions: the presence or absence of a characteristic or the occurrence or nonoccurence of an event.

When we talked about the parameters of a distribution of continuous data in Chapter 2, we used Greek letters to represent the population's parameters. We continue with this convention when thinking about the parameter of a distribution of nominal data. For the probability of the event, we use the Greek letter theta (θ). Equation {6.1} illustrates how we would calculate θ if we were able to observe the entire population.

$$\theta = \frac{\lambda}{N} \qquad \{6.1\}$$

where

θ = (theta) the probability of an event or characteristic in the population

λ = (lambda) the number of events or persons with the characteristic in the population

N = total number of persons in the population

Point Estimates

When calculating estimates of the population's parameters, we use English, rather than Greek letters. Equation {6.2} illustrates in mathematical language the sample's estimate of the population's probability of the event or characteristic.

$$\theta \triangleq p = \frac{a}{n} \qquad \{6.2\}$$

where

p = probability of the event or characteristic in the sample

a = number of events or persons with the characteristic in the sample

n = total number of persons in the sample

Equation {6.2} shows how to calculate the point estimate for the probability in the population. In addition to this general formula for a probability, there are two special probabilities that we use in health research, especially when the event of interest is having a particular disease. These special probabilities are called **prevalence** and **risk**.

In its most common form, prevalence is the probability that someone in a population has a particular disease at a particular point in time[2]. It is estimated from the sample's observations by dividing the number of persons in the sample with the disease by the total number of persons in the sample (Equation{6.3}).

$$\text{Prevalence} = \frac{\text{Number of persons with the disease at time } t}{\text{Total number of persons}} \qquad \{6.3\}$$

Risk is the probability that a person will develop a particular disease over a specified period of time. It is estimated from the sample's observations by dividing the number of persons in a sample that develop the disease over the time period by the total number of disease-free persons in the sample at the beginning of the time period (Equation{6.4}). The number of disease-free persons in a sample at the beginning of a time period is called the number "at risk."

$$\text{Risk}_{\Delta t} = \frac{\text{Number of persons developing the disease over } \Delta t}{\text{Total number of disease-free persons at the beginning of time period}} \qquad \{6.4\}$$

Both prevalence and risk are probabilities with properties just like those described for probabilities in Chapter 1. For example, prevalence or risk can have any value between zero and one. The distinction between prevalence and risk is that prevalence addresses the proportion of persons with a characteristic at a point in time while risk addresses the proportion of persons who develop a disease over a specified period of time. This is an important distinction, for prevalence can be estimated from a single examination of a sample while estimation of risk involves an examination to determine which persons do and do not have the characteristic and a second examination after a period of time to discover how

---

[2] More precisely, this is called a point prevalence.

many persons have developed the characteristic during the time interval. This distinction is illustrated in the next example.

Example 6-1 Suppose we are interested in the probability of retinopathy among diabetics. At one point in time, we examine 500 persons with diabetes and find 6 persons who have diabetic retinopathy. Five years later, we re-examine the 494 persons who did not have retinopathy at the initial examination and find that 68 have developed retinopathy during the five-year period of time. From those observations, let us estimate the prevalence and risk of diabetic retinopathy in the population from which these persons were sampled.

There are two different points in time for which we could estimate the prevalence of retinopathy. One of those is at the time of the initial examination. At that point in time, 6 out of the 500 persons examined had retinopathy. Thus, the prevalence of retinopathy at the first examination is calculated using Equation {6.3} as follows:

$$\text{Prevalence} = \frac{\text{Number of persons with the disease at the initial examination}}{\text{Total number of persons}} = \frac{6}{500} = 0.012$$

We can also estimate the prevalence of retinopathy at the time of the final examination. At that time, the original six persons who had retinopathy at the initial examination still have retinopathy plus an additional 68 people have developed retinopathy during the five-year time period. Thus, the prevalence of retinopathy at the final examination is (using Equation {6.3}):

$$\text{Prevalence} = \frac{\text{Number of persons with the disease at the final examination}}{\text{Total number of persons}} = \frac{6+68}{500} = 0.148$$

Although we can estimate two different prevalences of retinopathy (corresponding to the time of each of the two examinations), we can estimate only one risk. Since risk, in this example, is the probability of developing diabetic retinopathy over a five-year time period, our interest is confined to persons who do not have retinopathy at the beginning of the time period. Otherwise, the person is not "at risk" of developing retinopathy. The purpose of the first examination is to identify the persons who already have retinopathy. In this case, six persons were found to have retinopathy at the first examination. Thus, the number of persons "at risk" of developing retinopathy was 500 - 6 = 494. The purpose of the second examination is to find out how many of the 494 persons without retinopathy at the beginning of the five-year period developed that condition during the five-year period. Thus, our estimate of the five-year risk of diabetic retinopathy is (using Equation {6.4}):

$$\text{Risk}_{5yr} = \frac{\text{Number of persons developing the disease over 5-year period}}{\text{Total number of disease-free persons at the beginning of 5-year period}} = \frac{68}{500-6} = 0.138$$

Although the most commonly used parameter for a distribution of nominal data is the probability of the event or condition, there is one circumstance in which a probability may not be the best choice. That is when the likelihood of seeing the event represented by the nominal dependent variable is affected by time. To be affected by time, a nominal dependent variable has to meet two criteria.

The first criterion for being affected by time is that the event represented by the nominal dependent variable is more likely to be observed the longer the period of time spent looking for it. In Example 6-1, the event was development of retinopathy. That event satisfies this first criterion for being affected by time. The longer the period of time, the more new cases of retinopathy we would expect to observe. In health research, most events in which we are interested meet this first criterion for being affected by time.

The second criterion for a nominal dependent variable being affected by time is that different persons in a study must be followed for different periods of time. In Example 6-1, everyone who was at risk for developing retinopathy was followed for five years. Thus, this second criterion is not met in Example 6-1, and we need not consider the nominal dependent variable to be affected by time. For this reason, it is appropriate for us to describe the development of retinopathy using risk. It would not have been appropriate to use risk, however, if some people were not followed for the entire five-year period.

There are two ways in which persons in a study might be followed for different periods of time. One of these is due to persons withdrawing from a study before its planned end. To statisticians, the term "withdrawing" subsumes all reasons that a person might not be examined at the end of a period of follow-up. One of those reasons might be that the person chooses not to be examined, but it also includes the person moving or even someone dying before the end of the study.

Alternatively, individuals may be followed for different periods of time if they entered a study at different times. It is not unusual in health research to take a long period of time to find a sufficient number of persons who are eligible to be in the study. In this case, there is a period during which persons are recruited into the study. This feature of a study is called **staggered admission**, and it is a very common feature of clinical trials.

The reason that staggered admission causes different individuals to be followed for different periods of time is that follow-up usually ends for everyone in the study at the same point in time, regardless of when they were recruited. So, those persons who entered the study later are followed for a shorter period of time than individuals who entered the study earlier. In Example 6-1, we would have staggered admission, and, thus, different periods of follow-up for different persons, if, to be eligible for recruitment, a person had to be a newly diagnosed diabetic. If that were the case, we would need to have a period of time over which we were watching for newly diagnosed diabetics. Figure 6-2 shows a pattern of staggered admission that would lead to a nominal dependent variable affected by time if the event is more likely to be observed the longer we look for it.

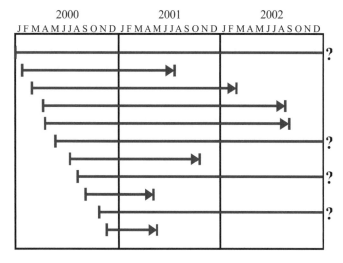

Figure 6-2 Staggered admission of 11 subjects during the first year of a 3-year study. Symbols used are: ⊢ indicates the time at which the individual entered the study (and consequently, the time at which follow-up began), ▶ indicates follow-up ending because of occurrence of the event of interest, and ? indicates end of follow-up without the event (because the study was concluded). Staggered admission is a feature of studies that can result in a nominal dependent variable being affected by time.

In Figure 6-2, there are four persons who have question marks on the outside of the time chart. For those persons, the study ended before they were observed to have the outcome. These are called **censored** observations. As that name implies, we do not know when or if these persons would have the event. Censored observations are a common feature of a nominal dependent variable affected by time.

When a nominal dependent variable is affected by time, we usually describe the nominal dependent variable using a rate instead of a probability.[3] Probabilities and rates differ according to the information that is used in their denominators. For a probability, the denominator reflects the number of persons who are candidates for having the event. For a rate, the denominator reflects the number of persons as well as how long each person was followed.

Having time in the denominator of a rate gives it 1/time as its units of measure. Probabilities, on the other hand, have no units of measure. Having time in the denominator of a rate also changes the range of possible values. In Chapter 1, we learned that a probability can have any value between zero and one. A rate, on the other hand, can have any value between zero and infinity.[4]

When we are interested in the rate of disease occurrence, we use a special name for the rate at which new cases appear in a population. We call this rate the **incidence** of the disease. Equation {6.5} shows how an incidence is calculated:

---

[3] In Chapter 12, we will look at life-table analysis. This is a statistical method that allows us to estimate probabilities from a nominal dependent variable affected by time.

[4] One way to think of the reason for this is to realize that the denominator of an incidence can be infinitely small if we express the incidence in an infinitely long period of time. For instance, one person-year is equal to 0.1 person-decades or 0.001 person-millennia.

$$\text{Incidence}=\frac{\text{Number of new cases of disease}}{\sum_{i=1}^{n}(\text{Time of follow-up for }i^{\text{th}}\text{ person})} \qquad \{6.5\}$$

where

$$\sum_{i=1}^{n}$$ = sum of values (e.g., follow-up times) for individuals from the first individual ($i=1$) to the nth individual

There are two ways in which we commonly calculate the follow-up time used in the denominator of a rate. The best way is to simply add up each person's individual follow-up time. A person's follow-up time begins when he or she enters the study. It ends either when the person has the event or when the person is no longer followed. The other way to calculate follow-up time is to assume that follow-up ended half-way between the time that the person was last seen without the event and the time at which the person either had the event or disappeared. This way of estimating follow-up time is called the **actuarial method**. The actuarial method is used only when we do not know the actual time follow-up ends, but we are able to identify two points in time between which follow-up ended. The next example illustrates both methods of determining follow-up time.

Example 6-2 Suppose that Figure 6-2 shows the results of following 11 individuals for up to three years looking for the development of retinopathy at monthly examinations. The following table shows, for each of those 11 persons, the month at which follow-up began, when it ended, and whether or not the person had the event.

Patient	Date Began	Date Ended	Event?
TH	1/00	12/02	No
IS	2/00	8/01	Yes
JU	3/00	3/02	Yes
ST	4/00	8/02	Yes
GE	4/00	9/02	Yes
TS	5/00	12/02	No
BE	7/00	11/01	Yes
TT	8/00	12/02	No
ER	9/00	5/01	Yes
DU	10/00	12/02	No
DE	11/00	6/01	Yes
TOTAL			7 events

Now, let us estimate the incidence of retinopathy using the actuarial method to approximate the total follow-up time.

In this set of data, we know the month during which each individual had the event, but we do not know exactly when it occurred. When this is the case, we need to make an assumption about the time at which the event occurred. The assumption in the actuarial method is that, on the average, events occur in the middle of the time period between examinations. To reflect this assumption, we allow each person who had the event to contribute to the overall follow-up time only half of the time (in this case, ½ month) from the examination at which they first had the event and the previous examination. The following table shows those data as they would appear if the actuarial method were used to determine the length of follow-up:

Patient	Date Began	Date Ended	Follow-up Length (months)	Event?
TH	1/00	12/02	36	No
IS	2/00	8/01	18+1/2=18.5	Yes
JU	3/00	3/02	24+1/2=24.5	Yes
ST	4/00	8/02	28+1/2=28.5	Yes
GE	4/00	9/02	29+1/2=29.5	Yes
TS	5/00	12/02	32	No
BE	7/00	11/01	16+1/2=16.5	Yes
TT	8/00	12/02	29	No
ER	9/00	5/01	8+1/2=8.5	Yes
DU	10/00	12/02	27	No
DE	11/00	6/01	7+1/2=7.5	Yes
TOTAL			257.5	7 events

The total follow-up time, using the actuarial method, is equal to 257.5 months (or 257.5/12=21.5 years). Notice how the follow-up time for those individuals who had the event is reduced by ½ month. This represents the assumption that, in the actuarial method, persons who had the event had it at the middle of the time between examinations. With that information and the fact that seven persons developed retinopathy, we can use Equation {6.5} to calculate the estimated incidence.

$$\text{Incidence} = \frac{\text{Number of new cases of disease}}{\sum_{i=1}^{n} (\text{Time of follow-up for } i^{th} \text{ person})} = \frac{7}{\frac{257.5}{12}} = \frac{7}{21.5} = 0.33 \text{ per year}$$

Prevalence, risk, and incidence are measurements of disease frequency. Most of the diseases of interest to health researchers are rare. Therefore, values of prevalence, risk, and incidence are generally small numbers. For instance, the prevalence of pancreatic cancer in the United States in 1999 was about 0.00008. To keep us from having to deal with all the zeros in these small numbers, prevalence and risk are often presented as a larger number times 10^{-5} (so many cases per 10^5 persons)[5] and incidence is frequently given as a larger number times 10^{-5} years (number of cases per 10^5 person-years). In the case of pancreatic cancer, we would report that the prevalence is equal to 8 x 10^{-5} (or 8 cases per 10^5 persons). For more common diseases, prevalence and risk are usually expressed as a percentage (i.e., prevalence x 100%). For example, the prevalence of heart disease among women in the United States is about 0.29 or 29%. Since incidence has the units 1/time, it cannot be expressed as a percentage.

Sampling Distributions

To take chance into account, we need to consider the sampling distribution for estimates of the probability or the rate of occurrence of an event in the population. To begin, let us consider a nominal dependent variable represented by the probability of the event. Later, we will discuss the sampling distribution for the rate of an event.

When we discussed the sampling distribution for estimates of the mean of a distribution of continuous data we assumed that the sampling distribution is a Gaussian distribution. We are comfortable with that assumption if the sample is not too small; since the central limit theorem tells us that sampling distributions for estimates of the mean tend to be Gaussian distributions, with that tendency increasing as the size of the samples increases. The sampling distribution for estimates of the probability of an event (θ), however, is not assumed to be a Gaussian distribution. Instead, the sampling distribution for estimates of θ is a **binomial distribution**.[6]

The binomial distribution is different from the Gaussian distribution in three ways. First, the binomial distribution is a discrete, rather than continuous, distribution. This is because there are a limited number of possible estimates of (θ) from samples of a given size. For instance, samples with 20 observations must provide one of 21 different estimates. This limited number of estimates is due to the fact that the numerator of an estimate of the

---

[5] This is known as scientific notation. 10^{-5} is equal to one over ten to the fifth power or 1/100,000. 10^5 is equal to ten to the fifth power or 100,000.

[6] This is not an assumption, but rather a statement of fact. The sampling distribution for estimates of θ will always be a binomial distribution.

probability of the event must be an integer (i.e., a whole number) between zero and the total number of observations. There are 21 integers in the interval between zero and twenty.

Recognition of the binomial distribution as a discrete distribution is reflected in the way in which binomial distributions are presented graphically. Recall from Chapter 2 that bar graphs are used for discrete data. Figure 6-3 shows a bar graph for a binomial sampling distribution.

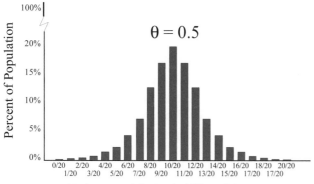

Figure 6-3 A graphical representation of the binomial sampling distribution for estimates of θ from all possible samples with 20 observations when the population's value of θ is equal to 0.5.

The second way in which the binomial distribution is different from the Gaussian distribution is that the binomial distribution has a discrete range of possible values whereas the Gaussian distribution has (theoretically) an infinite range of possible values. The reason that this distinction is important is that a distribution with a discrete range of possible values is symmetric only when its parameter is in the middle of that range. In Figure 6-3, θ is equal to 0.5, which is in the middle of the range of possible values for a probability (i.e., 0 to 1). Consequently, the binomial distribution in Figure 6-3 is symmetric. If we were to change the value of θ to some other value, however, the binomial distribution would no longer be symmetric. Figure 6-4 shows a binomial distribution for 20 observations and with θ equal to 0.25. That distribution is asymmetric.

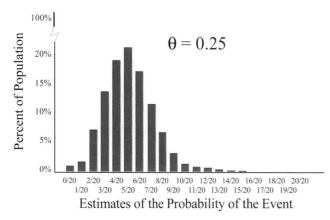

Figure 6-4 A graphical representation of the binomial sampling distribution for estimates of θ from all possible samples with 20 observations when the population's value of θ is equal to 0.25.

The third way in which the binomial distribution is different from the Gaussian distribution is in the number of parameters that is needed to mathematically define those distributions.

A Gaussian distribution is defined by two parameters: the mean and the variance (or standard deviation). A particular binomial distribution, on the other hand, requires only one parameter to distinguish it from other binomial distributions. This single parameter is θ, the probability of the event in the population.[7] θ is analogous to the mean of a Gaussian distribution.[8] Thus, we think of θ as a parameter of location of the binomial distribution. This parameter of location is the only value needed to identify a particular binomial distribution.

Statistical methods that address the binomial distribution itself are called **exact methods**. These methods are computationally cumbersome and, as a result, are not the way in which we usually analyze a nominal dependent variable.[9] More frequently, we use methods that are based on a **normal approximation**. In a normal approximation, we recognize that probabilities calculated using the actual sampling distribution for a parameter of a nominal dependent variable are, under certain circumstances, not very different from probabilities calculated assuming a Gaussian sampling distribution. When that is the case, we can use statistical methods based on a Gaussian sampling distribution to take the role of chance into account in estimating θ from the sample's observations (Figure 6-5).

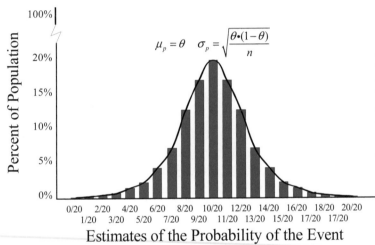

$$\mu_p = \theta \qquad \sigma_p = \sqrt{\frac{\theta \cdot (1 - \theta)}{n}}$$

Figure 6-5 When the normal approximation to the binomial is used to take into account the role of chance in estimating θ, we think of the sampling distribution as being approximated by a Gaussian distribution.

Estimates of the Probability of the Event

We are comfortable with a normal approximation when the sample is not too small. For a symmetric binomial distribution, samples of ten or more observations can be analyzed using the normal approximation. For an asymmetric binomial distribution, the sample's size needs to be larger than 10 observations. How much larger depends on the degree of asymmetry. The rule of thumb we use is that at least 5 events and at least 5 nonevents are required to use

---

[7] θ is the parameter of the distribution of nominal data (Figure 6-1) as well as the binomial sampling distribution.

[8] If we were to represent the occurrence of the event with the number one and the nonoccurrence of the event with zero, the mean of those values would be equal to θ.

[9] With the fast computers that we use today, this really is not a good excuse for using a method other than an exact method. Even so, changing the way in which statisticians traditionally analyze data is a slow process.

the normal approximation to the binomial distribution. If, for example, θ is equal to 0.10, then the minimum number of observations required to use the normal approximation is 50. Among those 50 persons, 5 would have the event (since the probability of having the event is 0.1) and 45 would not have the event.

In a normal approximation to the binomial distribution, we think about the binomial sampling distribution as if it were a Gaussian sampling distribution. If the sampling distribution were a Gaussian distribution, we would need two parameters to mathematically define that sampling distribution: a mean and a standard error. The ways in which we would calculate those parameters, if we observed the entire population, are shown in Equations {6.6} and {6.7}.

$$\mu_p = \theta \qquad\qquad \{6.6\}$$

$$\sigma_p = \sqrt{\frac{\theta \cdot (1-\theta)}{n}} \qquad\qquad \{6.7\}$$

where

μ_p = mean of the sampling distribution for estimates of θ when the normal approximation to the binomial is used to take chance into account

σ_p = standard error for estimates of θ when the normal approximation to the binomial is used to take chance into account

Equations {6.6} and {6.7} suggest that the sampling distribution has two parameters, but a closer look at those equations reveals only a single parameter: θ. For any particular value of the mean (θ), there is only one standard error possible, since the standard error is simply an algebraic function of θ. This is unlike the standard error for estimates of the mean for continuous data. For a particular value of the mean of a distribution of continuous data, the variance and, hence, the standard error for the sampling distribution for that mean can be equal to any value. Thus, we say that there is an independent role of chance in estimating the variance of a distribution of continuous data. There is not, however, an independent role of chance in estimating a variance of a distribution of nominal data. With nominal data, there is one, and only one, possible value for the variance with any particular value of θ.

The independent role of chance in estimating the variance of a distribution of continuous data is the reason that Student's t distribution was used in Chapter 4. Student's t distribution takes into account this independent role of chance by using degrees of freedom to reflect how much information the sample contains that can be used to estimate the variance. Since there is no independent role of chance in estimating the variance when we are using a normal approximation for a nominal dependent variable, we do not use Student's t distribution for a nominal dependent variable. Instead, we use the standard normal distribution when we are performing a normal approximation.

The sampling distribution for an estimate of a probability is a binomial distribution. When a nominal dependent variable is represented as a rate, however, we cannot use the binomial distribution. The problem is that the binomial distribution takes chance into account for estimates that can range from zero to one and that have no unit of measure. Rates have zero as their lower bound, but rates have no upper bound. Rates also have 1/time as their units of measure. Thus, to take chance into account for estimates of the rate of an event, we need to use a different sampling distribution.

The problem with rates stems from the fact that time is in their denominators. The solution to this problem is to use a sampling distribution that is not affected by what is in the denominator. The **Poisson distribution**[10] is the sampling distribution we use most often to take into account the role of chance in estimating a rate. The parameter of a Poisson distribution is the number of events. That is to say, the parameter is the numerator of the rate. We symbolize this parameter with the Greek letter lambda (λ).[11] This is the same as the numerator of θ in Equation{6.1}. The point estimate of θ calculated from the sample's observations is symbolized with the letter a. This is the same as the numerator of p in Equation{6.2}.

$$\lambda \stackrel{\triangle}{=} a \qquad \{6.8\}$$

To take the role of chance into account when estimating the rate at which events occur, we can perform an exact procedure that uses the Poisson distribution itself or we can use a normal approximation to the Poisson distribution. The same reason that motivated us to use the normal approximation to the binomial distribution also motivates us to use the normal approximation to the Poisson distribution. Namely, normal approximations are computationally less complicated.

Since the Poisson distribution has no upper bound, the Poisson distribution tends to be very asymmetric. Figure 6-6 shows an example of the Poisson distribution.

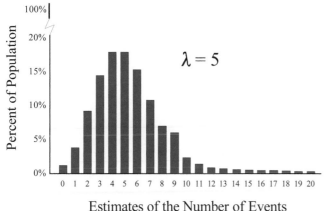

Estimates of the Number of Events

Figure 6-6 A graphical representation of the Poisson sampling distribution for estimates of λ from all possible samples with 20 observations when the population's value of λ is equal to 5.

If we were to use a normal approximation for the Poisson distribution shown in Figure 6-6,

---

[10] We always capitalize "Poisson," since this is the name of the French mathematician who derived this distribution.

[11] The Poisson distribution can also be used as a sampling distribution for probabilities of rare events, but when performing normal approximations, it is better to use the binomial distribution for probabilities.

we would need to have a relatively large sample to overcome the asymmetry of the distribution. Instead, what we do is to use a **transformation** for the number of events and, then, do a normal approximation for the transformed number of events. What statisticians mean by a transformation is performing a mathematical operation on dependent variable values so that they are easier to use in statistical analyses. The transformation we use for the number of events in the normal approximation to the Poisson distribution is the **square root transformation**.

The way that this transformation works is that we take the square root of the number of events and perform our statistical analysis on that transformed value. Then, after the statistical analysis is complete, the results of the analysis are changed back to the original scale by squaring the estimates. We will see how this works later, but for now, let us take a look at the parameters we use when performing a normal approximation to the Poisson distribution.

The mean and standard error of the sampling distribution for the square root of the number of events are illustrated in Equations {6.9} and {6.10}.

$$\mu_{\sqrt{a}} = \sqrt{\lambda} \qquad \{6.9\}$$

$$\sigma_{\sqrt{a}} = \frac{1}{2} \qquad \{6.10\}$$

where

$\mu_{\sqrt{a}}$ = mean of the sampling distribution for estimates of the square root of λ when the normal approximation to the Poisson is used to take chance into account

$\sigma_{\sqrt{a}}$ = standard error for estimates of the square root of λ when the normal approximation to the Poisson is used to take chance into account

As in estimation of the parameters in the normal approximation to the binomial (Equations {6.6} and {6.7}), estimation of the parameters in the normal approximation to the Poisson involves only a single role of chance. That role is the effect of chance on estimation of the mean of the distribution. When we discussed the normal approximation to the binomial, we found that there was no independent role of chance for estimation of the variance, since the variance was merely an algebraic form of the mean of the distribution (Equation {6.7}). In the normal approximation to the Poisson, the lack of an independent role of chance in estimating the variance is even clearer than it was in the normal approximation to the binomial. In the normal approximation to the Poisson, the variance is equal to a constant and, thus, requires no estimation at all.

Now that we are familiar with the sampling distributions for the normal approximations to the binomial and Poisson distributions, we are ready to see how we can use those sampling distributions to take chance into account through the processes of interval estimation and hypothesis testing.

Interval Estimation

In Chapter 3, we used the standard normal distribution to calculate a confidence interval for the mean of a distribution of continuous data. That method is not appropriate for a continuous dependent variable, but it is appropriate for calculating a confidence interval for the probability of an event, since there is no independent role of chance in estimating the variance of a distribution of nominal data. Equation {6.11} shows how a two-sided confidence interval for θ is calculated in the normal approximation to the binomial.

$$\theta \triangleq p \pm \left(z_{\alpha/2} \cdot \sqrt{\frac{\theta \cdot (1-\theta)}{n}} \right) \triangleq p \pm \left(z_{\alpha/2} \cdot \sqrt{\frac{p \cdot (1-p)}{n}} \right) \qquad \{6.11\}$$

The standard error in Equation {6.11} is a little different from the standard error in Equation {6.7}. Equation {6.7} uses the population's value of θ instead of the sample's estimate (p) to calculate the standard error. When we are calculating a confidence interval from the sample's observations, we do not know the value of θ. Our best guess for the value of θ is the point estimate (p). Thus, Equation {6.11} uses p instead of θ in the standard error.

Now, let us take a look at an example of how we calculate a confidence interval for the probability of an event represented by a nominal dependent variable.

Example 6-3 In Example 6-1, we estimated the five-year risk of developing retinopathy to be equal to 0.138 from a group of 494 persons without retinopathy at the beginning of the five-year period of follow-up. Now, let us calculate a 95%, two-sided confidence interval for that risk.

To calculate that confidence interval, we use Equation {6.11}:

$$\theta \triangleq p \pm \left(z_{\alpha/2} \cdot \sqrt{\frac{p \cdot (1-p)}{n}} \right) = 0.138 \pm \left(1.96 \cdot \sqrt{\frac{0.138 \cdot (1-0.138)}{494}} \right) = 0.108 \text{ to } 0.168$$

Thus, we can have 95% confidence that the actual five-year risk of developing retinopathy in the population is between 0.108 and 0.168

As we found out earlier in this chapter, normal approximations are used to analyze a nominal dependent variable because exact methods involve cumbersome calculations. If we are calculating a confidence interval by hand, the normal approximation is easier. However, the difficulty of the calculation is not an issue when the computer is doing the calculating.

To analyze a univariable sample with a nominal dependent variable, we use SAS's FREQ procedure. That procedure gives us two confidence intervals for an estimated probability. One is calculated using the exact method. The other one uses the normal approximation in Equation{6.11}. The next example shows these confidence intervals.

Example 6-4 In Example 6-3, we calculated a 95% two-sided confidence interval for the five-year risk of developing retinopathy using the normal approximation. Now, let us take a look at the confidence intervals calculated by SAS.

The following is the result of using SAS to analyze the data in Example 6-1:

```
                          The FREQ Procedure


                     Cumulative     Cumulative
    RETINOPATHY   Frequency      Percent     Frequency      Percent

    DISEASE            68         13.77            68         13.77
    NORMAL            426         86.23           494        100.00



                      Binomial Proportion for
                       RETINOPATHY = DISEASE

              Proportion                 0.1377
              ASE                        0.0155
              95% Lower Conf Limit       0.1073
              95% Upper Conf Limit       0.1680

                      Exact Conf Limits
              95% Lower Conf Limit       0.1085
              95% Upper Conf Limit       0.1712
```

The first part of the SAS output from the FREQ procedure gives us a table of the frequencies and percents corresponding to whether or not a person has retinopathy. These include both the simple frequency and percent and the **cumulative** values as well. Cumulative frequency tells the number of observations in that category and all previously listed categories combined. Similarly, cumulative percent tells the percentage of observations in that category and all previously listed categories.

The next part of the output from the FREQ procedure gives the confidence interval for the risk of retinopathy. The first interval is calculated using the normal approximation to the binomial. It is the same as the interval calculated in Example 6-3, except for a small rounding error. The second interval is the exact confidence interval. It is very close in value to the approximate confidence interval. This will be true when the sample is large. The better interval to report in a publication is the exact interval.

SAS will calculate confidence intervals for probabilities, but it does not calculate confidence interval for rates. Thus, we need to calculate these by hand. Using a normal approximation to calculate a confidence interval for the rate at which events occur involves three steps, but we can perform all three of those steps using a single equation. Equations {6.12} and {6.13} show the first two steps in deriving Equation{6.14}. In practice, we perform all three of those steps in the single calculation illustrated in Equation{6.14}.

The first step in this process is to calculate a confidence interval for the square root of the number of events. This step is shown in Equation{6.12}:

$$\sqrt{\lambda} \triangleq \sqrt{a} \pm \left(z_{\alpha/2} \cdot \frac{1}{2} \right) \qquad \{6.12\}$$

In the next step, we change the limits of that confidence interval from the square of the number of events to the number of events by squaring the limits. Equation {6.13} shows how Equation {6.12} changes to reflect this step:

$$\lambda \triangleq \left[\sqrt{a} \pm \left(z_{\alpha/2} \cdot \frac{1}{2} \right) \right]^2 \qquad \{6.13\}$$

Finally, we change the limits of that confidence interval so that they reflect the rate at which new events are occurring by dividing the limits by the total time of follow-up in the sample.

$$\text{Incidence} \triangleq \frac{\left[\sqrt{a} \pm \left(z_{\alpha/2} \cdot \frac{1}{2} \right) \right]^2}{\sum_{i=1}^{n} \text{Length of follow-up for the } i^{th} \text{ person}} \qquad \{6.14\}$$

Equation {6.14} includes all three steps in a single equation. In the next example, we will take a look at how we can use Equation {6.14} to calculate an interval estimate for a rate:

Example 6-5   In Example 6-2, we considered the results of 11 persons followed for up to three years looking for the development of diabetic retinopathy. Among these 11 persons, seven developed retinopathy during the follow-up period. The total time of follow-up for the eleven persons was 21.8 years. Using that information, we estimated in Example 6-2 that the incidence of retinopathy in the population is equal to 0.32 cases per person-year. Now, let us calculate a 95%, two-sided confidence interval for the incidence of retinopathy in the population.

We calculate the confidence interval for a rate by using Equation{6.14}:

$$\text{Incidence} \triangleq \frac{\left[\sqrt{a} \pm \left(z_{\alpha/2} \cdot \dfrac{1}{2}\right)\right]^2}{\displaystyle\sum_{i=1}^{n} \text{Length of follow-up for the } i^{th} \text{ person}} = \frac{\left[\sqrt{7} \pm \left(1.96 \cdot \dfrac{1}{2}\right)\right]^2}{21.8} = 0.13 \text{ to } 0.60 \text{ per year}$$

Thus, we have 95% confidence that the incidence of retinopathy in the population is between 0.13 and 0.60 new cases per person-year.

_____

Hypothesis Testing

In Chapter 3, we learned that using hypothesis testing as a way to take the role of chance into account depends on our ability to formulate a testable null hypothesis. A testable null hypothesis is one that makes a specific statement about the population, and that is also an interesting hypothesis to test. Often, this cannot be done for a univariable sample. In Chapter 4, we learned that a univariable sample with a continuous dependent variable is a candidate for hypothesis testing if the data are from a paired study. For mean differences, it makes sense to test the null hypothesis that the mean difference between two measurements for each individual is equal to zero. Otherwise, taking chance into account for a univariable sample of a continuous dependent variable is limited to interval estimation.

For the same reasons, we usually take chance into account by calculating a confidence interval when the dependent variable in a univariable data set represents nominal data. There is one exception. This is when each person in the study is exposed to both of the two nominal categories represented by the nominal dependent variable and the one considered to be "better" for each individual is recorded. Studies of this type are called **preference studies**. In a preference study, each person selects the nominal category he or she prefers more. Then, the data are summarized by determining the proportion of persons preferring a particular category.

The null hypothesis in a preference study is that half of the persons will choose a particular category (i.e., H_0: $\theta = 0.5$). This null hypothesis is the same as saying that there is no overall preference for either of the two categories. To test this null hypothesis, we can use either an exact test or a normal approximation. If offered the results of both, the exact test is the better method. If we are performing the calculation by hand, however, the normal approximation is easier.

For the normal approximation, the observed proportion preferring a selected category is converted to a standard normal deviate using Equation {6.15}.

$$z = \frac{p - \theta_0}{\sqrt{\dfrac{\theta_0 \cdot (1 - \theta_0)}{n}}} = \frac{p - 0.5}{\sqrt{\dfrac{0.5 \cdot (1 - 0.5)}{n}}} \qquad \{6.15\}$$

where

θ_0 = proportion of persons preferring a particular category of the nominal dependent variable according to the null hypothesis. In a preference study, this proportion is equal to 0.5.

In Equation{6.15}, the value of the θ used in calculation of the standard error is the value stated in the null hypothesis. The reason for this is that, when we are preparing to calculate *P*-values, we assume that the null hypothesis is true (see Equation 3.10). Since the standard error in the normal approximation to the binomial is an algebraic function of θ, the value of that standard error reflects the value of θ in the null hypothesis rather than the observed probability preferring a particular category. Thus, the standard error in hypothesis testing (Equation {6.15}) is different from the standard error in interval estimation (Equation {6.11}).

The next example illustrates a preference study and how the null hypothesis can be tested using the normal approximation to the binomial.

Example 6-6   Suppose we are interested in comparing two types of anti-nausea medication (called "A" and "B"). To make this comparison, we randomly assign one of the medications to 12 persons who have chronic nausea to use on that day. Then, they are instructed to use the other medication on another day. Suppose that 8 of the 12 persons reported better control of nausea with medication "A." From those observations, let us test the null hypothesis that, in the population, there is no preference for either of the medications, versus the alternative hypothesis that there is a preference. In testing this null hypothesis we will allow a 5% chance of making a type I error (i.e., $\alpha = 0.05$).

The null hypothesis that there is no preference for either of the two medications in the population is the same as saying that half of the persons in the population would prefer medication "A" and the other half of the persons in the population would prefer medication "B." In terms of the parameter of a distribution of nominal data (θ), that null hypothesis is:

$$H_0 : \theta = 0.5$$

To test this null hypothesis using the normal approximation to the binomial, we need to have at least five events (preferring "A") and five nonevents (preferring "B"). In this sample, there are 8 persons preferring "A" and 4 persons preferring "B." At first, this might seem to be insufficient to permit us to use the normal approximation, since there are only 4 persons preferring "B." However, when using hypothesis testing, we think about how many persons would prefer "B" if the null hypothesis were true. The null hypothesis tells us that half of the individuals prefer "B" (and the other half prefer "A"). With a sample of 12, we would expect 6 persons preferring each medication. This is sufficient to use the normal approximation.

Having decided to use the normal approximation to the binomial, we use Equation

{6.15} to convert the observed proportion preferring "A" (8/12=0.67) into a standard normal deviate (i.e., a z-value).

$$z = \frac{p - \theta_0}{\sqrt{\dfrac{\theta_0 \bullet (1 - \theta_0)}{n}}} = \frac{0.67 - 0.5}{\sqrt{\dfrac{0.5 \bullet (1 - 0.5)}{12}}} = 1.15$$

If we look up 1.15 in Table B.1, we find that it is associated with a probability in the upper tail of the standard normal distribution equal to 0.1251. Since the alternative hypothesis (i.e., that there is a preference) is two-sided, we need to double that probability to get the P-value. Thus, the P-value is equal to 0.2502. Since this is larger than α (0.05), we fail to reject the null hypothesis (i.e., we cannot draw a conclusion about the null hypothesis from this sample). From a biologic perspective, we cannot conclude that one medication is preferred over the other.[12]

In Example 6-6, we tested the null hypothesis that there is no preference for either of the medications by performing the calculations by hand. We can use SAS to test this same null hypothesis by using SAS's FREQ procedure as shown in the next example:

Example 6-7   In Example 6-6, we were interested in comparing two types of anti-nausea medication (called "A" and "B"). To make this comparison, we randomly assign each of 12 persons one of the medications on one day and the other on the next day. Then, we tested the null hypothesis that the probability of preferring either of those medications is equal to 0.5. Now, let us use the FREQ procedure to test that same null hypothesis.

The first part of the output from SAS reports frequencies and percentages as we saw in Example 6-4.

```
                          The SAS System
                        The FREQ Procedure

                                    Cumulative    Cumulative
    PREFER    Frequency    Percent   Frequency     Percent

      A           8         66.67         8         66.67
      B           4         33.33        12        100.00
```

The next part of the output gives us confidence intervals and the results of hypothesis

---

[12] It is important to keep in mind that this is not the same as saying that there is no preference. To conclude that there is no preference would be to accept the null hypothesis as true. We do not accept null hypotheses as being true so that we can avoid type II errors. This is discussed in Chapter 3.

testing.[13]

```
                    Binomial Proportion for PREFER = A
                    ─────────────────────────────────────

                    Proportion (P)                    0.6667
                    ASE                               0.1361
                    95% Lower Conf Limit              0.3999
                    95% Upper Conf Limit              0.9334


                    Exact Conf Limits
                    95% Lower Conf Limit              0.3489
                    95% Upper Conf Limit              0.9008


                       Test of H0: Proportion = 0.5

                    ASE under H0                      0.1443
                    Z                                 1.1547
                    One-sided Pr >  Z                 0.1241
                    Two-sided Pr > |Z|                0.2482


                    Exact Test
                    One-sided Pr >=  P                0.1938
                    Two-sided = 2 * One-sided         0.3877


                         Sample Size = 12
```

This output gives us two sets of P-values for the test of the null hypothesis that the probability of preferring medication A is equal to 0.5 in the population. The first has a two-sided P-value equal to 0.2482. This P-value is from a normal approximation.[14] Since that P-value is greater than 0.05, we fail to reject the null hypothesis. Aside from some rounding error, this is the same as the result in Example 6-6 where we performed the test by hand.

The second set of P-values is from an exact test. The two-sided exact P-value is equal to 0.3877. Since that P-value is greater than 0.05, we fail to reject the null hypothesis. This is the same conclusion as we drew using the P-value from the approximation. If these conclusions differ, the one based on the exact P-value is the more appropriate one.

Although the purpose of this example is to test the null hypothesis that the probability of preferring either of those medications is equal to 0.5, let us take a look at the confidence intervals calculated by SAS. There are two features of those confidence intervals that are notable. One is that the value in the null hypothesis (0.5) is included in those confidence intervals. We learned in Chapter 3 that this is consistent with failing to reject the null

---

[13] The results of hypothesis testing were also originally included in the output we examined in Example 6-4 (determining the five-year risk of developing retinopathy), but we removed them. The null hypothesis that the risk is equal to 0.5 does not make biological sense. There is no sensible null hypothesis to test when we are estimating a probability other than in a preference study.

[14] We can tell that this is a normal approximation because it is based on a z-value. Also, the value for ASE is an "approximate standard error." There is no standard error in an exact calculation.

hypothesis.[15]

The second thing to note about the confidence intervals is that the limits based on the normal approximation are not as close to the limits in the exact interval as those limits seen in Example 6-4. The reason for this difference is the difference in the sizes of the samples in the two examples. There were 494 observations in Example 6-4, but only 12 observations in this example. This should remind us that the normal approximation gives us an approximate result. The larger the size of the sample, the better is that approximation. Even though this sample of 12 persons was large enough to use the normal approximation in hypothesis testing, it is not considered large enough to use the normal approximation in interval estimation. The reason for this distinction is that the rule-of-thumb that states that at least 5 events and at least 5 nonevents are required to use the normal approximation to the binomial distribution is based on $\theta=0.5$ in hypothesis testing and is based on $\theta \triangleq p$ in interval estimation. In this example, p is equal to 0.67. That corresponds to 8 events and 4 nonevents. Four nonevents are fewer than the required five.

Taking chance into account for an estimate of the rate at which events occur is limited to interval estimation. The reason for this limitation is that it is impossible to formulate a testable null hypothesis for a rate. That is because we cannot select a specific value for a rate that is biologically interesting to test.

Now we have completed our look at univariable analysis. We are ready to begin Part Three of this text, which addresses bivariable analyses.

---

[15] In the normal approximation to the binomial, this will not always be the case. The reason for this inconsistency is the fact that the standard error is a function of θ. When testing the null hypothesis that $\theta=0.5$, the standard error is based on $\theta=0.5$ (see Equation{6.15}). When calculating a confidence interval however, the standard error is based on $\theta=p$ (see Equation{6.11}).

PART THREE
Bivariable Analyses

In the introduction to Part Two, we learned that variables serve either of two functions. One function is to represent the data of primary interest. This function is served by the dependent variable. To identify the dependent variable, we ask ourselves, "For which data we want to make an estimate or test a hypothesis?" The answer to that question identifies the data represented by the dependent variable. Every set of data must have some of the data values represented by the dependent variable.[1]

The other function served by variables is to specify the conditions under which we are interested in examining the dependent variable. This function is served by the independent variable(s). It is not necessary that a set of data has some of its data values represented by an independent variable. In univariable analyses (the subject of Part Two), there are no independent variables. This implies that there are no special conditions under which we are interested in examining the dependent variable in univariable analysis. Instead, we are interested in making estimates of or testing hypotheses about the dependent variable in general. This situation changes in bivariable analyses.

In bivariable analyses we have conditions that define our interest in examining the dependent variable. The nature of those conditions is determined by the type of data represented by the independent variable. In most cases, independent variables represent either continuous or nominal data.

When an independent variable represents continuous data, dependent variable values are arrayed along the continuum of independent variable values. As an example, suppose that we are interested in the ability of various dosages of a medication to lower diastolic blood pressure. In that case, the decrease in diastolic blood pressure is represented by the dependent variable and dose is represented by a continuous independent variable. Our interest in the decrease in diastolic blood pressure is how the dependent variable values are arrayed throughout the continuum of doses.

There are two aspects of the relationship between a dependent variable and a continuous independent variable that might be of interest. One of those is the strength of the association between the dependent and independent variables. In the example, the strength of the association between dose of a medication and the decrease in diastolic blood pressure would reflect how consistently the decrease in diastolic blood pressure changes as the dose changes.

Another aspect of the relationship between a dependent variable and a continuous independent variable that might be of interest is the ability to estimate dependent variable values that correspond to particular values of the continuous independent variable. In the example, we would be interested in this aspect of the relationship if we wanted to be able to calculate the decrease in the diastolic blood pressure we would expect to observe if a person were given a particular dose of the medication.

---

[1] If a set of data does not have some of its data values represented by a dependent variable, the implication is that there are no data for which we are interested in calculating an estimate or testing a hypothesis. In that case, we have no need for statistical analyses.

When an independent variable represents nominal data, the nominal independent variable values divide the dependent variable values into two groups. Our interest, then, is to compare estimates of or test hypotheses about the parameters in those two groups. As an example, suppose that we are interested in the change in diastolic blood pressure between persons who received a new medication and persons who received standard therapy. The value of the nominal independent variable, in that case, indicates which a person received.

The type of data represented by the independent variable helps to determine the statistical method that is appropriate to analyze those data. In each of the three chapters in Part Three of this text, the continuations of the flowchart will begin by deciding the type of data represented by the independent variable.

CHAPTER 7

Bivariable Analysis of a Continuous Dependent Variable

As shown in Flowchart 5, bivariable analysis of a continuous dependent variable can involve an independent variable that represents either continuous data or nominal data. We will begin by considering a bivariable data set in which both the dependent and independent variables represent continuous data.

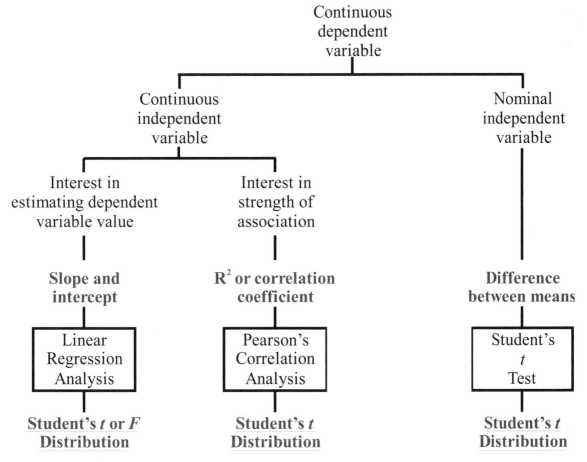

Flowchart 5 Flowchart showing bivariable analysis of a continuous dependent variable. The point estimate that is most often used to describe the dependent variable is in color. The common name of the statistical test is enclosed in a box. The standard distributions that are used to test hypotheses and calculate confidence intervals are in color and underlined.

CONTINUOUS INDEPENDENT VARIABLE

When the independent variable represents continuous data, the effect is to array dependent variable values along the continuum of independent variable values. This is easiest to appreciate if we examine the relationship between those variables graphically. The type of graph we use to look at this relationship is called a **scatter plot**. Figure 7-1 illustrates a scatter plot:

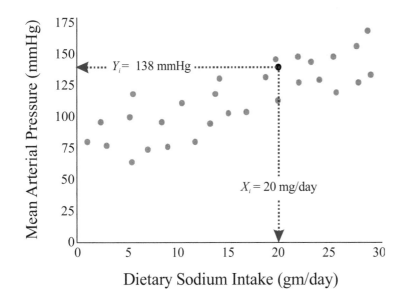

Figure 7-1 Scatter plot showing the relationship between dietary sodium intake (the independent variable) and mean arterial blood pressure (the dependent variable). Each point in the scatter plot tells us the value of both of those variables for an individual. For example, the indicated point corresponds to a dietary sodium intake of 20 gm/day and a mean arterial pressure of 138 mmHg.

The convention we use in drawing a scatter plot is to put the independent variable values on the horizontal axis (the abscissa) and the dependent variable values on the vertical axis (the ordinate). These are also called the X-axis and the Y-axis, respectively. The reason for these names is the fact we represent independent variable values with the letter X and dependent variable values with the letter Y.

Examination of the scatter plot tells us a number of things about the relationship between dietary sodium intake and mean arterial blood pressure. For one thing, we can see that the numeric magnitude of blood pressure increases as dietary sodium intake increases. We call this a **direct association**, when both variables change in the same direction. An **inverse association** occurs when values of the dependent variable decrease in numeric magnitude as values of the independent variable increase. For example, we would expect to observe an inverse association between the dose of an antihypertensive medication (the independent variable) and arterial pressure (the dependent variable). In that case, the mean arterial pressure would decrease as the dose of the medication increases.

REGRESSION ANALYSIS

Another thing we can do with continuous data in a scatter plot is to estimate the value of the dependent variable that, on the average, is associated with a particular value of the independent variable. When we are interested in estimating values of the dependent variable that correspond to specific values of the independent variable, we are interested in performing a **regression analysis**.[1]

There are two ways in which we can do a regression analysis. One of these is a graphic approach and the other is a mathematic approach. In the graphic approach, the scatter plot is

---

[1] When referring to estimation of dependent variable values in regression analysis, statisticians often use the term "predict" rather than "estimate." This implies that there is a difference between estimating dependent variable values in regression analysis and estimating other parameters. There is no difference.

used to estimate dependent variable values. For example, we might be interested in using the data in Figure 7-1 to determine the most likely mean arterial pressure for a person with a particular dietary sodium intake level of, say, 15 gm/day. Figure 7-2 shows us how we might use the scatter plot to make that estimate.

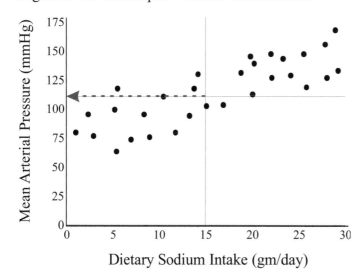

Dietary Sodium Intake (gm/day)

Figure 7-2 Illustration of how a scatter plot can be used to estimate the value of the dependent variable that is associated (on the average) with a particular value of the independent variable. First, a vertical line is drawn to represent the value of the independent variable. Then, a horizontal line is drawn to represent where the vertical line crosses the data points. That horizontal line corresponds to the dependent variable value. In this case, the mean arterial blood pressure associated with a dietary sodium intake of 15 gm/day is estimated to be approximately 110 mmHg.

Linear regression equation

Estimating values of the dependent variable that correspond to a particular value of the independent variable can be more precise if we use a mathematic approach instead of a graphic approach. To use the mathematic approach, we need to select a mathematical equation that represents the relationship between the dependent and independent variables. Most often, the mathematic equation we use is for a straight line. Thus, it is called a **linear regression** equation. Equation {7.1} shows the equation for a straight line relationship between a continuous dependent variable and a continuous independent variable in the population.[2]

$$\mu_{Y|X} = \alpha + \beta X_i \qquad \{7.1\}$$

where

$\mu_{Y|X}$ = mean of the dependent variable corresponding to a particular value of the independent variable (X_i)

α = value of the dependent variable in the population (on the average) when the independent variable is equal to zero. It is called the **intercept** of the straight line equation.

---

[2]In statistics, we use symbols in the equation for a straight line differently from the equation we learned in algebra. In algebra, the equation for a straight line was: $y = m x + b$. In the statistical equation, α is used in place of b and β is used in place of m.

β = amount that the dependent variable value in the population changes (on the average) when the independent variable value is increased by one unit. It is called the **slope** of the straight line equation.

X_i = a particular value of the independent variable

The statistical equation for a straight line probably looks different from what you might have expected. For one thing, Greek letters are used for the slope (β) and intercept (α). The reason for this is that Equation {7.1} represents the straight line relationship in the population and, following the usual convention, we use Greek letters to represent the population's parameters. Even more surprising might be the use of $\mu_{Y|X}$ to represent the dependent variable. As we know from Chapter 2, the Greek letter μ is used to represent the mean of the dependent variable values in the population. It represents the same thing here, except instead of a single mean, the dependent variable has different values for its mean corresponding to different values of the independent variable. The implication is that, in the population, there is a distribution of dependent variable values for each specific value of the independent variable and that $\mu_{Y|X}$ is the mean of each of those distributions. Figure 7-3 illustrates the population's regression line and the distributions of dependent variable values corresponding to each value of the independent variable.

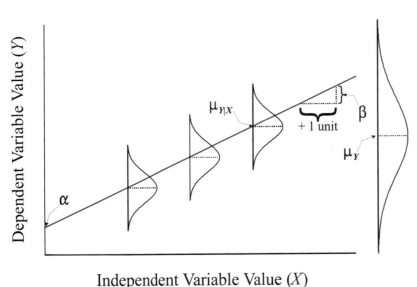

Figure 7-3 The regression line in the population indicating the slope (β), the intercept (α), and the mean of dependent variable values corresponding to a specific value of the independent variable ($\mu_{Y|X}$). The small Gaussian distributions on the regression line correspond to the distribution of dependent variable values that occur in persons with a particular independent variable value. The large Gaussian distribution to the right of the regression line corresponds to the distribution of dependent variable values for all values of the independent variable.

Figure 7-3 also illustrates the way in which the slope (β) and the intercept (α) mathematically describe the regression line. The slope indicates how quickly and in which direction values of the dependent variable change as the value of the independent variable increases. The numeric magnitude of the slope tells us how many units the dependent variable changes for a one-unit change in the numeric magnitude of the independent variable. A slope with a value that is greater than zero (i.e., a positive value) indicates that the dependent variable values increase as values of the independent variable increase. Thus, a positive slope indicates a direct association. In contrast, a slope with a value less than zero indicates that dependent variable values decrease as the value of the independent variable increases. Thus, a negative slope indicates an inverse association. The intercept reflects the elevation of the regression line, specifically by indicating the mean of the dependent variable values that correspond to an independent variable value of zero.[3]

Equation {7.1} illustrates the regression equation in the population. In practice, we use our sample's observations to estimate those parameters. Equation {7.2} shows the regression equation estimated from the sample's observations.

$$\mu_{Y|X} \triangleq \hat{Y}_i = a + bX_i \qquad \{7.2\}$$

where

$\mu_{Y|X}$ = mean of the dependent variable in the population corresponding to a particular value of the independent variable (X_i)

$\hat{Y}_i$ = estimated value of the dependent variable corresponding to a particular value of the independent variable (X_i)

a = sample's estimate of the intercept of the regression line

b = sample's estimate of the slope of the regression line

X_i = a particular value of the independent variable

With the addition of $\hat{Y}_i$ in Equation{7.2}, we now have three ways to think about dependent variable values in a sample. First, we can think of the dependent variable values that are actually observed in the sample. We use Y_i to symbolize those observed dependent variable values. Second, we can summarize all of the dependent variable values in the sample by referring to the mean of those values. We use $\overline{Y}$ to symbolize that mean. To these, we add $\hat{Y}$ which is the estimated value of the dependent variable that we obtain by using a particular independent variable value in the regression equation (Equation{7.2}). Figure 7-4 illustrates these three dependent variable values on a scatter plot.

---

[3]Thus, we could symbolize the intercept as $\mu_{Y|X=0}$ instead of α.

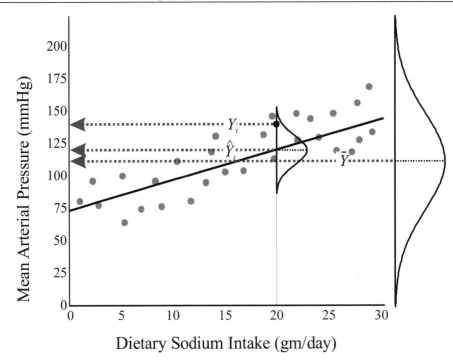

Figure 7-4 Scatter plot showing the relationship among an observed value of the dependent variable (Y_i = 138 mmHg), an estimated value $\hat{Y}_i$, and the mean $\bar{Y}$ of the dependent variable. The small Gaussian distribution corresponds to the distribution of dependent variable values that occur in persons with a dietary sodium intake of 20 gm/day. The large Gaussian distribution corresponds to the distribution of dependent variable values for all values of the independent variable.

Estimation of the slope and intercept

If we were to draw a straight line on a scatter plot to represent the relationship between the dependent and independent variables, we would draw that line to accomplish two things. First, we would want to draw a line in a way that the differences between observed and estimated values of the dependent variable balance (i.e., so that positive differences were equal to the negative differences). Second, we would draw the line in a way that would minimize the differences between the observed and estimated values of the dependent variable.

The mathematic procedure we use to estimate the slope and the intercept is based on those same two criteria. Mathematically, the way we represent these criteria is by using a method that minimizes the sum of the squared differences between the observed and estimated values of the dependent variable.[4] The value we want to minimize is illustrated in Equation{7.3}.

---

[4]In the first criterion, we draw a regression line so that positive and negative differences are balanced. If those differences are balanced, then the sum of these differences will be equal to zero. Thus, in the mathematical approach we need to square each of the differences so that they do not add up to zero.

$$\sum (Y_i - \hat{Y}_i)^2 \qquad \{7.3\}$$

where

Y_i = a particular observed value of the dependent variable

$\hat{Y}_i$ = estimated value of the dependent variable corresponding to a particular value of the independent variable (X_i)

Estimates of the slope and intercept that are calculated in a way that minimizes the sum of the squared differences in Equation {7.3} are called **least squares** estimates.[5] The least squares method that we use to estimate the slope of the regression equation is illustrated in Equation{7.4}.

$$\beta \triangleq b = \frac{\dfrac{\sum (Y_i - \bar{Y})(X_i - \bar{X})}{n-1}}{s_X^2} \qquad \{7.4\}$$

where

β = slope of the regression line in the population

b = sample's estimate of the population's slope

Y_i = a particular observed value of the dependent variable

$\bar{Y}$ = sample's mean of the dependent variable

X_i = a particular observed value of the independent variable

$\bar{X}$ = sample's mean of the independent variable

n = number of observations in the sample

s_X^2 = sample's estimate of the variance of independent variable values

In the numerator of Equation {7.4} is the **sum of cross-products** ($\sum (Y_i - \bar{Y}) \cdot (X_i - \bar{X})$) divided by the degrees of freedom (n-1). This value is the sample's estimate of the

---

[5]The method of least squares is one of two logical approaches we use to calculate estimates in statistics. The method of least squares is the more commonly used approach. The other approach, called the method of maximum likelihood, is used most often in multivariable analysis of a nominal dependent variable. We will discuss that approach in Chapter 12.

covariance. The covariance tells us the degree to which the dependent and independent variables vary relative to each other.[6]

To estimate the intercept of the regression line, we use the estimate of the slope obtained in Equation {7.4} and the fact that every least squares regression line will pass through the point corresponding to the means of the dependent and independent variables. At that point, the regression equation can be written as:

$$\bar{Y} = a + b\bar{X} \qquad\qquad \{7.5\}$$

where

$\bar{Y}$ = mean of the dependent variable values in the sample

a = sample's estimate of intercept of the regression line

b = sample's estimate of the slope of the regression line (from Equation {7.4})

$\bar{X}$ = mean of the independent variable values in the sample

The only term in Equation {7.5} that has not yet been estimated from the sample's observations is the intercept of the regression equation. Thus, we can estimate the intercept by algebraically rearranging Equation{7.5}. The calculation is illustrated in Equation {7.6}.

$$\alpha \stackrel{\wedge}{=} a = \bar{Y} - b\bar{X} \qquad\qquad \{7.6\}$$

where

α = intercept of the regression line in the population

Now, let us take a look at an example showing how we can estimate the slope and intercept of a regression equation from a sample's observations.

---

[6]Variance tells us how values of a variable vary among themselves by adding up the squared differences between each of the data values and the mean. Covariance tells us how values of the dependent variable vary with values of the independent variable. We can think of covariance as being like a combination of the variances of the dependent and independent variables in that covariance adds up the difference of each dependent variable value from its mean multiplied by the corresponding difference of the independent variable value from its mean.

Example 7-1 The data in the following table are the data that were used to draw the scatter plots in Figures 7-1, 7-2, and 7-4:

Patient	Dietary Sodium (X_i) gm/day	Arterial Pressure (Y_i) mmHg
TH	1.0	78
ER	2.3	93
EI	2.9	75
SN	5.2	97
OT	5.4	62
HI	5.5	115
NG	7.0	72
ON	8.4	93
EA	9.0	74
RT	10.5	108
HL	11.8	78
IK	13.3	92
EA	13.8	115
NI	14.2	127
CE	15.1	100
RE	16.9	101
GR	18.8	128
ES	19.8	142
SI	20.0	110
ON	20.2	136
TO	22.0	144
CH	22.1	124
EE	23.3	140
RS	24.1	126
TA	25.5	144
TI	25.8	116
ST	27.8	152
IC	28.0	124
IA	28.9	164
NS	29.2	130

Let us use these data to estimate the parameters of a straight line that can be used, in turn, to estimate mean arterial pressure corresponding to particular levels of dietary sodium intake.

To prepare, we make the calculations appearing in the following table:

Patient	X_i	Y_i	$X_i - \overline{X}$	$(X_i - \overline{X})^2$	$Y_i - \overline{Y}$	$\sum (Y_i - \overline{Y}) \cdot (X_i - \overline{X})$
TH	1.0	78	-14.93	222.81	-34	507.50
ER	2.3	93	-13.63	185.69	-19	258.91
EI	2.9	75	-13.03	169.69	-37	481.99
SN	5.2	97	-10.73	115.06	-15	160.90
OT	5.4	62	-10.53	110.81	-50	526.33
HI	5.5	115	-10.43	108.72	3	-31.28
NG	7.0	72	-8.93	79.69	-40	357.07
ON	8.4	93	-7.53	56.65	-19	143.01
EA	9.0	74	-6.93	47.98	-38	263.21
RT	10.5	108	-5.43	29.45	-4	21.71
HL	11.8	78	-4.13	17.03	-34	140.31
IK	13.3	92	-2.63	6.90	-20	52.53
EA	13.8	115	-2.13	4.52	3	-6.38
NI	14.2	127	-1.73	2.98	15	-25.90
CE	15.1	100	-0.83	0.68	-12	9.92
RE	16.9	101	0.97	0.95	-11	-10.71
GR	18.8	128	2.87	8.26	16	45.97
ES	19.8	142	3.87	15.00	30	116.20
SI	20.0	110	4.07	16.59	-2	-8.15
ON	20.2	136	4.27	18.26	24	102.56
TO	22.0	144	6.07	36.89	32	194.35
CH	22.1	124	6.17	38.11	12	74.08
EE	23.3	140	7.37	54.37	28	206.45
RS	24.1	126	8.17	66.80	14	114.43
TA	25.5	144	9.57	91.65	32	306.35
TI	25.8	116	9.87	97.48	4	39.49
ST	27.8	152	11.87	140.98	40	474.93
IC	28.0	124	12.07	145.77	12	144.88
IA	28.9	164	12.97	168.31	52	674.61
NS	29.2	130	13.27	176.18	18	238.92
Total	477.8	3,360	0.00	2,234.24	0	5,574.19

Now we are ready to calculate estimates of the slope and intercept of the regression equation describing the relationship between dietary sodium intake and mean arterial pressure. First, we estimate the slope using Equation {7.4} and the values from the previous table.

$$\beta \triangleq b = \frac{\frac{\sum (Y_i - \bar{Y})(X_i - \bar{X})}{n-1}}{s_X^2} = \frac{\frac{\sum (Y_i - \bar{Y})(X_i - \bar{X})}{n-1}}{\frac{\sum (X_i - \bar{X})^2}{n-1}} = \frac{\frac{5,574.19}{30-1}}{\frac{2,234.24}{30-1}} = 2.49 \text{ mmHg/gm/day}$$

Next, we use Equation {7.6} to estimate the intercept of the regression equation:

$$\alpha \triangleq a = \bar{Y} - b\bar{X} = \frac{\sum Y_i}{n} - (b \cdot \frac{\sum X_i}{n}) = \frac{3,360}{30} - (2.49 \cdot \frac{447.8}{30}) = 112 - (2.49 \cdot 15.9) = 72.3 \text{ mmHg}$$

Thus, the regression equation is:

$$\hat{Y} = a + bX = 72.3 + (2.49 \cdot X)$$

This regression equation can be used to estimate dependent variable values associated with particular values of the independent variable. For instance, suppose that we want to estimate the mean arterial blood pressure associated with a dietary sodium intake of 15 gm/day. Using that value of the independent variable in the regression equation allows us to make the following estimate.

$$\hat{Y} = a + bX = 72.3 + (2.49 \bullet 15) = 109.7 \text{ mmHg}$$

So, on the average we expect persons with a dietary sodium intake of 15 gm/day to have a mean arterial blood pressure equal to 109.7 mmHg. This is consistent with the corresponding values from the graphic approach to estimation of dependent variable values (Figure 7-2).

Taking chance into account for the slope and intercept

Now that we know how to calculate and interpret estimates of the slope and the intercept, we are almost ready to see how we can take chance into account for those estimates. There is one thing, however, that we need to think about first. That is the way in which we can think about variation of continuous dependent variable values now that we have an independent variable.

There are two ways in which we can think of the variation of dependent variable values. One way is without regard to the value of the independent variable (i.e., without taking that independent variable's value into account). This is the **univariable variance** of the dependent variable and it is the same as the variance we first encountered in Chapter 2 (Equation 2.3). In bivariable analysis, this univariable variance is symbolized as s_Y^2 to distinguish the variance of the dependent variable from the variance of the independent variable (s_X^2). The population's value of this univariable variance of the dependent variable is illustrated in Equation{7.7}.

$$\sigma_Y^2 = \frac{\sum (Y_i - \mu_Y)^2}{N} \tag{7.7}$$

where

σ_Y^2 =   variance of the distribution of dependent variable values in the population (same as σ^2 in Equation {2.3})

Y_i =   a value of the dependent variable

μ_Y =   mean of the distribution of dependent variable values in the population (same as μ in Equation {2.3})

N =   number of data values in the population

The other way to think about variation in dependent variable values is to consider only those dependent variable values that correspond to a particular value of the independent variable. $\sigma_{Y|X}^2$ is the way in which we symbolize that variance. Equation {7.8} illustrates that variance in mathematical language.

$$\sigma_{Y|X}^2 = \frac{\sum (Y_i - \mu_{Y|X})^2}{N} \tag{7.8}$$

where

$\sigma_{Y|X}^2$ =   variance of the distribution of dependent variable values in the population that corresponds to a particular value of the independent variable (X)

$\mu_{Y|X}$ =   mean of the distribution of dependent variable values in the population that corresponds to a particular value of the independent variable (X)

This is the **bivariable variance** of the dependent variable. When we want to take chance into account for estimates we have made in a bivariable analysis, it is the bivariable variance that we use to represent variation in dependent variable values. Figure 7-5 indicates the distributions of dependent variable values that are addressed by these two measures of variation.

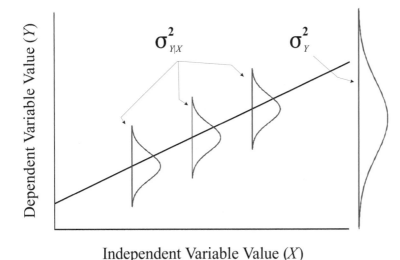

Figure 7-5 The Gaussian distributions on the regression line correspond to values of the dependent variable that occur in persons with a particular value of the independent variable. The variance of these distributions is called the variance of Y "given X," and is symbolized as $\sigma^2_{Y|X}$.

The large Gaussian distribution to the right of the regression line corresponds to the distribution of dependent variable values for all values of the independent variable. Its variance is symbolized as σ^2_Y.

Equations {7.7} and {7.8} as well as Figure 7-5 illustrate the population's values of the univariable and bivariable variance of dependent variable values. In practice, these are unknown and must be estimated from the sample's observations. We saw how this is done for the univariable variance in Chapter 3 (Equation {3.4}). In regression, however, we use some new terms to refer to variance estimates and the values from which they are calculated.

Understanding bivariable (and multivariable) analysis of a continuous dependent variable is easier if we take some time to learn these new terms. First, there is a new term for the variance estimate itself. It is called a **mean square**. To refer to the univariable variance estimate in particular, we use the term **"total" mean square**." The total mean square is calculated by dividing the **total sum of squares** by the **total degrees of freedom**. Equation {7.9} shows how these new terms relate to the sample's estimate of the univariable variance of dependent variable values (i.e., the total mean square).

$$\sigma^2_Y \triangleq s^2_Y = \frac{\sum(Y_i - \bar{Y})^2}{n-1} = \frac{\text{Total Sum of Squares}}{\text{Total Degrees of Freedom}} = \text{Total Mean Square} \qquad \{7.9\}$$

where

s^2_Y = sample's estimate of the variance of the distribution of dependent variable values

Y_i = a value of the dependent variable observed in the sample

$$\bar{Y} \quad = \quad \text{sample's estimate of the mean of the dependent variables values in the population}$$

$$n \quad = \quad \text{number of observations in the sample}$$

The sample's estimate of the bivariable variance of dependent variable values is called the **"error" mean square**.[7] Equation {7.10} shows how the estimate of the bivariable variance of dependent variable values (i.e., the error mean square) is calculated.

$$\sigma_{Y|X}^2 \triangleq s_{Y|X}^2 = \frac{\sum(Y_i - \hat{Y}_i)^2}{n-2} = \frac{\text{Error Sum of Squares}}{\text{Error Degrees of Freedom}} = \text{Error Mean Square} \qquad \{7.10\}$$

where

$$s_{Y|X}^2 \quad = \quad \text{sample's estimate of the variance of the distribution of dependent variable values that corresponds to a particular value of the independent variable}$$

$$\hat{Y}_i \quad = \quad \text{estimated value of the mean of dependent variable values that corresponds to a particular value of the independent variable}$$

Notice that the error degrees of freedom in Equation {7.10} are equal to n-2 instead of n-1, as used in estimating the univariable variance. The reason for this difference is that at least 2 observations are required to estimate the univariable variance, but at least 3 observations are required to estimate the bivariable variance. This is because the error mean square reflects how observed values of the dependent variable differ from values estimated from the regression equation. If the sample contained only two observations, the regression line would go through both points corresponding to the two observations and, thus, the two points would show no variation from the regression line.

Let us take another look at the error sum of squares in the numerator of Equation {7.10}. This is the same as the value in Equation {7.3}. It is this value that is minimized in the process of least squares estimation. Thus, the method of least squares as used in estimating the parameters of the regression equation has the effect of minimizing the bivariable variance of dependent variable values.

Now, we are ready to take into account the role of chance in estimating the slope and the intercept. First, we must think about the sampling distributions for estimates of the slope and the intercept. As with the sampling distribution for estimates of the mean, the sampling distributions for the slope and the intercept tell us about probabilities associated with various estimates of those parameters. Fortunately, as with the sampling distribution of estimates of

---

[7]The error mean square is often called the "residual mean square" in textbooks. We will use "error mean square" to be consistent with the terminology used in SAS and many other statistical analysis programs.

the mean, the sampling distributions for the slope and intercept are also influenced by the central limit theorem.[8] This implies that we can use the same sort of approach to take chance into account for the slope and intercept as we used for the mean. Namely, we can test a null hypothesis or calculate a confidence interval for either the slope or the intercept by using Student's t distribution in the same way we used it for the mean in Chapter 4 (Equation 4.3). The following equations illustrate how we can test the null hypothesis that the population's slope (Equation{7.11}) or that the population's intercept (Equation {7.12}) is equal to a specific value.

$$t = \frac{b - \beta_0}{s_b} \qquad \{7.11\}$$

where

t = Student's t-value that corresponds to the sample's estimate of the slope

b = sample's estimate of the slope

β_0 = slope of the regression line in the population according to the null hypothesis

s_b = standard error for estimates of the slope

$$t = \frac{a - \alpha_0}{s_a} \qquad \{7.12\}$$

where

t = Student's t-value that corresponds to the sample's estimate of the intercept

a = sample's estimate of the intercept

α_0 = intercept of the regression line in the population according to the null hypothesis

s_a = standard error for estimates of the intercept

To calculate a confidence interval for the slope or intercept, we use the same sort of calculations we used to calculate a confidence interval for the mean in Chapter 4 (Equation 4.4). The following equations show how that calculation applies to the estimate of the slope (Equation{7.13}) and to the estimate of the intercept (Equation{7.14}).

---

[8]Recall that the central limit theorem states that a sampling distribution tends to be a Gaussian distribution with that tendency increasing as the size of the sample increases.

$$\beta \overset{\wedge}{=} b \pm (t_{\alpha/2} \cdot s_b) \qquad \{7.13\}$$

where

$t_{\alpha/2}$ = Student's t-value with n-2 degrees of freedom that corresponds to α split between the two tails of Student's t distribution

$$\alpha \overset{\wedge}{=} a \pm (t_{\alpha/2} \cdot s_a) \qquad \{7.14\}$$

where

$t_{\alpha/2}$ = Student's t-value with n-2 degrees of freedom that corresponds to α (the chance of making a type I error) split between the two tails of Student's t distribution

In practice, a computer will calculate the standard errors for the intercept and the slope for us, so we are seldom in the position of having to calculate these standard errors by hand. It is helpful to our understanding of precision in regression analysis, however, to take a look at the way we could calculate the standard error if it were not supplied by a computer program. Equation {7.15} shows the standard error for estimates of the slope.[9]

$$\sigma_b \overset{\wedge}{=} s_b = \sqrt{\frac{s_{Y|X}^2}{\sum (X_i - \overline{X})^2}} \qquad \{7.15\}$$

where

s_b = standard error for estimates of the slope

$s_{Y|X}^2$ = sample's estimate of the variance of dependent variable values corresponding to a particular value of the independent variable (i.e., the error mean square)

$\sum (X - \overline{X})^2$ = sum of squares for the independent variable

Notice in Equation {7.15} that the standard error for estimates of the slope is influenced by

---

[9] The standard error for estimates of the intercept contains the error mean square and the sum of squares for the independent variable, as well as other information.

the dispersions of both the dependent and independent variables. The dispersion of dependent variable values is represented by the error mean square. As the dispersion of dependent variable values increases, the error mean square increases and, consequently the standard error for estimates of the slope increases, indicating a decrease in the precision with which we estimate the population's slope from the sample's observations. This relationship makes sense: as the variability of the data increases, the precision with which we estimate the slope decreases.[10]

Now, take a look at how dispersion of independent variable values influences the standard error of the slope. That dispersion is represented by the sum of squares of the independent variable values in the sample. The surprising part is that the sum of squares of the independent variable is in the <u>denominator</u> of the standard error. That implies that the precision with which we estimate the slope increases as the dispersion of independent variable values in the sample increases. This is the opposite of the effect of the dispersion of dependent variable values.

Although we might find this relationship surprising, it makes sense as we consider it more carefully. This increase in precision of the estimate of the slope that occurs with an increase in the dispersion of independent variable values is reflecting the same logic we would use when selecting two points through which we draw a straight line. In that case, we know that our ability to precisely draw a line increases as the two points we use to draw it become further apart. This influence of the dispersion of independent variable values on the standard error of the slope is a mathematical representation of that same logical process.

In the next example, we will calculate the standard error for the estimate of the slope and see how we can use that standard error to calculate a confidence interval.

Example 7-2 Let us use the data in Example 7-1 to calculate a 95%, two-sided confidence interval for the slope of the regression equation describing the relationship between dietary sodium intake and mean arterial blood pressure

---

The point estimate of the slope, calculated in Example 7-1, is 2.5 mmHg/gm /day. Before we can calculate a confidence interval for the slope, we need to calculate its standard error. To do that, we need to know the sum of squares for the independent variable. In Example 7-1, the sum of squares for dietary sodium intake (the independent variable) was found to be equal to 2,234.24 gm/day^2.

Also needed to calculate the standard error of the slope is the error mean square (i.e., the sample's estimate of the variance of dependent variable values corresponding to a particular value of the independent variable). Equation {7.10} shows us that the error mean square is equal to the error sum of squares divided by the error degrees of freedom. The error degrees of freedom are equal to n-2, or in this case, 30-2=28. The error sum of squares is calculated by estimating the dependent variable value corresponding to each observed value of the independent variable ($\hat{Y}_i$), subtracting that estimated value from the observed

---

[10] Precision of an estimate is equal to the inverse of the variance of the estimate (i.e., the inverse of the square of the standard error)

value of the dependent variable (Y_i), and adding up the squares of those differences. These calculations are summarized in the following table:

Patient	X_i	Y_i	$\hat{Y}_i$	$(Y_i - \hat{Y}_i)$	$(Y_i - \hat{Y}_i)^2$
TH	1.0	78	74.8	3.2	10.5
ER	2.3	93	78.0	15.0	224.9
EI	2.9	75	79.5	-4.5	20.2
SN	5.2	97	85.2	11.8	138.3
OT	5.4	62	85.7	-23.7	563.4
HI	5.5	115	86.0	29.0	841.8
NG	7.0	72	89.7	-17.7	314.3
ON	8.4	93	93.2	-0.2	0.0
EA	9.0	74	94.7	-20.7	429.3
RT	10.5	108	98.5	9.5	90.9
HL	11.8	78	101.7	-23.7	561.9
IK	13.3	92	105.4	-13.4	180.8
EA	13.8	115	106.7	8.3	69.0
NI	14.2	127	107.7	19.3	372.8
CE	15.1	100	109.9	-9.9	98.8
RE	16.9	101	114.4	-13.4	180.3
GR	18.8	128	119.2	8.8	78.0
ES	20.0	110	122.2	-12.2	147.9
SI	19.8	142	121.7	20.3	413.6
ON	20.2	136	122.7	13.3	177.9
TO	22.0	144	127.2	16.8	283.8
CH	22.1	124	127.4	-3.4	11.6
EE	23.3	140	130.4	9.6	92.2
RS	24.1	126	132.4	-6.4	40.9
TA	25.5	144	135.9	8.1	65.9
TI	25.8	116	136.6	-20.6	425.7
ST	27.8	152	141.6	10.4	107.7
IC	28.0	124	142.1	-18.1	328.4
IA	28.9	164	144.4	19.6	385.4
NS	29.2	130	145.1	-15.1	228.5
Total	477.8	3,360			6,884.9

Using the error sum of squares from that table (6,884.9 mmHg^2), we calculate the error mean square by using Equation {7.10}:

$$s_{Y|X}^2 = \frac{\sum (Y_i - \hat{Y}_i)^2}{n-2} = \frac{6,884.9}{30-2} = 245.9 \text{ mmHg}^2$$

Next we use Equation {7.15} to calculate the standard error for the estimate of the slope:

$$s_b = \sqrt{\frac{s_{Y|X}^2}{\sum(X_i - \bar{X})^2}} = \sqrt{\frac{245.9}{2,234.24}} = 0.33 \text{ mmHg/gm/day}$$

Now, we are ready to calculate the 95%, two-sided interval estimate for the slope. To perform this calculation, we use Equation{7.13}.

$$\beta = b \pm (t_{\alpha/2} \cdot s_b) = 2.49 \pm (2.048 \cdot 0.33) = 1.82 \text{ to } 3.17 \text{ mmHg/gm/day}$$

Thus, we are 95% confident that the population's slope is between 1.82 and 3.17 mmHg/gm/day

---

The *F*-ratio

So far, we have taken chance into account by considering sampling distributions for the slope and intercept and using Student's *t* distribution to test a hypothesis or to calculate a confidence interval. These procedures are the same as other procedures we have used to take chance into account for a continuous dependent variable in that they involve examination of the sample's estimate of a particular parameter in the population. There is another approach to examining the relationship between a continuous dependent variable and a continuous independent variable, however. This approach is to examine the amount of variation in dependent variable values that is explained by the association with the independent variable.

Earlier, we distinguished between the univariable variation of dependent variable values (called the "total" variation) and the bivariable variation of dependent variable value (called the "error" variation). Actually, there is another way to think about the bivariable variation of a continuous dependent variable. The "error" variation is the variation in dependent variable values that is "leftover" after we have used the regression equation to estimate the dependent variable values that correspond to particular values of the independent variable. The other way in which we can think about the bivariable variation of dependent variable values is to consider the variation that is "explained" by using the regression equation to estimate dependent variable values. The "explained" variation is called the **model** variation. The actual amount of explained variation is called the **model sum of squares** and the average explained variation is called the **model mean square**. As with the total and error mean squares, the model mean square is calculated by dividing the model sum of squares by the model degrees of freedom, as shown in Equation{7.16}.

$$\text{Model Mean Square} = \frac{\text{Model Sum of Squares}}{\text{Model Degrees of Freedom}} = \frac{\sum(\hat{Y}_i - \bar{Y})^2}{1} \quad \{7.16\}$$

Let us take a moment to examine Equation{7.16}. Perhaps the first thing you notice is that the model degrees of freedom is equal to one. Actually, the model degrees of freedom is equal to the number of independent variables that are used to estimate values of the dependent variable. In bivariable regression analysis, we have one independent variable. Thus, the model degrees of freedom are equal to one in bivariable analyses.[11]

Another interesting aspect of Equation {7.16} is that the model sum of squares, unlike the total and error sums of squares, does not consider the observed values of the dependent variable (Y_i). Instead, it includes the estimated values of the dependent variable ($\hat{Y}_i$) and the mean of the dependent variable ($\bar{Y}$). The mean of the dependent variable values can be considered the estimate of the dependent variable we would use if we did not know about the relationship between the dependent and independent variables. The estimated values of the dependent variable, on the other hand, are the values we use to estimate the dependent variable values when we take into account this relationship with the independent variable. Thus, the model sum of squares compares bivariable estimates ($\hat{Y}_i$) to the univariable estimate ($\bar{Y}$) for the dependent variable.[12] The bigger this difference, the more variability of the dependent variable is explained by the relationship with the independent variable.

To interpret the numeric magnitude of the model mean square as a reflection of how well the independent variable explains the variation of the dependent variable, we need to consider what we would expect to see if there were no relationship between those variables in the population. Since chance influences the selection of dependent variable values, we would expect to observe some apparent explained variation in the sample, even when the independent variable does not explain any variation of the dependent variable in the population. How much apparent explained variation we observe in a sample depends on how much variation there is among dependent variable values in the population. The more variation in dependent variable values, the greater the apparent explained variation we can expect to see in a sample due to chance alone. Thus, we would expect to see, on the average, the model mean square (the average explained variation) equal to the error mean square (the average unexplained variation) in samples from a population within which there is no association between those variables.

So, a way in which we can examine the relationship between a continuous dependent variable and a continuous independent variable is to compare the model mean square to the error mean square. The way in which we compare mean squares is by examining their ratio.[13] The result is called an **F-ratio**. Equation {7.17} illustrates calculation of the F-ratio in regression analysis.

---

[11]The model degrees of freedom will no longer be equal to one in multivariable regression analysis, since in multivariable regression analysis, by definition, we have more than one independent variable to estimate dependent variable values.

[12]Another way to calculate the model sum of squares is to subtract the error sum of squares from the total sum of squares. This also works with degrees of freedom. Namely, the error degrees of freedom added to the model degrees of freedom equals the total degrees of freedom. It does not work, however, to add the error mean square to the model mean square and get the total mean square.

[13]When comparing the model mean square to the error mean square, we always put the model mean square in the numerator of the ratio and the error mean square in the denominator of the ratio.

$$F = \frac{\text{Model Mean Square}}{\text{Error Mean Square}} \qquad \{7.17\}$$

If the independent variable does not help to estimate dependent variable values, we expect that the F-ratio will be equal to one (on the average) in the sample. If the independent variable does help to estimate dependent variable values, the F-ratio will be greater than one, indicating that more variation in the dependent variable is explained by the independent variable than can be attributed to chance.

The way in which we interpret the numeric magnitude of the F-ratio is by testing the **omnibus null hypothesis**. The omnibus null hypothesis states that the independent variable does not help estimate dependent variable values. When the omnibus null hypothesis is true, the F-ratio will be equal to one (on the average). When the omnibus null hypothesis is not true, the F-ratio will be greater than one.[14] The larger the F-ratio, the less likely it is that the omnibus null hypothesis is true.

To test the omnibus null hypothesis, we can compare the F-ratio calculated from the sample's observations to the value in a table of the F distribution. In this text, the F distribution is described in Table B.4.

The F distribution is a member of the Gaussian family of distributions. It comes from Student's t distribution with two features that distinguish it from Student's t. First, there are no negative values in the F distribution. This is an important feature of the F distribution because it is impossible for an F-ratio to be negative.[15] To get rid of negative numbers as we go from Student's t distribution to the F distribution we use the same old trick statisticians use so often to get rid of negative values: we square t-values to get F-values.

In addition, a second parameter is added to the t distribution to make it the F distribution. This parameter is called "degrees of freedom," but it is not the same as the parameter called "degrees of freedom" that was added to the standard normal distribution to create Student's t distribution. The degrees of freedom that is a parameter of Student's t distribution takes into account the role of chance in estimating the variance of dependent variable values. This same number of degrees of freedom is also associated with the error mean square in the F distribution. Since the error mean square is always in the denominator of the F-ratio, this is called the **denominator degrees of freedom**.

The degrees of freedom added as a parameter to create the F distribution is the degrees of freedom associated with the model mean square. Recall from our introduction to the model mean square that the model degrees of freedom tell us how many independent variables are used to estimate dependent variable values. In bivariable regression analysis, we have only one independent variable, so the model degrees of freedom is equal to one.

---

[14]When we are using the F-ratio to test the omnibus null hypothesis, we use an F-*value* that corresponds to all of α in the upper tail. That is because the alternative hypothesis for the F-ratio is one-sided; if F is not equal to one, it must be greater than one, at least on the average (an F-ratio in a particular sample can be less than one, but this is considered to be a reflection of the null hypothesis).

[15]For the F-ratio to be negative, one of the mean squares would need to be negative. Remember that a mean square is another name for a variance estimate. Variances are always positive.

Since the model mean square is always in the numerator of the F-ratio, this number of degrees of freedom is called the **numerator degrees of freedom**. The next example illustrates how we can use the F-ratio to examine the relationship between a continuous dependent variable and a continuous independent variable.

Example 7-3 Let us use the F-ratio to examine the relationship between dietary sodium intake and mean arterial blood pressure as reflected by the data in Example 7-1. Let us do that by testing the omnibus null hypothesis that knowing dietary sodium intake does not help to estimate mean arterial blood pressure.

To calculate the F-ratio, we need to know the values of the error mean square and of the model mean square. In Example 7-2, the error mean square was found to be equal to 245.9 $mmHg^2$. To calculate the model mean square, we need to compare the estimated values of the dependent variable ($\hat{Y}_i$ from Example 7-2) to the mean of the dependent variable ($\bar{Y}$). The following table summarizes those comparisons:

Patient	X_i	Y_i	$\hat{Y}_i$	$(\hat{Y}_i - \bar{Y})$	$(\hat{Y}_i - \bar{Y})^2$
TH	1.0	78	74.8	-37.2	1,386.9
ER	2.3	93	78.0	-34.0	1,155.8
EI	2.9	75	79.5	-32.5	1,056.3
SN	5.2	97	85.2	-26.8	716.2
OT	5.4	62	85.7	-26.3	689.7
HI	5.5	115	86.0	-26.0	676.7
NG	7.0	72	89.7	-22.3	496.0
ON	8.4	93	93.2	-18.8	352.6
EA	9.0	74	94.7	-17.3	298.6
RT	10.5	108	98.5	-13.5	183.3
HL	11.8	78	101.7	-10.3	106.0
IK	13.3	92	105.4	-6.6	42.9
EA	13.8	115	106.7	-5.3	28.2
NI	14.2	127	107.7	-4.3	18.6
CE	15.1	100	109.9	-2.1	4.3
RE	16.9	101	114.4	2.4	5.9
GR	18.8	128	119.2	7.2	51.4
ES	19.8	142	121.7	9.7	93.4
SI	20.0	110	122.2	10.2	103.3
ON	20.2	136	122.7	10.7	113.7
TO	22.0	144	127.2	15.2	229.6
CH	22.1	124	127.4	15.4	237.2

EE	23.3	140	130.4	18.4	338.4
RS	24.1	126	132.4	20.4	415.8
TA	25.5	144	135.9	23.9	570.5
TI	25.8	116	136.6	24.6	606.8
ST	27.8	152	141.6	29.6	877.5
IC	28.0	124	142.1	30.1	907.3
IA	28.9	164	144.4	32.4	1,047.6
NS	29.2	130	145.1	33.1	1,096.6
Total	477.8	3,360		0.0	13,907.1

Using the model sum of squares from this table (13,907.1 mmHg^2), we calculate the model mean square by using Equation{7.16}.

$$\text{Model Mean Square} = \frac{\sum(\hat{Y}_i - \bar{Y})^2}{1} = \frac{13,907.07}{1} = 13,907.1 \text{ mmHg/gm/day}^2$$

Next we use Equation {7.17} to calculate the F-ratio:

$$F = \frac{\text{Model Mean Square}}{\text{Error Mean Square}} = \frac{13,907.1}{245.9} = 56.6$$

Thus, the F-ratio that represents the model mean square relative to the error mean square is equal to 56.6. That F-ratio has one degree of freedom in the numerator and 28 (30-2) degrees of freedom in the denominator.

To interpret the F-ratio, we need to compare it to values in the table for the F distribution. The F distribution is in Table B.4, which includes many pages of tables, each page corresponding to the number of degrees of freedom in the numerator of the F-ratio. In this case, the model degrees of freedom are equal to one, so it is the first page of the F distribution that is used in bivariable regression analysis. In this table, we look for the F-value in the body of the table that corresponds to 28 denominator degrees of freedom and an α equal to 0.05.

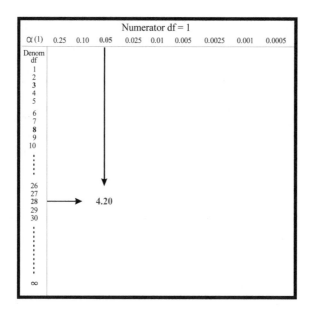

In Table B.4, we find that an F-ratio of 4.20 is associated with one degree of freedom in the numerator, 28 degrees of freedom in the denominator, and an α of 0.05. This is the critical value to which we need to compare our calculated F-ratio (56.6). Since the calculated value is larger than the critical value, we reject the omnibus null hypothesis and, through the process of elimination, accept the alternative hypothesis that states that knowing dietary sodium intake (the independent variable) helps to estimate mean arterial blood pressure (the dependent variable).

So, we find in Example 7-3 that we are able to reject the omnibus null hypothesis that the independent variable does not help to estimate dependent variable values. With that in mind, let us take a moment to imagine what the population's regression line looks like when the omnibus null hypothesis is true. If knowing the value of the independent variable does not help to estimate dependent variable values, the implication is that the same value of the dependent variable would be estimated for all values of the independent variable. For that to be true, the regression line would have to have a slope of zero (i.e., a horizontal line). If that is the case, we must ask ourselves, "How is testing the omnibus null hypothesis different from testing the null hypothesis that the slope is equal to zero?"

In bivariable analysis, testing the omnibus null hypothesis and testing the null hypothesis that the slope is equal to zero are exactly the same thing. One way to prove that this is true is to take the square root of the F-ratio. This square root is exactly equal to Student's t-value used in testing the null hypothesis that the slope is equal to zero (we will see this in SAS output in the next example). In bivariable analysis, the omnibus null hypothesis adds no new information. When we get to multivariable regression analysis in Chapter 10, however, testing the omnibus null hypothesis will provide very useful information about the relationship between the dependent and independent variables.

Examples 7-1 and 7-3 show how regression analysis can be performed by hand. We went through these calculations to help us to understand how regression analysis works. In practice, however, we will be using a computer to do these calculations. To perform a regression analysis in SAS, we can use the REG procedure. The next example shows the results of using the REG procedure to analyze the data presented in Example 7-1.

Example 7-4   Let us use SAS's REG procedure to analyze the data in Example 7-1.

The following is the result of analyzing the data in Example 7-1:

```
                          The REG Procedure
                           Model: MODEL1
                      Dependent Variable: DBP

                        Analysis of Variance

                               Sum of         Mean
   Source              DF      Squares        Square     F Value    Pr > F
   Model                1        13907         13907       56.56    <.0001
   Error               28   6884.93353     245.89048
   Corrected Total     29        20792

              Root MSE              15.68090    R-Square    0.6689
              Dependent Mean       112.00000    Adj R-Sq    0.6570
              Coeff Var             14.00080

                        Parameter Estimates

                        Parameter     Standard
   Variable    DF       Estimate       Error     t Value    Pr > |t|
   Intercept    1       72.26457       6.00940     12.03     <.0001
   NA           1        2.49490       0.33175      7.52     <.0001
```

At the top of this output, under the heading "Analysis of Variance" are the univariable and bivariable sources of variation of a continuous dependent variable. The degrees of freedom (DF), sums of squares, and mean squares are listed and agree with the values obtained in the previous examples. Along with those values are "F value" and "Prob>F." The "F value" is the F-ratio testing the omnibus null hypothesis. The "Prob>F" is the P-value associated with the F-ratio. Since this P-value is provided by the computer, we do not need to use Table B.4 to evaluate the F-ratio. Instead, we can reject the omnibus null hypothesis if "Prob>F" is equal to or less than our chosen value of α (usually 0.05).

In the middle of the SAS output are five values with various labels. These values are not part of regression analysis as we are considering it.[16]

At the bottom of this output, under the heading "Parameter Estimates" are the estimates of the slope and the intercept and the values associated with these estimates. The values

---

[16]Often the biggest help in interpreting computer output is to know which values can be ignored.

corresponding to the intercept are listed in the row labeled "INTERCEP." The values corresponding to the slope are listed in the row that is headed by the name we have given to the independent variable. In this case, the independent variable is dietary sodium intake, which we have named "NA." For both the slope and the intercept, SAS provides us with the point estimate (labeled "Parameter Estimate"), the standard error, Student's t-value testing the null hypothesis that the parameter is equal to zero in the population (labeled "T for H0: Parameter=0"), and the P-value associated with that value of Student's t (labeled "Pr > |t|").[17] We can use the point estimates of the slope and intercept to write the regression equation:

$$\hat{Y} = a + bX = 72.3 + (2.49 \cdot X)$$

This regression equation is the same as one we got in Example 7-1. The standard errors provided by SAS can be used in Equations {7.13} and {7.14} to calculate confidence intervals for the slope and the intercept. For the slope, the 95% confidence interval has the same limits as the interval calculated by hand in Example 7-2:

$$\beta = b \pm (t_{\alpha/2} \cdot s_b) = 2.4949 \pm (2.048 \cdot 0.33175) = 1.82 \text{ to } 3.17$$

$$\alpha = a \pm (t_{\alpha/2} \cdot s_a) = 72.26457 \pm (2.048 \cdot 6.0094) = 59.95 \text{ to } 84.57$$

The P-values test the null hypotheses that the intercept is equal to zero and that the slope is equal to zero in the population. Both of these P-values are less than 0.0001, so both null hypotheses can be rejected.

_____

CORRELATION ANALYSIS

Another aspect of the relationship between a continuous dependent variable and a continuous independent variable is the strength of the association between the variables. What we imply by the "strength" of the association is the consistency with which changes in the value of the dependent variable are associated with changes of a given amount in the value of the independent variable. This strength of the association between two continuous variables can be examined graphically in a scatter plot.

In Figure 7-1, we saw a tendency for mean arterial blood pressure values to increase with increases in dietary sodium intake, but there were exceptions. There are quite a few of these exceptions in Figure 7-1, so the strength of that relationship can be considered to be of

_____

[17]Also provided for each estimate is the number of degrees of freedom (labeled "DF"). This is not the degrees of freedom used by the t-tests. The number of degrees of freedom used by the t-tests is the same as the error degrees of freedom. Instead, the number of degrees of freedom listed here tells us how many independent variables were used to represent the variable. This is almost always equal to one. The situation in which this might change is when more than one nominal independent variable is used to represent a collection of nominal data and when the programmer used a single variable name to represent those nominal independent variables. We will not do that in this text.

a moderate degree. For comparison, Figure 7-6 shows a relationship that is considered to be strong and Figure 7-7 shows a relationship that is considered to be weak. Notice that there are fewer and numerically smaller exceptions for the strong association and more and numerically larger exceptions for weak association.

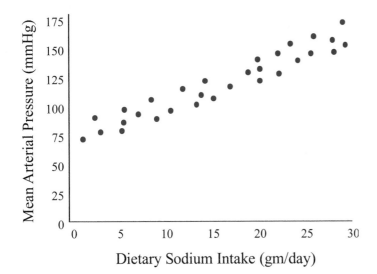

Figure 7-6 Scatter plot showing a strong association between dietary sodium intake and mean arterial blood pressure. There is a strong association when the dependent variable values change in a highly consistent manner as independent variable values increase.

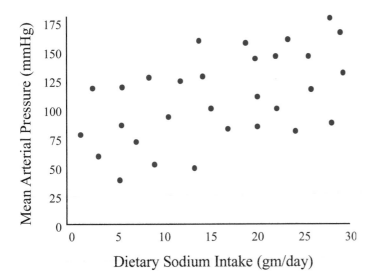

Figure 7-7 Scatter plot showing a weak association between dietary sodium intake and mean arterial blood pressure. There is a weak association when dependent variable values do not change in a consistent manner as independent variable values increase.

Examination of scatter plots is one way in which we might investigate the strength of the association between two continuous variables, but it is not the only way. Another way to look at the strength of the association is numerically, by calculating a number that reflects the strength of the association. One number that does this is the covariance. We encountered the covariance in our discussion of regression analysis, where covariance was used in the numerator of the estimate the slope of the regression line (Equation {7.4}).

As the name implies, covariance tells us how two continuous variables vary together. It is equal to a positive value when there is a direct association between the variables and a negative value when there is an inverse association between those variables.[18] Further, the numeric magnitude of the covariance is an indication of how strong the association is.

To see how this works, take a look at the scatter plot in Figure 7-8 to which a grid has been added to separate the scatter plot into four quadrants, based on the means of the dependent and independent variables. In the upper right quadrant, the values of the dependent and independent variables are larger than their means. Consequently, data values in this quadrant contribute positive values to the numerator of the covariance (when the mean of each variable is subtracted from each observed data value). In the lower left quadrant, both the dependent and independent variable values are less than their respective means. Since both the differences are negative and because these negative differences are multiplied together, they also contribute positive values to the numerator of the covariance. In the remaining two quadrants, one of the data values is greater than its mean and the other is less than its mean. Data in these quadrants contribute negative values to the numerator of covariance.

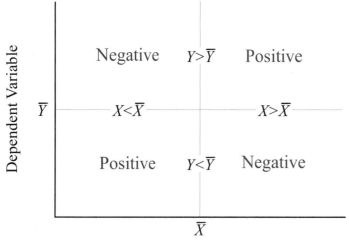

Figure 7-8 **Contributions of data values in the four quadrants of a scatter plot to the numerator of the covariance.**

In a direct association, most of the data values fall in the upper right and lower left quadrants of the scatter plot. These are the quadrants in which data contribute positive values to the numerator of the covariance. Therefore, data in these quadrants will cause the covariance to have a positive numeric value. In an inverse association, most of the data fall in the upper left and lower right quadrants of the scatter plot, giving the covariance a negative value. This is why a direct association is indicated by a positive covariance and an inverse association is indicated by a negative covariance.

Covariance tells us more than just the direction of the association. It also tells us the strength of the association, with larger numeric values corresponding to stronger associations. To examine this, let us take a look at Figures 7-9, 7-10, and 7-11.

---

[18]The concept of direct and inverse associations was introduced earlier in this chapter when we were discussing regression analysis. There, a direct association was identified by a positive slope and an inverse association was identified by a negative slope.

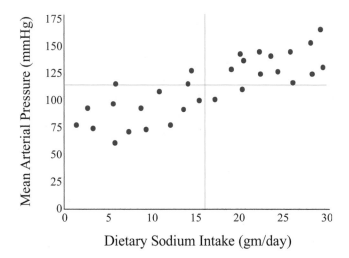

Figure 7-9 Scatter plot from Figure 7-1 showing a moderate association between dietary sodium intake and mean arterial pressure. The means of the dependent and independent variables are used to separate the scatter plot into four quadrants. Data points in the upper right and lower left quadrants contribute positive values to the covariance. Data points in the upper left and lower right quadrants contribute negative values to the covariance. Most of the data points in this example are in the upper right and lower left quadrants, resulting in a covariance with a moderately high positive value.

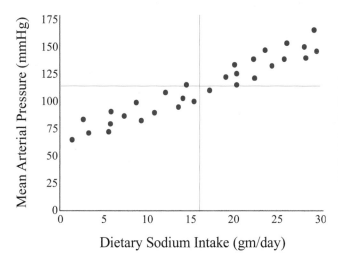

Figure 7-10 Scatter plot from Figure 7-6 showing a strong association between dietary sodium intake and mean arterial pressure. Almost all of the data points in this example are in the upper right and lower left quadrants, resulting in a covariance with a high positive value.

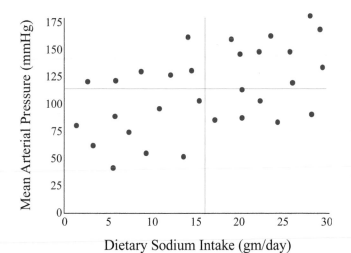

Figure 7-11 Scatter plot from Figure 7-7 showing a weak association between dietary sodium intake and mean arterial pressure. Although most of the data points in this example are in the upper right and lower left quadrants, quite a few are in the upper left and lower right quadrants. Thus, the covariance will have a small positive value.

All three scatter plots in Figures 7-9 through 7-11 show direct associations of different strengths. Notice that the stronger the direct association, the more the data values are confined to the lower left and upper right quadrants. For a weaker direct association, there are also data values in the upper left and lower right quadrants (see Figure 7-11). Since these are the quadrants that contribute negative values to the numerator of the covariance, they decrease the numeric magnitude of the covariance in a direct association.

For inverse associations, just the opposite is true: most of the data values are in the upper left-hand and lower right-hand quadrants. These are the quadrants that contribute negative values to the covariance. For weaker inverse associations, data will also fall in the other two quadrants, which contribute positive values to the covariance.

So, covariance can tell us about both the direction and the strength of the association between a continuous dependant variable and a continuous independent variable. The strength of the association is reflected by the numeric magnitude of the covariance. Unfortunately, the numeric value of the covariance also reflects the scale on which the dependant and independent variables were measured. Consequently, interpretation of the numeric magnitude of the covariance varies for different data and for the same data measured on different scales (e.g., weight measured in pounds as opposed to weight measured in kilograms). This feature substantially reduces the utility of covariance as a measure of the strength of the association between two continuous variables.

What we need is a dimensionless index that reflects only the strength of the association and not the scale of measurement. Fortunately, we can calculate such an index by dividing the covariance by its maximum possible value. That maximum value is equal to the square root of the product of the variances of the two variables. The index of the strength of the association calculated in this way is called the **correlation coefficient**. Equation {7.18} shows how the population's correlation coefficient (ρ) is estimated from the sample's observations.

$$\rho \triangleq r = \frac{\dfrac{\sum (Y_i - \bar{Y})(X_i - \bar{X})}{n-1}}{\sqrt{s_Y^2 \bullet s_X^2}} \qquad \{7.18\}$$

where

ρ = population's correlation coefficient (rho)

r = sample's estimate of the correlation coefficient

s_Y^2 = sample's estimate of the variance of dependant variable values

s_X^2 = sample's estimate of the variance of independent variable values

Since the square root of the product of the variance estimates is the maximum numeric magnitude for the covariance, the correlation coefficient will be equal to +1 when the covariance is at its maximum positive value. The minimum numeric magnitude of the covariance is equal to the negative square root of the product of the variances. Thus, the maximum negative value of the correlation coefficient is -1 when the covariance is at its maximum negative value.

A perfect direct association is represented by a correlation coefficient of +1 and a perfect inverse association is represented by a correlation coefficient of -1. Also, no association between the variables results in a correlation coefficient equal to zero. Interpretation of a correlation coefficient for those three values is fairly straightforward. Unfortunately, interpretation of other numeric values of the correlation coefficient (i.e., between zero and positive one and between zero and negative one) is a little more complicated.

For instance, what does a correlation coefficient of 0.5 tell us about the strength of the association between two continuous variables? Since 0.5 is half way between zero and +1, we might expect that the strength of that association to be half as strong as a perfect direct association. This is not the case, since the correlation coefficient does not have a linear (i.e., straight line) relationship with the strength of association between two continuous variables.[19] Fortunately, we can change the correlation coefficient into a value that does have a linear relationship with the strength of the association between two continuous variables. This is done by squaring the correlation coefficient. This square of the correlation coefficient is called the **coefficient of determination** or, more commonly, **R-squared (R^2)**. Equation {7.19} illustrates the calculation of the coefficient of determination.

$$R^2 = r^2 \qquad \{7.19\}$$

where

R^2 = sample's estimate of the coefficient of determination

r = sample's estimate of the correlation coefficient

R^2 tells us the proportion of variation of the dependent variable that is associated with the independent variable. Although it is part of correlation analysis, R^2 can be calculated from the results of regression analysis.[20] Equation {7.20} shows how this calculation can be performed:

$$R^2 = \frac{\text{Model Sum of Squares}}{\text{Total Sum of Squares}} \qquad \{7.20\}$$

---

[19] Actually 0.5 is one-quarter of the way between no association and a perfect direct association! We will soon see why this is true.

[20] This is one reason why most computer programs for regression analysis include the coefficient of determination in the output. If we look back at Example 7-4, we can see that the coefficient of determination is part of the information in the middle of the output that we ignored when we were concentrating on information relevant to regression analysis. It is the value labeled "R-square."

Equation {7.20} does a pretty good job of illustrating what we mean when we say that R^2 tells us the proportion of variation in the dependent variable that is associated with the independent variable. The total variation in the dependent variable is represented by the total sum of squares. The total sum of squares consists of the model sum of squares (the variation of dependent variable values "explained" by the independent variable in the regression equation) and the error sum of squares (the variation of dependent variable values not "explained" by the independent variable in the regression equation). R^2 tells us what proportion of the total variation is the "explained" variation.

The next example illustrates calculation and interpretation of a correlation coefficient:

Example 7-5   Let us calculate a correlation coefficient to examine the strength of the association between dietary sodium intake and mean arterial blood pressure using the data described in Example 7-1.

To calculate a correlation coefficient, we need an estimate of the covariance and estimates of the univariable variances of the dependent and independent variables. The covariance can be estimated from the sum of cross products calculated in Example 7-1.

$$\frac{\sum(Y_i - \bar{Y})(X_i - \bar{X})}{n-1} = \frac{5,574.2}{30-1} = 192.2 \text{ mmHg}\cdot\text{gm/day}$$

Also from information in Example 7-1, we can estimate the variance of the independent variable:

$$s_X^2 = \frac{\sum(X_i - \bar{X})^2}{n-1} = \frac{2,234.24}{30-1} = 77.04 \text{ gm/day}^2$$

We also need to estimate the univariable variance estimate for the dependent variable. The following table summarizes the calculations we perform in preparation to estimate this variance:

Patient	X_i	Y_i	$\Sigma(Y_i - \bar{Y})$	$\Sigma(Y_i - \bar{Y})^2$
TH	1.0	78	-34	1,156
ER	2.3	93	-19	361
EI	2.9	75	-37	1,369
SN	5.2	97	-15	225
OT	5.4	62	-50	2,500
HI	5.5	115	3	9
NG	7.0	72	-40	1,600
ON	8.4	93	-19	361

EA	9.0	74	-38	1,444
RT	10.5	108	-4	16
HL	11.8	78	-34	1,156
IK	13.3	92	-20	400
EA	13.8	115	3	9
NI	14.2	127	15	225
CE	15.1	100	-12	144
RE	16.9	101	-11	121
GR	18.8	128	16	256
ES	19.8	142	30	900
SI	20.0	110	-2	4
ON	20.2	136	24	576
TO	22.0	144	32	1,024
CH	22.1	124	12	144
EE	23.3	140	28	784
RS	24.1	126	14	196
TA	25.5	144	32	1,024
TI	25.8	116	4	16
ST	27.8	152	40	1,600
IC	28.0	124	12	144
IC	28.0	124	12	144
IA	28.9	164	52	2,704
NS	29.2	130	18	324
Total	477.8	3,360	0	20,792

The sample's estimate of the univariable variance is:

$$\sigma_Y^2 \triangleq s_Y^2 = \frac{\sum (Y_i - \bar{Y})^2}{n-1} = \frac{20,792}{30-1} = 717.0 \text{ mmHg}^2$$

Now, we are ready to use Equation {7.18} to calculate the sample's estimate of the population's correlation coefficient.

$$\rho \triangleq r = \frac{\dfrac{\sum (Y_i - \bar{Y})(X_i - \bar{X})}{n-1}}{\sqrt{s_Y^2 \cdot s_X^2}} = \frac{\dfrac{5,574.2}{30-1}}{\sqrt{717.0 \cdot 77.04}} = 0.818$$

Thus, the sample's estimate of the correlation coefficient is equal to 0.818. To interpret that correlation coefficient, we use Equation {7.19} to calculate the coefficient of determination (i.e., R^2).

$$R^2 = r^2 = 0.818^2 = 0.669$$

That coefficient of determination tells us that 0.669 (or 66.9%) of the variation in mean arterial pressure is associated with variation in dietary sodium intake.

_____

Taking chance into account

Under certain conditions, we can take chance into account for the sample's estimate of the population's correlation coefficient using the same kind of Gaussian approach we have used for means, slopes, and intercepts. This can be done when the population's correlation coefficient is equal to zero.[21]

At first, this might seem to be an unrealistic restriction, but the most commonly used null hypothesis for the correlation coefficient is that the population's value is equal to zero. Since we always assume that the null hypothesis is true when taking chance into account using hypothesis testing, we can use the Gaussian approach to test the null hypothesis.

When we assume that the population's correlation coefficient is equal to zero, the sampling distribution has a mean equal to zero and a standard error equal to the following:

$$\sigma_r \triangleq s_r = \sqrt{\frac{1-r^2}{n-2}} \qquad \{7.21\}$$

where

$\quad s_r \quad = \quad$ standard error for the sample's estimate of the correlation coefficient

$\quad r \quad = \quad$ sample's estimate of the correlation coefficient

To test the null hypothesis that the population's correlation coefficient is equal to zero, we can apply the usual Gaussian approach in which we convert the sample's estimate to a value from a distribution with a mean equal to zero and a standard deviation of one. Since we are also estimating the variances of the dependent and independent variables, we need to use Student's t distribution to take into account the independent role of chance in making these estimates.[22] Equation {7.22} shows this calculation.

_____

[21]The reason for this is that the correlation coefficient has a restricted range of possible values (from -1 to +1), but means, slopes, and intercepts vary (theoretically) from $-\infty$ to $+\infty$. The effect of this restricted range of possible values is to make the sampling distribution for the correlation coefficient symmetric only when the mean of that sampling distribution is equal to the midpoint of its range of possible values (when the correlation coefficient is equal to zero).

[22]At first, it may seem as if we are not estimating either variance in Equation{7.21}, but those variance estimates are included in $1-r^2$ in the numerator of the standard error. There, r^2 is an algebraic simplification of including the covariance and the two variances in calculation of the standard error.

$$t = \frac{r - \rho_0}{s_r} \qquad \{7.22\}$$

where

t = Student's t-value with n-2 degrees of freedom

r = sample's estimate of the correlation coefficient

ρ_0 = population's correlation coefficient, according to the null hypothesis (i.e., equal to zero)

s_r = standard error for the sample's estimate of the correlation coefficient (from Equation{7.21})

Now, let's take a look at an example in which we take chance into account for the sample's estimate of the population's correlation coefficient.

Example 7-6 In Example 7-5 we found that the sample's estimate of the population's correlation coefficient representing the strength of the association between dietary sodium intake and mean arterial blood pressure is equal to 0.818. Now, let us take chance into account by testing the null hypothesis that the population's correlation coefficient is equal to zero versus the alternative hypothesis that is not equal to zero. Let us allow a 5% chance of making a Type 1 error.

First, we use Equation {7.21} to calculate the standard error for estimates of the correlation coefficient.

$$s_r = \sqrt{\frac{1 - r^2}{n - 2}} = \sqrt{\frac{1 - 0.818^2}{30 - 2}} = 0.1087$$

Next, we convert the sample's estimate to Student's t-value using Equation{7.22},

$$t = \frac{r - \rho_0}{s_r} = \frac{0.818 - 0}{0.1087} = 7.53$$

To interpret that value, we compare it to a value from Table B.2 that corresponds to 28 degrees of freedom and a two-sided α of 0.05 (i.e, the critical value). That t-value is 2.048. Since 7.52 is larger than 2.048, we reject the null hypothesis and, through the process of elimination, accept the alternative hypothesis (i.e., that the population's correlation coefficient is not equal to zero).

Example 7-5 and Example 7-6 illustrate how we can perform correlation analysis by hand. In practice, we use a computer to perform these calculations for us. In SAS, correlation analysis is usually done using the CORR procedure. The next example shows the output from that procedure when the data from Example 7-1 are analyzed by SAS.

Example 7-7   In Example 7-5 we found that the sample's estimate of the population's correlation coefficient representing the strength of the association between dietary sodium intake and mean arterial blood pressure is equal to 0.818 and in Example 7-7 we rejected the null hypothesis that the correlation coefficient is equal to zero in the population. Now, let us use SAS to analyze these same data.

The following is the result of analyzing the data in Example 7-1 using the CORR procedure:

```
                           The CORR Procedure

                2  Variables:     DBP       NA

                          Simple Statistics

Variable       N         Mean        Std Dev          Sum      Minimum      Maximum
DBP           30    112.00000       26.77621         3360     62.00000    164.00000
NA            30     15.92667        8.77740    477.80000      1.00000     29.20000


               Pearson Correlation Coefficients, N = 30
                   Prob > |r| under HO: Rho=0


                             DBP              NA
              DBP        1.00000         0.81784
                                          <.0001
              NA         0.81784         1.00000
                          <.0001
```

This output contains quite a bit more information than is necessary to estimate the population's correlation coefficient and test the null hypothesis that it is equal to zero. The upper part of that output provides some univariable estimates for each of the variables. The lower part of the output provides the results of correlation analysis.

There are a couple of things to notice about the lower part of this output. First, the bottom part of the output is labeled, "Pearson Correlation Coefficient." This is a more formal name for the correlation coefficient shown in Equation{7.18}. SAS uses the more formal label so that this type of correlation analysis can be distinguished from other correlation analyses that can be performed by SAS.

Second, notice that the correlation coefficients are presented in a table with separate columns and rows for each of the variables. This arrangement of correlation coefficients is called a **correlation matrix**. To find a particular correlation coefficient, find the column corresponding to one of the variables (either one) and the row corresponding to the other variable. The correlation coefficient comparing the two variables is at the intersection of that row and column. The number of columns and rows in a correlation matrix will change depending on how many variables are in the data set.[23]

At the intersection of a row and a column in the correlation matrix, two numbers are given. The number on top is the sample's estimate of the population's correlation coefficient. The number on the bottom is the *P*-value resulting from a test of the null hypothesis that the correlation coefficient is equal to zero in the population. If this *P*-value is less than or equal to α (usually 0.05), we can reject the null hypothesis. The *P*-value in the output is equal to "<.0001."[24] Since that *P*-value is less than α (i.e., 0.05), we can reject the null hypothesis that the correlation coefficient is equal to zero in the population.

The CORR procedure is designed specifically to perform correlation analyses, but these same results are included in other SAS procedures. For example, the output in Example 7-4 shows us the result of a regression analysis on these same data. Included in that output is the coefficient of determination (i.e., R^2). If you take the square root of that R^2, you would find that is equal to the correlation coefficient in the output from the CORR procedure in Example 7-7. Further, the *P*-value associated with the *F*-ratio testing the omnibus null hypothesis in the REG output is the same as the *P*-value testing the null hypothesis that the population's correlation coefficient is equal to zero in the CORR output.

Naturalistic versus purposive samples

In Flowchart 5, the choice between performing regression analysis or correlation analysis appears to be determined by the purpose of the analysis. If dependent variable values are to be estimated, regression analysis is the right choice. If the strength of the association between the dependent and independent variables is our interest, we should choose correlation analysis. In the latter case, however, there is an additional criterion that must be met if the strength of the association between the two variables in the population is being estimated. This is because the sample's estimate of the population's correlation coefficient is influenced by how independent variable values are sampled.

There are two ways in which we can sample independent variable values from the population. One possibility is to select a sample that contains a random subset of the independent variable values in the population.[25] When independent variable values are

---

[23]There are two characteristics of the correlation matrix that might, at first, be confusing. The first of these is the appearance of correlation coefficients equal to one on the left-to-right diagonal. These correlation coefficients are for each of the variables compared to itself. By definition, a variable compared to itself will always have a correlation coefficient of one. The second characteristic is that each correlation coefficient appears twice in the matrix: once with a particular variable specifying a column and once with that same variable specifying a row.

[24] 0.0001 is the smallest *P*-value SAS will print. When we see a *P*-value of "<.0001" in SAS output, we say that the *P*-value is "less than 0.0001."

[25]This is distinct from a random sample of dependent variable values. As discussed in Chapter 2, all statistical procedures assume that the dependent variable has been sampled randomly. Now, we are referring to how the independent variable has been sampled. Few statistical procedures assume that the independent variable has been sampled randomly as well.

selected randomly, the distribution of independent variable values in the sample represents the distribution of independent variable values in the population, at least on the average. We call a sample that is the result of randomly sampling independent variable values a **naturalistic sample**.

In contrast to sampling independent variable values randomly, these values can be selected so that they have a distribution in the sample that is different from their distribution in the population. Such a sample is called a **purposive sample**. There are a number of reasons a researcher might choose to take a purposive sample. A common reason is to "over-sample" values of the independent variable that do not occur very often in the population. For example, the National Hospital Discharge Survey (NHDS) planned to include all of the very largest hospitals in the United States while lower percentages of smaller hospitals were included. One reason for this is that there are very few of these largest hospitals in the population. To be able to describe the discharges at the largest hospitals and smaller hospitals with the same precision, a greater proportion of the larger hospitals had to be included in the sample. As a result, the distribution of hospital sizes in the sample was not representative of their distribution in the population. Thus, the NHDS uses a purposive sample of hospital size in its sample.

The following example illustrates the distinction between a naturalistic sample and a purposive sample:

Example 7-8 Suppose that we are interested in the relationship between age and renal clearance rates. Further suppose that the relationship in the population is represented in the following scatter plot:

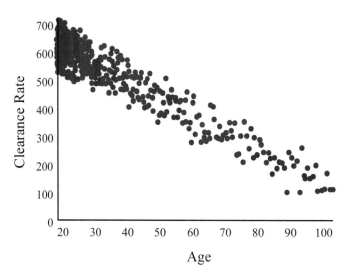

The scatter plot shows the renal clearance rate (measured as plasma/min/1.73 $m^{2)}$ decreasing with increasing age. It also demonstrates that there are fewer persons in the population in older age groups. This is evident by the fact that there are fewer points in the scatter plot for each higher decade of life.

Now, let us consider how to sample this population and the implications of our choice on interpretation of the estimate of the correlation coefficient.

One choice is to take a naturalistic sample. To take a naturalistic sample, members of the population are selected without regard to their age. When the value of the independent variable does not influence the probability of being included in the sample, chance will create a distribution of independent variable values in the sample that, on the average, reflects the population's distribution. The following scatter plot illustrates a naturalistic sample taken from that population. The points in darker color represent the individuals in the population who are selected to be in the sample.

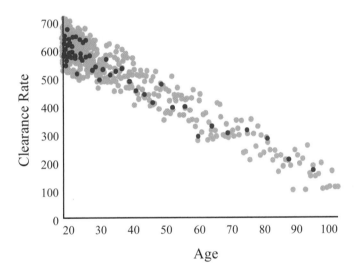

This naturalistic sample shows the same age distribution as the population's age distribution; namely, there are fewer persons in each older age group. With this naturalistic sample, renal clearance rates can be estimated with fair precision for younger persons, but they cannot be estimated with much precision for older persons, since there are few older persons in the sample.

If we are interested in more precisely estimating clearance rates for older persons we need to determine each person's age before we can decide whether or not they should be included in the sample. Then, we need to select persons for the sample according to their age (i.e., take a **stratified** sample), making the probability of being selected higher for older persons than for younger persons. The following scatter plot illustrates a sample that would be selected from the population in this way:

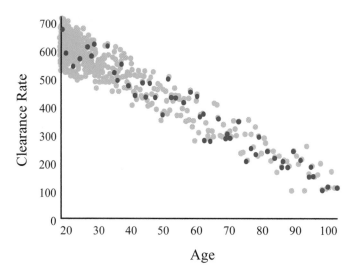

This over-sampling of older persons results in a sample with approximately the same number of persons throughout the range of ages studied. Consequently, estimates for older persons to have the same precision as estimates for younger persons. This sample, however, is a purposive sample. This fact limits the kind of analysis that would be appropriate for these data (i.e., correlation analysis would not be appropriate).

Another approach to sampling a population such as this one is to limit the range of independent variable values to those values that are well represented in the population (i.e., take a **restricted** sample). For this population, suppose we decided to eliminate persons 60 years old or older from the sampling process, and then take a naturalistic sample of persons between the ages of 20 and 50 years. The following scatter plot illustrates a restricted sample:

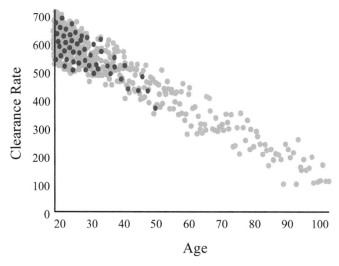

This sampling method confines the ages in the sample to those that are well represented in the population. It does not allow estimates for older persons; instead it focuses on the younger persons for whom precise estimates can be made without over-sampling. Between the ages of 20 and 59 years, the distribution of ages in the sample represents the distribution of ages in the population in that age range. Thus, relative to persons between 20 and 59 years of age in the population, this is a naturalistic sample. Relative to the initial population, however, this is a purposive sample.

When we have a purposive sample we can perform a regression analysis that can be interpreted relative to the population. That is to say, such analyses provide unbiased estimates of the slope in the population. The only effect of purposive sampling on the estimate of the slope is to change the precision of this estimate.[26] It will not have an effect on the value of the estimate itself (i.e., on the average, samples' estimates will be equal to the population's parameters).

This is not the case for the sample's estimate of the population's correlation coefficient. Estimates of the correlation coefficient will change in value as the distribution of independent variable values in the sample changes. Only naturalistic samples produce estimates of the correlation coefficient that are equal, on the average, to the population's correlation coefficient. With purposive samples, the estimate of the correlation coefficient will be higher than the population's value (even on the average) when the ages of persons in the sample are more dispersed than the ages of persons in the population (as in the first purposive sample in Example 7-6 in which older persons were over-sampled). Similarly, the estimate of the correlation coefficient will be lower than the population's value when the ages of persons in the sample are less dispersed (as in the second purposive sample in Example 7-6 in which older persons were excluded from the sample). The ways in which methods of sampling independent variable values affects estimates of the slope, intercept, and correlation coefficient is illustrated in the next example.

Example 7-9   In Example 7-8, we considered a naturalistic and two purposive samples from a population with fewer persons of older ages. We were interested in the relationship between age and renal clearance rates   This population was generated in a computer simulation that assumed that the population's regression equation had an intercept equal to 700 cc of plasma/min/1.73 m^2 and a slope equal to -6 cc of plasma/min/1.73 m^2/year. The coefficient of determination (R^2) in this simulated population was equal to 0.9 (which corresponds to a correlation coefficient of approximately 0.95). Now, let us see what the estimates for the slope, intercept, and correlation coefficient are for each of the three samples taken from that population.

---

[26]The precision of the estimates of the slope and intercept increase as the variability of independent variable values in the sample increases. This is illustrated mathematically (for the slope) in Equation{7.15}, where the sum of squares for the independent variable values in the sample is included in the denominator of the standard error calculation.

To begin, let us take a look at the first sample in Example 7-8. That was a naturalistic sample, so we expect all of the estimates to be close to the population's values. The following SAS output came from analyzing those data using the REG procedure:

```
                        The REG Procedure
                     Model: NATURALISTIC SAMPLE
                     Dependent Variable: clearance

                       Analysis of Variance

                            Sum of         Mean
  Source          DF       Squares       Square    F Value    Pr > F
  Model            1        686677       686677     531.16     <.0001
  Error           48         62053   1292.77854
  Corrected Total 49        748731

            Root MSE            35.95523    R-Square    0.9171
            Dependent Mean     489.78879    Adj R-Sq    0.9154
            Coeff Var            7.34097

                       Parameter Estimates

                     Parameter      Standard
    Variable    DF    Estimate         Error    t Value    Pr > |t|
    Intercept    1   706.99334      10.70865      66.02      <.0001
    age          1    -6.26329       0.27176     -23.05      <.0001
```

At the bottom of this output, we can see that the naturalistic sample's estimate of the intercept and slope are 706.99334 cc of plasma/min/1.73 m^2 and -6.26329 cc of plasma/min/1.73 m^2/year. These are close to the actual values (700 and -6). In addition, if we were to continue taking naturalistic samples from this population, we would find that the means of the slope and intercept from these samples would be, in the long run, exactly equal to the population's values. Thus, the estimates of the slope and intercept from a naturalistic sample are unbiased estimates[27] of the slope and intercept in the population.

The sample's estimate of the correlation coefficient is equal to the square root of the estimate of R^2 that is included in the output from the REG procedure. In this sample, the estimate of R^2 is 0.9171, which is very close to the actual value in the population (0.9).

Similar to the estimates of the slope and intercept, the mean of estimates of the correlation coefficient from repeated naturalistic samples would be exactly equal to the population's value. Thus, naturalistic samples provide unbiased estimates of the slope, intercept and correlation coefficient.

Next, let us take a look at the first purposive sample in Example 7-8, which resulted from over-sampling persons of older ages. The following is the result of using the REG procedure to analyze these data:

---

[27] Recall from Chapter 2 that an unbiased estimate is equal to the population's value on the average.

```
                        The REG Procedure
                    Model: PURPOSIVE SAMPLE 1
                    Dependent Variable: clearance

                       Analysis of Variance

                                  Sum of          Mean
   Source            DF          Squares        Square    F Value   Pr > F
   Model              1          1027659       1027659     726.72   <.0001
   Error             48            67877    1414.10189
   Corrected Total   49          1095536

           Root MSE              37.60455   R-Square    0.9380
           Dependent Mean       345.91926   Adj R-Sq    0.9368
           Coeff Var             10.87090

                      Parameter Estimates

                      Parameter       Standard
   Variable     DF     Estimate          Error   t Value   Pr > |t|
   Intercept     1    706.99334       10.70865     66.02    <.0001
   age           1     -6.26329        0.27176    -23.05    <.0001
```

As in the naturalistic sample, this purposive sample gives us an estimate of the slope (-6.29827) that is close in value to the actual slope (-6). The intercept (725.58134) is not as close to the actual intercept (700) as that from the naturalistic sample, but this is due the role of chance in selecting this sample from the simulated population.[28] Even so, if we were to take all possible samples of this kind from the population, the mean of the estimates of the slope and the intercept from those samples would be exactly equal to the actual slope and the intercept. Taking a purposive sample does not bias the point estimates of the slope and intercept.

The estimate of R^2 (0.9380), however, is larger than the actual value in the population (0.9).[29] This would be true even if we were to take all possible samples like this one and calculate the mean of the estimates of the correlation coefficient from each sample. In that case, the mean would be larger than the actual value. This purposive sample has increased the variation in ages by over-sampling older persons and, as a result, over-estimates the population's correlation coefficient.

Finally, let us take a look at the second purposive sample in Example 7-8. This sample resulted from restricting the sample to persons 50 years old or younger. The following is the result of using the REG procedure to analyze those data:

---

[28] In a simulation, chance is used to select a particular sample. Thus, we can see the effect of this role of chance in a simulation by occasionally obtaining estimates that are not very close to the value of the population's parameter. On the average, however, those estimates would be exactly equal to the parameter.

[29] At first, 0.9380 does not seems to be very much larger than 0.9, but we need to keep in mind that R^2 has an upper limit of +1. 0.9380 represents an increase that is more than 1/3 (0.0380/0.1000) of the maximum possible increase

```
                            The REG Procedure
                         Model: PURPOSIVE SAMPLE 2
                       Dependent Variable: clearance

                           Analysis of Variance

                              Sum of          Mean
     Source            DF     Squares        Square    F Value    Pr > F
     Model              1      140985        140985     109.64    <.0001
     Error             48       61723    1285.88764
     Corrected Total   49      202708

                Root MSE            35.85928    R-Square    0.6955
                Dependent Mean     532.44989    Adj R-Sq    0.6892
                Coeff Var            6.73477

                          Parameter Estimates

                         Parameter     Standard
     Variable     DF      Estimate        Error    t Value    Pr > |t|
     Intercept     1     713.05020     17.97786      39.66      <.0001
     age           1      -6.62744      0.63294     -10.47      <.0001
```

Like the previous two samples, this purposive sample gives us estimates of the slope (-6.62744) and the intercept (713.05020) that are close in value to the actual slope (-6) and intercept (700). Also like the previous two samples, the mean of the estimates of the slope and the intercept from all possible samples of this same type would be exactly equal to the actual slope and the intercept. The estimate of R^2 (0.6955), however, is smaller than the actual value of R^2 (0.9). This would be true even if we were to take all possible samples like this one and calculate the mean of the estimates of the correlation coefficient from each sample. This purposive sample has decreased the variation in ages by excluding older persons and, as a result, under-estimates the population's R^2 (and correlation coefficient).

ORDINAL INDEPENDENT VARIABLE

When a bivariable sample contains a continuous dependent variable, we can choose among a variety of statistical procedures for continuous or nominal independent variables. There are not, however, any well-accepted procedures used in health research for a sample consisting of a continuous dependent variable and an ordinal independent variable. Such a sample is analyzed either by converting the continuous dependent variable to an ordinal scale and using techniques discussed in Chapter 8, or by creating a collection of nominal variables from the ordinal independent variable and using statistical procedures described in Chapter 10.

NOMINAL INDEPENDENT VARIABLE

When the independent variable represents nominal data, the effect is to separate dependent variable values into two groups.[30] Suppose, for instance, that we conduct a clinical trial of an antihypertensive medication to compare a new treatment to standard therapy.   The independent variable, in this case, is a nominal variable indicating group membership (new or standard therapy) and dependent variable is the change in blood pressure. Figure 7-12 illustrates the way in which we think about the distribution of continuous dependent variable values when the independent variable represents nominal data.

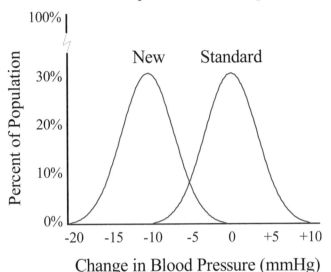

Figure 7-12 **Distribution of continuous dependent variable values divided into two groups by a nominal independent variable.**

Estimating the Difference Between the Groups

The most common method of comparing two groups of continuous dependent variable values is by comparing the means of the groups. The way in which we compare means is by examining their difference.   For example, when comparing changes in blood pressure measurements between persons who received a new drug versus those who received standard therapy, we would make the comparison by examining the difference between the mean of the change in blood pressure values in the two treatment groups.[31]

To estimate the difference between the means of the groups in the population, we take the difference between the sample's estimates of those means (Equation{7.23}). This is an unbiased estimate of the difference between the means in the population.

---

[30]Remember that a nominal variable can represent only two possible values. Therefore, a single nominal independent variable divides a sample into two, and only two, groups. If the sample contains more than two groups, those groups must be represented by more than one nominal independent variable.

[31]One reason we compare means as a difference is that a linear combination (such as a sum or difference) of measures of location of a distribution (like means) will have a Gaussian distribution if the components of the linear combination have Gaussian distributions. In other words, we can apply the central limit theorem to linear combinations of measures of location just as we can apply it to these measures of location themselves.

$$\mu_1 - \mu_2 \triangleq \overline{Y}_1 - \overline{Y}_2 = \frac{\sum Y_{1_i}}{n_1} - \frac{\sum Y_{2_i}}{n_2} \qquad \{7.23\}$$

where

μ_1 =   population's mean in group 1

μ_2 =   population's mean in group 2

$\overline{Y}_1$ =   sample's estimate of the mean in group 1

$\overline{Y}_2$ =   sample's estimate of the mean in group 2

Taking Chance into Account

We can take chance into account for the estimate of the difference between means either by testing a null hypothesis or calculating a confidence interval for that difference. In either case, we need to consider the sampling distribution for differences between the means (i.e., the distribution of differences between the means from all possible samples of the same size). This sampling distribution tends to be a Gaussian distribution, so we can use the same approach to conducting hypothesis testing and interval estimation we have used for other Gaussian sampling distributions.

    If the sampling distribution for the differences between the means is a Gaussian distribution, its parameters must be a mean and a standard error. The mean of this sampling distribution is equal to the difference between the population's means.[32] The standard error of the sampling distribution of the difference between two means is calculated from the standard errors of the univariable sampling distributions for each of the means[33] as illustrated in Equation{7.24}.

$$\sigma_{\overline{Y}_1 - \overline{Y}_2} \triangleq s_{\overline{Y}_1 - \overline{Y}_2} = \sqrt{s_{\overline{Y}_1}^2 + s_{\overline{Y}_2}^2} = \sqrt{\frac{s_1^2}{n_1} + \frac{s_2^2}{n_2}} \qquad \{7.24\}$$

---

[32]For any unbiased estimate, the mean of the sampling distribution is equal to the population's value being estimated. This is what we imply when we say that an unbiased estimate is equal to the population's value, "on the average."

[33]Another aspect of a linear combination that makes it attractive as a way to compare measures of location is that the standard error of the combination can be calculated from the standard errors of its components.

where

$$s_{\bar{Y}_1 - \bar{Y}_2} = \text{standard error for the difference between the means in two groups of continuous dependent variable values}$$

$$s_{\bar{Y}_1}^2, s_{\bar{Y}_2}^2 = \text{sample's estimate of the squared univariable standard errors for the means in groups 1 and 2}$$

$$s_1^2, s_2^2 = \text{sample's estimates of the variances of dependent variable values in groups 1 and 2}$$

$$n_1, n_2 = \text{numbers of observations in groups 1 and 2}$$

We will take a look at an example in which we calculate this standard error shortly, but first we need to consider how we will go about estimating the variance of dependent variable values when there are two groups of these values. In Figure 7-12, the dispersions of the two distributions of dependent variable values are identical. This is done for simplicity. Having the dispersions of these two distributions equal to the same value implies that we can use all of the data in our sample to estimate that single, common variance. The alternative is to use the sample's observations in each group by themselves to estimate the population's variance of values in that group.[34]

If we can assume that the variances are equal in the two groups of dependent variable values, then we can use all of the observations in the sample (i.e., dependent variable values associated with both groups) to estimate a single variance in the population that applies to both groups, rather than having to estimate separate variances for each of the two groups. As a result, we can have greater confidence in that estimate and greater statistical power (i.e., greater ability to avoid a type II error in statistical inference). Assuming that the variances are the same for different groups of dependent variable values is known as the assumption of **homoscedasticity**.

When we assume homoscedasticity, we can use information from both groups to estimate the population's variance. It is important to keep in mind that assuming homoscedasticity does not require that the sample's estimates of the variance observed in each of the two groups have the same value. Rather, we expect that the sample's observations in each of those groups will give us different variance estimates by chance alone, even if they are estimating the same variance in the population. The issue here is whether or not the observed variances (i.e., the sample's estimates) are different enough for us to suspect that they are estimating different values in the population. We will consider how to decide about this assumption shortly. For now, let us say that we are willing to assume homoscedasticity. In that case, we want to arrive at a single estimate of the variance.

To understand how we derive a single estimate of the population's variance from the sample's two estimates, we need to learn about an important statistical concept. That is the

---

[34]This implies that there are three ways in which chance can influence the sample. The first is in the estimates of the difference between the means of the two distributions. The second and third ways are in the variance estimates for each of the two groups of dependent variable values.

concept of a **weighted average**.

In everyday language, the terms "average" and "mean" are considered to be synonyms. In statistics, we draw a distinction between the two. An average (more often called a weighted average) is the sum of the products of each observation or estimate times a particular number (called a weight) divided by the sum of those weights. This is easier to appreciate if we look at Equation{7.25}.

$$\text{Weighted Average} = \frac{\sum w_i \bullet Y_i}{\sum w_i} \qquad \{7.25\}$$

where

$$w_i \quad = \quad \text{weight for the } i^{th} \text{ observation or estimate}$$

$$Y_i \quad = \quad \text{value of the } i^{th} \text{ observation or estimate}$$

In contrast, a mean is a special type of weighted average in which each observation is given a weight equal to one.[35] The use of a weighted average with weights equal to one implies that we are unable to say that one observation is closer to the population's mean than is any other observation. Thus, each observation is given the same weight as every other observation when estimating the mean.

Now, let us apply this principle of weighted averages to estimation of the population's variance of the distribution of data when we have estimates of that variance from two groups of dependent variable values.

We know from Chapter 4 that the number of degrees of freedom in a sample is used as a parameter of Student's t distribution to reflect the degree of precision with which we can estimate the population's variance of the distribution of data. The greater the number of degrees of freedom, the less the penalty that must be paid for estimating the population's variance from the sample's observations.[36] Since degrees of freedom can be used in that context to reflect how precisely we can estimate the population's variance, it makes sense for us to use degrees of freedom as the weights for the variance estimates from each of the two groups in the sample. The weighted average of those two variance estimates using degrees of freedom as the weights is called the **pooled estimate** of the variance. The following equation shows us how we can calculate the pooled estimate of the variance of the distribution of data in the population from the sample's observations.

---

[35]Mathematically, the mean can be presented as a weighted average as follows: $\overline{Y} = \dfrac{\sum 1 \bullet Y_i}{\sum 1} = \dfrac{\sum Y_i}{n}$

[36]Recall from Chapter 4 that the "penalty" applied by Student's t distribution is to make it harder to reject the null hypothesis (by making the P-value larger) and to make confidence intervals wider.

$$\sigma_Y^2 \overset{\wedge}{=} s_{\text{pooled}}^2 = \frac{\sum (n_i - 1) \cdot s_i^2}{\sum (n_i - 1)} = \frac{((n_1 - 1) \cdot s_1^2) + ((n_2 - 1) \cdot s_2^2)}{(n_1 - 1) + (n_2 - 1)} \qquad \{7.26\}$$

where

σ_Y^2 = variance of the distribution of dependent variable values in the population

s_{pooled}^2 = pooled estimate of the variance of dependent variable values

$(n_i - 1)$ = degrees of freedom in the ith group of dependent variable values

s_i^2 = variance estimate in the ith group of dependent variable values

When we assume homoscedasticity, we can use the pooled estimate of the variance to calculate the standard error of the difference between the means rather than use the separate variance estimates. Equation {7.27} shows how Equation {7.24} is modified to use the pooled estimate in calculating the standard error for the differences between the means.

$$\sigma_{\bar{Y}_1 - \bar{Y}_2} \overset{\wedge}{=} s_{\bar{Y}_1 - \bar{Y}_2} = \sqrt{s_{\bar{Y}_1}^2 + s_{\bar{Y}_2}^2} = \sqrt{\frac{s_{\text{pooled}}^2}{n_1} + \frac{s_{\text{pooled}}^2}{n_2}} \qquad \{7.27\}$$

where

$s_{\bar{Y}_1 - \bar{Y}_2}$ = standard error for the difference between the means in two groups of continuous dependent variable values

s_{pooled}^2 = pooled estimate of the variance of dependent variable values from Equation {7.26}

n_1, n_2 = number of observations in groups 1 and 2

So, there are two ways to calculate the standard error for the differences between the means of two groups of continuous dependent variable values. Equation {7.27} is the way we calculate the standard error if we are willing to assume that the population's variances of the distributions of data are equal in the two groups (i.e., when we assume homoscedasticity). In that case, we use the pooled estimate of the population's variance in calculating the standard error. If we are unwilling to assume homoscedasticity, however, we use the separate, group-specific estimates of the population's variance in each group of dependent variable values. That calculation is shown in Equation{7.24}.

Now that we understand the choices for the standard error of the difference between two means, we are ready to take chance into account for the sample's estimate of that difference. To do this, we can either test a null hypothesis[37] or calculate a confidence interval for the difference between the means in the population. In either case, we use Student's t distribution so that we can have degrees of freedom to take into account the independent role(s) of chance in estimating the population's variance(s) of the distributions of data in each group. Equations {7.28} (for hypothesis testing) and {7.29} (for interval estimation) illustrate these calculations.

$$t = \frac{(\overline{Y}_1 - \overline{Y}_2) - (\mu_1 - \mu_2)}{s_{\overline{Y}_1 - \overline{Y}_2}} \qquad \{7.28\}$$

$$\mu_1 - \mu_2 = (\overline{Y}_1 - \overline{Y}_2) \pm (t_{\alpha/2} \bullet s_{\overline{Y}_1 - \overline{Y}_2}) \qquad \{7.29\}$$

where

t = Student's t-value representing the observed difference between the means

$t_{\alpha/2}$ = Student's t-value representing 1-α confidence

$\overline{Y}_1, \overline{Y}_2$ = sample's estimate of the means in groups 1 and 2

$\mu_1 - \mu_2$ = population's means in groups 1 and 2

$s_{\overline{Y}_1 - \overline{Y}_2}$ = standard error for the difference between the means calculated from Equation {7.24} when we cannot assume homoscedasticity or from Equation {7.27} when we can assume homoscedasticity

When we assume homoscedasticity, the degrees of freedom for Student's t-value are equal to n_1+n_2-2. This is the same as the value that is used in the denominator when we calculate the pooled estimate of the variance (Equation{7.26}). It is equal to the sum of the univariable degrees of freedom (i.e., n_i-1) in each group.

When we are unwilling to assume that the variances are equal in the two groups, we have an additional role of chance. In that case, chance can have an independent influence on the estimates of both variances. This additional role of chance is reflected in the degrees of freedom we use to identify a t-value. The degrees of freedom will be fewer than n_1+n_2-2

---

[37]The most commonly addressed null hypothesis for a difference between means is that the difference in the population is equal to zero. This is tantamount to hypothesizing that the means for the two groups are equal to each other.

when we are unwilling to assume homoscedasticity.[38] The effect of having fewer degrees of freedom, with all else being equal, is to make rejecting the null hypothesis harder and to make confidence intervals wider.

In the next example, we see how we can take chance into account in examining the difference between the means of dependent variable values in two groups specified by a nominal independent variable.

Example 7-10 Suppose that we are interested in comparing mean arterial blood pressure values between two groups of persons: one group of 30 persons who follow a low-sodium diet and a second group of 50 persons who do not try to control their dietary sodium intake. Imagine that we observed the following results:

Group	n	Arterial Blood Pressure $\bar{Y}$	s^2
Diet	30	104.6	392.34
Control	50	117.9	650.78

While assuming that the variances are equal to the same value in the population, let us test the null hypothesis that the difference between the mean arterial blood pressure is equal to zero (versus the alternative hypothesis that the difference between the means is not equal to zero) while allowing a 5% chance of making a type I error.

Since we are told to assume that the variances are equal to the same value in the population, we will calculate a standard error based on the pooled estimate of the variance of dependent variable values. In preparation, we use Equation {7.26} to calculate the pooled estimate of that variance:

$$\sigma_Y^2 \triangleq s_{\text{pooled}}^2 = \frac{((n_1-1) \cdot s_1^2) + ((n_2-1) \cdot s_2^2)}{(n_1-1) + (n_2-1)} = \frac{((30-1) \cdot 392.34) + ((50-1) \cdot 650.78)}{(30-1) + (50-1)} = 554.70 \text{ mmHg}^2$$

So, our best estimate of the variance of dependent variable values is equal to 554.70 mmHg^2. This value is closer to the variance estimate among controls than it is to the estimate among persons on the diet. The reason for this is that the estimate of the variance is more precise (i.e., more individuals and thus, more degrees of freedom) among controls.

---

[38]The calculation of the degrees of freedom when we are not willing to assume homoscedasticity is a bit complicated, so we will not present it in this text. In practice, the computer does this calculation for us.

Next, we use Equation {7.27} to calculate the standard error for the difference between two means:

$$\sigma_{\bar{Y}_1 - \bar{Y}_2} \overset{\wedge}{=} s_{\bar{Y}_1 - \bar{Y}_2} = \sqrt{\frac{s^2_{pooled}}{n_1} + \frac{s^2_{pooled}}{n_2}} = \sqrt{\frac{554.70}{30} + \frac{554.70}{50}} = 5.44 \text{ mmHg}^2$$

Now, we are ready to convert the observed difference between the means to a t-value. To do that, we use Equation {7.28}.

$$t = \frac{(\bar{Y}_1 - \bar{Y}_2) - (\mu_1 - \mu_2)}{s_{\bar{Y}_1 - \bar{Y}_2}} = \frac{(104.6 - 117.9) - 0}{5.44} = -2.44$$

To interpret this value, we can compare it to the value in Table B.2 (Student's t distribution) that corresponds to a two-sided $\alpha = 0.05$ and 78 degrees of freedom. There is no listing for that number of degrees of freedom in Table B.2. Instead, we find a t-value of 1.992 for 75 degrees of freedom and of 1.990 for 80 degrees of freedom. Our calculated value (-2.44) is larger (for a two-sided test, we ignore the sign of the calculated t-value) than either of those values. Thus, we can reject the null hypothesis and accept, through the process of elimination, the alternative hypothesis that the difference between the two means is not equal to zero.

In Example 7-10, we assumed that the variances for the groups are equal in the population. When you looked at the estimates of that variance, you might have been concerned that they were not similar enough to assume homoscedasticity. Deciding how similar estimates of the population's variance have to be to make it sensible to use a pooled estimate is a bit tricky. What most people do is to test the null hypothesis that the population's variances are equal to each other. This may not be the best method, since it is affected by statistical power.[39] Its use, however, is encouraged by computer programs that provide the results of this hypothesis test any time Student's t-test is performed. For now, we will use that criterion for assuming homoscedasticity.

To have SAS perform Student's t-test for the difference between two means, we can use the TTEST procedure. This procedure performs the t-test first assuming homoscedasticity, and then again without assuming homoscedasticity. In addition, it provides the result of testing the null hypothesis that the variances are equal in the two groups and also provides confidence intervals for each of the means, their difference, and each of the standard

---

[39]Statistical power will determine how different the sample's estimates of the variance need to be before the null hypothesis stating that they are equal can be rejected. The problem with this is that the sample's estimates of the variance can be quite different in a small sample without rejecting the null hypothesis. On the other hand, estimates that are numerically similar can lead to rejection of the null hypothesis if the sample is large. Thus, this criterion for assuming homoscedasticity has different results for samples of different sizes.

deviations. Example 7-11 shows the result of performing SAS's TTEST procedure on the data presented in Example 7-10.

Example 7-11 If we were to use the TTEST procedure to analyze the data described in Example 7-10, we would observe the following output:

```
                          The TTEST Procedure

                              Statistics

                   Lower CL              Upper CL  Lower CL            Upper CL
   Variable GROUP    N     Mean    Mean    Mean    Std Dev  Std Dev  Std Dev  Std Err
   MAP      CONTROL 50   110.63  117.88  125.12    21.31    25.51    31.789   3.6077
   MAP      DIET    30   97.229  104.63  112.02    15.775   19.808   26.628   3.6164
   MAP      Diff (1-2)   2.4216  13.25   24.078    20.366   23.552   27.929   5.4391

                               T-Tests

           Variable    Method         Variances     DF    t Value   Pr > |t|
           MAP         Pooled         Equal         78      2.44     0.0171
           MAP         Satterthwaite  Unequal      72.8     2.59     0.0115


                         Equality of Variances

           Variable    Method      Num DF    Den DF    F Value   Pr > F
           MAP         Folded F       49        29       1.66    0.1471
```

Let us interpret this output.

This output provides us with a lot of useful information. In the first table (labeled "Statistics") we find point and interval estimates for means and standard deviations and point estimates of standard errors. Before we look more closely at these estimates, a word of caution is needed. The formatting of this table makes it easy to select the lower limit of the interval estimate, mistakenly thinking that it is the point estimate. This is a common mistake when interpreting the output from SAS's TTEST procedure. The reason this mistake is easy to make is because the point estimate is displayed between the lower and upper limits of its corresponding interval estimate. This is the only output in the current version of SAS that displays point and interval estimates like that.

The first two rows of this table give us univariable values and the last row gives us bivariable values. Both of those types of information are useful, but for different purposes. When describing the means in the two groups, the univariable values are appropriate (117.88 mmHg for controls and 104.63 for persons on the diet). When comparing those means, however, the bivariable results should be used (i.e., the mean difference of 13.25 mmHg).

It is not uncommon to find persons who try to use univariable estimates to draw a bivariable conclusion. They do this by determining if two univariable confidence intervals overlap. In this example, the univariable confidence intervals for the mean arterial blood pressure are 110.63 to 125.12 mmHg for controls and 97.229 to 112.02 mmHg for persons on the diet. Since the lower limit for controls is less than the upper limit for persons on the diet, the univariable confidence intervals overlap. The common, but incorrect, interpretation of this overlap of univariable confidence intervals is to say that the means are not statistically different (a bivariable statement). This is not a reliable method of bivariable inference. Instead, the bivariable confidence interval (i.e., for the difference between the means) should be examined to draw a bivariable conclusion. This bivariable confidence interval is 2.4216 to 24.078 mmHg. This confidence interval does not include zero (the null value),[40] so we conclude that these means are statistically different, contrary to the conclusion based on univariable confidence intervals.

The estimate of the standard deviation in the last row of this table (23.552 mmHg) is the square root of the pooled estimate of the variance we calculated in Example 7-10 (554.70 $mmHg^2$). The standard error in that row has been calculated using this pooled estimate. It is this standard error that has been used to calculate the confidence interval for the difference between the means. Thus, we must be willing to assume homoscedasticity if we are to accept SAS's confidence interval for the difference between the means.

The next table in the output (labeled "T-Tests") shows the result of performing Student's t-tests. The results in the first row (labeled "Equal" in the "Variances" column) are from the t-test that assumes homoscedasticity. The results in the second row (labeled "Unequal" in the "Variances" column) are for Student's t-test when homoscedasticity is not assumed. The P-values for both of these tests (0.0171 when assuming homoscedasticity and 0.0115 when not assuming homoscedasticity) are less than 0.05, so the null hypothesis that the means are equal in the population can be rejected, regardless of whether or not we assume homoscedasticity.

Let us take a moment to consider the degrees of freedom for the two tests of the null hypothesis that the difference between the mean is equal to zero in the population. When assuming homoscedasticity, the degrees of freedom are equal to $n_1 + n_2 - 2 = 78$. When we do not assume homoscedasticity, the degrees of freedom are equal to 72.8.[41] This reduction in the degrees of freedom results in a decrease in statistical power.[42]

The final table in this output (labeled "Equality of Variances") displays the result of testing the null hypothesis that the variances in the two groups are equal to the same value in the population. The result of this test is the most commonly used indication of our willingness to assume homoscedasticity. If we use this test to determine whether or not we will assume homoscedasticity, the usual practice is to make that assumption if the P-value

---

[40] We learned in Chapter 3 that, if the value in the null hypothesis is outside the limits of the confidence interval, this is the same as rejecting the null hypothesis.

[41] When degrees of freedom are adjusted to take into account the independent roles of chance in estimating two separate variances, the degrees of freedom often contains a decimal value.

[42] Here, the P-value for the test that does not assume homoscedasticity is lower than the P-value for the test that makes that assumption. The reason for this is the fact that the two groups each have a different number of observations. The larger group (controls) has the higher variance estimate. When a weighted average of variance estimates is determined, the estimate in the larger group will have a greater influence on the pooled estimate than will the lower estimate from the smaller group (dieters).

for this test (here, 0.1471) is greater than 0.05. In this case, we cannot reject the null hypothesis that the variances are equal, so the convention says that we can assume homoscedasticity.

In the next chapter, we will take a look at bivariable analysis of an ordinal dependent variable. Those analyses are the nonparametric methods that correspond to the analyses presented in this chapter.

CHAPTER 8
Bivariable Analysis of an Ordinal Dependent Variable

When we begin a chapter that addresses an ordinal dependent variable, we can expect to see methods that we could use as nonparametric analyses for a continuous dependent variable. With that expectation, we look for methods that are parallel to those we encountered in Chapter 7. In that chapter, we learned about regression and correlation analyses for a continuous dependent variable with a continuous independent variable and about Student's t test for a continuous dependent variable with a nominal independent variable.

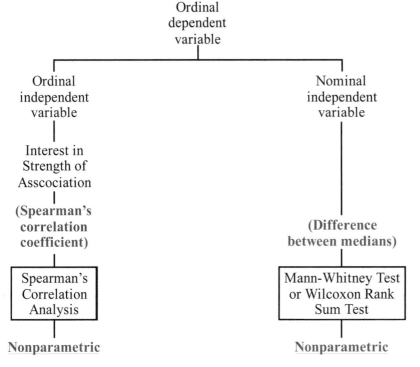

Flowchart 6   **Flowchart showing bivariable analysis of an ordinal dependent variable. The point estimate that is most often used to describe the dependent variable is in color. The common name of the statistical test is enclosed in a box. The general procedure that is used to test hypotheses and calculate confidence intervals is in color and underlined.**

If we look at Flowchart 6 with the expectation of finding nonparametric methods for regression, correlation, and Student's t test, we will be disappointed. The most obvious feature of this flowchart is that it describes two, rather than three types of statistical approaches. The missing method is a nonparametric approach that is parallel to regression analysis. There are no truly nonparametric methods for regression analysis. The reason for this is the fact that a slope cannot be defined for ordinal data.[1] Without a slope, we cannot have regression analysis, since it is the purpose of regression analysis to estimate values of dependent variable corresponding to particular values of the independent variable.

---

[1]Recall from Chapter 7 that the slope tells us how much the value of the dependent variable changes for each unit change in the value of the independent variable. When the dependent variable is represented on an ordinal scale, we no longer consider how far apart dependent variable values are from each other; we only consider their rank order. Without considering how far apart dependent variable values are, we cannot think about how much the dependent variable values change. Thus, a slope has no meaning on an ordinal scale.

ORDINAL INDEPENDENT VARIABLE

Even though we are unable to perform a regression analysis for an ordinal dependent variable, we still can consider the strength of the association between the dependent and independent variables. On an ordinal scale, however, the nature of the association is different from the association between two continuous variables.[2] On a continuous scale, an association has two properties. The first property of an association between two continuous variables is the consistency with which the values of the dependent variable change in a particular direction as the values of the independent variable increase.[3] The more consistent the direction of change in the values of the dependent variable, the stronger is the association between the variables. The second property of an association between continuous variables is the consistency with which the numeric magnitude of the dependent variable values change as the values of the independent variable increase. The more consistent the amount of the change in the values of the dependent variable as the values of the independent variable increase by a given amount, the stronger is the association between the two variables.

Pearson's correlation coefficient is the correlation coefficient we use to assess the strength of the association between two continuous variables (see Equation 7.18). A perfect association between two continuous variables is indicated by Pearson's correlation coefficient being equal to one (+1 for a direct association or -1 for an inverse association). Figure 8-1 illustrates direct associations between two continuous variables and their corresponding values of Pearson's correlation coefficient.

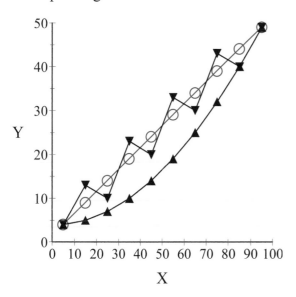

Figure 8-1 Scatter plot showing the aspects of an association between a continuous dependent variable (Y) and a continuous independent variable (X). The circles (in color) represent a perfect direct association between the variables: the value of the dependent variable increases by the same amount as the value of the independent variable increases ($r=1.00$). The ▲s represent an association in which the <u>magnitude</u> of the change in dependent variable values varies ($r=0.97$). The ▼s represent an association in which the <u>direction</u> of change of the dependent variable values varies ($r=0.97$).

---

[2]This difference will be true regardless of whether the independent variable is represented by a continuous or an ordinal variable. The convention, however, is to consider both variables to be ordinal.

[3]Recall from Chapter 7 that, for a <u>direct</u> association, this would be the consistency with which the value of the dependent variable <u>increases</u> as the value of the independent variable increases. For an <u>inverse</u> association, this would be the consistency with which the value of the dependent variable <u>decreases</u> as the value of the independent variable increases.

In Figure 8-1, the only values that have a perfect association are those in which both the direction and the magnitude of the change in the values of the dependent variable are constant. When either the direction (▼s) or the magnitude (▲s) of the changes in the value of the dependent variable varies, the association is less than perfect. This is reflected by Pearson's correlation coefficient having a value closer to zero.

When we think about the association between two ordinal variables, the direction of the change in dependent variable values can be considered, but the magnitude of that change cannot. This is due to the fact that the magnitude of differences between data values is lost when continuous data are converted to an ordinal scale. This is illustrated in Figure 8-2.

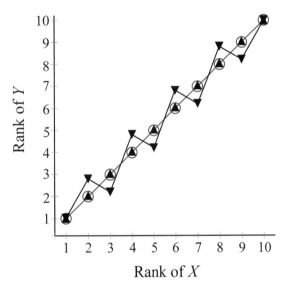

Figure 8-2 Scatter plot showing the continuous variables from Figure 8-1 when they are represented by their relative ranks. Now, both the circles (linear on the continuous scale) and the ▲s (changing magnitude on the continuous scale) represent perfect direct associations on an ordinal scale ($r_S=1.00$). The ▼s (changing direction on the continuous scale), however, have an imperfect association on an ordinal scale. This is because the ordinal scale has information about direction but not magnitude of an association.

So, a correlation coefficient for ordinal variables should take only the direction of change in dependent variable values into account. There are several correlation coefficients that satisfy this criterion, but the one that is used most often in analysis of health research data is called **Spearman's correlation coefficient**. This correlation coefficient is the one that is most similar to Pearson's correlation coefficient, but is not influenced by the magnitude of changes in dependent variable values. In fact, Spearman's correlation coefficient can be calculated using the same equation that is used to calculate Pearson's correlation coefficient (Equation 7.19), substituting the ranks of the data values for the actual values of the data on the continuous scale. If there are no tied ranks,[4] Spearman's correlation coefficient is easier to calculate using the following shortcut equation:[5]

---

[4]Recall from Chapter 5 that the term "tied ranks" refers to two (or more) data values that are equal to the same value on the continuous scale. Each of those observations is assigned the mean of the ranks that they would be assigned if they had close, but not identical, values.

[5]If there are tied ranks, the "shortcut" is fairly complicated. In that circumstance, it is easier to use Equation 7.19, substituting the ranks for the data values.

$$\rho_S \stackrel{\triangle}{=} r_S = 1 - \frac{6 \cdot \sum d_i^2}{n \cdot (n^2 - 1)} \qquad \{8.1\}$$

where

ρ_S	=	population's value of Spearman's correlation coefficient
r_S	=	sample's estimate of Spearman's correlation coefficient
d_i	=	difference between the rank of the dependent variable and the rank of the independent variable for the ith observation
n	=	sample's size

Soon, we will look at how Spearman's correlation coefficient can be estimated using this shortcut formula, but before we do, let us consider how we can interpret its numeric value.

To begin, let us recall from Chapter 7 how Pearson's correlation coefficient is interpreted. Pearson's correlation coefficient (r) is converted to a coefficient of variation (R^2) by squaring it. Then, the coefficient of variation is interpreted as the proportion of variation in the dependent variable that is associated with variation in the independent variable. Since Spearman's correlation coefficient is the same as Pearson's correlation coefficient, except that it is calculated from the ranks of the data, interpretation of Spearman's correlation coefficient is easier if we square it. Then, we can interpret the square of Spearman's correlation as the degree of association between the variables on an ordinal scale.[6]

Another aspect of the interpretation of Spearman's correlation coefficient is how it compares with the value of Pearson's correlation coefficient calculated on the same data. Usually, Spearman's correlation coefficient will be close to or larger (in either a positive or negative direction) than Pearson's correlation coefficient. Keeping in mind that Pearson's correlation coefficient reflects the consistency in the change of magnitude of the dependent variable while Spearman's correlation coefficient is not affected by the magnitude of changes, we can interpret the relative values of these two correlation coefficients as a reflection of the consistency of the change in magnitude of the dependent variable. When the two correlation coefficients are close in value, this suggests that the magnitude of change of the dependent variable is consistent. In other words, this suggests that the relationship between the dependent and independent variables is linear. If the value of Spearman's correlation coefficient is larger (in absolute magnitude) than the value of Pearson's correlation coefficient, however, this indicates that Pearson's correlation coefficient is

---

[6]Strictly speaking, the square of Spearman's correlation indicates the proportion of variance in the ranks of the dependent variable that is associated with variation in the ranks of the independent variable.

affected by inconsistencies in the change in magnitude of the dependent variable.[7] That will be the case when the relationship between the variables is not linear. This is illustrated by the ▲s in Figures 8-1 and 8-2.

Now, let us take a look at an example of using the shortcut formula to estimate Spearman's correlation coefficient.

Example 8-1 In Example 7-5, we calculated Pearson's correlation coefficient as reflection of the strength of the association between dietary sodium intake and mean arterial blood pressure in a sample of 30 persons. That correlation coefficient was equal to 0.818. Now, let us use the shortcut formula (Equation {8.1}) to estimate Spearman's correlation coefficient for these data.

To begin, we need to convert the data for both the independent and dependent variables to an ordinal scale. This is done by representing the data values with their relative ranks. This process is illustrated in the following table:

Patient	Dietary Sodium (X_i)	Rank of X_i	Arterial Pressure (Y_i)	Rank of Y_i	d_i	d_i^2
TH	1.0	1.0	78.0	5.5	-4.5	20.25
ER	2.3	2.0	93.0	8.5	-6.5	42.25
EI	2.9	3.0	75.0	4.0	-1.0	1.00
SN	5.2	4.0	97.0	10.0	-6.0	36.00
OT	5.4	5.0	62.0	1.0	4.0	16.00
HI	5.5	6.0	115.0	15.5	-9.5	90.25
NG	7.0	7.0	72.0	2.0	5.0	25.00
ON	8.4	8.0	93.0	8.5	-0.5	0.25
EA	9.0	9.0	74.0	3.0	6.0	36.00
RT	10.5	10.0	108.0	13.0	-3.0	9.00
HL	11.8	11.0	78.0	5.5	5.5	30.25
IK	13.3	12.0	92.0	7.0	5.0	25.00
EA	13.8	13.0	115.0	15.5	-2.5	6.25
NI	14.2	14.0	127.0	21.0	-7.0	49.00
CE	15.1	15.0	100.0	11.0	4.0	16.00
RE	16.9	16.0	101.0	12.0	4.0	16.00
GR	18.8	17.0	128.0	22.0	-5.0	25.00
ES	19.8	18.0	142.0	26.0	-8.0	64.00
SI	20.0	19.0	110.0	14.0	16.0	256.00

---

[7]Sometimes, Pearson's correlation coefficient is larger (i.e., farther from zero) than Spearman's correlation coefficient. When this happens, it is because there is quite a bit of variation of independent variable values. For instance, this occurs when only extreme values of the independent variable are represented in the sample.

ON	20.2	20.0	136.0	24.0	-5.0	25.00
TO	22.0	21.0	144.0	27.5	-7.5	56.25
CH	22.1	22.0	124.0	18.5	2.5	6.25
EE	23.3	23.0	140.0	25.0	-3.0	9.00
RS	24.1	24.0	126.0	20.0	3.0	9.00
TA	25.5	25.0	144.0	27.5	-3.5	12.25
TI	25.8	26.0	116.0	17.0	8.0	64.00
ST	27.8	27.0	152.0	29.0	-3.0	9.00
IC	28.0	28.0	124.0	18.5	8.5	72.25
IA	28.9	29.0	164.0	30.0	-2.0	4.00
NS	29.2	30..0	130.0	23.0	6.0	36.00
Total						1,068.50

Now, let us use Equation {8.1} to estimate Spearman's correlation coefficient.

$$\rho_s \triangleq r_s = 1 - \frac{6 \cdot \sum d_i^2}{n \cdot (n^2 - 1)} = 1 - \frac{6 \cdot 1,068.50}{30 \cdot (30^2 - 1)} = 0.762$$

In these data, there are five pairs of tied ranks. The presence of these tied ranks makes the estimate derived from the shortcut formula a biased estimate. Specifically, the estimate is closer to zero than is the actual value of Spearman's correlation coefficient. If we were to use a method that corrects for these tied ranks, we would get 0.810; a value much closer to Pearson's correlation coefficient estimated for these data (0.818).

We can use the method demonstrated in Example 8-1 if we need to estimate Spearman's correlation coefficient manually. In practice, however, we will be using a computer program to estimate Spearman's correlation coefficient. There are two ways in which we can use a computer to estimate Spearman's correlation coefficient. If you are using software that calculates Pearson's correlation coefficient, but not Spearman's correlation coefficient (e.g., calculators, spreadsheets, etc.), Spearman's correlation coefficient can be calculated by changing the variables to ranks and calculating Pearson's correlation coefficient for those ranks. The result will be the estimate of Spearman's correlation coefficient. The other way is by using software that will calculate Spearman's correlation coefficient directly from continuous data. SAS will do this by using the SPEARMAN option in the CORR procedure. Example 8-2 shows the result of using SAS to calculate Spearman's correlation coefficient for the data in Example 8-1.

Example 8-2 In Example 8-1, we were told that the sample's estimate of Spearman's correlation coefficient is equal to 0.810 (when correcting for tied ranks). This value came from SAS's CORR procedure when Spearman's correlation analysis was specifically selected (the default is Pearson's analysis). Let us take a look at this output.

The following is the result of analyzing the data in Example 8-1 using the CORR procedure:

```
                         The CORR Procedure

                  2  Variables:    DBP      NA

                        Simple Statistics

Variable      N        Mean      Std Dev         Sum      Minimum      Maximum
DBP          30   112.00000     26.77621        3360     62.00000    164.00000
NA           30    15.92667      8.77740     477.80000     1.00000     29.20000


              Spearman Correlation Coefficients, N = 30
                     Prob > |r| under HO: Rho=0

                            DBP             NA
                DBP     1.00000        0.80979
                                        <.0001
                 NA     0.80979        1.00000
                         <.0001
```

This output looks very much like the output we saw in Example 7-7 when we asked for Pearson's correlation analysis. As in that output, the intersection of a row and a column in the correlation matrix provides the estimate of the correlation coefficient (here, Spearman's correlation coefficient) and the P-value testing the null hypothesis that the correlation coefficient is equal to zero in the population. The P-value in the output is equal to "<.0001" (i.e., less than the smallest P-value SAS will print), so we can reject the null hypothesis that the correlation coefficient is equal to zero in the population. In other words, we can conclude that, as dietary sodium intake increases, so does diastolic blood pressure.

If we estimate Spearman's correlation coefficient using a computer program that does not provide a P-value (e.g., a spreadsheet), we can test the null hypothesis that it is equal to zero in the population by using a statistical table. The next example shows how this is done.

Example 8-3 In Example 8-1, we used the shortcut formula to estimate Spearman's correlation coefficient to reflect the strength of the association on an ordinal scale between dietary sodium intake and mean arterial blood pressure in a sample of 30 persons. That estimate was equal to 0.76 (not correcting for ties). Now, let us use a statistical table to test the null hypothesis that Spearman's correlation coefficient in the population is equal to zero.

We use Table B.5 to test this null hypothesis. Across the top of the table are one- and two-sided values of α. Sample sizes are listed down the left-most column. In the body of the table are the corresponding values of Spearman's correlation coefficient. The easiest way to use this table is to find the critical value for the correlation coefficient by identifying the row that corresponds to our sample's size ($n = 30$) and the column that corresponds to our selected value of α ($α(2) = 0.05$). Where this row and column intersect, the critical value of Spearman's correlation coefficient is found.

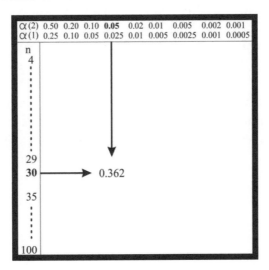

The critical value is equal to 0.362. Since our calculated value (0.76) is greater than the critical value (0.362), we can reject the null hypothesis that there is no association between dietary sodium intake and mean arterial blood pressure in the population.

In Chapter 7, we learned that the correlation coefficient in the sample can be assumed to estimate the correlation coefficient in the population only if the distribution of independent variable values in the sample represents their distribution in the population. A sample in which this is true is called a "naturalistic" sample. This principle applies to Spearman's correlation coefficient just as it does to Pearson's correlation coefficient. Thus, Spearman's correlation analysis should be used only when a naturalistic sample has been taken.

NOMINAL INDEPENDENT VARIABLE

When the independent variable represents nominal data, that independent variable divides dependent variable values into two groups. The purpose, then, is to compare those two groups. When we had a continuous dependent variable (i.e., in Chapter 7), we compared the means of the two groups by estimating their difference and by testing the null hypothesis that the difference between the means is equal to zero in the population. Student's t test was used to test this null hypothesis. The commonly used nonparametric tests that parallel Student's t test are the **Mann-Whitney test** and the **Wilcoxon Rank Sum test**.

Both the Mann-Whitney test and the Wilcoxon Rank Sum test begin by converting the dependent variable values to an ordinal scale by ranking them. This ranking of dependent variable values is done without regard to which group the dependent variable values belong. We will see how this is done in the next example, but before we do, we need to learn how to calculate and interpret statistics associated with each of those tests.

Calculations are easier for the Wilcoxon Rank Sum test. All that is required is to add the ranks of the dependent variable values separately for each of the two groups of dependent variable values. An unusual feature of the Wilcoxon Rank Sum test is that P-values get smaller for smaller values of the test statistic. Most statistics have just the opposite relationship with P-values: as those test statistics get larger, the P-values get smaller.[8]

The Mann-Whitney test gives us the same answer as the Wilcoxon Rank Sum test, except that the Mann-Whitney test uses the sums of ranks in a calculation that produces a test statistic (U) that behaves as most test statistics do; namely, the P-value gets smaller as the test statistic gets bigger. Equation {8.2} illustrates that calculation:

$$U = (n_1 \cdot n_2) + \frac{n_1 \cdot (n_1 + 1)}{2} - R_1 \qquad \{8.2\}$$

where

U = Mann-Whitney test statistic

n_1 = number of observations in group 1 (chosen arbitrarily)

n_2 = number of observations in group 2

R_1 = sum of the ranks of the dependent variable values in group 1

The choice of which group is considered to be group 1 in Equation {8.2} is arbitrary, but that choice affects the value of U. When we are performing a two-sided test, the Mann-Whitney test statistic is calculated both ways and then the larger of the two values is compared to the critical value in a table of Mann-Whitney test statistics. To calculate the second value of U, Equation {8.2} can be used again, or the following shortcut formula can be used:

$$U' = (n_1 \cdot n_2) - U \qquad \{8.3\}$$

---

[8]This is also true for the Wilcoxon Signed Rank test that we encountered as the nonparametric parallel to the paired t test in Chapter 4. There is no commonly used alternative to the Wilcoxon Signed Rank test, but the Mann-Whitney test is a common alternative to the Wilcoxon Rank Sum test.

where

U' = Mann-Whitney test statistic value when the second group of dependent variable values is considered to be group 1

n_1 = number of observations in group 1

n_2 = number of observations in group 2

U = Mann-Whitney test statistic from Equation {8.2}

Now, let us take a look at an example of how to perform and interpret this nonparametric parallel to Student's t test.

Example 8-4 Suppose that we were to compare blood pressure values between 12 persons who received a new medication intended to lower blood pressure and 8 persons who received standard therapy. Imagine that we were to observe the following results from that study:

New	Standard
130	137
114	130
121	143
127	146
115	134
124	150
113	142
110	138
126	
116	
125	
119	

Let us use these data to test the null hypothesis that blood pressure is the same in the two treatment groups.

To begin, we need to convert the blood pressure values to an ordinal scale. We do that by ranking the dependent variable values from both groups. This is illustrated in the next table:

New	Rank	Standard	Rank
130	12.5	137	15
114	3	130	12.5
121	7	143	18
127	11	146	19
115	4	134	14
124	8	150	20
113	2	142	17
110	1	138	16
126	10	Total	131.5
116	5		
125	9		
119	6		
Total	78.5		

The sums of the ranks are equal to 78.5 in the new treatment group and 131.5 for the standard treatment group. If we were performing the Wilcoxon Rank Sum test, we would compare the smaller of those sums (i.e., 78.5) to values in a table of Wilcoxon Rank Sum test statistics. Alternatively, we can use those sums in Equation {8.2} to calculate the Mann-Whitney test statistic. Choosing the new treatment group as group 1, we get:

$$U = (n_1 \cdot n_2) + \frac{n_1 \cdot (n_1 + 1)}{2} - R_1 = (12 \cdot 8) + \frac{12 \cdot 13}{2} - 78.5 = 95.5$$

The value of 95.5 is obtained if we arbitrarily assign the new treatment group to be group 1. If we had assigned the standard treatment group as group 1, we would have gotten the following test statistic (using Equation {8.3}:

$$U' = (n_1 \cdot n_2) - U = (12 \cdot 8) - 95.5 = 0.5$$

For a two-sided test, we select the larger of those two test statistics (95.5). Then, we compare that calculated value to the corresponding value in a table of Mann-Whitney U statistics (e.g., Table B.6).

Table B.6 has in its left-most column the number of observations in each of the two groups of dependent variable values. These are listed under the headings "n_S" and "n_L." "n_S" corresponds to the group with the fewer observations and "n_L" corresponds to the group with the greater number of observations. In this example, the standard treatment group has 8 observations and the new treatment group has 12 observations. Thus, we need to find the row that has 8 in the "n_S" column and 12 in the "n_L" column. The critical value of the U statistic is in that row and in the column corresponding to a two-sided α of 0.05. This value is equal to 74.

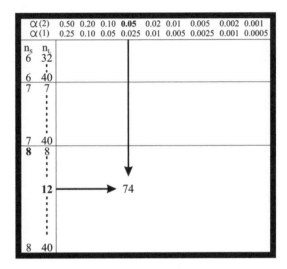

Since the calculated value of U (95.5) is greater than the value from the table (74), we can reject the null hypothesis and accept, through the process of elimination, the alternative hypothesis that the blood pressure is not the same in the two groups

Even though the calculations involved in nonparametric tests are relatively easy to do by hand, it is even easier to let the computer do them for us. In SAS, the Wilcoxon Rank Sum and Mann-Whitney tests are done in the NPAR1WAY procedure. Example 8-5 shows the result of analyzing the data in Example 8-4.

Example 8-5 Let us use SAS's NPAR1WAY procedure to analyze the data presented in Example 8-4.

```
                        The NPAR1WAY Procedure

                Wilcoxon Scores (Rank Sums) for Variable BP
                       Classified by Variable GROUP

                          Sum of     Expected      Std Dev         Mean
    GROUP         N       Scores     Under H0      Under H0        Score
    ─────────────────────────────────────────────────────────────────────
    New          12        78.50       126.0      12.956608      6.541667
    Standard      8       131.50        84.0      12.956608     16.437500

                   Average scores were used for ties.
```

```
                      Wilcoxon Two-Sample Test

                Statistic              131.5000

                      Normal Approximation
                Z                        3.6275
                One-Sided Pr >  Z        0.0001
                Two-Sided Pr >  |Z|      0.0003

                        t Approximation
                One-Sided Pr >  Z        0.0009
                Two-Sided Pr >  |Z|      0.0018

          Z includes a continuity correction of 0.5.

                      Kruskal-Wallis Test

                Chi-Square               13.4402
                DF                             1
                Pr > Chi-Square          0.0002
```

SAS has performed the Wilcoxon rank-sum test. The "Statistic" is the sum of the ranks (see Example 8-4). The P-values provided are for two approximations. This is not ideal, since we are probably using this nonparametric analysis because the sample is too small for us to be comfortable assuming that the sampling distribution is Gaussian. The output also provides the results of the Kruskal-Wallis test. This gives us the same result as the Wilcoxon rank-sum test and the Mann-Whitney test, but it can be used to compare more than two groups of dependent variable values.[9] The P-value for the Kruskal-Wallis test (0.0002) is probably the best choice for the Wilcoxon rank-sum test or the Mann-Whitney test.

The next chapter is the last one on bivariable analysis. It discusses bivariable analysis of a nominal dependent variable.

---

[9]We will see the Kruskal-Wallis test again when we consider multivariable analysis of an ordinal dependent variable (Chapter 11).

CHAPTER 9
Bivariable Analysis of a Nominal Dependent Variable

Nominal data, which can only be equal to either of two possible values, are the simplest type of data we encounter in health research. Even so, Flowchart 7 reveals a greater diversity of bivariable statistical methods for nominal dependent variables than we have seen for either continuous or ordinal dependent variables. The reason for this diversity is the simplicity of nominal data. Because nominal data are comparatively simple, we understand these data better than other types of data. This better understanding allows us to interpret nominal dependent variables in a variety of ways. We will find this to be true especially when the independent variable also represents nominal data.

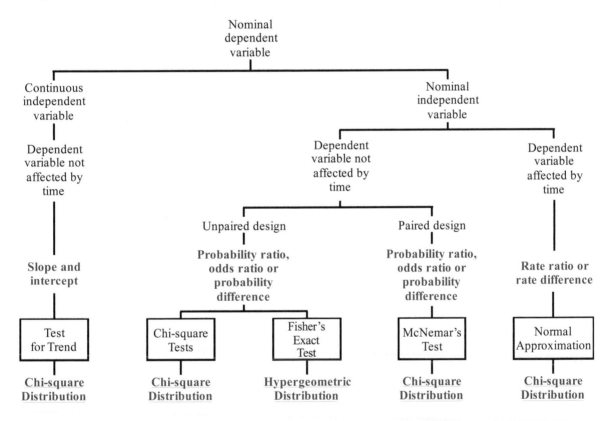

Flowchart 7 Flowchart showing bivariable analysis of a nominal dependent variable. The point estimate that is most often used to describe the dependent variable is in color. The common name of the statistical test is enclosed in a box. The standard distributions that are used to test hypotheses and calculate confidence intervals are in color and underlined.

CONTINUOUS INDEPENDENT VARIABLE

When we are analyzing a set of data that has a nominal dependent variable and a continuous independent variable, our interest most often is in estimating the probability of the event addressed by the dependent variable (e.g., probability of cure) along the continuum of independent variable values (e.g., dose of medication). Figure 9-1 illustrates this sort of relationship graphically:

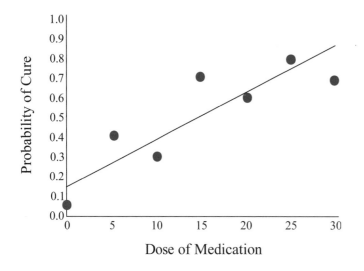

Figure 9-1 Scatter plot showing the relationship between a nominal dependent variable and a continuous independent variable.

The implication in Figure 9-1 is that the relationship between the nominal dependent variable and the continuous independent variable is a linear (i.e., straight-line) one. This is not the only possible relationship, but it is the one that is assumed by the **test for trend**, a statistical method that is often used to describe how the probability of the event represented by a nominal dependent variable changes as the value of a continuous independent variable changes. Mathematically, this relationship can be described as shown in Equation{9.1}.

$$\theta = \alpha + \beta X \qquad \{9.1\}$$

where

θ = probability of the event in the population when the independent variable is equal to X

α = population's intercept of the line, indicating the probability of the event when the continuous independent is equal to zero in the population

β = population's slope of the line, indicating how much the probability of the event changes as the value of the independent variable increases by one unit

X = value of the independent variable

Other than the fact that the dependent variable is represented by θ instead of by μ, Equation {9.1} looks like the population's regression equation we considered for a continuous dependent variable and a continuous independent variable in Chapter 7 (Equation {7.1}). Namely, dependent variable values are equal to the intercept plus the slope times the value of the independent variable.

Estimation

Not only does Equation {9.1} look like a regression equation, but the parameters of that equation are estimated from the sample's observations in the same way in which we estimate the parameters of a linear regression line. Specifically, we use the method of least squares, which minimizes the squared differences between observed and estimated values of the dependent variable.

An important difference between a continuous dependent variable and a nominal dependent variable is that a continuous dependent variable represents quantitative information (i.e., numeric magnitude), while a nominal dependent variable represents qualitative information (i.e., categories). A regression equation estimates the numeric magnitude of the dependent variable. Thus, to have a regression equation that relates to a nominal dependent variable, that nominal dependent variable must be represented numerically.

There are two ways to satisfy this need for a numeric representation of a nominal variable. One is to make multiple observations of the nominal dependent variable for each distinct value of the independent variable. Then, the number of times the event is observed among those multiple observations can be expressed as the probability of the event occurring when the independent variable is equal to that specific value. This approach is illustrated in the following example.

Example 9-1 Suppose that the data in Figure 9.1 are from a study in which we are interested in the probability that an infection is cured for different doses of an antibiotic. In this study, we randomly assign 10 persons to each of 7 doses of the antibiotic (1, 5, 10, 15, 20, 25, 30 mg. Imagine that observed the following results:

Dose in mg (X)	Number of persons observed (n)	Number of persons cured (a)
1	10	1
5	10	4
10	10	3
15	10	7
20	10	6
25	10	8
30	10	9

From these results, let us calculate the probability of being cured for each of the seven groups of observations.

The probability of having the event represented by a nominal dependent variable is calculated in the same way that we calculated univariable probabilities in Chapter 6 (Equation 6.2). These calculations are summarized in the following table:

Dose in mg (X)	Number of persons observed (n)	Number of persons cured (a)	Probability of cure (p)
1	10	1	0.1
5	10	4	0.4
10	10	3	0.3
15	10	7	0.7
20	10	6	0.6
25	10	8	0.8
30	10	9	0.9

The probabilities of being cured in this table correspond to the ●s in Figure 9.1.

When this approach is used to represent a nominal dependent variable quantitatively, the sample's estimates of the slope and the intercept of the equation describing the association between the nominal dependent variable and the continuous independent variable (i.e., Equation {9.1}) are calculated as shown in Equations {9.2} and {9.3}, respectively.

$$\beta \triangleq b = \frac{\sum n_i \cdot (p_i - \bar{p}) \cdot (X_i - \bar{X})}{\sum n_i \cdot (X_i - \bar{X})^2} \qquad \{9.2\}$$

where

β =   population's slope

b =   sample's estimate of the slope

n_i =   number of observations in the ith group

p_i =   probability of the event in the ith group

$\bar{p}$ =   probability of the event in all groups combined

X_i =   independent variable value in the ith group

$$\overline{X} = \text{mean of the independent variable values in all groups combined}$$

$$\alpha \triangleq a = \overline{p} - b\overline{X} \qquad \{9.3\}$$

where

α = population's intercept

a = sample's estimate of the intercept

The next example shows how this method can be used to estimate the slope and the intercept of the straight line equation that describes the relationship between a nominal dependent variable and a continuous independent variable.

Example 9-2 Let us estimate the parameters of the equation that describes the relationship between the probability of an infection being cured and the dose of an antibiotic for the data in Example 9-1.

To begin, we need to estimate the mean of the independent variable values and the overall probability of the event. In preparation, we need to add up the number of events, the number of observations, and the product of the number of observations and the values of the independent variable (we need this product to calculate the mean of the independent variable values because each group has n_i observations of its independent variable value). The following table summarizes these calculations.

Dose in mg (X_i)	Number of persons observed (n_i)	Number of persons cured (a_i)	Probability of cure (p_i)	$X_i \cdot n_i$
1	10	1	0.1	10
5	10	4	0.4	50
10	10	3	0.3	100
15	10	7	0.7	150
20	10	6	0.6	200
25	10	8	0.8	250
30	10	9	0.9	300
Total	70	38		1,060

Now, we can estimate the mean of the independent variable values:

$$\bar{X} = \frac{\sum n_i \cdot X_i}{\sum n_i} = \frac{1,060}{70} = 15.14 \text{ mg}$$

and the overall probability of the event:

$$\bar{p} = \frac{\sum a_i}{\sum n_i} = \frac{38}{70} = 0.54$$

Next, we use these two estimates to calculate the values we will need to estimate the slope and the intercept. The following table summarizes these calculations:

X_i	n_i	a_i	p_i	$X_i - \bar{X}$	$p_i - \bar{p}$	$n_i \cdot (X_i - \bar{X}) \cdot (p_i - \bar{p})$	$n_i \cdot (X_i - \bar{X})^2$
1	10	1	0.1	-14.14	-0.44	62.63	2,000.20
5	10	4	0.4	-10.14	-0.14	14.49	1,028.78
10	10	3	0.3	-5.14	-0.24	12.49	264.49
15	10	7	0.7	-0.14	0.16	-0.22	0.20
20	10	6	0.6	4.86	0.06	2.78	235.92
25	10	8	0.8	9.86	0.26	25.35	971.63
30	10	9	0.9	14.86	0.36	53.06	2,207.35
Total	70	38				170.57	6,708.57

Now, we are ready to use Equations {9.2} and {9.3} to estimate the slope and the intercept.

$$\beta \overset{\wedge}{=} b = \frac{\sum n_i \cdot (p_i - \bar{p}) \cdot (X_i - \bar{X})}{\sum n_i \cdot (X_i - \bar{X})^2} = \frac{170.57}{6,708.57} = 0.025$$

$$\alpha \overset{\wedge}{=} a = \bar{p} - b\bar{X} = 0.54 - (0.025 \cdot 15.14) = 0.158$$

These estimates of the slope and intercept can be used to estimate the probability of being cured for a particular dose. To make an estimate, the dose is substituted for X in the following equation (this is the sample's estimate of Equation {9.1}).

$$\theta = \alpha + \beta X \overset{\wedge}{=} \hat{p} = a + bX = 0.158 + (0.025 \cdot X)$$

Thus, for a dose of 7.5 mg, we would expect to see the following proportion of the people treated with that dose to be cured.

$$\hat{p} = a + bX = 0.158 + (0.025 \cdot 7.5) = 0.35$$

In other words, we estimate that 35% of the people receiving a dose of 7.5 mg will be cured.

We have taken a look at one way in which we can estimate the slope and intercept of the straight line equation we use in the test for trend to describe the relationship between a nominal dependent variable and a continuous independent variable. That way was to represent the nominal dependent variable as the probability of the event occurring in a group of persons all of whom have the same, specific value of the continuous independent variable (e.g., they all have the same dose of medication). Another way is to represent the nominal dependent variable numerically and, then use the same methods that were used in Chapter 7 to estimate the slope and the intercept for a continuous dependent variable.

The trick in this approach is to pick numeric values for the nominal dependent variable that are qualitative and not quantitative. We cannot represent the nominal dependent variable with numbers that convey any quantitative value, because nominal data are not quantitative. We cannot say, for instance, that having the event is twice the value used for not having the event. Instead, we need to select numeric values that separate those observations in which the event occurs from those observations in which the event does not occur.

The key to solving this problem is to use zero to represent one value of the nominal dependent variable and to use the number one to represent the other value. When we do this, the numeric variable that represents the nominal variable is called an **indicator** or **dummy variable**. If we represent the nominal dependent variable with an indicator variable, then we can use linear regression calculations to estimate the slope and the intercept. This approach will give us exactly the same estimates as those obtained using the first method.[1]

If we are using a computer to estimate the slope and intercept for us, this second method becomes important. SAS, like most statistical packages, does not have a straightforward method for the test for trend. Instead, we can use a regression procedure (e.g., REG) while representing the dependent variable with an indicator variable. The next example shows the result of using this approach for the data in Examples 9-1 and 9-2.

Example 9-3 Let us use SAS to estimate the slope and intercept as part of a test for trend. To do this, we represent being cured with an indicator variable equal to one and not being cured with that indicator variable equal to zero. Then, we use SAS's REG procedure with the indicator variable as the dependent variable and observe the following output:

---

[1]This second approach is the same as the first approach with each "group" containing only one observation. If the observation is an event, the probability of having the event in that "group" is equal to one. If the observation is not an event, the probability of having the event in that "group" is equal to zero. Then, Equations 9.2 and 9.3 become identical to Equations 7.4 and 7.6, which were used to estimate the slope and the intercept for a continuous dependent variable.

```
                            The REG Procedure
                            Model: MODEL1
                       Dependent Variable: CURE
                       Frequency: GROUP_SIZE

                          Analysis of Variance

                                Sum of          Mean
Source                  DF      Squares        Square     F Value    Pr > F
Model                   1       4.33693       4.33693      22.63     <.0001
Error                   68     13.03450       0.19168
Corrected Total         69     17.37143


            Root MSE              0.43782    R-Square     0.2497
            Dependent Mean        0.54286    Adj R-Sq     0.2386
            Coeff Var            80.65051

                          Parameter Estimates

                    Parameter      Standard
Variable     DF     Estimate         Error     t Value    Pr > |t|
Intercept    1       0.15784       0.09639       1.64      0.1061
DOSE         1       0.02543       0.00535       4.76      <.0001
```

Most of information in this output is not applicable to analysis of a nominal dependent variable, but the estimates of the intercept and slope are the same as those calculated in the test for trend in Example 9-2.

The *t*-values in the output in Example 9-3 that test the null hypotheses that the slope or intercept are equal to zero in the population are not interpretable for a nominal dependent variable. Similarly, the *F*-ratio that tests the omnibus null hypothesis is not interpretable for a nominal dependent variable.[2] Instead, we need to use a special procedure to test these null hypotheses. This procedure is what we will consider next.

Hypothesis Testing

Although the methods for estimating the slope and the intercept in the test for trend are the same as the methods used for regression analysis of a continuous dependent variable, the method for testing hypotheses is not the same. When we discussed regression analysis in

---

[2]The reason that these tests are inappropriate for a nominal dependent variable is that both the *t* and *F* distributions take into account the role of chance in estimating the variance of dependent variable values in the population. With a nominal dependent variable, however, there is no independent role of chance in estimating the variance. This was addressed in Chapter 6 where we discussed the normal approximation to the binomial.

Chapter 7, one method of hypothesis testing we encountered used an F ratio to compare the model mean square (the average explained variation in the dependent variable) to the error mean square (the average unexplained variation in the dependent variable) as shown in Equation 7.17. The F-ratio, however, cannot be applied to a nominal dependent variable.[3]

The null hypothesis that is of interest in the test for trend is that the independent variable does not help estimate the probability of the event. This is parallel to the omnibus null hypothesis in regression analysis.[4] The way in which we test this null hypothesis for a nominal dependent variable is by comparing the amount of variation in the dependent variable values that is explained by the relationship with the independent variable to the univariable (i.e., "total") variance of dependent variable values. These values are the same as the model sum of squares and the total mean square in regression analysis. They are compared as a ratio, but it is not an F ratio. Instead it is a **chi-square** statistic. Equation {9.4} shows us how this chi-square statistic is calculated from the output of the REG procedure[5] or when groups of observations are made for each value of the independent variable.

$$\chi^2 = \frac{\sum n_i \cdot (\hat{p}_i - \overline{p})^2}{\overline{p} \cdot (1 - \overline{p})} = \frac{\text{Model Sum of Squares}}{\text{Total Mean Square}} = \frac{\text{Model Sum of Squares}}{\dfrac{\text{Total Sum of Squares}}{\text{Total Degrees of Freedom}}} \quad \{9.4\}$$

where

χ^2 = chi-square statistic

n_i = number of observations in the ith group

$\hat{p}_i$ = estimated probability of the event in the ith group

p_i = observed probability of the event in the ith group

---

[3]To use a single value for the unexplained variation in the dependent variable (i.e., a single error mean square) requires the assumption that the unexplained variation is the same regardless of the value of the independent variable. This is the assumption of homoscedasticity. When we learned about the normal approximation to the binomial in Chapter 6, however, we found that the variation of a nominal dependent variable changes as the probability of the event changes. Thus, it does not make sense to assume homoscedasticity in hypothesis testing for a nominal dependent variable.

[4]Recall from Chapter 7 that the test of the omnibus null hypothesis in bivariable regression analysis is the same as testing the null hypothesis that the slope is equal to zero in the population. The same is true when the dependent variable represents nominal data. The test of this parallel hypothesis also tests the null hypothesis that the slope in Equation 9.1 is equal to zero.

[5]This hypothesis test can also performed in the FREQ procedure, but the FREQ procedure does not provide estimates of the slope and intercept and it uses the ranks of the independent variable values as if they were continuous data, instead of their actual values. We recommend that the REG procedure be used instead.

$$\bar{p} \quad = \quad \text{overall probability of the event (for all groups combined)}$$

The chi-square distribution is a member of the Gaussian family of standard statistical distributions. This is the fourth member of that family that we have encountered.[6] The first of these was the standard normal distribution, which is a Gaussian distribution with a mean equal to zero and a standard deviation equal to one (Chapter 2). The chi-square distribution comes from the standard normal distribution, but is distinguished from it by two features. First, the chi-square values are the square of standard normal deviates.[7] This is to prevent the occurrence of negative values. Second, an additional parameter is added to the mean and standard deviation of the standard normal distribution. This parameter is called degrees of freedom. These degrees of freedom reflect how much information the sample contains for estimation of the probability of the event. That amount of information is equal to the number of independent variables. In bivariable analysis, we have only one independent variable. Thus, the number of degrees of freedom for chi-square statistics in bivariable analysis is equal to one.[8]

Now, we are ready to take a look at an example of how we can perform hypothesis testing in the test for trend.

Example 9-4 Let us test the null hypothesis that knowing a patient's dose of antibiotic does not help to estimate the probability that the patient's infection will be cured. As an alternative hypothesis, let us consider that knowing the dose does help estimate the probability of cure. Also, suppose that we are willing to take a 5% chance of making a type I error.

To calculate the chi-square statistic in Equation{9.4}, we need the model sum of squares, total sum of squares, and total degrees of freedom. From the output in Example 9-3, we know that these values are 4.33693, 17.37143, and 69 respectively. Substituting these values in Equation{9.4}, we get the following result:

$$\chi^2 = \frac{\text{Model Sum of Squares}}{\dfrac{\text{Total Sum of Squares}}{\text{Total Degrees of Freedom}}} = \frac{4.33693}{\dfrac{17.37143}{69}} = 17.23$$

---

[6]The other members of the Gaussian that we have encountered are the standard normal, Student's t distribution, and the F distribution.

[7]We encountered this feature in Chapter 6 when we looked at output from proc FREQ to test the null hypothesis that the proportion of persons in the population preferring one thing over another is equal to 0.5.

[8]This is the same as the degrees of freedom in the numerator of the F-ratio used to test the omnibus hypothesis in regression analysis with a continuous dependent variable (Equation 7.17).

To evaluate a chi-square statistic, we compare our calculated value to a value in a table of the chi-square distribution that corresponds to a two-sided α and one degree of freedom. Table B.7 is such a table. From that table, we find that the critical value of chi-square is equal to 3.841.

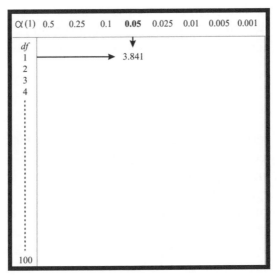

Since the calculated chi-square value (17.23) is greater than the critical value (3.841), we can reject the null hypothesis that knowing dose does not help us estimate the probability of cure and accept, through the process of elimination, the alternative hypothesis that knowing the dose helps estimate the probability of cure.

NOMINAL INDEPENDENT VARIABLE

A look at Flowchart 7 reveals that there are a variety of methods for estimation and inference when both the dependent and independent variables represent nominal data. The choice of methods is determined in part by whether or not the nominal dependent variable is affected by time. What it means for a nominal dependent variable to be affected by time was discussed in Chapter 6, when we were thinking about univariable analysis of a nominal dependant variable. In essence, we use rates, rather than probabilities, to represent events when more events are observed the longer we look for them and if we have looked longer in some cases than in others. In the current chapter, we will begin by thinking about dependent variables that are not affected by time and, then we will see how these methods apply to nominal dependent variables affected by time.

DEPENDENT VARIABLE NOT AFFECTED BY TIME: UNPAIRED DESIGN

When the independent variable represents nominal data and the nominal dependent variable is not affected by time, there is another distinction between the statistical methods we use. This is whether or not the data were collected in a paired or in an unpaired design. The choice of design affects hypothesis testing and some estimation processes. First, we will consider the unpaired design. Then, we will see how a paired design affects these statistical methods.

Estimation

A nominal independent variable has the effect of dividing dependent variable values into two groups; we want to compare estimates of the population's parameters between these groups. When the nominal dependent variable is not affected by time, the parameter estimates we compare are probabilities or related measures.

In Chapter 7, we compared means by looking at the difference between two means. The reason that we took this approach is that differences between means are easier for the statistician to consider than are ratios of means. The same is true of probabilities: differences between probabilities are easier for the statistician than are ratios of probabilities. Even so, we often wish to compare two probabilities by looking at their ratio, especially when these probabilities are measures of disease frequency (i.e., prevalence or risk).

The reason for this interest in ratios is the fact that probabilities that reflect disease frequency are usually small in numeric magnitude. When we take the difference between two small probabilities, the difference is also a small number. Ratios of small probabilities, on the other hand, can be large. For example, suppose that the risk of developing lung cancer during a certain period of time is 0.00001 if you smoke and 0.000001 if you do not smoke. The difference between those probabilities is 0.000009. That gives us a very different perspective on the risk of lung cancer among smokers compared to nonsmokers than if we examined the ratio of these two probabilities. That ratio is equal to 10. That implies that smokers are at 10 times the risk of developing lung cancer than are nonsmokers!

Neither of our choices (a difference or a ratio of probabilities or rates) is the better choice in all applications. Which measure we choose to reflect the relationship between two groups of nominal data depends on the question we are asking.

If we are interested in the <u>actual</u> distinction between two groups of nominal dependent variable values, we should estimate the difference between probabilities or rates. For example, if we wish to determine the practicality of treating two diseases, we would want estimates that reflected both the efficacy of the treatments and the underlying risks of the diseases. In this application, we would be more impressed with the treatment of a disease with a relatively large difference between the probabilities of recovery than we would be for a disease with a small difference, even if the ratios of those probabilities were the same for the two diseases (e.g., probabilities of recovery of 0.000001 and 0.0000001 versus probabilities of recovery of 0.01 and 0.1).

If, on the other hand, we are interested in the <u>relative</u> distinction between two groups of nominal dependent variable values, we should estimate the ratio of probabilities or rates. For example, if we wish to determine how strongly a particular exposure is associated with a disease, we would not want estimates that reflect the underlying frequency of the disease. In this application, it does not matter if the event is rare or common in a particular population, the biologic relationship is the same.

When we have a nominal dependent variable and a nominal independent variable, we have a particular way in which we organize our observations in preparation for analysis. This organization is called a **contingency table** or, more commonly, a **2 × 2 table** (pronounced "2 by 2" table). A 2 × 2 table contains two rows and two columns. Although it is not a rule that is consistently followed in the medical literature, SAS expects columns to correspond to the event (e.g., disease) and the rows to correspond to the groups (e.g., exposure). Table 9-1 shows a general 2 × 2 table set up in that way.

Outcome

	Event	No Event	
Group 1	a	b	a+b
Group 2	c	d	c+d
	a+c	b+d	n

Group

Table 9-1   A general 2 × 2 table for the organization of observations of a nominal dependent variable and a nominal independent variable.   The letters a, b, c, and d represent the frequencies (i.e., counts) of each specific value of the variables. n is the sample's size.

The frequencies in each of the four boxes (called **cells**) in the 2 × 2 table are called the **cell frequencies**. a, b, c, and d represent these cell frequencies. The frequencies on the outside of the 2 × 2 table are called the **marginal frequencies**. Each of the marginal frequencies is equal to the sum of two cell frequencies, except the one in the lower right corner. There, we find the sample's size.

With our observations arranged in a 2 × 2 table, calculation of probabilities and their differences and ratios is rather straightforward. For example, the probability of the event in group 1 is a/(a+b) and the probability of the event in group 2 is c/(c+d). Thus, the difference between and the ratio of two probabilities can be expressed using the notation from a 2 × 2 table as shown in Equations {9.5} and {9.6}, respectively.[9]

$$\text{Probability Difference} = \theta_1 - \theta_2 \triangleq p_1 - p_2 = \frac{a}{a+b} - \frac{c}{c+d} \qquad \{9.5\}$$

where

$\theta_1 - \theta_2$ = difference between the probabilities of the event in the population

$p_1 - p_2$ = difference between the probabilities of the event in the sample

---

[9]These equations assume that the 2 x 2 table is arranged as shown in Table 9-1.

a = number of observations in group 1 with the event

b = number of observations in group 1 without the event

c = number of observations in group 2 with the event

d = number of observations in group 2 without the event

$$\text{Probability Ratio} = \frac{\theta_1}{\theta_2} \triangleq \frac{p_1}{p_2} = \frac{\dfrac{a}{a+b}}{\dfrac{c}{c+d}} \qquad \{9.6\}$$

where

$\dfrac{\theta_1}{\theta_2}$ = ratio of the probabilities of the event in the population

$\dfrac{p_1}{p_2}$ = ratio of the probabilities of the event in the sample

Now, let us take a look at an example in which we calculate and interpret a probability difference and a probability ratio.

Example 9-5 In a clinical trial of a treatment for coronary artery disease, 100 persons were given the experimental treatment and 36 of them died within the study period. In addition, another 100 persons were given the standard treatment and, of those persons, 54 died within the same period of time. Let us compare the risk of dying with the experimental treatment to the risk of dying with the standard treatment.

First, let us organize these observations in a 2 × 2 table:

Outcome

Treatment		Died	Survived	
	Standard	54	46	100
	New	36	64	100
		90	110	200

The risks of death for those two treatment groups are:

$$p(\text{death}|\text{standard treatment}) = \frac{a}{a+b} = \frac{54}{100} = 0.54$$

$$p(\text{death}|\text{new treatment}) = \frac{c}{c+d} = \frac{36}{100} = 0.36$$

We can compare these risks either by examining their difference or by examining their ratio. If we were interested in the practicality of the new treatment (i.e., taking into account the number of lives saved), it would be better to examine the risk difference (Equation {9.5}) than the risk ratio, since the risk difference takes into account the underlying risk of death in coronary artery disease patients.

$$\theta_1 - \theta_2 \triangleq p_1 - p_2 = p(\text{death}|\text{standard treatment}) - p(\text{death}|\text{new treatment}) = 0.54 - 0.36 = 0.18$$

This risk difference tells us that, for every 100 patients treated with the new treatment, 18 (or 18%) more persons will survive the period of time studied than would have survived that period of time if they had been given the standard treatment.

If, on the other hand, we are interested in the relative efficacy of the new treatment compared to the standard treatment (i.e., the biologic relationship), the risk ratio (Equation {9.6}) is the better choice, since it is not influenced by the underlying risk of death in coronary artery disease patients.

$$\frac{\theta_1}{\theta_2} \triangleq \frac{p_1}{p_2} = \frac{p(\text{death}|\text{standard treatment})}{p(\text{death}|\text{new treatment})} = \frac{0.54}{0.36} = 1.50$$

This risk ratio tells us that the risk of death (in the period of time studied) for persons given the standard treatment is 1.5 times the risk of death for persons given the new treatment.

As a further demonstration of the distinction between a probability difference and a probability ratio, let us change the underlying risk of death in the sample from 0.45 to 0.225 (i.e., half of what it was). Then, the 2 × 2 table would be:

Outcome

		Died	Survived	
	Standard	27	73	100
Treatment				
	New	18	82	100
		45	155	200

Now, the risks of death for those two treatment groups are:

$$p(\text{death}|\text{standard treatment}) = \frac{a}{a+b} = \frac{27}{100} = 0.27$$

$$p(\text{death}|\text{new treatment}) = \frac{c}{c+d} = \frac{18}{100} = 0.18$$

Finally, let us use Equation {9.5} to estimate the risk difference and Equation {9.6} to estimate the risk ratio from the data in this 2×2 table.

$$\theta_1 - \theta_2 \triangleq p_1 - p_2 = p(\text{death}|\text{standard treatment}) - p(\text{death}|\text{new treatment}) = 0.27 - 0.18 = 0.09$$

$$\frac{\theta_1}{\theta_2} \triangleq \frac{p_1}{p_2} = \frac{p(\text{death}|\text{standard treatment})}{p(\text{death}|\text{new treatment})} = \frac{0.27}{0.18} = 1.50$$

Reducing the overall risk of death reduced the risk difference by the same amount. Instead of preventing 18 out of 100 (18%) deaths by using the new treatment, now only 9 out of 100 (9%) deaths are prevented. This change is not because of a change in efficacy (the risk of death is still 1.5 times as likely using the standard treatment), but instead due to a reduction of the risk of death regardless of which treatment is used. The risk ratio is unchanged.

_____

In addition to probabilities and rates, nominal dependent variables can be expressed as **odds**. Odds are the number of observations that had the event divided by the number of observations that did not have the event (Equation {9.7}).

$$\text{Odds of event in Group 1} = \frac{\text{Events in Group 1}}{\text{Nonevents in Group 1}} = \frac{a}{b} \qquad \{9.7\}$$

Odds are not rates, because they do not contain time in the denominator. Neither are odds probabilities, because the numerator is not contained in the denominator. When the probability of an event is small, however, odds have a value that is very close to the value of the probability of the event. For example, if the probability of an event is 0.5, this implies that, for every two observations, one observation will have the event and the other observation will not. The odds for that event would be equal to 1/1 or 1.0. If, on the other hand, the probability of an event is 0.05, then only one out of every 20 observations would have the event and the remaining 19 of those 20 observations would not. The odds of that event would be equal to 1/19 or 0.053, which is much closer to the corresponding probability.

We did not discuss odds in Chapter 6 when were thinking about univariable samples with a nominal dependent variable because odds are used in health statistics only to compare nominal dependent variables between groups. Then, the odds of an event in the two groups are compared only as a ratio. This ratio is called an **odds ratio**. Equation {9.8} illustrates how the odds ratio is estimated from 2 × 2 table data.

$$OR \triangleq \widehat{OR} = \frac{\text{Odds of event in Group 1}}{\text{Odds of event in Group 2}} = \frac{\frac{a}{b}}{\frac{c}{d}} = \frac{a \cdot d}{b \cdot c} \qquad \{9.8\}$$

where

OR = ratio of the odds of the event in the population

$\widehat{OR}$ = ratio of the odds of the event in the sample

a = number of observations in group 1 with the event

b = number of observations in group 1 without the event

c = number of observations in group 2 with the event

d = number of observations in group 2 without the event

Now, let us take a look at an example of calculating and interpreting an odds ratio.

Example 9-6 In Example 9-5, we looked at data from a clinical trial of a new treatment for coronary artery disease. Those data are summarized in the following table.

Outcome

		Died	Survived	
Treatment	Standard	54	46	100
	New	36	64	100
		90	110	200

Let us calculate an odds ratio to reflect the association between treatment group and outcome.

To calculate the odds ratio, we use Equation {9.8}.

$$OR \triangleq \widehat{OR} = \frac{\text{Odds of death in Group 1}}{\text{Odds of death in Group 2}} = \frac{\frac{a}{b}}{\frac{c}{d}} = \frac{a \cdot d}{b \cdot c} = \frac{54 \cdot 64}{46 \cdot 36} = 2.09$$

That odds ratio tells us that the odds of dying if someone receives the standard treatment is about twice that of dying if someone receives the new treatment.

The odds ratio is an important estimate of the relationship between two groups of nominal variables for several reasons. To the statistician, odds ratios are attractive because they have statistical properties that make analysis easier. To the health researcher, odds ratios are attractive because they are less affected by certain types of bias[10] and because they are the only sensible way to compare nominal dependent variables in **case-control studies**.

A case-control study is a very useful approach to studying common characteristics (that we call risk factors) and their relationships to rare diseases. In this type of study, the researcher identifies a certain number of persons with the disease (the cases) and a certain number of persons without the disease (the controls). Since disease status defines the groups to be compared, the independent variable in a case-control study is an indicator of whether a person is a case or a control. In case-control studies, the researcher always determines the numbers of cases and controls to be included.[11] Thus, case-control studies always use purposive sampling.

Once cases and controls have been identified, the researcher determines the frequency of some characteristic (or risk factor) believed to influence the occurrence of the disease of interest. Since the frequency of the risk factor is what is being determined here, the dependent variable in a case-control study is the presence or absence of this risk factor. At first, this might seem to be backwards since, as health researchers, we are primarily interested in disease frequency, not presence or absence of some risk factor. It is important to recognize, however, that the dependent variable must be randomly sampled from the population. In a case-control study, only the presence or absence of the risk factor meets this criterion.

Table 9-2, shows observations from a case-control study arranged in a 2×2 table.

---

[10]For example, samples' odds ratios are unbiased estimates of the population odds ratio under the condition of nondifferential (i.e., the same in both groups) sampling bias. If nondifferential sampling bias exists however, sample estimates of differences and ratios of probabilities and rates are biased estimates of their corresponding population values.

[11]Since case-control studies are applied to diseases that occur rarely, researchers usually include all persons who develop the disease over a specified period of time. Controls are selected so that there usually are between one and four controls per case in the sample. Thus, the researcher selects the proportion of persons in the sample who have the disease and that proportion is between 0.5 (one control per case) and 0.2 (4 controls per case). This results in a purposive sample.

Disease Groups

		Cases	Controls	
Risk Factor	Exposed	a	b	$a+b$
	Not Exposed	c	d	$c+d$
		$a+c$	$b+d$	n

Table 9-2 A 2 × 2 table for observations from a case-control study. Here, disease status is the independent variable and the presence or absence of some characteristic (called a risk factor) is the dependent variable.

The next example shows the calculation and interpretation of an odds ratio in a case-control study.

Example 9-7 Suppose we conducted a case-control study of the relationship between consumption of a particular food preservative and stomach cancer. In this study we identified 100 persons with stomach cancer and 100 persons without stomach cancer and asked them about their consumption of food containing the preservative. Among those persons with stomach cancer, 25 ate foods containing the preservative. Among those persons without stomach cancer, 14 ate foods containing the preservative. Let us compare the odds of consumption of the preservative between cases and controls.

First, we organize this information in a 2 × 2 table:

Disease Group

		Cases	Controls	
Food Preservative	Exposed	25	14	39
	Not Exposed	75	86	161
		100	100	200

To calculate the odds ratio, we use Equation {9.8}.

$$OR \triangleq \widehat{OR} = \frac{\text{Odds of exposure among cases}}{\text{Odds of exposure among controls}} = \frac{\frac{a}{c}}{\frac{b}{d}} = \frac{a \cdot d}{b \cdot c} = \frac{25 \cdot 86}{14 \cdot 75} = 2.05$$

This odds ratio tells us that the odds of being exposed to the food preservative is about twice as high among the cases as among the controls.

If we wanted to estimate probabilities from observations in a case-control study, we could only calculate the probability of having the risk factor for cases and controls since the frequency of the risk factor is the only variable that has been randomly sampled. The probability of having the risk factor, however, is not really of interest to us. Rather, we would like to compare estimates of the probabilities of having the disease for persons who have the risk factor relative to persons who do not have the risk factor. Unfortunately, we cannot estimate probabilities of having the disease from case-control data since the researcher has determined how many cases and how many controls were included in the sample.

There is a similar limitation with odds in case-control studies. We would like to compare the odds of having the disease between persons with and without the risk factor, but we only can estimate the odds of having the risk factor for cases and controls for the same reason we are limited to estimating probabilities of having the risk factor. When we compare odds in an odds ratio, however, we find that the ratio of the odds for having the risk factor (i.e., from a case-control study) is identical to the odds for having the disease (i.e., from other types of studies). With the odds ratio, it does not matter which variable is the dependent variable and which is the independent variable; the odds ratio will have exactly the same value. In addition, when the disease we are studying is rare, the odds ratio is very close in value to the ratio of probabilities of having the disease.[12]

Hypothesis Testing

Regardless of which estimate is used to represent the association between the nominal dependent and independent variables, the null hypothesis that is usually tested is that those variables are statistically independent of each other. What is meant by statistical independence here is exactly the same thing that was meant when we first encountered that term in Chapter 1. Namely, statistical independence implies that the probability of one event is the same whether or not another event occurs. Generically, statistical independence can be described as shown in Equation {9.9} (same as Equation {1.8}).

$$p(B \mid A) = p(B \mid \overline{A}) = p(B) \qquad \{9.9\}$$

where

$p(B \mid A)$ =   probability of event B occurring given that event A occurs

$p(B \mid \overline{A})$ =   probability of event B occurring given that event A does not occur

$p(B)$ =   probability of event B occurring regardless of whether or not event A occurs (i.e., the unconditional probability of event B occurring)

Equation {9.10} shows how this description of statistical independence applies to 2×2 table data by using the terminology in Table 9-1.

---

[12]Thus, we can think of an odds ratio in a case-control study similar to a risk ratio in a cohort study.

$$p(\text{event}|\text{group 1})=p(\text{event}|\text{group 2})=p(\text{event}) \qquad \{9.10\}$$

where

$p(\text{event}|\text{group 1})$	=	probability of the event represented by the dependent variable occurring for persons in group 1
$p(\text{event}|\text{group 2})$	=	probability of the event represented by the dependent variable occurring for persons in group 2
$p(\text{event})$	=	probability of the event represented by the dependent variable occurring for persons in both groups combined

Since statistical independence is defined as having the probability of the event equal to the same value in each of the two groups, testing the null hypothesis of statistical independence is the same as testing the null hypothesis that the probability difference is equal to zero or that the probability or odds ratios are equal to one.

In Chapter 1, we were interested in statistical independence when we considered the multiplication rule of probability theory: the way in which the probability of the intersection of events is calculated. The importance of statistical independence in the multiplication rule is to permit the probability of the intersection to be calculated by multiplying unconditional probabilities. A general form of this calculation is shown in Equation {9.11} (a simplified version of Equation 1.12).

$$p(A \text{ and } B)= p(A)\cdot p(B) \qquad \{9.11\}$$

where

$p(A \text{ and } B)$	=	probability that both events A and B will occur in the same observation (i.e., the intersection of events A and B)
$p(A)$	=	probability that event A will occur regardless of whether or not event B occurs (i.e., the unconditional probability of event A)
$p(B)$	=	probability that event B will occur regardless of whether or not event A occurs (i.e., the unconditional probability of event B)

Equation {9.12} shows this same relationship, but in terms of a 2 × 2 table.

$$p(\text{event and group 1})= p(\text{event})\cdot p(\text{group 1}) \qquad \{9.12\}$$

where

$p(\text{event and group 1})$	=	probability that a person has the event represented by the dependent variable and is in group 1 (i.e., the intersection of having the event and being in group 1)

$$p(\text{event}) \quad = \quad \text{probability that the event represented by the dependent}$$
variable will occur regardless of in which group a person is
(i.e., the unconditional probability of the event occurring)

$$p(\text{group 1}) \quad = \quad \text{probability that a person is in group 1 regardless of whether}$$
or not the event represented by the dependent variable occurs
(i.e., the unconditional probability of being in group 1)

In a 2 × 2 table, the probability of the intersection of being in a particular group and having the event is the same as the probability of an observation being in a particular cell of the table. The probability of having the event and being in group 1 to the left of the equals sign in Equation {9.12} equals the probability of an observation being in the upper left-hand cell of the table. The unconditional probabilities relate to the marginal frequencies of that table. Table 9-3 shows how those probabilities relate to the frequencies in a 2 × 2 table.

Table 9-3 A 2 × 2 table that shows the probabilities that, when multiplied by the sample's size (n), are equal to the cell and marginal frequencies in a 2 × 2 table.

Outcome

	Event	No Event	
Group 1	$p(\text{event and group 1})$	$p(\overline{\text{event}} \text{ and group 1})$	$p(\text{group 1})$
Group 2	$p(\text{event and group 2})$	$p(\overline{\text{event}} \text{ and group 2})$	$p(\text{group 2})$
	$p(\text{event})$	$p(\overline{\text{event}})$	1

(left margin label: **Group**)

In Table 9-3, we can see that the probabilities associated with each of the four cells of the 2 × 2 table are the probabilities of someone in the sample being in one of the groups specified by the independent variable and either having or not having the event represented by the dependent variable. If any of those four probabilities is multiplied by the total number of observations in the sample (i.e., n), the product would be equal to the corresponding cell frequency (a, b, c, or d). The probabilities on the margins of the 2 × 2 table represent the unconditional probabilities of either being in a particular group or having (or not having) the event.

The way in which we test the null hypothesis of statistical independence is by using the unconditional probabilities on the margins of the 2 × 2 table to calculate the probabilities in the cells of that table. Then, these calculated probabilities for the cells of the 2 × 2 table are multiplied by the sample's size to obtain the cell frequencies we would expect to observe, on the average, if the variables are statistically independent (i.e., if the null hypothesis is true). Equations {9.13} through {9.16} illustrate how these expected values are calculated.

$$E(a) = p(\text{event}) \cdot p(\text{group 1}) \cdot n = \frac{a+b}{n} \cdot \frac{a+c}{\cancel{n}} \cdot \cancel{n} = \frac{(a+b) \cdot (a+c)}{n} \qquad \{9.13\}$$

$$E(b) = p(\overline{\text{event}}) \cdot p(\text{group 1}) \cdot n = \frac{a+b}{n} \cdot \frac{b+d}{n} \cdot n = \frac{(a+b) \cdot (b+d)}{n} \qquad \{9.14\}$$

$$E(c) = p(\text{event}) \cdot p(\text{group 2}) \cdot n = \frac{c+d}{n} \cdot \frac{a+c}{n} \cdot n = \frac{(c+d) \cdot (a+c)}{n} \qquad \{9.15\}$$

$$E(d) = p(\overline{\text{event}}) \cdot p(\text{group 2}) \cdot n = \frac{c+d}{n} \cdot \frac{b+d}{n} \cdot n = \frac{(c+d) \cdot (b+d)}{n} \qquad \{9.16\}$$

where

$E(a), E(b), E(c), E(d)$	=	cell frequencies that are expected in a 2 × 2 table, on the average, if the null hypothesis of statistical independence is true (i.e., the expected values)
$p(\text{group 1}), p(\text{group 2})$	=	unconditional probability that a person is in group 1 (or group 2) as specified by the independent variable
$p(\text{event}), p(\overline{\text{event}})$	=	unconditional probability that a person has (or does not have) the event represented by the dependent variable
$(a+b), (c+d), (a+c), (b+d)$	=	marginal frequencies from the 2 × 2 table
n	=	total number of observations (i.e., sample's size) $= a+b+c+d$

Now, let us take a look at an example that illustrates how we can calculate these expected values for the cell frequencies in a 2 × 2 table.

Example 9-8 In Examples 9-5 and 9-6, we looked at data from a clinical trial of a treatment for coronary artery disease. Those data are summarized in the following table:

Outcome

		Died	Survived	
Treatment	Standard	54	46	100
	New	36	64	100
		90	110	200

These are the observed frequencies for the 2 × 2 table. Now, let us calculate the cell frequencies that we would expect to observe (on the average) if the dependent and independent variables were statistically independent.

To calculate these expected frequencies, we use the marginal frequencies in the 2×2 table and Equations {9.13} through {9.16}.

$$E(a) = p(\text{event}) \cdot p(\text{group 1}) \cdot n = \frac{a+b}{n} \cdot \frac{a+c}{n} \cdot n = \frac{(a+b) \cdot (a+c)}{n} = \frac{100 \cdot 90}{200} = 45$$

$$E(b) = p(\overline{\text{event}}) \cdot p(\text{group 1}) \cdot n = \frac{a+b}{n} \cdot \frac{b+d}{n} \cdot n = \frac{(a+b) \cdot (b+d)}{n} = \frac{100 \cdot 110}{200} = 55$$

$$E(c) = p(\text{event}) \cdot p(\text{group 2}) \cdot n = \frac{c+d}{n} \cdot \frac{a+c}{n} \cdot n = \frac{(c+d) \cdot (a+c)}{n} = \frac{100 \cdot 90}{200} = 45$$

$$E(d) = p(\overline{\text{event}}) \cdot p(\text{group 2}) \cdot n = \frac{c+d}{n} \cdot \frac{b+d}{n} \cdot n = \frac{(c+d) \cdot (b+d)}{n} = \frac{100 \cdot 110}{200} = 55$$

A convenient way to organize these expected frequencies is to include them in the cells of the 2×2 table along with the corresponding observed values. To distinguish the expected values from the observed values, the expected values appear in brackets:

Outcome

		Died	Survived	
	Standard	54 {45}	46 {55}	100
Treatment				
	New	36 {45}	64 {55}	100
		90	110	200

In Examine 9-8, we can see that there is a difference between the observed cell frequencies and those that we expect to see (on the average) if survival outcome is statistically independent of the treatment group. The question now is, "Are these differences large enough to lead us to reject the null hypothesis?" The way in which we answer this question is by calculating a chi-square value. That chi-square value represents the difference between each observed cell frequency and its corresponding expected cell frequency, relative to the magnitude of the expected frequency for each cell. This calculation is illustrated in Equation {9.17}.

$$\chi^2 = \frac{(a - E(a))^2}{E(a)} + \frac{(b - E(b))^2}{E(b)} + \frac{(c - E(c))^2}{E(c)} + \frac{(d - E(d))^2}{E(d)} \quad \text{\{9.17\}}$$

where

$$\chi^2 \quad = \quad \text{chi-square statistic (with 1 degree of freedom)}$$

$$a, b, c, d \quad = \quad \text{cell frequencies observed in the sample}$$

$$\begin{aligned} E(a), E(b), \quad &= \quad \text{cell frequencies expected, on the average, if the null hypothesis of}\\ E(c), E(d) \quad & \qquad \text{statistical independence is true} \end{aligned}$$

To test the null hypothesis that the dependent and independent variables are statistically independent, the chi-square value calculated in Equation {9.17} is compared to the value from Table B.7 that corresponds to one degree of freedom and α=0.05. This process is illustrated in the next example.

Example 9-9 In Example 9-8 we calculated the expected cell frequencies and organized them in a 2 × 2 table:

Outcome

		Died	Survived	
Treatment	Standard	54 {45}	46 {55}	100
	New	36 {45}	64 {55}	100
		90	110	200

Now, let us test the null hypothesis that the dependent and independent variables are statistically independent

To test the null hypothesis of statistical independence, we use Equation {9.17} to calculate a chi-square statistic

$$\chi^2 = \frac{(a-E(a))^2}{E(a)} + \frac{(b-E(b))^2}{E(b)} + \frac{(c-E(c))^2}{E(c)} + \frac{(d-E(d))^2}{E(d)}$$

$$= \frac{(54-45)^2}{45} + \frac{(46-55)^2}{55} + \frac{(36-45)^2}{45} + \frac{(64-55)^2}{55} = 6.545$$

Thus, the calculated value of chi-square is equal to 6.545. To test the null hypothesis that the dependent and independent variables are statistically independent, we compare this calculated value to a value from Table B.7 that corresponds to one degree of freedom and

$\alpha=0.05$. That value is equal to 3.841. Since the calculated value (6.545) is larger than the value from the table (3.841), we reject the null hypothesis and accept, through the process of elimination, the alternative hypothesis. The alternative hypothesis states that the dependent and independent variables in the population are not statistically independent. In other words, the risk of dying is different for the two treatments.

The chi-square test is a normal approximation. Although it is the test we encounter most often to test the null hypothesis of statistical independence for data in a 2 × 2 table, there are two other tests based on normal approximations that are used often enough in health research that they deserve mention. One of these is a normal approximation for the difference between the two probabilities. Equation {9.18} shows how a standard normal deviate is calculated to represent the observed difference between the probability estimates.

$$z = \frac{(p_1 - p_2) - (\theta_1 - \theta_2)}{\sqrt{\dfrac{\bar{\theta} \cdot (1-\bar{\theta})}{n_1} + \dfrac{\bar{\theta} \cdot (1-\bar{\theta})}{n_2}}} \qquad \{9.18\}$$

where

z = standard normal deviate representing the observed difference between the probabilities

p_1, p_2 = observed probabilities of the event represented by the dependent variable

θ_1, θ_2 = actual probabilities of the event represented by the dependent variable in the population

$\bar{\theta}$ = overall (univariable) probability of the event in the population

n_1, n_2 = number of observations in groups 1 and 2

Although Equations {9.17} and {9.18} look like different tests, they are not. Not only do they test the same null hypothesis,[13] but they also are numerically identical, except for the fact that the chi-square value is equal to the square of the standard normal deviate.

A third normal approximation test for 2 × 2 table data is the **Mantel-Haenszel test**.[14] It can be used to test the same null hypotheses that are tested by the chi-square test and the normal approximation for the difference between two probabilities. It is very similar (but not identical) to these tests. Equation {9.19} illustrates the Mantel-Haenszel chi-square test.

---

[13]These hypotheses are: H_0: $\theta_1 - \theta_2 = 0$, H_0: $\theta_1 / \theta_2 = 1$, H_0: $OR = 1$, and H_0: the dependent and independent variables are statistically independent

[14]Sometimes the Mantel-Haenszel test statistic is presented as a standard normal deviate, rather than as a chi-square value. This standard normal deviate is the square root of the chi-square value.

$$\chi^2 = \frac{(a - E(a))^2}{\dfrac{(a+b)\cdot(c+d)\cdot(a+c)\cdot(b+d)}{n^2\cdot(n-1)}}$$ {9.19}

where

χ^2 = chi-square statistic representing the difference between the observed and expected frequencies for any one of the cells in a 2 × 2 table

a = observed frequency in the upper left-hand cell in a 2 × 2 table

$E(a)$ = expected frequency for the upper left-hand cell, assuming that the dependent and independent variables are statistically independent (from Equation {9.13})

$(a+b), (c+d),$ = marginal frequencies from the 2 × 2 table
$(a+c), (b+d)$

n = total number of observations in the 2 × 2 table

The next example compares these three tests for a 2 × 2 table.

Example 9-10   In Example 9-9, we used the chi-square test to test the null hypothesis that the dependent and independent variables are statistically independent for the data in the following 2 × 2 table:

Outcome

		Died	Survived	
	Standard	54	46	100
Treatment	New	36	64	100
		90	110	200

Now, let us test this same null hypothesis using the normal approximation for the difference between the probabilities and the Mantel-Haenszel test.

First, let us take a look at the normal approximation for the difference between the probabilities of death for the two treatment groups. This test uses Equation{9.18}:

$$z = \frac{(p_1 - p_2) - (\theta_1 - \theta_2)}{\sqrt{\dfrac{\overline{\theta} \cdot (1 - \overline{\theta})}{n_1} + \dfrac{\overline{\theta} \cdot (1 - \overline{\theta})}{n_2}}} = \frac{(0.54 - 0.36) - 0}{\sqrt{\dfrac{0.45 \cdot (1 - 0.45)}{100} + \dfrac{0.45 \cdot (1 - 0.45)}{100}}} = 2.56$$

This standard normal deviate is compared to a value from Table B.1 that corresponds to 0.05 split between the two tails of the standard normal distribution. That value from the table is equal to 1.96. Since the calculated value (2.56) is larger than the critical value (1.96), we can reject the null hypothesis and accept, through the process of elimination, the alternative hypothesis that states that the dependent and independent variables are not statistically independent. This is the same conclusion we drew in Example 9.9 using the chi-square test. In fact, the square of this standard normal deviate (2.56^2) is exactly equal to the chi-square value calculated in Example 9-9.

Next, let us test this same null hypothesis using the Mantel-Haenszel test from Equation {9.19}.

$$\chi^2 = \frac{(a - E(a))^2}{\dfrac{(a+b) \cdot (c+d) \cdot (a+c) \cdot (b+d)}{n^2 \cdot (n-1)}} = \frac{(54 - 45)^2}{\dfrac{90 \cdot 110 \cdot 100 \cdot 100}{200^2 \cdot (199)}} = 6.513$$

This result (6.513) is very close, but not identical, to the result from the chi-square test (6.454) and the square of the result from the normal approximation for the difference between the probabilities (also 6.454). This difference is due to a slightly different approximation used in the Mantel-Haenszel test.

_____

The three hypothesis tests we have considered are all normal approximations applied to the **hypergeometric distribution**. The hypergeometric distribution is the actual sampling distribution for 2 x 2 tables. It is a discrete distribution (i.e., represented graphically using a bar graph), while the Gaussian distribution is a continuous distribution (i.e., represented graphically using a frequency polygon). Some statisticians think that we can get a better approximation if we correct for the lack of continuity in the hypergeometric distribution. The most common **continuity correction** involves subtracting ½ from the absolute difference between observed and expected cell frequencies.[15] The corrected calculation for the chi-square test is illustrated in Equation {9.20} and in the next example.

$$\chi^2 = \frac{(|a - E(a)| - \frac{1}{2})^2}{E(a)} + \frac{(|b - E(b)| - \frac{1}{2})^2}{E(b)} + \frac{(|c - E(c)| - \frac{1}{2})^2}{E(c)} + \frac{(|d - E(d)| - \frac{1}{2})^2}{E(d)} \qquad \{9.20\}$$

_____

[15]This is sometimes called **Yate's correction**.

Example 9-11   In Example 9-9, we used the chi-square test to test the null hypothesis that the dependent and independent variables are statistically independent for the data in the following 2 × 2 table:
Now, let us perform that chi-square test using the correction for continuity.

We us Equation {9.20} to obtain the corrected calculation of chi-square:

$$\chi^2 = \frac{(|a-E(a)|-\frac{1}{2})^2}{E(a)} + \frac{(|b-E(b)|-\frac{1}{2})^2}{E(b)} + \frac{(|c-E(c)|-\frac{1}{2})^2}{E(c)} + \frac{(|d-E(d)|-\frac{1}{2})^2}{E(d)}$$

$$= \frac{(|54-45|-\frac{1}{2})^2}{45} + \frac{(|36-45|-\frac{1}{2})^2}{45} + \frac{(|46-55|-\frac{1}{2})^2}{55} + \frac{(|64-55|-\frac{1}{2})^2}{55} = 5.838$$

This chi-square corrected for continuity (5.838) is less than the uncorrected chi-square (6.545), but it is still greater than the value from Table B.7 corresponding to one degree of freedom and α=0.05 (3.841).   Thus, we draw the same conclusion: we reject the null hypothesis.

The advantage of using normal approximations for a nominal dependent variable is that normal approximations are easier to calculate than using the actual sampling distribution (i.e., the hypergeometric distribution for a 2 × 2 table).   However, with computers to perform these calculations for us, their difficulty should be moot.   Given a choice, we should use the actual sampling distribution.   We learned in Chapter 6, using the actual sampling distribution for a nominal dependent variable is called an exact procedure.   In the case of 2 × 2 tables, this exact procedure is called **Fisher's exact test**.

    We will see the result of Fisher's exact test in the next example.   This example uses SAS's FREQ procedure to analyze the 2 × 2 table data we have considered in previous examples.

Example 9-12   Let us use SAS to compare survival outcome compared between our two treatment groups.

The following is output from the FREQ procedure:

```
                         The FREQ Procedure

                    Table of treatment by event

                 treatment        event

                 Frequency |
                 Percent   |
                 Row Pct   |
                 Col Pct   | YES      | NO       |    Total
                 ----------+----------+----------+
                 YES       |       54 |       46 |      100
                           |    27.00 |    23.00 |    50.00
                           |    54.00 |    46.00 |
                           |    60.00 |    41.82 |
                 ----------+----------+----------+
                 NO        |       36 |       64 |      100
                           |    18.00 |    32.00 |    50.00
                           |    36.00 |    64.00 |
                           |    40.00 |    58.18 |
                 ----------+----------+----------+
                 Total            90        110        200
                               45.00      55.00     100.00


              Statistics for Table of treatment by event

           Statistic                    DF      Value      Prob
           --------------------------------------------------------
           Chi-Square                    1     6.5455     0.0105
           Likelihood Ratio Chi-Square   1     6.5831     0.0103
           Continuity Adj. Chi-Square    1     5.8384     0.0157
           Mantel-Haenszel Chi-Square    1     6.5127     0.0107
           Phi Coefficient                      0.1809
           Contingency Coefficient              0.1780
           Cramer's V                           0.1809


                         Fisher's Exact Test
                  ------------------------------------
                  Cell (1,1) Frequency (F)        54
                  Left-sided Pr <= F          0.9966
                  Right-sided Pr >= F         0.0077
                  Table Probability (P)       0.0043
                  Two-sided Pr <= P           0.0155


              Estimates of the Relative Risk (Row1/Row2)

     Type of Study              Value      95% Confidence Limits
     -----------------------------------------------------------------
     Case-Control (Odds Ratio)  2.0870     1.1839        3.6789
     Cohort (Col1 Risk)         1.5000     1.0916        2.0612
     Cohort (Col2 Risk)         0.7187     0.5552        0.9306
```

The 2 × 2 table we get from SAS looks different from the 2 × 2 tables we have seen in previous examples. The reason for this is that SAS gives us more than just the cell frequencies. The other numbers in each cell are: percent of all observations that are in the cell, the percent of observations in that row that are in the cell, and the percent observations in that column that are in the cell.

Immediately following the 2 × 2 table are tests of the null hypothesis that death is unrelated to treatment group. Here, we find two of the three normal approximations we have considered namely, the chi-square test and the Mantel-Haenszel test), plus another (the likelihood ratio chi-square). In addition, the chi-square corrected for continuity is provided. The P-values for the normal approximations are very close in magnitude for all, except the continuity corrected chi-square. The continuity corrected chi-square will always have a larger P-value (corresponding to a smaller chi-square value) than the uncorrected chi-square.

In the next table, the results of the exact test are reported. The bottom line here is the P-value in the last row (0.0155). Since that P-value is less than 0.05, we can reject the null hypothesis. If we compare this P-value to the P-values in the normal approximations, we can see that it is closest in value to the P-value for the corrected chi-square. This observation supports the idea that a correction for continuity makes the result of a normal approximation closer to the exact P-value.

The last table in this output lists point and interval estimates for the odds ratio (labeled "Case-Control" and the probability ratio (labeled "Cohort"). There are two values for the probability ratio, because SAS does not know which column corresponds to the event. In this case, the event (death) is in the first column of the 2 × 2 table. Therefore, the probability ratio applicable to these data is the one in the row labeled "Cohort (Col1 Risk)."

DEPENDENT VARIABLE NOT AFFECTED BY TIME: PAIRED DESIGN

When we make two measurements of the dependent variable on each individual or on two individuals who are essentially identical, we call it a **paired design**. The purpose of a paired design is to control for some of the person-to-person variability and, as a result, to provide more precise estimates of differences between groups. For a continuous dependent variable, we did this by taking the difference between the two measurements for each pair (i.e., as in the paired-t test discussed in Chapter 4). For a nominal dependent variable, we have a different way to represent paired data. That is by numerating different outcomes for each pair of observations.

For each pair, there are four possible outcomes. First, both members of a pair could have the event represented by the nominal dependent variable. Second, neither member of a pair could have that event. These first two types of pairs are called **concordant pairs**. The more concordant pairs we observe, the more effective was the pairing. That is to say, the pairing resulted the selection of two persons who had about the same likelihood of having the event.

The concordant pairs do not, however, reflect the difference between the groups being compared. This difference is reflected by the **discordant pairs**. These are the pairs in which one member of the pair had the event while the other member of that pair did not have the event. The discordant pairs are those pairs between which group membership is more likely to be reflected in the outcomes of the members of the pairs. This is because pairing intends to match individuals who are identical in all aspects related to the outcome, except for group membership.

Since this paired analysis tracks the outcomes by pairs, we organize the events in a different type of 2×2 table. This **paired 2×2 table** distinguishes between the two groups specified by the nominal independent variable by having one group represented by the columns and the other group represented by the rows. Then, each column for the first group and each row for the second group specify the outcome for that member of the pair. This format is illustrated in Table 9-4.

Group 1

		Event	No Event	
Group 2	Event	A	B	b
	No Event	C	D	d
		a	c	n_p

Table 9-4   A paired 2×2 table. The letters A, B, C, and D in the cells of the paired 2×2 table represent the frequencies of each possible outcome for a pair. The letters a, b, c, and d represent the frequencies of each outcome for the individuals who make up the pairs as shown in Figure 9-2. n_p is the number of pairs in the sample ($n_p = n/2$).

The next example illustrates data organized in a paired 2×2 table and how they relate to an unpaired 2×2 table.

Example 9-13   In previous examples, we examined data from a clinical trial of a treatment for coronary artery disease in which 100 persons were given the experimental treatment (36 of whom died within the study period) and another 100 persons were given the standard treatment (54 of whom died within the same period of time). The following 2×2 table was used in Example 9-5 to organize these data:

Outcome

		Died	Survived	
Treatment	Standard	54	46	100
	New	36	64	100
		90	110	200

Now, let us suppose that these data come from a paired design in which each of the 100 persons in the new treatment group is matched to one of the 100 persons in the standard treatment group.

The unpaired and paired 2 × 2 tables are related in that the cell frequencies of the unpaired table are the marginal frequencies of the paired table. Therefore, the paired table contains all of the information in the unpaired table. That is to say, both tables tell us what happened to the 200 individuals in the study. In addition, the paired table tells us what happened to each pair. The following is an example of how the paired table could appear for these data:

		Standard Treatment Group		
		Died	Survived	
New Treatment Group	Died	30	6	36
	Survived	24	40	64
		54	46	100

This table tells us that there were 30 pairs in which both members of the pair died and 40 pairs in which both members of the pair survived. These are the concordant pairs. The discordant pairs are those in which one member of the pair died and the other member of the pair survived. In 24 of these pairs, it was the member who received the standard treatment who died. In 6 of these pairs, it was the member who received the standard treatment who died.

Estimation

Having a paired study does not affect the point estimates of the probability difference or of the probability ratio. We still use Equations {9.5} and {9.6} and the cell frequencies from the unpaired 2 × 2 table (or marginal frequencies from the paired table). It does not matter whether the study is paired or not; these estimates will be identical. The point estimate of the odds ratio, on the other hand, is affected by the paired design. Thus, we must use the paired 2 × 2 table to estimate the odds ratio when the study has a paired design. Equation {9.21} illustrates how the point estimate of the odds ratio is calculated from a paired 2 × 2 table.[16]

---

[16]Equation {9.21} assumes that the paired 2 × 2 table has the group in the numerator of the odds ratio specifying columns. If that group is specifying rows, take the inverse of this equation (B/C).

$$OR \triangleq \widehat{OR} = \frac{C}{B} \qquad \{9.21\}$$

where

OR	$=$	population's value of the odds ratio
$\widehat{OR}$	$=$	sample's estimate of the odds ratio
B	$=$	number of discordant pairs in which the member in group 1 did not have the event and the member in group 2 had the event
C	$=$	number of discordant pairs in which the member in group 1 had the event and the member in group 2 did not have the event

The next example shows how these point estimates are calculated from the paired 2×2 table.

Example 9-14   In Example 9-13, we organized the data from a clinical trial of a treatment for coronary artery disease as if it had a paired design in which one member from each of 100 pairs of persons was given the experimental (i.e., new) treatment and the other member was given the standard treatment. The particular paired 2×2 table selected in Example 9-13 as follows:

		Standard Treatment Group		
		Died	Survived	
New Treatment Group	Died	30	6	36
	Survived	24	40	64
		54	46	100

Now, let us calculate point estimates of the probability difference, probability ratio, and odds ratio comparing survival in the two treatment groups.

First, we use Equation {9.5} to estimate the probability difference. When the data appear in a paired 2×2 table, we can perform this calculation using the frequencies in the margins of the paired table (see Table 9-4). For this particular table we get:

$$\theta_1 - \theta_2 \triangleq p_1 - p_2 = \frac{a}{a+c} - \frac{b}{b+c} = \frac{54}{54+46} - \frac{36}{36+64} = 0.18$$

Then, we use Equation {9.6} to estimate the probability ratio from the paired 2 × 2 table.

$$\frac{\theta_1}{\theta_2} \triangleq \frac{p_1}{p_2} = \frac{\dfrac{a}{a+c}}{\dfrac{b}{b+d}} = \frac{\dfrac{54}{54+46}}{\dfrac{36}{36+64}} = 1.5$$

These values are the same as the probability difference and the probability ratio point estimates obtained from the unpaired 2 × 2 table in Example 9-5.

Now, we calculate the point estimate for the odds ratio. When the study has a paired design, we cannot use Equation{9.8}, since it applies only to the unpaired 2 × 2 table. Instead we use Equation {9.21} to estimate the odds ratio from the paired table.

$$OR \triangleq \widehat{OR} = \frac{C}{B} = \frac{24}{6} = 3.0$$

This is not the same as the estimate of the odds ratio that we calculated from the unpaired 2 × 2 table in Example 9.6. That unpaired odds ratio was equal to 2.09. In general, odds ratios from paired studies will be further from one in numeric magnitude (i.e., larger in absolute value) than the corresponding odds ratios from unpaired studies. This difference between paired and unpaired odds ratio estimates reflects the advantage of pairing.

_____

Hypothesis Testing

The principal advantage of using a paired design is to increase statistical power (i.e., improve our chance of rejecting a false null hypothesis). This advantage applies equally to probability differences, probability ratios, and odds ratios. Equation {9.22} shows how we can test the null hypotheses that the probability difference is equal to zero, that the probability ratio is equal to one, that the odds ratio is equal to one, or that there is statistical independence between group membership and the outcome.[17]

_____

[17]Earlier in this chapter we learned that, if any of these null hypotheses are rejected, then all of four are rejected.

$$\chi^2 = \frac{(C-B)^2}{C+B} \qquad \{9.22\}$$

where

χ^2 = chi-square value with one degree of freedom

B = number of discordant pairs in which the member in group 1 did not have the event and the member in group 2 had the event

C = number of discordant pairs in which the member in group 1 had the event and the member in group 2 did not have the event

The statistical test that uses Equation {9.22} on data from a paired 2 × 2 table is called **McNemar's test**. The following example shows McNemar's test applied to the paired 2 × 2 table in Example 9-13.

Example 9-15   In Example 9-13, we organized the data from a clinical trial of a treatment for coronary artery disease as if it had a paired design in which one member from each of 100 pairs of persons was given the experimental (i.e., new) treatment and the other member was given the standard treatment.   The particular paired 2 × 2 table selected in Example 9-13 as follows:

		Standard Treatment Group		
		Died	Survived	
New Treatment Group	Died	30	6	36
	Survived	24	40	64
		54	46	100

Now, let us use these data to test the null hypothesis that the probability ratio is equal to one in the population.

Since these data are from a study with a paired design, we need to test this null hypothesis using McNemar's test. From Equation {9.22} we get:

$$\chi^2 = \frac{(C-B)^2}{C+B} = \frac{(24-6)^2}{24+6} = 10.8$$

The chi-square value calculated by using McNemar's test has one degree of freedom, so we compare it to a value from Table B.7 for α=0.05 and one degree of freedom. This value is equal to 3.841. Since 10.80 is larger than 3.841, we reject the null hypothesis that the probability ratio in the population is equal to one and accept, through the process of elimination, that it is not equal to one. The fact that this test has greater statistical power than the chi-square test for unpaired data (Equation {9.17}) is illustrated by the fact that McNemar's test yields a larger chi-square value (10.80) than does the unpaired chi-square test in Example 9-9 (6.55). A larger chi-square value implies that it is easier to reject the null hypothesis.

Example 9.15 illustrated how McNemar's test can be performed by hand. This test can also be performed by SAS, but SAS requires that the data be formatted in a different way than when performing an unpaired analysis. This programming can take more time than calculating the chi-square statistic by hand!

DEPENDENT VARIABLE AFFECTED BY TIME

In Chapter 6, we considered a nominal dependent variable to be affected by time if two criteria are met. The first criterion is that the event represented by the dependent variable is observed more often the longer we look for it. This is true of most events we encounter in health research and practice. The second criterion is that we look longer for the event in some cases than we do in others. If both of these criteria are met, we need to use special statistical methods that take time into account. In Chapter 6, we did that by using rates (i.e., incidence), rather than probabilities, as estimates of the frequency of events. We take that same approach in bivariable analysis.

When we have nominal dependent and independent variables and the dependent variable is not affected by time, we organize the observations in a 2 × 2 table. We do something similar when the dependent variable is affected by time, but we do not keep track of the number of observations in which the event does not occur. Figure 9.6 illustrates the way in which we organize data from a bivariable sample when the nominal dependent variable is affected by time.

Independent Variable

		Group 1	Group 2	
Dependent Variable	Events	a	b	$a+b$
	Person-Time	PT_1	PT_2	

Table 9-5   A table for organizing of observations for a nominal dependent variable and a nominal independent variable when the dependent variable is affected by time. The letters a and b represent the frequencies (i.e., counts) of the events in each of two groups. PT_1 and PT_2 represent the total amount of follow-up time ("person-time") over which events were observed in each group.

In bivariable analysis, when the independent variable represents nominal data, we can estimate the incidence of the event in each of the two groups specified by the nominal independent variable. The way in which we make those estimates is the same as the way we did in univariable analysis (Equation {6.5}). When we have two estimates of the incidence of an event, however, our interest is in comparing the estimates.   We can make this comparison either by considering the difference between, or the ratio of, the estimates. These estimates are illustrated in Equations {9.23} and {9.24}.

$$ID \triangleq \widehat{ID} = \frac{a}{PT_1} - \frac{b}{PT_2} \qquad \{9.23\}$$

where

ID = population's incidence difference

$\widehat{ID}$ = sample's estimate of the incidence difference

a, b = number of events observed in groups 1 and 2 respectively, in the sample

PT_1, PT_2 = amount of follow-up time spent looking for events in groups 1 and 2, respectively, in the sample

and

$$IR \triangleq \widehat{IR} = \frac{\dfrac{a}{PT_1}}{\dfrac{b}{PT_2}} \qquad \{9.24\}$$

where

IR = population's incidence ratio

$$\widehat{IR} \quad = \quad \text{sample's estimate of the incidence ratio}$$

a, b = number of events observed in groups 1 and 2, respectively, in the sample

PT_1, PT_2 = amount of follow-up time spent looking for events in groups 1 and 2, respectively, in the sample

When the nominal dependent variable is not affected by time, the choice between a probability difference and a probability ratio is based on whether or not we want the measure to reflect the underlying frequency of the event. The same is true in bivariable analysis when the nominal dependent is affected by time. The incidence difference is used to compare rates when we want to reflect the underlying rate of disease and the incidence ratio is used to compare rates when we do not want to reflect the underlying rate of disease. We will take a look at an example of how to calculate and interpret these estimates shortly, but first, let us see how we can take chance into account for two rates.

Regardless of whether we are interested in the difference between or the ratio of two rates, the method that we use to take chance into account is the same, as long as the null hypothesis corresponds to the rates being equal to the same value in the population. For the difference between rates, the null hypothesis is that the difference is equal to zero. For the ratio of two rates, the corresponding null hypothesis is that the ratio is equal to one. Equation 9.25 illustrates the method for testing these null hypotheses.

$$\chi^2 = \frac{\left(a - \dfrac{(a+b)\cdot PT_1}{PT_1 + PT_2}\right)^2}{\dfrac{(a+b)\cdot PT_1 \cdot PT_2}{(PT_1 + PT_2)^2}} \qquad \{9.25\}$$

where

χ^2 = chi-square value with 1 degree of freedom

a, b = number of events observed in groups 1 and 2, respectively

PT_1, PT_2 = amount of follow-up time spent looking for events in groups 1 and 2, respectively

Now, let us take a look at an example in which we compare two rates.

Example 9-16   In Example 6-2, we followed 11 persons for up to three years looking for the development of retinopathy and found 7 new cases during a total of 21.8 person-years. That led to an estimate of the rate at which new cases of retinopathy appear in the population equal to 0.32 per year. Now, let us suppose that these 11 persons represent a group who has been diagnosed with diabetes and that we have another group of 11 persons without diabetes among whom 6 cases of retinopathy were observed over a total of 40 person-years of follow-up. Let us compare those rates between the two groups.

First, let us organize these data in a table like Table 9-5.

		Diabetes		
		Yes	No	
Retinopathy	Cases	7	6	13
	Person-Year	21.8	40.0	

Next, we need to decide whether or not we want to make this comparison in a way that reflects the underlying rate of disease. Most likely we would be interested only in how strongly associated retinopathy and diabetes are (i.e., without reflecting the underlying incidence of retinopathy). If this is the case, we want to make the comparison by calculating a rate ratio using Equation{9.24}.

$$IR \triangleq \widehat{IR} = \frac{\dfrac{a}{PT_1}}{\dfrac{b}{PT_2}} = \frac{\dfrac{7}{21.8}}{\dfrac{6}{40.0}} = \frac{0.32}{0.15} = 2.14$$

This implies that persons with diabetes develop retinopathy at more than twice the rate at which persons without diabetes do. Now, let us take chance into account by testing the null hypothesis that the incidence of retinopathy is the same in these two groups. We do that by using Equation {9.25}.

$$\chi^2 = \frac{\left(a - \dfrac{(a+b) \cdot PT_1}{PT_1 + PT_2}\right)^2}{\dfrac{(a+b) \cdot PT_1 \cdot PT_2}{(PT_1 + PT_2)^2}} = \frac{\left(7 - \dfrac{13 \cdot 21.8}{21.8 + 40.0}\right)^2}{\dfrac{13 \cdot 21.8 \cdot 40.0}{(21.8 + 40.0)^2}} = 1.96$$

To test the null hypothesis that the rate ratio in the population is equal to one, we compare that calculated chi-square value to one from Table B.7 that corresponds to $\alpha = 0.05$ and one degree of freedom. This chi-square value is 3.841. Since 1.96 is less than 3.841, we fail to reject the null hypothesis.

We have finished discussing bivariable methods that are commonly used in the health research literature. Now, we are ready to take a look at multivariable methods.

PART FOUR
Multivariable Analyses

If there is one thing on which we can all agree, it is the fact that the science of health and disease is complex. There are few (if any) measurements that we can make on individuals that are not related to other characteristics of these individuals. To do justice to this complexity, our analyses of data from health research should take these interrelationships into account. This can be done by considering more than one independent variable. When we have a data set with more than one independent variable, we call it a **multivariable** data set.

Usually, we conduct statistical analyses with one independent variable of primary interest. We know that independent variables specify conditions under which we wish to examine the dependent variable. These conditions are defined for one of two reasons. The first reason is that we wish to examine the relationship between the dependent variable and independent variable. For example, in data from a clinical trial of a therapeutic intervention, we have a nominal independent variable that specifies to which treatment group someone has been assigned. Our interest in analyzing these data is to compare values of the dependent variable between the treatment groups. In bivariable analyses, every independent variable has served this purpose.

The second reason we might want to use independent variables to specify conditions is to examine the relationship between the dependent variable and one or more independent variables while taking into account or controlling for the effects of other characteristics. For example, if we were interested in the relationship between dose of an antihypertensive medication and diastolic blood pressure, we would probably want to control for any differences in age among the persons at different doses. The reason for this is that diastolic blood pressure increases with age. If the persons who received the higher doses were younger than persons who received the lower doses, we would see an apparent dose-response relationship, even if the dose of the medication does not change diastolic blood pressure. An apparent association that is caused by another characteristic like this is most often called **confounding**.

In health research, there are two approaches to decrease the impact of confounding on observed associations. First, we can design a study with features that reduce the impact of confounding. One such feature is **matching**. In matching, two (or more) measurements are made on the same individual or on individuals who are the same as far as characteristics that are potential confounders. If there is no difference in these characteristics, they cannot be confounders.

The second design feature that can be used to decrease the impact of confounding is **randomization**. In randomization, persons are randomly assigned to groups. This tends to make the groups similar in all characteristics, including those that are potential confounders. Unlike matching however, randomization does not guarantee that potential confounders will have the same distribution in the groups. Just by chance, there could still be confounding.

The second approach to controlling confounding is to include potential confounders as independent variables in multivariable analyses. In the next three chapters, we will see how independent variables can serve this important function.

CHAPTER 10
Multivariable Analysis of a Continuous Dependent Variable

In Chapter 7, we discussed bivariable analysis of a continuous dependent variable. In that chapter we considered, in turn, continuous and nominal independent variables. When the independent variable represents continuous data, the choices for bivariable analysis include regression analysis and correlation analysis. The same is true in multivariable analysis, only they now include more than one continuous independent variable and are called **multiple regression analysis** and **multiple correlation analysis**.

When the independent variable represents nominal data, the bivariable analysis we use is Student's *t* test. The purpose of this test is to compare dependent variable values between the two groups specified by the nominal independent variable. In multivariable analysis, we can have more than one nominal independent variable and, as a result, more than two groups of dependent variable values. The multivariable methods that we use to compare these groups include **analysis of variance** and **posterior tests**.

Multivariable analysis of a continuous dependent variable includes statistical methods for which there is not a bivariable parallel. These methods are used when a data set includes a mixture of continuous and nominal independent variable. The multivariable method used in this case is called **analysis of covariance**. These statistical methods are summarized in Flowchart 8.

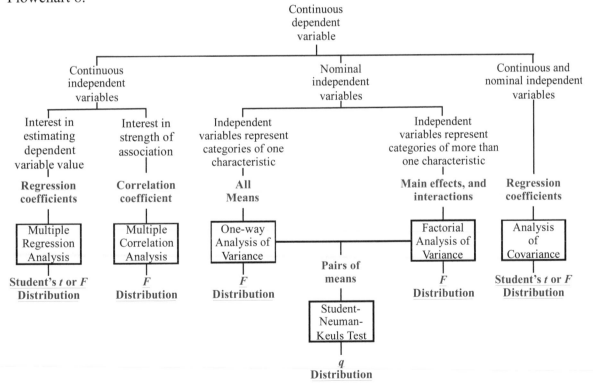

Flowchart 8 Flowchart showing multivariable analysis of a continuous dependent variable. The point estimate that is most often used to describe the dependent variable is in color. The common name of the statistical test is enclosed in a box. The standard distribution that is used to test hypotheses and calculate confidence intervals is in color and underlined.

CONTINUOUS INDEPENDENT VARIABLES

One thing that statisticians like is a linear relationship. We saw this in bivariable regression and correlation analyses when the relationship between a continuous dependent variable and a continuous independent variable was considered to be a straight line. Even though there is more than one continuous independent variable in multiple regression and correlation analyses, the assumed relationship between the dependent variable and those continuous independent variables continues to be linear. However, with more than one independent variable, the relationship is more complicated than can be described as a straight line. In this case, the linear relationship includes the effects of each of the independent variables added together. This is easiest to see in the context of multiple regression analysis.

Multiple Regression Analysis

In multiple regression analysis, we have a continuous dependent variable and more than one continuous independent variable. The way in which the independent variables are related to the dependent variable is by adding their effects. This is illustrated in Equation{10.1}.

$$\mu_{Y|X_1,X_2,...,X_k} = \alpha + \beta_1 \cdot X_1 + \beta_2 \cdot X_2 + ... + \beta_k \cdot X_k \qquad \{10.1\}$$

where

$\mu_{Y|X_1,X_2,...,X_k}$ = mean of the dependent variable in the population corresponding to a particular set of values for each of the k independent variables

α = intercept of the population's multiple regression equation

β_i = regression coefficient (i.e., slope) for the ith (out of k) independent variable in the population

X_i = value of the ith (out of k) independent variable

Estimation of Regression Coefficients

In multiple regression analysis, we tend to use the term "**regression coefficient**" instead of "slope" to refer to the number by which we multiply independent variable values. The reason for this is that "slope" implies a two-dimensional relationship. That fits a bivariable regression equation, but multivariable regression equations have more than two dimensions.

Equation {10.2} shows the multiple regression equation as it is estimated from the sample's observations.

$$\hat{Y} = a + b_1 \cdot X_1 + b_2 \cdot X_2 + ... + b_k \cdot X_k \qquad \{10.2\}$$

Estimates of the intercept and regression coefficients in the multiple regression equation are based on the same least squares approach we used to estimate the slope and intercept of the bivariable regression equation in Chapter 7.[1] In that chapter, we took a look at the mathematical equation that is used in the method of least squares to estimate the slope of the bivariable regression equation. We did this as an aid to understanding, rather than as a suggestion that we will, in practice, be determining the value of that estimate by hand. We recognize that the computer will be doing the calculations for us when we are actually analyzing data. Now that we are considering multiple regression analysis, we need to rely on other methods to help us understand the logic behind estimation of the regression coefficients, since having more than one independent variable makes the math virtually useless for most of us as a method to understand the logic. So, we will leave these calculations to the computer.

Control of Confounding

Since multiple regression analysis involves two or more independent variables, we now must confront an issue that does not exist when we have only one independent variable. This is how the relationship between the dependent variable and each of the independent variables is influenced by the inclusion of the other independent variables in the analysis. The way that multiple regression analysis (and all other multivariable analyses) does this is to take into account the relationship between the dependent variable and all of the other independent variables before considering the relationship between the dependent variable and a particular independent variable.

To see how this works, let us consider a multiple regression equation with only two independent variables. Suppose that we are interested in examining the relationship between diastolic blood pressure (the dependent variable) and dietary sodium intake and age (the independent variables). Equation {10.3} shows the estimated regression equation for those three variables.

$$\widehat{DBP} = a + b_1 \cdot NA + b_2 \cdot AGE \qquad \{10.3\}$$

where

$\widehat{DBP}$ = estimated diastolic blood pressure (dependent variable)

a = sample's estimate of the intercept

NA = dietary sodium intake (independent variable)

b_1 = sample's estimate of the regression coefficient for dietary sodium intake

---

[1] In Chapter 7, we found that the least squares method of estimation involves calculations that minimize the sum of the squared differences between observed and estimated values of the dependent variable.

AGE = age (independent variable)

b_2 = sample's estimate of the regression coefficient for age

Now suppose that the research question for these data is, "How does dietary sodium intake affect diastolic blood pressure?" Then, the reason age is included as an independent variable is to control for its effect on diastolic blood pressure. The concern is that diastolic blood pressure increases with age and that dietary sodium intake increases with age as well. If that is true, an observed association between diastolic blood pressure and dietary sodium intake might only be due to the relationship of both to age. This can lead to a type of bias known as confounding.[2] By including age as an independent variable in the multiple regression equation, we can control for its effect as a confounder before considering the relationship between dietary sodium intake and diastolic blood pressure. The next example shows how this process affects estimates of regression coefficients.

Example 10-1   Suppose that we determine diastolic blood pressure (DBP) and average dietary sodium intake (NA) for 40 persons between 30 and 69 years of age. Imagine that we use SAS's REG procedure to perform a bivariable regression analysis on these data and observe the following results:

```
                         The REG Procedure
                           Model: MODEL1
                       Dependent Variable: DBP

                         Analysis of Variance

                                Sum of          Mean
 Source              DF        Squares        Square     F Value    Pr > F
 Model                1     3100.41622     3100.41622       14.94    0.0004
 Error               38     7887.18378      207.55747
 Corrected Total     39        10988

              Root MSE              14.40685    R-Square     0.2822
              Dependent Mean        97.40000    Adj R-Sq     0.2633
              Coeff Var             14.79143

                         Parameter Estimates

                      Parameter       Standard
 Variable      DF      Estimate          Error    t Value    Pr > |t|
 Intercept      1      -8.15717       27.40642      -0.30      0.7676
 NA             1       0.04103        0.01062       3.86      0.0004
```

---

[2]Confounding occurs when there is a correlation between independent variables, but not all of the independent variables have biologic relationships with the dependent variable. In that circumstance, there can be a statistical association that does not reflect a biologic relationship.

From this regression analysis, it appears that dietary sodium intake helps to estimate diastolic blood pressure. The regression coefficient is equal to 0.04103 mmHg/mg and is statistically different from zero ($P = 0.0004$).

Now, let us include age as an additional independent variable and use the REG

```
                          The REG Procedure
                           Model: MODEL1
                       Dependent Variable: DBP

                          Analysis of Variance

     Source              DF        Squares        Square    F Value    Pr > F
     Model                2      5963.18579    2981.59289      21.96    <.0001
     Error               37      5024.41421     135.79498
     Corrected Total     39         10988


                   Root MSE              11.65311    R-Square     0.5427
                   Dependent Mean        97.40000    Adj R-Sq     0.5180
                   Coeff Var             11.96418


                          Parameter Estimates

                          Parameter      Standard
     Variable     DF       Estimate         Error    t Value    Pr > |t|
     Intercept     1       30.94403      23.74742       1.30      0.2006
     AGE           1        1.03160       0.22468       4.59      <.0001
     NA            1        0.00197       0.01209       0.16      0.8712
```

Now that there are two independent variables in the regression equation, we are provided with separate parameter estimates for each (i.e., their corresponding regression coefficients). The estimate of the regression coefficient for dietary sodium intake is now equal to 0.00197 mmHg/mg. That is substantially closer to zero than the regression coefficient from the bivariable regression equation (0.04103 mmHg/mg). Also, this regression coefficient is no longer significantly different from zero ($P=0.8712$). This reduction in the magnitude of the regression coefficient and the increase in the magnitude of the P-value for dietary sodium intake reflect the fact that dietary sodium intake has little impact on estimation of diastolic blood pressure values when we control for the effect of age.

From this example, we can see how controlling for age affects the regression coefficient for dietary sodium intake. Now, let us take a closer look at the regression coefficient for age.

Multiple regression analysis cannot discriminate between independent variables that are included in a multiple regression equation because they address the research question (like dietary sodium intake) and those that have been included to control for their confounding (like age). Thus, the regression coefficient for age in the multiple regression equation reflects the relationship between age and diastolic blood pressure after controlling for the potential confounding effect of dietary sodium intake just like the regression coefficient for dietary sodium intake reflects the relationship between dietary sodium intake and diastolic blood pressure after controlling for the potential confounding effect of age. It works both ways. This is illustrated in the next example.

Example 10-2   The following output is the result of using the REG procedure to perform a bivariable regression analysis with age as the only independent variable:

```
                        The REG Procedure
                         Model: MODEL1
                      Dependent Variable: DBP

                        Analysis of Variance

                              Sum of          Mean
    Source          DF       Squares        Square    F Value    Pr > F
    Model            1     5959.56773    5959.56773      45.04    <.0001
    Error           38     5028.03227     132.31664
    Corrected Total 39        10988

              Root MSE             11.50290    R-Square    0.5424
              Dependent Mean       97.40000    Adj R-Sq    0.5303
              Coeff Var            11.80996

                        Parameter Estimates

                        Parameter      Standard
    Variable     DF     Estimate         Error    t Value    Pr > |t|
    Intercept     1     34.48405       9.54957       3.61      0.0009
    AGE           1      1.05741       0.15756       6.71      <.0001
```

Let us interpret this output, comparing it to the multiple regression equation in Example 10-1.

The regression coefficient for age is equal to 1.05741 mmHg/mg when it is the only independent variable in a bivariable regression analysis. This is of higher numeric magnitude than when dietary sodium intake is also included in the multiple regression equation (1.03160 mmHg/mg). The difference between the two regression coefficients for age is much smaller than the difference between the regression coefficients for dietary sodium intake. This implies that controlling for dietary sodium intake does affect the relationship between diastolic blood pressure and age, but it does not have a substantial impact on that relationship.

Estimates of the regression coefficients for independent variables in a multiple regression equation reflect the relationship between the corresponding independent variable and the dependent variable after taking into account all of the other independent variables. The fact that some independent variables are included in a multiple regression equation because they reflect the research question (like dietary sodium intake) and others are included to control for their effect as a confounder (like age) is reflected in the way in which the results are interpreted, not in the way calculations are performed. Estimation for all independent variables in a multiple regression equation is based on the same logic process.

Variability of Dependent Variable Values

What we saw happen to the regression coefficients for age and dietary sodium intake when we compared bivariable and multivariable regression equations in Examples 10-1 and 10-2 is the result of a relationship between those independent variables that we call **multicollinearity**.[3] Multicollinearity affects the results of multivariable analyses when independent variables have two characteristics. First, for multicollinearity to exist, the independent variables need to be correlated with each other. By being correlated, we mean that the independent variables share some of their variability. Second, some of that shared variability needs to include variability that is used to "explain" (i.e., estimate) the dependent variable. When two or more independent variables have both of those characteristics, we say that they are **collinear**.

The usual result of multicollinearity on estimates of regression coefficients is to reduce the absolute numeric magnitude of the regression coefficients for the collinear independent variables. The magnitude of that reduction depends on how much of the variability used by a particular independent variable to estimate dependent variable values is correlated with the other independent variable(s) in the multiple regression equation. The key to understanding how to interpret the results of multiple regression analysis is to understand the relationships between the variability of the independent variables and how that variability contributes to estimation of dependent variable values.

As in bivariable regression analysis, we can think of the variability of dependent variable values in multiple regression analysis as being divided between variation that is explained by the relationship with the independent variables and variation that is not explained by that relationship. Also, as in bivariable regression analysis, the explained variation is called the **model** variation and the unexplained variation is called the **error** variation. Unlike bivariable regression analysis however, a multiple regression equation contains two or more independent variables. Thus, we can consider how much of the variation in dependent variable values is explained by all of the independent variables taken together, or how much is explained by individual independent variables taking the other independent variables into account.[4] The latter is a feature of multivariable analyses that is referred to as the **independent contribution** of an independent variable.

---

[3]This is also called **collinearity**. Collinearity and multicollinearity mean the same thing.

[4]We could also consider the contribution of subsets of independent variables, but this would be useful only if those subsets represent interesting biologic relationships.

In the example of age, dietary sodium intake, and diastolic blood pressure, most of the variability in dietary sodium intake that is used to estimate diastolic blood pressure values is associated with age. We know that this is the case because the regression coefficient for dietary sodium intake is much closer to zero in the multiple regression equation than in the bivariable regression equation. Because the regression coefficient is close to zero, the estimated value of diastolic blood pressure changes very little as dietary sodium intake increases in value. Thus, dietary sodium intake has little independent contribution to estimation of diastolic blood pressure values.

The same is not true for age. Since the regression coefficient for age is not much closer to zero in the multiple regression equation than in the bivariable regression equation, we can conclude that little of the variability in diastolic blood pressure explained by age is the same as the variability associated with dietary sodium intake. Thus, age has a considerable independent contribution to estimation of diastolic blood pressure values.

To see how this works, let us take a look at the R^2 values in the SAS output in Examples 10-1 and 10-2. We learned in Chapter 7 that these values tell us the proportion of the variation in the dependent variable that is associated with the independent variable.[5] Table 10-1 summarizes the R^2 values from the three regression analyses in these two examples.

Regression equation	R^2	Difference
$\widehat{DBP} = a + b_1 \cdot NA + b_2 \cdot AGE$	0.5427	--
$\widehat{DBP} = a + b \cdot AGE$	0.5424	0.0003
$\widehat{DBP} = a + b \cdot NA$	0.2822	0.2605

Table 10-1 R^2 values for the regression equations in Examples 10-1 and 10-2. The column labeled "Difference" is the R^2 value for the corresponding equation subtracted from the R^2 value for the equation including both independent variables.

Notice that the R^2 value for the regression equation that includes both independent variables ("called the **"full model"**") is larger than the values for either of the regression equations excluding one of independent variables (called a **"reduced model"**). This will always be the case. Adding more independent variables, even if they are just random numbers, will cause the R^2 value to increase. This is because; every independent variable will be associated to some degree with the dependent variable, if only by chance.

These relationships also can be represented graphically. In this graphic approach, the variability of a variable is represented as a rectangle and associations between variables are represented by overlap of their rectangles. The amount of overlap of the rectangles relative to the size of the rectangles reflects the strength of these associations. Figures 10-1 through 10-3 are graphic representations of the associations among diastolic blood pressure, dietary sodium intake, and age seen in Examples 10-1 and 10-2.

---

[5]The R^2 value is really a part of correlation analysis, rather than regression analysis. For R^2 to reflect the proportion of variation in dependent variable explained by the independent variables in the population, the independent variables must all be from a naturalistic sample. Here, we are interested in the amount of explained variation in the sample, without extrapolating the results to the population.

$$\widehat{DBP} = a + b \cdot AGE$$

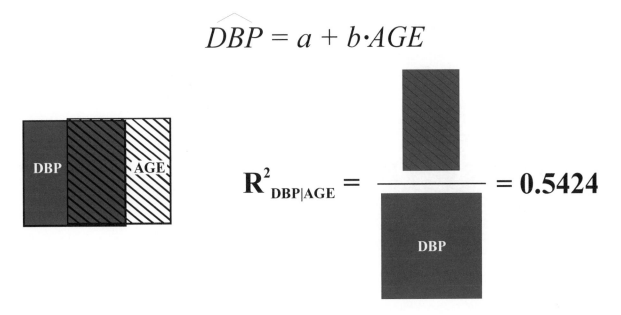

Figure 10-1 Graphic representation of the bivariable regression equation that estimates diastolic blood pressure (in color) from age (▨). The area of overlap represents the association between the variables. The R^2 value for this regression equation corresponds to the area in which the rectangle for age overlaps the rectangle for diastolic blood pressure divided by the entire rectangle for diastolic blood pressure

$$\widehat{DBP} = a + b \cdot NA$$

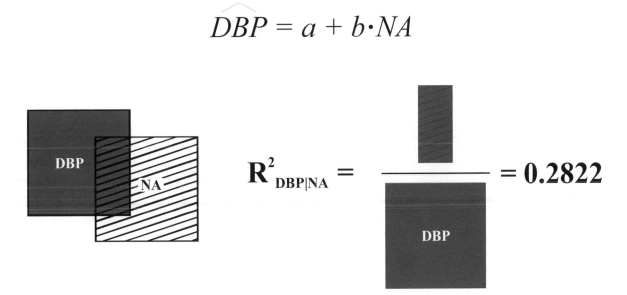

Figure 10-2 Graphic representation of the bivariable regression equation that estimates diastolic blood pressure (in color) from dietary sodium intake (▨). The area of overlap represents the association between the variables. The R^2 value for this regression equation corresponds to the area in which the rectangle for dietary sodium intake overlaps the rectangle for diastolic blood pressure divided by the entire rectangle for diastolic blood pressure.

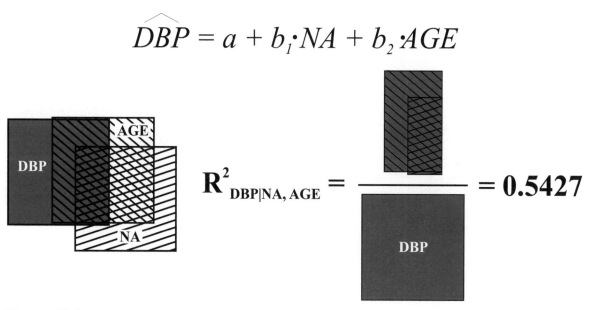

Figure 10-3 Graphic representation of the multivariable regression equation that estimates diastolic blood pressure (in color) from the combination of dietary sodium intake (▨) and age (▧). The areas of overlap represent the associations among the variables. The R^2 value for this regression equation corresponds to the area in which the rectangles for dietary sodium intake and/or age overlap the rectangle for diastolic blood pressure divided by the entire rectangle for diastolic blood pressure.

Table 10-1 also looks at how much larger the R^2 value in the equation that includes both independent variables is compared to the equations including only one of the independent variables. Differences between these R^2 values are presented in the last column of this table. The difference is very small for age (0.0003) and not very small for dietary sodium intake (0.2605). At first, it might seem that this indicates that dietary sodium intake is associated with the greater proportion of variation in diastolic blood pressure, but just the opposite is true. The difference of 0.0003 for the equation that includes only age tells us that dietary sodium intake contributes only 0.0003 over and above that contributed by age in the equation that includes both of the independent variables. Earlier, we learned that this is often referred to as the "independent contribution" of an independent variable. The independent contribution of dietary sodium intake is that it explains 0.0003 of the variation in diastolic blood pressure over and above the variation explained by age. Likewise, the independent contribution of age is that it explains 0.2605 of the variation in diastolic blood pressure over and above the variation explained by dietary sodium intake. Figures 10-4 and 10-5 show how these independent contributions of the independent variable relate to variation in diastolic blood pressure (the dependent variable).

Independent Contribution of Age

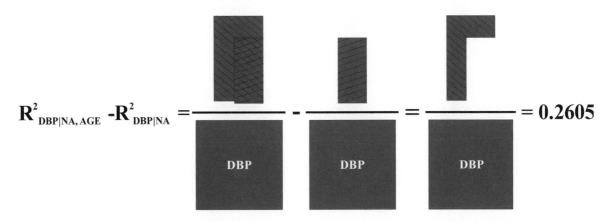

$$R^2_{DBP|NA,\,AGE} - R^2_{DBP|NA} = \frac{}{} - \frac{}{} = \frac{}{} = 0.2605$$

Figure 10-4 Graphic representation of the regression equation that estimates diastolic blood pressure (in color) from dietary sodium intake (▨) and age (▧). The areas of overlap represent the association among the variables. The difference in R^2 values indicates the independent contribution of AGE to the regression equation.

Independent Contribution of NA

$$R^2_{DBP|NA,\,AGE} - R^2_{DBP|AGE} = \frac{}{} - \frac{}{} = \frac{}{} = 0.0003$$

Figure 10-5 Graphic representation of the regression equation that estimates diastolic blood pressure (in color) from dietary sodium intake (▨) and age (▧). The areas of overlap represent the association among the variables. The difference in R^2 values indicates the independent contribution of dietary sodium intake to the regression equation.

This reduced overlap between diastolic blood pressure and dietary sodium intake in Figure 10-5 is consistent with the results of the multiple regression analysis in Example 10-1. Namely, when age was included as an independent variable in the multiple regression equation, very little variability in diastolic blood pressure was explained by dietary sodium intake.

For more general applications, we can calculate the independent contribution of any particular independent variable in a multiple regression equation by subtracting the R^2 value for the reduced model that includes all but that particular independent variable from the R^2 value for the full model that includes all of the independent variables. This difference is called the **partial R^2** or the **coefficient of partial determination**. It is illustrated in Equation{10.4}.

$$R^2_{\text{Partial}_i} = R^2_{Y|\text{all IVs}} - R^2_{Y|\text{all IVs except } X_i} \qquad \{10.4\}$$

where

$R^2_{\text{Partial}_i}$ = coefficient of partial determination for independent variable X_i

$R^2_{Y|\text{all IVs}}$ = R^2 from the full model (i.e., including all of the independent variables)

$R^2_{Y|\text{all IVs except } Xi}$ = R^2 from the reduced model that includes all of the independent variables except the one for which the partial R^2 is calculated (X_i)

Earlier in this chapter, we recalled from Chapter 7 that the R^2 in bivariable regression analysis tells us the proportion of variation in dependent variable values explained by the independent variable. R^2 in multivariable regression analysis tells us the proportion of variation in dependent variable values explained by all of the independent variable taken together and the partial R^2 tells us the proportion of variation in dependent variable values explained by a particular independent variable over and above the variation explained by the other independent variables.

Hypothesis Testing

In bivariable regression analysis, we took chance into account by testing three null hypotheses. These hypotheses were:

H_0: $\alpha = 0$ (i.e., that the population's intercept is equal to zero)

H_0: $\beta = 0$ (i.e., that the population's slope is equal to zero)

H_0 : The independent variable does not help estimate dependent variable values
   (i.e., the omnibus null hypothesis)

These same null hypotheses are tested in multiple regression analysis, but with some distinctions. The first of these is that there are separate null hypotheses to be tested for the regression coefficients for each of the independent variables. Also, the omnibus null hypothesis addresses all of the independent variables taken together instead of an individual independent variable.

In the bottom part of the SAS output from the REG procedure we find the sample's estimate of the intercept and the sample's estimates of the regression coefficients that correspond to each of the independent variables. Also in that part of the output, we find the standard errors for each of the estimates, Student's t-values resulting from a test of the null hypothesis that the corresponding population's value is equal to zero, and its P-value (labeled "Prob>|T|"). If that P-value is equal to or less than α, (which is usually equal to 0.05), we reject the null hypothesis and, through the process of elimination, accept the alternative hypothesis that the population's parameter is not equal to zero. This sounds like the way in which we interpret the P-values from bivariable regression analysis, but there is an important difference: these P-values in multiple regression analysis also reflect multicollinearity.

To see how this works, it helps to look at how Student's t-value can be used to test the null hypothesis that a particular regression coefficient is equal to zero in the population. One way to do this is by dividing the sample's estimate of the regression coefficient by its standard error just like in bivariable regression analysis (Equation {7.11}). This illustrated for multiple regression analysis in Equation{10.5}.

$$t_{\mathrm{H_0}:\beta_i=0} = \frac{b_i - \beta_{0_i}}{s_{b_i}} \qquad \{10.5\}$$

where

$t_{\mathrm{H_0}:\beta_i=0}$ = Student's t-value that corresponds to the sample's estimate of the regression coefficient for the ith independent variable

b_i = sample's estimate of the regression coefficient for the ith independent variable

β_{0_i} = value of the regression coefficient for the ith independent variable in the population according to the null hypothesis (equal to zero)

s_{b_i} = sample's estimate of the standard error for the estimate of the regression coefficient for the ith independent variable

It is helpful to our understanding of how to interpret the results of these tests, however, to consider another way in which those t-values could be calculated. This way uses the independent variable's unique contribution to estimation of dependent variable values as expressed by the partial R^2 (Equation{10.4}). The partial R^2 is multiplied by the total sum of squares to determine the amount of variation in the dependent variable explained by the independent variable and then compared (by division) to the unexplained variation (error mean square). The square root of that value is exactly equal to Student's t-value testing the null hypothesis that the corresponding regression coefficient is equal to zero in the population as shown in Equation{10.5}. This relationship is illustrated in Equation{10.6}.

$$t_{H_0 : \beta_i = 0} = \frac{b_i - \beta_{0_i}}{s_{b_i}} = \sqrt{\frac{R^2_{\text{Partial}_i} \cdot \text{Total SS}}{\text{Error MS}}} \qquad \{10.6\}$$

where

$t_{H_0 : \beta_i = 0}$ = Student's t-value used to test the null hypothesis that the regression coefficient for the ith independent variable is equal to zero in the population

$R^2_{\text{Partial}_i}$ = coefficient of partial determination for independent variable X_i (from Equation {10.4})

Total SS = total sum of squares from the multiple regression equation that includes all of the independent variables (i.e., the full model)

Error MS = error mean square from the multiple regression equation that includes all of the independent variables (i.e., the full model)

The numerator of Equation {10.6} reflects the unique contribution of that independent variable to estimation of dependent variable values. If that independent variable is collinear with one (or more) other independent variable(s) in the multiple regression equation, the numeric magnitude of the numerator will be reduced. The greater the degree of multicollinearity, the greater will be that reduction in numeric magnitude and, as a result, the smaller will be Student's t-value. A smaller value of Student's t makes it harder to reject the null hypothesis. Thus, multicollinearity affects hypothesis testing in multiple regression analysis by making it harder to reject the null hypothesis that a particular regression coefficient is equal to zero in the population. This effect is illustrated in the next example.

Example 10-3   Let us compare hypothesis testing for the regression coefficient of dietary sodium intake with and without age in the model to see how multicollinearity affects hypothesis testing.

To begin, we will look again at the result of testing the null hypothesis that the regression coefficient for dietary sodium intake is equal to zero when dietary sodium intake is the only independent variable (i.e., from bivariable regression analysis). The SAS output for that bivariable regression analysis is (as seen in Example 10-1):

```
                          The REG Procedure
                          Model: MODEL1
                       Dependent Variable: DBP

                         Analysis of Variance

                              Sum of          Mean
    Source           DF      Squares        Square    F Value    Pr > F
    Model             1    3100.41622    3100.41622      14.94    0.0004
    Error            38    7887.18378     207.55747
    Corrected Total  39       10988

             Root MSE              14.40685    R-Square     0.2822
             Dependent Mean        97.40000    Adj R-Sq     0.2633
             Coeff Var             14.79143

                        Parameter Estimates

                       Parameter     Standard
    Variable    DF      Estimate        Error    t Value    Pr > |t|
    Intercept    1      -8.15717     27.40642      -0.30      0.7676
    NA           1       0.04103      0.01062       3.86      0.0004
```

As we learned in Chapter 7, the *P*-value from the test of the null hypothesis that the regression coefficient (i.e., the slope) is equal to zero in the population appears in the last column of the bottom table in output from SAS's REG procedure. Here, that *P*-value is 0.0004, which is less than 0.05. Thus, we are able to reject the null hypothesis that the regression coefficient is equal to zero in the population.

Now, let us look at the same hypothesis test, but from multivariable regression analysis that includes age as another independent variable. The SAS output for this multivariable regression analysis is (as seen in Example 10-1):

```
                          The REG Procedure
                          Model: MODEL1
                       Dependent Variable: DBP

                         Analysis of Variance

    Source           DF      Squares        Square    F Value    Pr > F
    Model             2    5963.18579    2981.59289      21.96    <.0001
    Error            37    5024.41421     135.79498
    Corrected Total  39       10988

             Root MSE              11.65311    R-Square     0.5427
             Dependent Mean        97.40000    Adj R-Sq     0.5180
             Coeff Var             11.96418
```

```
                              Parameter Estimates

                        Parameter        Standard
     Variable     DF     Estimate          Error    t Value    Pr > |t|
     Intercept     1     30.94403       23.74742       1.30      0.2006
     AGE           1      1.03160        0.22468       4.59     <.0001
     NA            1      0.00197        0.01209       0.16      0.8712
```

In this output, the P-value testing the null hypothesis that the regression coefficient for dietary sodium intake is equal to zero in the populations is equal to 0.8712. This is much larger than the P-value from the bivariable regression analysis. When the P-value in multivariable analysis is larger than the P-value from bivariable analysis, this is an indication that multicollinearity exists between that independent variable and at least one other independent variable in the multivariable regression equation.

Now, let us use Equation {10.6} to calculate Student's t-value for the test of this null hypothesis. For the numerator of this equation, we need the partial R^2 for dietary sodium intake. We are told that this is equal to 0.0003 in Table 10-1.

$$t_{\mathrm{H}_0:\beta_i=0} = \sqrt{\frac{\text{Partial } R^2 \cdot \text{Total SS}}{\text{Error MS}}} = \sqrt{\frac{0.0003 \cdot 10,988}{135.79498}} = 0.1558$$

This result is the same as Student's t-value corresponding to the regression coefficient for dietary sodium intake at the bottom of the SAS output for the multiple regression analysis (when it is rounded to two decimals). Thus, testing the null hypothesis that a particular regression coefficient is equal to zero in the population using the partial R^2 is equivalent to using the point estimate of the regression coefficient and its standard error.

So, one way that hypothesis testing in multiple regression analysis differs from hypothesis testing in bivariable regression analysis concerns the test that a particular regression coefficient is equal to zero in the population. The difference is that the ability to reject this null hypothesis in multiple regression analysis can be reduced by multicollinearity. In essence, it is a test of the null hypothesis that the independent variable does not have a unique (i.e., independent) contribution to estimation of dependent variable values. It only considers the relationship between the dependent and an independent variable after taking all of the other independent variables into account.

Another null hypothesis that we tested in bivariable regression analysis was the omnibus null hypothesis. The omnibus null hypothesis in bivariable regression analysis is that the independent variable does not help estimate dependent variable values. In multiple regression analysis, the omnibus null hypothesis states that all of the independent variables taken together do not help estimate dependent variable values. The F-ratio and its corresponding P-value used to test the omnibus null hypothesis in multiple regression analysis appear in the first part of the output from the REG procedure just like they do in bivariable regression analysis.

In Chapter 7, we found that the test of the omnibus null hypothesis in bivariable regression analysis yields exactly the same result as the test of the null hypothesis that the slope is equal to zero in the population. Thus, the test of the omnibus null hypothesis in bivariable regression provides no new information. This is not the case in multiple regression analysis.

The omnibus null hypothesis in multivariable analysis tests the null hypothesis that all of the independent variables in a regression equation, taken together, do not help estimate dependent variable values. In bivariable regression analysis, only the single independent variable was considered. This made the test of the omnibus null hypothesis in bivariable regression analysis the same as the test that the slope is equal to zero. In multiple regression analysis, however, "all of the independent variables" refers to the entire collection of independent variables. Thus, the test of the omnibus null hypothesis in multiple regression analysis is no longer redundant. Instead, it addresses a unique aspect of the relationship between the dependent variable and the independent variables.

The F-ratio used to test the omnibus null hypothesis in multiple regression analysis is equal to the model mean square divided by the error mean square. This calculation appears in Equation{10.7}.

$$F = \frac{\text{Model Mean Square}}{\text{Error Mean Square}} \qquad \{10.7\}$$

Equation {10.7} is the same as the equation for the F-ratio in Chapter 7 (Equation {7.17}). A difference between these two F-ratios is in the degrees of freedom. In bivariable regression analysis, the degrees of freedom in the numerator of the F-ratio (i.e., the model degrees of freedom) are equal to one. In multivariable regression analysis, the degrees of freedom in the numerator of the F-ratio are greater than one. In the example of diastolic blood pressure being estimated from dietary sodium intake and age, the model degrees of freedom are equal to two (see the second output in Example 10-1 or Example 10-3). In general, the model degrees of freedom are equal to the number of independent variables in the regression equation. In bivariable regression analysis, there is one independent variable and, thus, one model degree of freedom. In multivariable regression analysis, there is more than one independent variable, corresponding to more than one model degree of freedom.

The F-ratio in multiple regression analysis considers all of the independent variables as a unit when the omnibus null hypothesis is tested. Since all of the independent variables are considered, the degree to which these independent variables share information used to estimate dependent variable values does not detract from the ability to reject the omnibus null hypothesis as it does when testing the null hypothesis for an individual regression coefficient. The test of the omnibus null hypothesis in multiple regression analysis is not influenced by multicollinearity in the way that a test of the null hypotheses for a particular regression coefficient is affected. This is because the influence of one independent variable is not "subtracted" from the influence of another independent variable when considering the omnibus null hypothesis. This can lead to apparent contradictions in the conclusions drawn from multiple regression analysis as illustrated in the next example.

Example 10-4   To take a closer look at how multicollinearity affects hypothesis testing in multiple regression analysis, let us add another independent variable to the multiple regression equation. To make this new independent variable collinear with age and dietary sodium intake, we will create it by squaring each person's age.[6] Then, the output from the REG procedure is as follows:

```
                         The REG Procedure
                          Model: MODEL1
                       Dependent Variable: DBP

                        Analysis of Variance

                               Sum of          Mean
    Source             DF      Squares        Square    F Value    Pr > F
    Model               3    6115.07376    2038.35792     15.06    <.0001
    Error              36    4872.52624     135.34795
    Corrected Total    39      10988

                Root MSE            11.63391    R-Square    0.5565
                Dependent Mean      97.40000    Adj R-Sq    0.5196
                Coeff Var           11.94447

                        Parameter Estimates

                     Parameter     Standard
    Variable    DF    Estimate        Error    t Value    Pr > |t|
    Intercept    1    -25.17086     58.03502      -0.43      0.6671
    AGE          1      2.97675      1.84984       1.61      0.1163
    AGE2         1     -0.01637      0.01545      -1.06      0.2965
    NA           1      0.00217      0.01207       0.18      0.8584
```

Let us take a look at the results of hypothesis testing from this output.

If we look at the bottom of this output, we see that we are not able to reject any of the null hypotheses that a particular regression coefficient is equal to zero in the population. To conclude from this observation that the independent variables do not contribute to estimating diastolic blood pressure would be a mistake. This is evident when we consider the F-ratio and P-value for the omnibus null hypothesis at the top of the output. This P-value is less than 0.0001. This tells us that we can reject the omnibus null hypothesis that the entire collection of independent variables does not help estimate dependent variable values.

---

[6]This creates what is called a **polynomial** regression equation. Polynomial regression analysis is used to allow the relationship between the independent and dependent variables to be curvilinear.

The reason for this apparent discrepancy is the fact that, with the addition of the square of age, the independent variables share practically all of the information they use to estimate dependent variable values. So, none of the independent variables provides sufficient independent information to allow rejection of the null hypothesis that its regression coefficient is equal to zero. When taken as a group, however, the independent variables are able to estimate dependent variable values. We draw this conclusion because of our ability to reject the omnibus null hypothesis. This implies that, although there is substantial overlap between the independent variables, the entire collection of independent variables accounts for a significant degree of variability of the dependent variable in the sample.

The apparent contradiction in the conclusions drawn in Example 10-4 leads some to suggest that correlated independent variables should not be included in the same regression equation. This is poor advice, since it ignores the fact that multicollinearity is an intentional feature built into multiple regression analysis, and all other multivariable analyses. It is multicollinearity that allows us to control for the confounding effects of some measurements by including them as independent variables. There is a danger in multicollinearity, but that danger is not the inclusion of collinear variables in the multivariable analysis. Instead, the danger is that we might try to interpret the results of multivariable analyses in the same way that we interpret the results of bivariable analyses. In regression analysis, we can avoid this mistake by examining the test of the omnibus null hypothesis as well as tests of null hypotheses about individual regression coefficients. When these seem to disagree (as they do in Example 10-4), we know that the independent variables are collinear.

Even though we do not want to eliminate all collinear independent variables from multivariable analyses, we should be aware that inclusion of an independent variable may make it harder to see relationships between other independent variables and the dependent variable. If we are including independent variables in the regression equation for which we do not intend to control, the multicollinearity should be reduced by removing those independent variables from the multiple regression equation. The square of age in Example 10.5 is such an independent variable. Since it seems to play no independent role in estimation of diastolic blood pressure, it should be excluded from the regression equation.[7]

Multiple Correlation Analysis

The purpose of correlation analysis is to estimate the strength of the association between independent and dependent variables. In multiple correlation analysis, the association between the dependent variable and the entire collection of independent variables is analyzed. The way in which these independent variables are organized into a collection is through the multiple regression equation. In essence, the **multiple correlation coefficient**

---

[7]This process of removing independent variables that seem to have little independent contribution to estimation of dependent variable values is called "**modeling**." You can learn more about modeling in *Building Multivariable Models* available from Stat-Aid.

reflects the strength of the association between the observed values of the dependent variable and the estimated values of the dependent variable that result when all of the independent variable values are used in the multiple regression equation. Since the regression equation is necessary to calculate the multiple correlation coefficient, multiple correlation analysis is conducted using the REG procedure. The square root of the R^2 from the REG procedure is equal to the multiple correlation coefficient. To test the null hypothesis that the multiple correlation coefficient is equal to zero in the population, we use the P-value from the test of the omnibus null hypothesis. This is illustrated in the next example:

Example 10-5   Let us use the output from Example 10-1 to perform multiple correlation analysis.

The following is the output from Example 10-1 in which diastolic blood pressure is the dependent variable and dietary sodium intake and age are the independent variables:

```
                          The REG Procedure
                            Model: MODEL1
                        Dependent Variable: DBP

                          Analysis of Variance

   Source              DF        Squares        Square   F Value   Pr > F
   Model                2     5963.18579    2981.59289     21.96   <.0001
   Error               37     5024.41421     135.79498
   Corrected Total     39        10988

              Root MSE             11.65311   R-Square    0.5427
              Dependent Mean       97.40000   Adj R-Sq    0.5180
              Coeff Var            11.96418

                         Parameter Estimates

                         Parameter     Standard
      Variable    DF      Estimate        Error   t Value   Pr > |t|
      Intercept    1      30.94403     23.74742      1.30     0.2006
      AGE          1       1.03160      0.22468      4.59     <.0001
      NA           1       0.00197      0.01209      0.16     0.8712
```

We can obtain the multiple correlation coefficient from the REG procedure by taking the square root of the R^2 value (0.5427). Thus, the multiple correlation coefficient is equal to 0.7367. We can test the null hypothesis that this correlation coefficient is equal to zero in the population by testing the omnibus null hypothesis. The P-value for this hypothesis test is less than 0.0001. Since it is less that 0.05, we can reject the null hypothesis that the multiple correlation coefficient is equal zero in the population.

The multiple correlation coefficient is part of the regression output because the regression equation is required to calculate it. This does not imply, however, that it is appropriate to interpret the correlation coefficient as a reflection of the strength of the association between the dependent and independent variables in the population. As with the bivariable correlation coefficient, the multiple correlation coefficient requires a naturalistic sample before it can be considered an estimate of the population's value. In the case of multivariable analysis, all of the independent variables in the sample need to be representative of their distributions in the population for the sample to be naturalistic.

NOMINAL INDEPENDENT VARIABLES

When we had a nominal independent variable in bivariable analysis, the independent variable had the effect of dividing the dependent variable values into two groups. In multivariable analysis, we have more than one nominal independent variable and, thus, more than two groups of dependent variable values. In general, k -1 nominal independent variables identify k groups of dependent variable values. The next example describes such a set of data.

Example 10-6   Suppose that we are interested in comparing serum cholesterol levels (the dependent variable) among persons in four geographic regions of the United States: Northeast (NE), Northwest (NW), Southeast (SE), and Southwest (SW). To do this, we select ten persons from each region and measure their serum cholesterol levels. Imagine that we make the following observations:

	NE	NW	SE	SW
	197	194	220	206
	183	185	202	196
	190	186	212	195
	212	212	221	222
	223	209	227	228
	202	194	224	205
	201	186	197	197
	202	196	201	203
	197	190	198	199
	213	218	218	219
Mean	202	197	212	207

This data set consists of four groups of dependent variable values. This is a multivariable data set, since it takes three nominal independent variables to specify these four groups of dependent variable values. For example, suppose that we have the following three nominal independent variables: NE, NW, SE. Further, suppose that NE is equal to "yes" if the person is from the northeast and equal to "no" if the person is not from the northeast. Likewise, NW and SE identify persons from the northwest and southeast. People from the southwest are identified when NE, NW, and SE are all equal to "no." Thus, three nominal independent variables are required to specify four groups of dependent variable values.

When we had only two groups of continuous dependent variable values (in Chapter 7), we were interested in comparing the means of those groups. Now that we have more than two groups of dependent variable values, we are still interested the means of those groups. The difference is that, in multivariable analysis we have more than two means to compare.

Analysis of Variance

As far as point estimation is concerned, the mean for each group of dependent variable values is estimated in the same way we estimated the mean for a single group of continuous dependent variable values (Equation 3.1). To test the null hypothesis that the population's means are equal to the same value, however, we need to use a new method. The name of the method we use to compare the means in multivariable analysis is **analysis of variance** which is often called **ANOVA**.

This might seem to be a strange name for a method used to compare means, but it refers to the fact that the variation of the means between the groups of dependent variable values is compared to the variation of dependent variable values within those groups. These two sources of variation of dependent variable values are illustrated graphically in Figure 10-6.

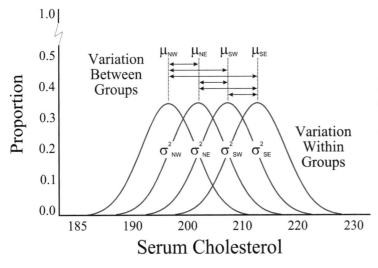

Figure 10-6 Illustration of the variation of dependent variable values between groups and the variation of dependent variable values within groups.

The variation of dependent variable values between groups reflects the differences between the means of the groups. If the means of the groups in the population are all equal to the same value (i.e., the null hypothesis is true), we would still expect to see some variation of the sample's estimates of those means just by chance. To test the null hypothesis that the population's means are all equal to the same value, we need to consider whether the observed differences between the groups' means in the sample are greater than we would expect to see simply due to chance.

The amount of variation among the sample's means that we would expect to see simply due to chance depends on how different the data values are from each other. In other words, it depends on the variance of the dependent variable values. The greater the variation in the data, the greater the variation we can expect to see between the sample's means by chance alone. As a matter of fact, the chance variation in the estimates of the means will be equal, on the average, to the variance of the dependent variable values. Thus, we can test the null hypothesis that the means of the groups in the population are all equal to the same value by seeing how close the observed variation between the means in the sample is to the sample's estimate of the variance of dependent variable values. This is where we get the name, "analysis of variance."

When we had just two groups of continuous dependent variable values (in Chapter 7), we estimated the variance of dependent variable values by assuming that the variances in the two groups were equal in the population. This is the assumption of homoscedasticity. We make that same assumption here as well. The only difference is that we now have more than two estimates of the variance. The method of estimating the variance is the same, however. That is, we use a weighted average of the group-specific variance estimates to represent our best estimate of the variance in the population (Equation {7.26}). The following equation illustrates how this is applied to more than two groups of dependent variable values.

$$\sigma_Y^2 \triangleq s_{Y|Xs}^2 = \frac{\sum (n_i - 1) \cdot s_{Y|X_i}^2}{\sum (n_i - 1)} \qquad \{10.8\}$$

where

σ_Y^2 = variance of the distribution of dependent variable values in the population

$s_{Y|Xs}^2$ = estimate of the variance of dependent variable values pooling estimates for each set of values of the independent variables

$(n_i - 1)$ = degrees of freedom in the ith group of dependent variable values

$s_{Y|X_i}^2$ = variance estimate in the ith group of dependent variable values

So, in analysis of variance we have two measures of the variation in dependent variable values. The one that reflects the variation between the means in the sample is usually called the **between mean square**. The one that is a pooled estimate of the variance in dependent variable values (Equation{10.8}) is called the **within mean square**. We test the null hypothesis that the population's means are all equal to the same value by comparing the between mean square to the within mean square. The comparison is done by calculating an F-ratio. Equation {10.9} illustrates that calculation in terms of the between mean square and the within mean square.

$$F = \frac{\text{Between Mean Square}}{\text{Within Mean Square}} \qquad \{10.9\}$$

If the null hypothesis that all of the means are equal to the same value in the population is true, we expect to observe, on the average, an F-ratio equal to one. That implies that the observed difference among the means is the same as we would expect to occur just by chance. If the null hypothesis is not true (i.e., that some of the means are not equal to the same value), we expect that, on the average, the between mean square will be greater than the within mean square. This is because the variation between groups due to differences between means in the population is added on to the differences between groups that is attributable to the variation in the dependent variable values themselves. So, the F-ratio will be greater than one (on the average) when the means of the groups in the population are not all equal to the same value.[8]

In SAS, we can use the ANOVA procedure to test the null hypothesis that the means are all equal to the same value in the population. The ANOVA procedure tests this null hypothesis using the F-ratio in Equation$\{10.9\}$, but SAS uses different names for the mean squares. Instead of "between mean square," SAS calls the mean square that reflects the variation of the means between groups the **model mean square.** Instead of "within mean square" SAS calls the mean square that reflects the variation of the data within groups the **error mean square**. These are the same terms that are used for the mean squares in regression analysis (Equation 10.7).[9] In the next example, we will take a look at the output from SAS's ANOVA procedure and see how to interpret it.

Example 10-7   In Example 10-6 we looked at serum cholesterol levels among persons in four geographic regions of the United States: Northeast (NE), Northwest (NW), Southeast (SE), and Southwest (SW). To do that, we selected ten persons from each region and measured their serum cholesterol levels. Now, suppose that we use proc ANOVA to analyze those data and that we observe the following output: Let us interpret this output.

The first part of this output looks like the first part of SAS output from the REG procedure. Namely, it lists degrees of freedom, sums of squares, and mean squares for the model, error, and total variation in dependent variable values. In the ANOVA procedure, the model variation is the same as the between variation and the error variation is the same as the within variation. Notice that the model degrees of freedom are equal to 3. This reflects the fact that three nominal independent variables are needed to specify the four groups of

---

[8]Occasionally, the calculated F-ratio can fall below one. When this happens, we interpret that result as being a random variation from an F-ratio of one.

[9]Later in this chapter we will see that regression analysis and analysis of variance are very closely related procedures. Using the same names for the mean squares in regression analysis and analysis of variance reflects this relationship.

dependent variable values (see Example 10-6).

The F-ratio following the model mean square is the same as the F-ratio in Equation{10.9}. It tests the null hypothesis that the means of serum cholesterol values in the four regions are equal to the same value in the population. Since the associated P-value is less than 0.05, we can reject that null hypothesis.

At the bottom of that output, the information from the model variation is described again. Here, the three nominal independent variables are combined under the name "REGION." The reason that the model variation is repeated will become clear when we look at a different type of analysis of variance. We will look at that type next.

_____

Factorial Analysis of Variance

The type of ANOVA we have been considering is called **one-way** ANOVA. That type of ANOVA is distinguished by the fact that the groups of dependent variables correspond to categories of a single characteristic. In the example of serum cholesterol values, the four groups were considered to be categories of a single characteristic: geographic location.

Sometimes, the groups of dependent variable values are specified by categories of more than one characteristic. For example, the four groups of serum cholesterol values in Example 10-6 that we thought of as representing four categories of a single characteristic (region) could also be thought of as representing two categories of each of two characteristics: north versus south and east versus west. The next example illustrates this way of thinking about the groups of dependent variable values.

_____

Example 10-8   The following table displays the data from Example 10-6 using two categories of two characteristics instead of four categories of one characteristic.

	North		South	
	East	West	East	West
	197	194	220	206
	183	185	202	196
	190	186	212	195
	212	212	221	222
	223	209	227	228
	202	194	224	205
	201	186	197	197
	202	196	201	203
	197	190	198	199
	213	218	218	219
Mean	202	197	212	207

The difference between this table and the table in Example 10-6 is in the way in which we label the means. Now, identifying a mean is a two step process. First, we specify whether the mean is for persons in the north or the south. Once we make that determination, we further specify whether the mean is for persons from the east or the west.

_____

In statistical terminology, the characteristics that are used to identify groups of dependent variable values are called **factors**. Example 10-7 shows a one-way analysis of variance. When we think about dependent variable values as categories of more than one factor, as in Example 10-8, the analysis is called **factorial analysis of variance**.

When we have dependent variable values divided according to two (or more) factors we have additional null hypotheses about the means that can be examined. These additional null hypotheses concern either **main effects** or **interactions**.

The **main effect** of a factor compares the means of the categories of that factor, combining the categories of the other factor(s). For instance, the main effect of the north/south factor in Example 10-8 compares the mean serum cholesterol among the 20 persons from the north, combining persons from the northeast and northwest ([202+197] / 2 = 199.5 mg/dL), to the mean among the 20 persons from the south, combining persons from the southeast and southwest ([212+207] / 2 = 209.5 mg/dL). The corresponding null hypothesis for the north-south main effect is that the mean serum cholesterol levels in the north are equal to the mean serum cholesterol levels in the south. Likewise we can compare the mean serum cholesterol levels among persons in the east to mean serum cholesterol levels among persons in the west combining persons from the north and south. This is the east-west main effect. The next example illustrates testing these main effects using SAS.

_____

Example 10-9   The following SAS output is the result of analyzing the data in Example 10-6 as a factorial analysis of variance in the ANOVA procedure.

```
                        The ANOVA Procedure

                      Class Level Information

                Class          Levels     Values
                NS                2       NORTH SOUTH
                EW                2       EAST WEST

                  Number of observations      40

Dependent Variable: CHOLESTEROL
                                   Sum of
   Source                DF        Squares      Mean Square    F Value    Pr > F
   Model                  3      1250.000000     416.666667       3.04     0.0413
   Error                 36      4934.000000     137.055556
   Corrected Total       39      6184.000000

              R-Square     Coeff Var      Root MSE     CHOLESTEROL Mean
              0.202135     5.724730       11.70707            204.5000
```

Source	DF	Anova SS	Mean Square	F Value	Pr > F
NS	1	1000.000000	1000.000000	7.30	0.0105
EW	1	250.000000	250.000000	1.82	0.1853
NS*EW	1	0.000000	0.000000	0.00	1.0000

Let us interpret this output.

The first part of that output is identical to the output in Example 10-7, when these data were analyzed as a one-way analysis of variance. That is to say that the model, error, and total variation are unchanged as well as the F-ratio testing the null hypothesis that the means for all four groups are equal to the same value in the population. The reason for this uniformity is that we have changed the way in which we think about the relationships between the four groups of dependent variable values, but not the groups themselves. So, when we test the null hypothesis that all four means are equal to the same value in the population we get exactly the same result regardless of the way the groups are defined.

The bottom of that output, however, is different from the output from the one-way analysis of variance in Example 10-7. Previously, there was only a single entry in the bottom table. The source of variation was indicated as "Region" and the degrees of freedom, sum of squares, and mean square for that entry were identical to the model degrees of freedom, sum of squares, and mean square in the table in the beginning of the output. In one-way analysis of variance, there is only one explanation for the differences among the means. That is that they differ because they were sampled from four different geographic regions.

In the output from the factorial analysis of variance, however, the values in the bottom table provide more information about the differences between the means. For instance, the means might differ between the north and the south. That possibility is examined by the north-south main effect (labeled "NS"). To test the null hypothesis that the mean of the serum cholesterol levels in the north are equal to the mean of the serum cholesterol levels in the south, we look at the P-value in the row headed by "NS" in the bottom table of the output (0.0105). Since that P-value is less than 0.05, we can reject the null hypothesis and conclude that those means are different in the population. In the same way, we can test the null hypothesis that the mean of the serum cholesterol values in the east is equal to the mean of the serum cholesterol values in the west by looking at the P-value in the row headed by "EW" in the bottom table of the output (0.1853). Since that P-value is greater than 0.05, we cannot reject that null hypothesis.

In one-way analysis of variance we learned that the means among the four geographic regions are different. In factorial analysis of variance, we learned that the differences can be attributed to different levels in the north compared to the south.

At the bottom of the SAS output in Example 10-9 is a row headed by "NS*EW." This is the **interaction** between the north-south effect and the east-west effect. The interaction tells us whether or not it makes sense to look at the means of the categories for one factor (i.e., the main effect) while ignoring categories of the other factor(s). This makes sense only if the relationships among categories of the factor are the same regardless of the category of the other factor(s). If there is an interaction, the implication is that these relationships are different. In that case, observation of the main effect of each factor is not helpful in understanding how the categories are related. This is illustrated in the next example.

Example 10-10 The following figure illustrates mean serum cholesterol levels in the population from which the sample in Example 10-6 might have come. The main effects in that figure are represented by the differences between the means on the outside of the figure. The north-south main effect is that serum cholesterol levels in the south average 10 mg/dL more than serum cholesterol in the north. The east-west main effect is that serum cholesterol levels in the west average 5 mg/dL less than serum cholesterol levels in the east.

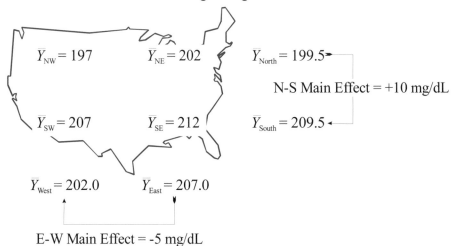

In this population, the main effects are enough to explain the differences between the means in the four geographic regions. For instance, if we know that the mean serum cholesterol level in the northwest is equal to 197 mg/dL, we can add 5 mg/dL to get the mean cholesterol level in the northeast or we can add 10 mg/dL to get the mean serum cholesterol level in the southwest. To get the mean in the southeast, we add both 5 mg/dL and 10 mg/dL to the mean in the northeast.

When we use the main effects in the sample to reflect the population's means in each group, we are assuming that there is no interaction between the factors. By this, we imply that it does not matter in which category of one factor the categories of another factor occur, the relationships among the means in the categories of that other factor will be the same.

In the case of this population, no interaction implies that the difference between the mean in the north and the mean in south will be 10 mg/dL, regardless of whether those means are from the east (212 - 202 = 10) or from the west (207 - 197 = 10). Likewise, it does not matter whether we compare the east to the west in the north or in the south, the difference between the means will be equal to 5 mg/dL.

Now, let us take a look at another possibility for mean serum cholesterol levels in four geographic regions in the population; one that illustrates an interaction.

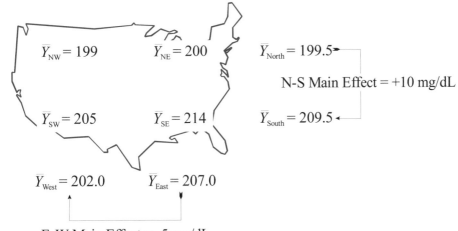

$\bar{Y}_{NW} = 199$ $\bar{Y}_{NE} = 200$ $\bar{Y}_{North} = 199.5$

N-S Main Effect = +10 mg/dL

$\bar{Y}_{SW} = 205$ $\bar{Y}_{SE} = 214$ $\bar{Y}_{South} = 209.5$

$\bar{Y}_{West} = 202.0$ $\bar{Y}_{East} = 207.0$

E-W Main Effect = -5 mg/dL

In this possibility, the main effects are the same as in the previous figure. Namely, there is a difference of 10 mg/dL between the serum cholesterol values in the north and the south and a difference of 5 mg/dL between the serum cholesterol values in the east and the west. Although the main effects are the same as the previous population, they can no longer be interpreted in the same way. Now, the main effects are not enough to explain the differences between the mean levels of serum cholesterol in the geographic regions. For instance, if we add the east-west main effect to the mean in the northwest, we get (199+5) 204 mg/dL. When we did this for the previous population, we got the mean for the northeast. This does not work when there is an interaction. Instead of the actual mean in the northeast (200 mg/dL), we get 204 mg/dL for the northeast by using the east-west main effect. Likewise, adding the north-south main effect to the mean in the northwest yields the mean for the southwest when there is no interaction, but not when there is an interaction. Instead of the actual mean in the southwest (205 mg/dL), we get (199+10) 209 mg/dL by adding the north-south main effect to the mean serum cholesterol level in the northwest. When there is an interaction, the main effects do not describe the differences between the means.

In Example 10-10, we saw that an interaction implies that main effects are not sufficient to describe the means in all the groups of dependent variable values. In that example, an interaction was assumed to exist as long as there were any differences not accounted for by the main effects. In practice, we expect to see some variation between the means not attributable the main effects just by chance, even if the main effects are sufficient to describe the differences between the means in the population. To decide whether or not the apparent interaction in the sample is indicative of interaction in the population, we can test the null hypothesis of no interaction in a factorial analysis of variance. The next example shows the test of the null hypothesis of no interaction for the data introduced in Example 10-10.

Example 10-11 In Example 10-10, we looked at two possibilities for mean serum cholesterol levels in four geographic regions in a population in which the main effects are an increase of 10 mg/dL between the north and south and a decrease of 5 mg/dL between the east and the west. Now, let us take a look at a set of data which might have come from the second population (i.e., the one with an interaction).

	North		South	
	East	West	East	West
	220	198	222	223
	199	199	199	205
	193	193	198	224
	191	215	211	202
	205	181	217	187
	199	189	223	213
	212	196	202	192
	183	194	226	203
	203	221	215	203
	195	204	227	198
Mean	200	199	214	205

The following SAS output is what we get when we analyze this new set of data using SAS's ANOVA procedure to perform a factorial analysis of variance.

```
                          The ANOVA Procedure

                       Class Level Information

                 Class        Levels     Values
                 NS              2        NORTH SOUTH
                 EW              2        EAST WEST

                 Number of observations     40

Dependent Variable: CHOLESTEROL
                                 Sum of
 Source                DF        Squares      Mean Square    F Value    Pr > F
 Model                  3     1410.000000     470.000000       3.60     0.0225
 Error                 36     4694.000000     130.388889
 Corrected Total       39     6104.000000

            R-Square     Coeff Var     Root MSE     CHOLESTEROL Mean
            0.230996     5.583763      11.41880          204.5000


 Source                DF       Anova SS      Mean Square    F Value    Pr > F
 NS                     1     1000.000000    1000.000000       7.67     0.0008
 EW                     1      250.000000     250.000000       1.92     0.1747
 NS*EW                  1      160.000000     160.000000       1.23     0.2753
```

Let us interpret this output.

The test of the null hypothesis that there is no interaction in the population is presented at the end of the output in the row headed "NS*EW." The last number in that row (0.2753) is the P-value for that null hypothesis. Since the P-value is greater than 0.05, we fail to reject the null hypothesis of no interaction. In that case, we assume that there is no interaction in the population and, thus, we can interpret the main effects as indicators of the differences between means. Here, we are able to reject the null hypothesis that the mean for the north is equal to the mean from the south ($P = 0.0088$), but we unable to reject the null hypothesis that the mean for the east is the same as the mean for the west ($P = 0.1747$).

So, the way in which we interpret the results of a factorial analysis of variance depends on the result of the test of the null hypothesis that there is no interaction between the factors in the population. If we fail to reject that null hypothesis, we can interpret the main effects as explanations for differences between means. This makes interpretation of the data easier, since each main effect can be examined without having to consider the other factor(s). If, on the other hand, we reject the null hypothesis of no interaction between the factors, the main effects cannot be interpreted as an explanation of the differences between means. In this case, we must consider differences between all of the means, as we do in one-way analysis of variance, testing the omnibus null hypothesis.

Posterior Testing

When the P-value for the test of the omnibus null hypothesis (i.e., that all of the means in the population are equal to the same value) in one-way analysis of variance is less than our usual α of 0.05, we reject that null hypothesis and, through the process of elimination, accept the alternative hypothesis. That alternative hypothesis must include all possible relationships among the means, except for the relationship specified in the null hypothesis.[10] Thus, the alternative hypothesis is that at least two of the means are different in the population. Exactly how many means are different and which means are different is not specified by this alternative hypothesis. To determine where the differences are, we need to use an additional type of analysis; one that reveals which means are different from each other. Such a test is called a **posterior test** because it is performed after the analysis of variance has indicated that there are differences between the means.

The way in which we discover which means are different is to test null hypotheses that the difference between a pair of means is equal to zero. This could be done by performing

---

[10]This is the principle we first encountered in Chapter 3. Since the alternative hypothesis is accepted through the process of eliminating the null hypothesis, the null and alternative hypotheses must be a collectively exhaustive set of possible relationships among the means.

several bivariable analyses. For example, if we have four means to compare, we could use Student's *t* test to compare each pair of means. For four means, there are six pairs of means and, thus, six *t* tests.

Although this appears to be a viable solution, it is not our best choice. The problem with doing six *t* tests is that each one is associated with its own risks of making a type I or type II error (i.e., of rejecting a true null hypothesis or accepting a false null hypothesis). When we consider the entire collection of bivariable tests, the chance that we have made at least one error in the process performing those tests is higher than the chance of making an error on any single test.[11] If there are many bivariable tests required to examine each pair of means, the chance of making at least one error can be very high indeed. For instance, six *t* tests, each with a 5% chance of making a type I error can have as much as a 26% chance that at least one type I error has occurred.[12]

If the chance of drawing an incorrect conclusion in a series of statistical tests can be reduced, we should consider reducing it, but we need to be careful in selecting a method to do that. One of the methods that sometimes is used to reduce the overall type I error is to make the value of α smaller for each of the statistical tests, so that the overall α is equal to 0.05. The greater the number of statistical tests done, the smaller the value of α for each test must be. This approach is called the **Bonferroni** method. This method is not a good choice as a way to reduce the overall chance of making a type I error. The reason for this is the fact that lowering α makes it harder to reject null hypotheses that should be rejected. In other words, it increases the chance of making type II errors (i.e., it reduces the statistical power). So, the Bonferroni method simply trades one kind of error for another. This is not much of a bargain, especially since there are other posterior tests that can accomplish the same reduction in the overall chance of making at least one type I error with only a small reduction in statistical power.

One commonly used posterior test that controls the overall chance of making a type I error without much of a reduction in statistical power is the **Student-Neuman-Keuls test**. This test is quite a bit like performing Student's *t* tests to compare each pair of means. Equation {10.10} shows the calculation for comparing two means in the Student-Neuman-Keuls test.[13]

$$q = \frac{(\bar{Y}_1 - \bar{Y}_2) - (\mu_1 - \mu_2)}{\sqrt{\frac{s_{Y|Xs}^2}{2} \cdot (\frac{1}{n_1} + \frac{1}{n_2})}} \qquad \{10.10\}$$

---

[11]This is not unique to posterior testing. Any time we consider performing more than one statistical test, the chance of drawing an incorrect conclusion on at least one of the tests will be greater than the chance of drawing an incorrect conclusion on a single test. More generally, this simply says that the more times we do something with a chance of making a mistake, the greater the probability that on one (or more) of those times a mistake will occur.

[12]This calculation assumes that the null hypothesis is true for all six *t* tests and that the chance of making a type I error on each test is statistically independent of the chance of making a type I error on another test.

[13] Compare this to the calculation for Student's *t* test (Equation {7.28}).

where

q =   Student-Neuman-Keuls test statistic

$\overline{Y}_i$ =   observed mean in group i

μ_i =   population's mean in group i

$s^2_{Y|Xs}$ =   within (error) mean square

n_i =   number of observations in group i

There are two important features that make the Student-Neuman-Keuls test different from performing Student's t tests. The first is that there is a specific order in which the comparisons are made in the Student-Neuman-Keuls test. To begin, the means are arranged according to their numeric magnitudes. Then, the two most extreme means are compared. If the null hypothesis that those two means are the same in the population is rejected, then the next most extreme means are tested. If it is not rejected, then null hypotheses for the corresponding less extreme means are automatically not rejected as well. It is following this protocol for comparing means that accounts for much of the reduction in the overall chance of making a type I error.

The second feature is that the Student-Neuman-Keuls test uses a new standard distribution to determine statistical significance. This is the **q distribution**. The q distribution is like Student's t distribution, but it has an additional parameter k that specifies the number of means involved in the comparison. Although, in practice, we will use a computer to do the calculations, it is easier to understand the Student-Neuman-Keuls test by seeing it calculated by hand. The next example does that.

Example 10-12 Let us use the Student-Neuman-Keuls test to find out which means are significantly different for the data in Example 10-6.

The first step in the Student-Neuman-Keuls test is to arrange the means according to their numeric magnitudes.

REGION	NW	NE	SW	SE
MEAN	197	202	207	212

Next, we test the null hypothesis that the two most extreme means are equal to the same value (i.e., their difference is equal to zero). Those means are 197 mg/dL for persons from the NW and 212 mg/dL for persons from the SE.

$$H_0 : \mu_{NW} = \mu_{SE}$$

To make that comparison, we use Equation{10.10}. That equation includes the within (error) mean square ($s^2_{Y|Xs}$). We can find the error mean square (137.055556) in the SAS output from Example 10-7.

$$q = \frac{(\overline{Y}_{NW} - \overline{Y}_{SE}) - (\mu_{NW} - \mu_{SE})}{\sqrt{\dfrac{s^2_{Y|Xs}}{2} \cdot \left(\dfrac{1}{n_{NW}} + \dfrac{1}{n_{SE}}\right)}} = \frac{(197 - 212) - 0}{\sqrt{\dfrac{137.06}{2} \cdot \left(\dfrac{1}{10} + \dfrac{1}{10}\right)}} = -4.05$$

To interpret that result, we compare it to the q-value in Table B.8 that corresponds to $\alpha = 0.05$. The way Table B.8 is set up, there are separate pages for specific values of α, with that value of α specified in the top row. The second page of the table corresponds to $\alpha = 0.05$.

To find the critical value to which we need to compare the absolute value of our calculated value of q, we need to know the degrees of freedom and the value of k. The degrees of freedom are the within (error) degrees of freedom. In Example 10-7, we see that there are 36 degrees of freedom for the within (error) variation. 36 does not appear in Table B.8, so we use the next lower number of degrees of freedom (30).

The parameter k specifies the number of means involved in the comparison. We determine that value by counting the number of means being compared (always equal to two) and the number of means in-between the two being compared (here, equal to two). So, the value of k for the comparison of the means from the NW and SE is equal to four.

Now, we go to Table B.8 and find that the critical value corresponding to α of 0.05, 30 degrees of freedom, and k equal to four is equal to 3.845.

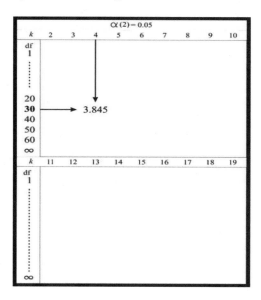

Then, we compare the calculated value (4.05) to the critical value (3.845). Since the calculated value is greater than the critical value, we can reject the null hypothesis that the mean serum cholesterol levels in the NW are equal to the mean serum cholesterol levels in the SE.

The fact that we reject this null hypothesis allows us to test null hypotheses for the next most extreme means. Those are the null hypothesis that the mean for persons from the NW is equal to the mean for persons from the SW

$$H_0 : \mu_{NW} = \mu_{SW}$$

and the null hypothesis that the mean for persons from the NE is equal to the mean for persons from the SE

$$H_0 : \mu_{NE} = \mu_{SE}$$

It does not matter which of those two null hypotheses we test first. To test each of them, we use Equation {10.10} to calculate the q-value.

$$q = \frac{(\overline{Y}_{NW} - \overline{Y}_{SW}) - (\mu_{NW} - \mu_{SW})}{\sqrt{\frac{s^2_{Y|Xs}}{2} \cdot \left(\frac{1}{n_{NW}} + \frac{1}{n_{SW}}\right)}} = \frac{(197 - 207) - 0}{\sqrt{\frac{137.06}{2} \cdot \left(\frac{1}{10} + \frac{1}{10}\right)}} = -2.70$$

$$q = \frac{(\overline{Y}_{NE} - \overline{Y}_{SE}) - (\mu_{NE} - \mu_{SE})}{\sqrt{\frac{s^2_{Y|Xs}}{2} \cdot \left(\frac{1}{n_{NE}} + \frac{1}{n_{SE}}\right)}} = \frac{(202 - 212) - 0}{\sqrt{\frac{137.06}{2} \cdot \left(\frac{1}{10} + \frac{1}{10}\right)}} = -2.70$$

To interpret these results, we compare the absolute value of the calculated q-value to the q-value in Table B.8 that corresponds to $\alpha = 0.05$, 30 degrees of freedom, and $k = 3$ (we now have the two means being compared with one mean between them. That critical value is equal to 3.486.

For the null hypothesis that the mean for the NW is equal to the mean for the SW, the calculated q-value (2.70) is less than the critical value (3.486), so we fail to reject the null hypothesis. When we fail to reject a null hypothesis in the Student-Neuman-Keuls test, we also fail to reject any null hypotheses for any two means that are both in between the means in the null hypothesis that we failed to reject. Thus, we fail to reject the following three null hypotheses even though only the first was actually tested.

$$H_0 : \mu_{NW} = \mu_{SW}$$

$$H_0 : \mu_{NW} = \mu_{NE}$$

$$H_0 : \mu_{NE} = \mu_{SW}$$

To keep track of the results of using the Student-Neuman-Keuls test, it is useful to draw a line connecting the means for which we fail to reject the null hypothesis that the means are equal as follows:

REGION	NW	NE	SW	SE
MEAN	197	202	207	212

Then, we know that any pair of means also connected by that line have their null hypothesis not rejected, even though they were not directly tested.

For the null hypothesis that the mean for the NE is equal to the mean for the SE, the calculated q-value (2.70) is less than the critical value (3.486), so we fail to reject this null hypothesis and any null hypotheses for any two means that are both in between the means in that null hypothesis. Thus, we fail to reject the following three null hypotheses:

$$H_0 : \mu_{NE} = \mu_{SE}$$

$$H_0 : \mu_{NE} = \mu_{SW}$$

$$H_0 : \mu_{SW} = \mu_{SE}$$

As before, we can keep track of these results by drawing a line connecting the means for which we fail to reject the null hypothesis that the means are equal:

REGION	NW	NE	SW	SE
MEAN	197	202	207	212

From that table, we know that the difference between any two means is not statistically significant if they are connected by a line. In this example, only the means for the NW and SE are significantly different.

Hopefully, Example 10-12 helps you to understand how the Student-Neuman-Keuls test works. Now, let us take a look at an example that shows the result of using SAS to carry out the Student-Neuman-Keuls test to look for pair-wise differences between means.

Example 10-13 Posterior testing can be performed in SAS as part of proc ANOVA. The following output is the result of asking SAS to use the Student-Neuman-Keuls[14] test to compare the means of the four geographic regions as part of the one-way analysis of

---

[14]SAS misspells "Neuman" as "Newman."

variance shown in Example 10-7.

```
                     The ANOVA Procedure

            Student-Newman-Keuls Test for CHOLESTEROL

NOTE: This test controls the Type I experimentwise error rate under the complete null
hypothesis but not under partial null hypotheses.

                  Alpha                     0.05
                  Error Degrees of Freedom    36
                  Error Mean Square      137.0556

         Number of Means          2          3          4
         Critical Range    10.618308  12.797271  14.100562

Means with the same letter are not significantly different.

         SNK Grouping        Mean      N    REGION

                      A     212.000    10    SE
                      A
                 B    A     207.000    10    SW
                 B    A
                 B    A     202.000    10    NE
                 B
                 B          197.000    10    NW
```

Let us interpret this output.

It is the table at the bottom of that output that tells us the results of the Student-Neuman-Keuls test. SAS has arranged the means for the four groups in order of their numeric magnitudes. The last column in that table tells us from which group each mean is. The letters to the left of those means indicate the results of comparing the means using the Student-Neuman-Keuls protocol. There are two ways in which we can use those letters. One is by imagining each string of letters representing a line connecting means that are not significantly different (like in Example 10-12).[15] The other way is to note which letters are assigned to each mean, then, as the output points out, any pair of means that have the same letter to their left are not statistically different from each other. The mean for the southeast (212.000), the mean for the southwest (207.000), and the mean for the northeast (202.000) all have "A" to their left. That tells us that we cannot reject the null hypotheses that compare those means to each other. Likewise, the means of the southwest, northeast, and northwest (197.000) all have a letter "B" to their left. This tells us that we cannot reject the null hypotheses that compare those means. The only null hypothesis that can be rejected is

---

[15]It is to facilitate this interpretation that letters appear in the spaces between means.

that the mean for the southeast is equal to the mean for the northwest. We can tell that this null hypothesis can be rejected by the fact that the mean for the southeast has only the letter "A" to its left and the mean for the northwest has only a letter "B" to its left. Means that have <u>different</u> letters to their left in this output have <u>statistically significant</u> differences.

The SAS output in Example 10-13 is what we could expect if we were performing a one-way analysis of variance or a factorial analysis of variance with a statistically significant interaction. If we are using a factorial analysis of variance design in which there is not a statistically significant interaction, means for each of the factors can be compared by their own separate analyses. The next example shows the result of the Student-Neuman-Keuls test for the factorial analysis of variance in Example 10-9.

Example 10-14   The following is the result of asking SAS to perform Student-Neuman-Keuls test on the main effects from the factorial ANOVA in Example 10-9:

```
                    The ANOVA Procedure

          Student-Newman-Keuls Test for CHOLESTEROL

NOTE: This test controls the Type I experimentwise error rate under the complete null
hypothesis but not under partial null hypotheses.

               Alpha                    0.05
               Error Degrees of Freedom   36
               Error Mean Square      130.3889

               Number of Means            2
               Critical Range       7.3233923

        Means with the same letter are not significantly different.

        SNK Grouping       Mean     N     NS

              A          209.500    20    SOUTH

              B          199.500    20    NORTH
```

```
                        The ANOVA Procedure

              Student-Newman-Keuls Test for CHOLESTEROL

NOTE: This test controls the Type I experimentwise error rate under the complete null
hypothesis but not under partial null hypotheses.

                    Alpha                          0.05
                    Error Degrees of Freedom         36
                    Error Mean Square          130.3889

                    Number of Means                   2
                    Critical Range            7.3233923

         Means with the same letter are not significantly different.

          SNK Grouping         Mean      N    EW

                   A         207.000     20    EAST
                   A
                   A         202.000     20    WEST
```

Let us interpret this output.

The first half of that output addresses the north-south main effect by comparing the overall mean for the south (209.500) with the overall mean for the north (199.500). Since those two means have different letters to their left, we are able to reject the null hypothesis that those mean are equal to the same value in the population. The second half of the output addresses the east-west main effect. Here, the means both have the letter "A" to their left. Thus, we are not able to reject the null hypothesis that the overall mean for the east (207.000) is the same as the overall mean for the west (202.000).

In this particular example, there are only two categories of each factor and, thus, only two means for each main effect. When there are only two categories, we do not need to perform a posterior test to determine which means are different. Instead, we know about these differences from the factorial analysis of variance test for the main effects. In Example 10-10, we were able to reject the null hypothesis of no main north-south main effect, but we were unable to reject the null hypothesis of no east-west main effect. These results are consistent with the Student-Neuman-Keuls tests. Namely, the means for the north and south are statistically different but the means for the east and west are not statistically different.

BOTH CONTINUOUS AND NOMINAL INDEPENDENT VARIABLES

When a set of data consists of a mixture of continuous and nominal independent variables, we analyze those data using the **analysis of covariance** or (**ANCOVA**). Analysis of covariance can be thought of in two ways. One way to think about it is as an analysis of variance in which the nominal independent variable(s) specify the groups to be compared and the continuous independent variable(s) are included to control for their effect on the dependent variable.[16] Another way to think about it is as a multiple regression analysis in which nominal independent variables are included in the regression equation. Although both ways are correct, it is this latter way that is the more frequent in modern statistical thinking. Thus, we will discuss analysis of covariance in terms of a parallel multiple regression.

As an illustration of the type of study in which we would use analysis of covariance to analyze the data, let us suppose that we are interested in looking at the relationship between two antihypertensive medications and diastolic blood pressure while controlling for the effect of time since diagnosis of hypertension. In this study, diastolic blood pressure is the continuous dependent variable, treatment (new treatment versus standard treatment) is a nominal independent variable, and time since diagnosis is a continuous independent variable. Then, we can think of the following multiple regression equation as representing the relationship among those variables in the population:

$$\mu_{DBP|TIME,TREATMENT} = \alpha + \beta_1 \cdot TIME + \beta_2 \cdot TREATMENT \qquad \{10.11\}$$

where

$\mu_{DBP|TIME,TREATMENT}$ = mean diastolic blood pressure value in the population that corresponds to persons with a certain time since diagnosis and assignment to a particular treatment group

$TIME$ = time since diagnosis of hypertension

$TREATMENT$ = treatment group to which a person was assigned

As in regression analysis, we would like to use the regression equation to estimate the mean of the dependent variable values that correspond to specific values of the independent variables. This is accomplished by substituting values for the independent variables in the regression equation. This will not work for Equation {10.11}, since *TREATMENT* is a nominal independent variable having values of "yes" or "no" (i.e., new treatment or standard treatment). Multiplying those values by a regression coefficient has no meaning as far as the regression equation is concerned. To have meaning, all of the independent variables in a regression equation must have a numeric value. So, to include it in a regression equation,

---

[16]It is this way of thinking about the analysis of covariance that gives it its name. Continuous independent variables are called "covariates" in (older) statistical terminology.

we need to represent the nominal independent variable numerically.

Indicator ("Dummy") Variables

The trick here is to represent the nominal independent variable numerically without assigning quantitative meaning to its inherent qualitative nature. We faced this same task in Chapter 9 when we wanted to use the REG procedure to perform a test for trend. In that instance, we created an **indicator** (or **dummy**) **variable** by making the number one represent an observation in which the event occurred and zero represent an observation in which the event did not occur[17] These two numbers (zero and one) are numeric, but they differ qualitatively instead of quantitatively.[18]

In our example of two treatment groups, we could set the indicator variable equal to one if the person received the new treatment and equal to zero if the person received the standard treatment. Equation {10.12} illustrates the multiple regression equation shown in Equation{10.11}, but with an indicator variable (*TX*) representing the nominal independent variable (*TREATMENT*).

$$\mu_{DBP|TIME,TX} = \alpha + \beta_1 \cdot TIME + \beta_2 \cdot TX \qquad \{10.12\}$$

where

TX = indicator variable that is equal to one if the person received the new treatment or equal to zero if the person received the standard treatment

To see how we can interpret the regression coefficients in Equation{10.12}, let us first think about persons who receive the standard treatment. For those persons, *TX* is equal to zero. Then, Equation {10.12} becomes the following:

$$\mu_{DBP|TIME,TX=0} = \alpha + \beta_1 \cdot TIME + \beta_2 \cdot 0 = \alpha + \beta_1 \cdot TIME \qquad \{10.13\}$$

Since *TX* is equal to zero in Equation{10.13}, the regression coefficient for the indicator variable (β_2) disappears from the regression equation. What are left are the intercept, one regression coefficient (β_1), and the independent variable *TIME*. Since there is only one independent variable in that equation, it is really just a bivariable regression equation with an intercept equal to α and with a slope equal to β_1.

---

[17]We will take a look at another method of defining these variables in the section of this chapter that considers the general linear model.

[18]We had a numbering system without the concept of zero for millennia. It is believed that the Babylonians first introduced the concept in the Old World and the Mayans independently introduced it in the New World. In the Old World, however, it was not a well accepted concept until much later. Around 450 BC Zeno of Elea, a Greek philosopher and cohort of Socrates, struggled with the concept of zero as part of a numbering system. In essence, his argument was that "nothing" cannot be included with "something."

Next, let us think about persons who receive the new treatment. They have a value of one for the indicator variable, and the resulting regression equation is:

$$\mu_{DBP|TIME,TX=1} = \alpha + \beta_1 \cdot TIME + \beta_2 \cdot 1 = \alpha + \beta_1 \cdot TIME + \beta_2 \qquad \{10.14\}$$

In Equation{10.14}, the indicator variable is equal to one, so that its regression coefficient remains in the regression equation. In fact, this is the only difference between the regression equation for persons who received the standard treatment (Equation{10.13}) and persons who received the new treatment (Equation{10.14}: their diastolic blood pressure values differ by the value of β_2. Like when the indicator variable is equal to zero, this is really a bivariable regression equation. In this case, the intercept is equal to $\alpha+\beta_2$ and the slope is equal to β_1. The relationship between these two bivariable regression equations is illustrated graphically in Figure 10-7.

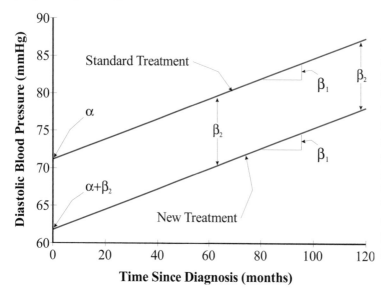

Figure 10-7 Illustration of how the regression coefficient for an indicator variable is interpreted. In this case, the indicator variable differentiates between two treatment groups. The regression coefficient for the indicator variable (β_2) specifies the difference between the means of the dependent variable for the two groups, regardless of the value of time since diagnosis. In this example, β_2 is a negative number, indicating that DBP is lower when the indicator variable is equal to one.

Interaction Variables

If nominal independent variables are represented only by indicator variables, the regression coefficients for those indicator variables specify differences between mean values of the dependent variable regardless of the value of the continuous independent variable(s) or other indicator variable(s). In other words, the regression lines for the groups are parallel to each other (as seen in Figure 10-7). To allow the regression lines to have different slopes, we need to include another kind of variable in the regression equation. The variables that create differences in slopes are called **interaction variables**. An interaction variable is created by multiplying an indicator variable by another independent variable. This other independent variable can be either a continuous independent variable or another indicator variable. Equation {10.15} shows the regression equation describing the relationship between time since diagnosis, treatment group, and diastolic blood pressure with inclusion of an interaction variable.

$$\mu_{DBP|TIME,TX=1} = \alpha + \beta_1 \cdot TIME + \beta_2 \cdot TX + \beta_3 \cdot TIME \cdot TX \qquad \{10.15\}$$

where

TX = indicator variable that is equal to one if the person received the new treatment or equal to zero if the person received the standard treatment

$TIME \cdot TX$ = interaction between time since diagnosis and treatment group, created by multiplying the continuous independent variable ($TIME$) by the indicator variable (TX).

To see how to interpret the regression coefficient for the interaction, let us first take a look at how Equation {10.15} appears when the indicator variable is equal to zero. In the example of diastolic blood pressure and its relationship to time since diagnosis and treatment group, the indicator variable is equal to zero for a person who receives the standard treatment. Equation {10.16} illustrates what happens to Equation {10.15} when the indicator variable is equal to zero.

$$\mu_{DBP|TIME,TX=0} = \alpha + \beta_1 \cdot TIME + \beta_2 \cdot 0 + \beta_3 \cdot TIME \cdot 0 = \alpha + \beta_1 \cdot TIME \qquad \{10.16\}$$

When the indicator variable is equal to zero (e.g., when a person receives the standard treatment), the interaction variable is also equal to zero. As a result, adding an interaction variable does not change the regression equation when the indicator is equal to zero. It is still a bivariable regression equation with an intercept equal to α and with a slope equal to β_1 .

When the indicator variable is equal to one, however, the interaction variable changes the regression equation. This is illustrated in Equation {10.17}.

$$\mu_{DBP|TIME,TX=1} = \alpha + \beta_1 \cdot TIME + \beta_2 \cdot 1 + \beta_3 \cdot TIME \cdot 1 = \alpha + \beta_1 \cdot TIME + \beta_2 + \beta_3 \cdot TIME \qquad \{10.17\}$$

To see how the regression coefficient for the interaction variable is interpreted, let us do a little algebra and rearrange Equation{10.17}:

$$\mu_{DBP|TIME,TX=1} = \alpha + \beta_1 \cdot TIME + \beta_2 + \beta_3 \cdot TIME = (\alpha + \beta_2) + (\beta_1 + \beta_3) \cdot TIME \qquad \{10.18\}$$

Now, let us compare Equation {10.18} to Equation {10.16} to see how the equations differ between the treatment groups. In Equation{10.16}, the slope of the regression line is equal to the regression coefficient for *TIME* (β_1). In Equation{10.18}, however, the slope of the regression line is equal to the sum of the regression coefficients for *TIME* and for the interaction variable ($\beta_1+\beta_3$). Thus, the regression coefficient for the interaction variable tells us about the difference between the slopes of the regression lines for persons in the two treatment groups.

Equation {10.18} also illustrates further how the regression coefficient for the indicator variable (β_2) is interpreted. Without an interaction variable in the regression equation (Equation{10.14}), the regression coefficient for the indicator variable told us about the difference between the mean diastolic blood pressure values in the two treatment groups, regardless of a person's time since diagnosis. Since the regression lines were parallel before we included the interaction variable, it really did not matter at what time since diagnosis the means were compared; the difference between the means was equal to the same value.

When there is an interaction and, as a result, a difference between the slopes of the regression lines, the difference between the mean diastolic blood pressure values will change for persons with different times since diagnosis. Thus, the means of dependent variable values need to be compared for a specific value of the continuous independent variable (e.g., for persons with a particular time since diagnosis). Only if the continuous independent variable is equal to zero does the regression coefficient for the indicator variable tell us the difference between the means. In other words, the regression coefficient for the indicator variable tells us the difference between the intercepts of the regression lines. This is illustrated graphically in Figure 10-8.

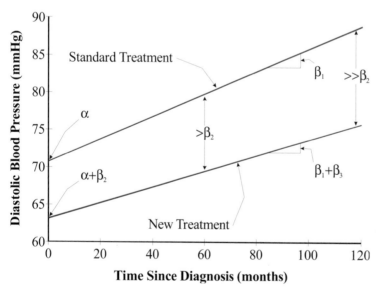

Figure 10-8 Illustration of how regression coefficients for an indicator variable and an interaction variable are interpreted. The regression coefficient for the indicator variable (β_2) differentiates between the intercepts of the two groups. The regression coefficient for the interaction variable (β_3) specifies the difference between the slopes of the regression lines for the two groups. In this example, β_2 and β_3 are negative numbers, indicating that the intercept and slope are lower when the indicator variable is equal to one.

When interpreting the results of an analysis of covariance, we must first consider the interaction variable(s). The reason for this is that, in the presence of an interaction, we cannot interpret the regression coefficient for the continuous independent variable (β_1) as the slope of the regression line without specifying which group is being considered. By definition, the presence of an interaction indicates that the slopes differ between the groups. Also, the presence of an interaction affects the way in which we interpret the regression coefficient for the indicator variable (β_2) as the difference in the means of the dependent variable values between the two groups. When there is an interaction, the difference between those means varies according to the value of the continuous independent variable. In that case, the regression coefficient for the indicator variable tells us the difference between means when the indicator variable is equal to zero. The next example illustrates how we can apply these principles when we use the REG procedure in SAS to perform an analysis of covariance.[19]

Example 10-15 In our discussion of analysis of covariance, we have been thinking about a study in which diastolic blood pressure (the dependent variable) is compared between persons who received a new antihypertensive medication and persons who received a standard treatment. Those two groups are represented by a nominal independent variable. Also, the comparison between diastolic blood pressure and treatment group is performed while controlling for time since diagnosis (a continuous independent variable).

Now, let us suppose that we have made these observations on 42 persons, 21 of whom were randomly assigned to receive the new treatment and 21 of whom were assigned to receive the standard treatment. To represent those treatment groups in the regression equation, we created an indicator variable (*TX*) that is equal to one if the person received the new treatment and equal to zero if the person received the standard treatment. Also, we created an interaction variable (*TIME_TX*) by multiplying time since diagnosis by the indicator variable. Now, suppose that we were to obtain the following output from the REG procedure when we analyze those data.

```
                         The REG Procedure
                          Model: MODEL1
                     Dependent Variable: DBP

                        Analysis of Variance

                              Sum of        Mean
    Source          DF       Squares       Square    F Value    Pr > F
    Model            3     1944.16147    648.05382     10.55    <.0001
    Error           38     2334.33853     61.42996
    Corrected Total 41     4278.50000


            Root MSE              7.83773    R-Square     0.4544
            Dependent Mean       74.50000    Adj R-Sq     0.4113
            Coeff Var            10.52044
```

---

[19]REG is not the only SAS procedure that can be used to perform an analysis of covariance. Another approach is to use the GLM procedure. We will take a look at output from the GLM procedure later in this chapter.

```
                             Parameter Estimates


                        Parameter        Standard
        Variable    DF   Estimate           Error    t Value    Pr > |t|
        Intercept    1   70.21645         3.30199      21.26      <.0001
        TIME         1    0.14957         0.04708       3.18      0.0030
        TX           1   -7.61472         4.66972      -1.63      0.1112
        TIME_TX      1   -0.02944         0.06657      -0.44      0.6609
```

Let us interpret this output.

As explained previously, the first thing we consider in analyses of covariance are the interactions. In this case there is only one: the interaction between time since diagnosis and treatment group. The last row in the SAS output tells us about that interaction. The last entry in that row (0.6609) is the *P*-value for the test of the null hypothesis that the regression coefficient for the interaction is equal to zero in the population. Since that *P*-value is greater than 0.05, we cannot reject the null hypothesis. In this circumstance, we can conclude that there is not an interaction between time since diagnosis and treatment group.

In Example 10-15, we considered an analysis of covariance in which the interaction term is not statistically significant. That implies that we cannot rule out the possibility that the regression coefficient in the population is equal to zero. Even so, the regression coefficient for the interaction term in the sample is <u>not</u> equal to zero. This means that the point estimates for the slopes of the regression lines are different. From Example 10-15, the slope for the regression line for persons who receive the standard treatment is equal to 0.14957 (the regression coefficient for the continuous independent variable, *TIME*). The slope for persons who receive the new treatment is equal to 0. 14957 – 0.02944 = 0.12013 (-0.02944 is the regression coefficient for the interaction). Those two estimates of slopes are not significantly different, but they <u>are</u> numerically different.

    If the interaction term is not significantly different from zero, it is often removed from the regression equation and the analysis repeated without it.[20] Then, there is only one estimate of the slope that can be applied to both groups. This makes the interpretation of the results of the analysis more straightforward. This is illustrated in the next example.

Example 10-16 In Example 10-15 we found that the regression coefficient for the interaction term was not significantly different from zero. That implies that the slopes of the regression equations for the two groups were not significantly different from each other. If we want to have a single estimate of the slope that can be applied to both regression

---

[20]To learn more about the process of selecting which variables to include in a regression equation (i.e., "modeling") see *Building Multivariable Models* available from Stat-Aid.

equations, we need to redo the analysis, leaving out the interaction term. When we do that, we get the following output from the REG procedure.

```
                        The REG Procedure
                          Model: MODEL1
                     Dependent Variable: DBP

                       Analysis of Variance

                             Sum of          Mean
Source              DF      Squares        Square    F Value    Pr > F
Model                2   1932.15108     966.07554      16.06    <.0001
Error               39   2346.34892      60.16279
Corrected Total     41   4278.50000


            Root MSE              7.75647    R-Square     0.4516
            Dependent Mean       74.50000    Adj R-Sq     0.4235
            Coeff Var            10.41137


                       Parameter Estimates

                       Parameter      Standard
Variable        DF      Estimate         Error    t Value    Pr > |t|
Intercept        1      71.09957       2.60222      27.32     <.0001
TIME             1       0.13485       0.03294       4.09     0.0002
TX               1      -9.38095       2.39370      -3.92     0.0003
```

Let us interpret this output.

Now, the two regression equations have the same slope (0.13485).[21] This makes interpretation of the results more straightforward. Now, the only difference between persons who received the new treatment and persons who received the standard treatment is that the mean diastolic blood pressure for persons who received the new treatment had a mean diastolic blood pressure that is 9.38095 less than the diastolic blood pressure for persons who received the standard treatment. Because the interaction term has been removed, this difference applied to persons regardless of time since diagnosis (as in Figure 10-7).

Removing the interaction term(s) from an ANCOVA model has the effect of simplifying the relationship(s) between variables, but it also has an effect on the independent contributions of the independent variables that were involved in the interaction. Since an interaction is created by multiplying the independent variables together, it is not a surprise that the interaction is correlated with those independent variables. If that correlated variation is used

---

[21] This is the mean of the separate slopes from the model in which the interaction was included (Example 10-15).

to estimate dependent variable values, there is multicollinearity among the independent variables and the interaction. When the interaction is removed from the regression equation, that multicollinearity is also removed. The effect of removing multicollinearity is to increase the independent contributions of the independent variables that remain in the model. We can see that effect by comparing the results in Example 10-16 to the results in Example 10-15. The *P*-values for each of the independent variables in Example 10-16 (without the interaction) are smaller than their *P*-values in Example 10-15 (with the interaction).[22] In fact, the reductions in *P*-values in Example 10-16 are great enough that the indicator of treatment group becomes statistically significant.[23]

General Linear Model

Thinking about analysis of covariance as a regression analysis leads to the use of indicator variables to represent nominal independent variables in a regression equation. Strictly speaking, an analysis of covariance includes at least one nominal independent variable and at least one continuous independent variable. In general, however, it is not necessary that the regression equation include any continuous independent variables. For instance, consider the following regression equation:

$$\mu_{CHOL} = \alpha + \beta_1 \cdot NS + \beta_2 \cdot EW + \beta_3 \cdot NS \cdot EW \qquad \{10.19\}$$

where

μ_{CHOL} = mean serum cholesterol level in the population

NS = indicator variable that is equal to one if the person is from the north or equal to zero if the person is from the south

EW = indicator variable that is equal to one if the person is from the east or equal to zero if the person is from the west

Equation $\{10.19\}$ consists of two indicator variables (NS and EW) representing two nominal independent variables. These nominal independent variables specify the geographic region in which a person lives. The dependent variable is a person's serum cholesterol level. This sounds like the example we used earlier in this chapter when we were discussing factorial analysis of variance. The next example compares that factorial analysis of variance to Equation $\{10.19\}$ using SAS's REG procedure.

---

[22]We learned earlier in this chapter that smaller *P*-values for individual independent variables indicate a greater independent contribution of the variables.

[23]The same thing can happen if an interaction is removed from a factorial ANOVA.

Example 10-17 In Example 10-9, we examined the following SAS output as result of analyzing the data in Example 10-6 as a factorial analysis of variance using the ANOVA procedure.

```
                        The ANOVA Procedure

                     Class Level Information

            Class         Levels    Values
            NS               2      NORTH SOUTH
            EW               2      EAST WEST

                Number of observations    40

                     The ANOVA Procedure

Dependent Variable: CHOLESTEROL
                                Sum of          Mean
   Source              DF       Squares        Square     F Value    Pr > F
   Model                3     1250.000000    416.666667      3.04    0.0413
   Error               36     4934.000000    137.055556
   Corrected Total     39     6184.000000


          R-Square     Coeff Var     Root MSE    CHOLESTEROL Mean
          0.202135     5.724730      11.70707        204.5000


   Source              DF      Anova SS     Mean Square    F Value    Pr > F
   NS                   1    1000.000000    1000.000000       7.30    0.0105
   EW                   1     250.000000     250.000000       1.82    0.1853
   NS*EW                1       0.000000       0.000000       0.00    1.0000
```

The values in this output that provide information about differences between the mean serum cholesterol levels are the F-ratio and corresponding P-value at the top of the output and the three F-ratios and corresponding P-values at the bottom of the output. At the top of the output, the F-ratio tests the omnibus null hypothesis (that all four means are equal to the same value in the population). Since the corresponding P-value (0.0413) is less than 0.05, we can reject that null hypothesis.

At the bottom of the output, the F-ratios test null hypotheses about main effects and the interaction. The first of those null hypotheses we need to consider states that there is no interaction between the north-south main effect and the east-west main effect. We test this null hypothesis by looking at the P-value in the row headed "NS*EW" (1.0000). Since that P-value is greater than 0.05, we fail to reject the null hypothesis of no interaction, and, as a result, we can examine each of the main effects.

To test the null hypothesis that the mean serum cholesterol levels in the north are equal to the mean serum cholesterol levels in the south (i.e., the north-south main effect), we look at the P-value in the row headed by "NS" (0.0105). Since that P-value is less than 0.05, we can reject the null hypothesis and conclude that the mean in the north is different from the mean in the south in the population. In the same way, we can test the null hypothesis that the mean serum cholesterol value in the east is equal to the mean serum cholesterol value in the west by looking at the *P*-value in the row headed by "EW" (0.1853). Since that *P*-value is greater than 0.05, we cannot reject the null hypothesis.

Now, let us reanalyze those same data using the REG procedure and the regression equation as it appears in Equation{10.19}. The following is the output we get from that analysis.

```
                          The REG Procedure
                   Dependent Variable: CHOLESTEROL

                        Analysis of Variance

                              Sum of          Mean
   Source              DF     Squares        Square    F Value    Pr > F
   Model                3  1250.00000     416.66667       3.04    0.0413
   Error               36  4934.00000     137.05556
   Corrected Total     39  6184.00000


            Root MSE              11.70707    R-Square     0.2021
            Dependent Mean       204.50000    Adj R-Sq     0.1356
            Coeff Var              5.72473


                        Parameter Estimates

                       Parameter      Standard
   Variable     DF      Estimate         Error    t Value    Pr > |t|
   Intercept     1     207.00000       3.70210      55.91      <.0001
   NS            1     -10.00000       5.23556      -1.91      0.0641
   EW            1       5.00000       5.23556       0.96      0.3459
   NS_EW         1             0       7.40420       0.00      1.0000
```

Let us interpret this output.

The *F*-ratio at the top of the REG procedure output tests the omnibus null hypothesis (that none of the independent variables help to estimate dependent variable values). That is the same as the omnibus null hypothesis that mean serum cholesterol values are the same in the four geographic regions (i.e., the null hypothesis addressing all of the groups of dependent variable values in analysis of variance). That *F*-ratio and corresponding *P*-value (0.0413) are the same in this output as in the previous output from the ANOVA procedure.

Now, let us take a look at the *t*-values and *P*-values at the bottom of the output from the REG procedure. Those values test the null hypothesis that the corresponding regression coefficient is equal to zero in the population. The *P*-values are not the same as those at the bottom of the output from the ANOVA procedure, so they must be testing different null hypotheses. Next, we will determine what those null hypotheses are and how they are different from hypotheses tested in analysis of variance. Our purpose in doing this is to gain a fuller understanding of both types of analysis.

_____

In Equation{10.19}, we represented the relationship between geographic region and serum cholesterol with a regression equation that included two indicator variables: *NS* and *EW*. Those indicator values were given values of zero and one. This is a common choice for the values of indicator variables, but it is not the only choice. Let us take a closer look at what these regression coefficients imply and, then, we will consider another way in which to represent nominal independent variables in a regression equation.

Table 10-2 shows how the regression coefficients for zero/one indicator variables relate to the estimated mean of the dependent variable for each group of dependent variable values. The intercept (*a*) estimates the mean in the group that corresponds to all of the indicator variables being equal to zero. For serum cholesterol levels, that group includes persons from the southeast. Thus, the estimate of the intercept in the regression output in Example 10-17 (207 mg/dL) is the estimate of the mean serum cholesterol level in the southwest.

Table 10-2 Interpretation of the estimated regression coefficients when two nominal independent variables are represented by indicator variables that have the values of either zero or one.

Region	$b_1 \cdot NS$	$b_2 \cdot EW$	$b_3 \cdot NS \cdot EW$	$\widehat{CHOL}$*	Mean
Southwest	$b_1 \cdot 0$	$b_2 \cdot 0$	$b_3 \cdot 0 \cdot 0$	a	207
Northwest	$b_1 \cdot 1$	$b_2 \cdot 0$	$b_3 \cdot 1 \cdot 0$	$a + b_1$	207-10=197
Southeast	$b_1 \cdot 0$	$b_2 \cdot 1$	$b_3 \cdot 0 \cdot 1$	$a + b_2$	207+5=212
Northeast	$b_1 \cdot 1$	$b_2 \cdot 1$	$b_3 \cdot 1 \cdot 1$	$a + b_1 + b_2 + b_3$	207-10+5+0=202

*Estimated value of the dependent variable

Now, let us consider the regression coefficients for the two indicator variables. Table 10-2 shows us that we add the regression coefficient for the north-south indicator variable ($b_1 = -10$ mg/dL) to the intercept ($a = 207$ mg/dL), to get the mean serum cholesterol level in the northwest (197 mg/dL). Thus, the regression coefficient for the north-south indicator variable tells us how much serum cholesterol levels change, on the average, as we go from the southwest to the northwest. Likewise, Table 10-2 shows us that we add the regression coefficient for the east-west indicator variable ($b_2 = 5$ mg/dL) to the intercept ($a = 207$ mg/dL), to get the mean serum cholesterol levels in the southeast (212 mg/dL). So, the regression coefficient for the east-west indicator variable tells us how serum cholesterol levels change, on the average, as we go from the southwest to the southeast.

If we know the intercept and the regression coefficients for the indicator variables, we can calculate estimates of the mean serum cholesterol levels among persons in the southwest, northwest, and southeast. This leaves only the mean in the northeast. To estimate that mean, we add both of the regression coefficients for the indicator variables (-10 mg/dL and 5 mg/dL) to the intercept and, then, we add to that sum the regression coefficient for the interaction ($b_3 = 0$ mg/dL).

In this example, the regression coefficient for the interaction is equal to zero. If the regression coefficient for the interaction is equal to zero in the population, that implies that the difference between the means in the north and south is the same in the east as it is in the west. That is to say, the regression coefficient for the north-south main effect is equal to the difference between the means in the northeast and southeast as well as the difference between the means in the northwest and southwest.

When testing null hypotheses in this regression model, we are testing null hypotheses about mean serum cholesterol levels. For instance, testing the null hypothesis that the intercept is equal to zero in the population is the same as testing the null hypothesis that the mean serum cholesterol in the southwest is equal to zero in the population. Testing the null hypothesis that one of the regression coefficients for an indicator is equal to zero in the population is the same as testing the null hypothesis that each of those means is equal to the mean for the southwest.   When testing the null hypothesis that the interaction's regression coefficient is equal to zero we are testing the hypothesis that the difference between the southwest and the northeast is equal to the difference between the southwest and northwest added to the difference between the southwest and the southeast. These null hypotheses are summarized in Table 10-3.

Table 10-3 Null hypotheses tested when two nominal independent variables are represented by indicator variables that are equal to either zero or one. Those null hypotheses are stated first in terms of the parameters of the regression equation and, then, in terms of the means for each group of dependent variable values.

Null Hypotheses in Terms of:

Regression Parameters	Means
$H_0 : \alpha = 0$	$H_0 : \mu_{SW} = 0$
$H_0 : \beta_1 = 0$	$H_0 : \mu_{SW} = \mu_{NW}$
$H_0 : \beta_2 = 0$	$H_0 : \mu_{SW} = \mu_{SE}$
$H_0 : \beta_3 = 0$	$H_0 : \mu_{NE} = \mu_{SW} + (\mu_{SW} - \mu_{NW}) + (\mu_{SW} - \mu_{SE})$ [24]

---

[24] Another way to state this null hypothesis is to say that $\mu_{SW} - \mu_{NW} = \mu_{SE} - \mu_{NE}$ (i.e., the difference between north and south is the same in the east as it is in the west) and $\mu_{SW} - \mu_{SE} = \mu_{NW} - \mu_{NE}$ (i.e., the difference between west and east is the same in the north as it is in the south).

Now, let us compare those null hypotheses to the null hypotheses tested in factorial analysis of variance. In factorial analysis of variance, we test null hypotheses that address the main effects of each of the factors and their interaction(s). One of those main effects in this example is the difference between serum cholesterol values in the north and the south. These means differ from the ones in the null hypotheses in Table 10-3 in that the comparison between the north and the south in factorial analysis of variance (i.e., the north/south main effect) is made without regard to whether it makes that comparison in the east or in the west. In Table 10-3, however, the comparison between north and south is restricted to persons from the west ($H_0 : \mu_{SW} = \mu_{NW}$). Likewise, the comparison between the east and the west in factorial analysis of variance is made without regard to whether it makes that comparison in the east or in the west. In Table 10-3, however, the comparison between east and west is restricted to persons from the south ($H_0 : \mu_{SW} = \mu_{SE}$). So, when we make the indicator variables in Equation {10.19} equal to zero and one, the regression coefficients tell us how the group represented by a value of one for a particular indicator variable differs from the group represented by the intercept (i.e., the group for which there is no indicator variable). This is not the way in which comparisons are made in factorial analysis of variance.

To make Equation {10.19} more like factorial analysis of variance, we need to make another choice for the values of indicator variables. Another choice is to use the values of positive one and negative one. Like zero and one, the values of positive and negative one do not imply a quantitative difference between groups, thus they are appropriate to represent the qualitative nature of nominal variables numerically. Equation {10.20} shows a regression equation with positive one/negative one indicator variables.

$$\mu_{CHOL} = \alpha + \beta_1 \cdot NS' + \beta_2 \cdot EW' + \beta_3 \cdot NS' \cdot EW' \qquad \{10.20\}$$

where

μ_{CHOL}	=	mean serum cholesterol level in the population
NS'	=	indicator variable that is equal to positive one if the person is from the north or equal to negative one if the person is from the south
EW'	=	indicator variable that is equal to positive one if the person is from the east or equal to negative one if the person is from the west

The next example illustrates the use of positive one/negative one indicator variables and how the regression coefficients relate to a factorial analysis of variance.

Example 10-18 The following SAS output is result of analyzing the data in Example 10-6 using SAS's REG procedure and representing the nominal independent variables in the regression equation with positive one/negative one indicator variables.

```
                          The REG Procedure
                      Dependent Variable: CHOLESTEROL

                          Analysis of Variance

                               Sum of        Mean
     Source             DF     Squares      Square    F Value    Pr > F
     Model               3   1250.00000   416.66667      3.04    0.0413
     Error              36   4934.00000   137.05556
     Corrected Total    39   6184.00000


             Root MSE                11.70707   R-Square     0.2021
             Dependent Mean         204.50000   Adj R-Sq     0.1356
             Coeff Var                5.72473


                          Parameter Estimates

                         Parameter      Standard
     Variable      DF     Estimate         Error    t Value    Pr > |t|
     Intercept      1    204.50000       1.85105     110.48      <.0001
     NS             1     -5.00000       1.85105      -2.70      0.0105
     EW             1      2.50000       1.85105       1.35      0.1853
     NS_EW          1            0       1.85105       0.00      1.0000
```

Let us interpret this output.

The *F*-ratio and corresponding *P*-value in the table at the top of this output are the same as those in the table at the top of the REG procedure output in Example 10-17. In both instances, these test the omnibus null hypothesis that all of the independent variables taken together do not help to estimate dependent variable values. Since all of the independent variables are nominal, this is the same as the ANOVA omnibus null hypothesis that the means in all of the groups of dependent variable values are equal to the same value in the population. The way in which we have defined the indicator variables does not change the fact that there are four groups of dependent variable values corresponding to four geographic regions. The only thing we have changed is the way in which those four groups of dependent variable values are represented in the regression equation.

The *t*-values and their corresponding *P*-values in the table at the bottom of this output are somewhat different from those values in the table at the bottom of the REG procedure output in Example 10-17. That difference is due to the way in which the four groups of dependent variable values are represented by the indicator variables in those analyses. If we compare the *P*-values in the table at the bottom of this output to the ones in the table at the bottom of the ANOVA procedure output in Example 10-17 however, we see that they match. Specifically, the *P*-value for the *NS* indicator variable in this example is the same as the one testing the north-south main effect in Example 10-17 (0.0105) and the *P*-value for the *EW* indicator variable in this example is the same as the one testing the east-west main effect in Example 10-17 (0.1853). Next, we will discover why this is the case.

The interpretation of regression coefficients for positive one/negative one indicator variables is different from the interpretation of the regression coefficients for zero/one indicator variables. To help us understand their interpretation, let us take a look at Table 10-4 in which the mean serum cholesterol values for the four geographic regions are represented by the positive one/negative one indicator variables in Equation {10.20}.

Table 10-4 Interpretation of the estimated regression coefficients when two nominal independent variables are represented by indicator variables that have the values of either positive one or negative one.

Region	$b_1 \cdot NS'$	$b_2 \cdot EW'$	$b_3 \cdot NS' \cdot EW'$	$\widehat{CHOL}$	Mean
Southwest	$b_1 \cdot -1$	$b_2 \cdot -1$	$b_3 \cdot -1 \cdot -1$	$a - b_1 - b_2 + b_3$	204.5-(-5)-2.5+0=207
Northwest	$b_1 \cdot +1$	$b_2 \cdot -1$	$b_3 \cdot +1 \cdot -1$	$a + b_1 - b_2 - b_3$	204.5+(-5)-2.5-0=197
Southeast	$b_1 \cdot -1$	$b_2 \cdot +1$	$b_3 \cdot -1 \cdot +1$	$a - b_1 + b_2 - b_3$	204.5-(-5)+2.5-0=212
Northeast	$b_1 \cdot +1$	$b_2 \cdot +1$	$b_3 \cdot +1 \cdot +1$	$a + b_1 + b_2 + b_3$	204.5+(-5)+2.5+0=202

When positive one/negative one indicator variables are used, the intercept no longer represents the mean of one of the groups of dependent variable values, as it does when zero/one indicators variables are used. Instead, the intercept represents the overall mean[25] of the dependent variable values (i.e., the mean of the groups' means).[26] Then, the regression coefficients represent differences from that overall mean.[27] The tests of the null hypotheses that these regression coefficients are equal to zero in the population are described in

---

[25]The overall mean is sometimes called the **grand mean**.

[26]That this is the case can be verified by adding the coefficients that correspond to all of the means and dividing by the number of means. For Table 10-3, this becomes:

$$\frac{\mu_{SW} + \mu_{NW} + \mu_{SE} + \mu_{NE}}{4} = \frac{(a - b_1 - b_2 + b_3) + (a + b_1 - b_2 - b_3) + (a - b_1 + b_2 - b_3) + (a + b_1 + b_2 + b_3)}{4} = \frac{4 \cdot a}{4} = a$$

[27]In Equation{10.20}, the regression coefficient for the north/south indicator variable (NS') indicates how far away from the mean of all of the means (μ_{means}) are the means for the north ($\mu_N = (\mu_{NE} + \mu_{NW})/2$) and south ($\mu_S = (\mu_{SE} + \mu_{SW})/2$). Likewise, the regression coefficient for the east/west indicator variable (EW') indicates how far away from the mean of all of the means (μ_{means}) are the means for the east ($\mu_E = (\mu_{NE} + \mu_{SE})/2$) and west ($\mu_W = (\mu_{NW} + \mu_{SW})/2$). The regression coefficient for the interaction indicates how far away the mean for the southwest is from the overall mean (μ_{means}) plus the effect of going from north to south ($\mu_{means} - \mu_N$) and the effect of going from east to west ($\mu_{means} - \mu_E$).

relationship to the differences in means in Table 10-5.

Table 10-5 Null hypotheses tested when two nominal independent variables are represented by indicator variables that are equal to either positive one or negative one. Those null hypotheses are stated first in terms of the parameters of the regression equation and, then, in terms of the means for each group of dependent variable values. μ_{Means} refers to the mean of all of the means.

Null Hypotheses in Terms of:

Regression Parameters	Means
$H_0 : \alpha = 0$	$H_0 : \mu_{\text{means}} = 0$
$H_0 : \beta_1 = 0$	$H_0 : \mu_S = \mu_N$
$H_0 : \beta_2 = 0$	$H_0 : \mu_W = \mu_E$
$H_0 : \beta_3 = 0$	$H_0 : \mu_{SW} = \mu_{\text{means}} + (\mu_{\text{means}} - \mu_N) + (\mu_{\text{means}} - \mu_E)$

So, zero/one indicator variables specify differences from the mean of the dependent variable values in one of the groups (when both indicator variables are equal to zero) and positive one/negative one indicator variables specify differences from the overall mean.

Thus, testing the null hypothesis that a regression coefficient for a positive one/negative one indicator variable is equal to zero is the same as testing a main effect in factorial analysis of variance. Likewise, testing the null hypothesis that a regression coefficient for an interaction between two positive one/negative one indicator variables is equal to zero is the same as testing for an interaction in factorial analysis of variance. From these observations, we can conclude that regression analysis and analysis of variance are really just different forms of the same type of analysis. In fact, this is true of all of the methods of analysis we have discussed for a continuous dependent variable; they can all be expressed as a regression equation.

This unity of methods used to analyze a continuous dependent variables is called the **general linear model**. This is reflected in SAS by the existence of the GLM procedure.[28] This procedure allows a regression equation to include nominal and/or continuous dependent variables. When nominal independent variables are included in the regression equation, the GLM procedure will automatically create indicator variables and interactions.[29] If those indicator variables are created by the GLM procedure, they will be of the positive one/negative one type.[30] The next example illustrates the output from the GLM procedure.

‖ **Example 10-19** The following SAS output is result of analyzing the data in Example 10-6

---

[28]GLM stands for **G**eneral **L**inear **M**odel.

[29]When the REG procedure is used with nominal independent variables, the programmer must create the indicator and interaction variables. In the GLM procedure and the ANOVA procedure the indicator and interaction variables are created by the SAS procedure.

[30]This is also true of the ANOVA procedure.

using the GLM procedure and allowing the procedure to choose how to represent the nominal independent variables in the regression equation.

```
                        The GLM Procedure

                    Class Level Information

              Class        Levels    Values
              NS              2       NORTH SOUTH
              EW              2       EAST WEST

                  Dependent Variable: CHOLESTEROL

                            Sum of
    Source              DF     Squares     Mean Square    F Value    Pr > F
    Model                3   1250.000000    416.666667      3.04     0.0413
    Error               36   4934.000000    137.055556
    Corrected Total     39   6184.000000

            R-Square     Coeff Var     Root MSE     CHOLESTEROL Mean
            0.202135     5.724730      11.70707          204.5000

    Source              DF   Type I SS     Mean Square    F Value    Pr > F
    NS                   1  1000.000000    1000.000000      7.30     0.0105
    EW                   1   250.000000     250.000000      1.82     0.1853
    NS*EW                1     0.000000       0.000000      0.00     1.0000

    Source              DF   Type III SS   Mean Square    F Value    Pr > F
    NS                   1  1000.000000    1000.000000      7.30     0.0105
    EW                   1   250.000000     250.000000      1.82     0.1853
    NS*EW                1     0.000000       0.000000      0.00     1.0000
```

Let us interpret this output.

These results are the same as those obtained in Example 10-18, illustrating that the GLM procedure uses positive one/negative one indicator variables to represent nominal independent variables in the regression equation.

The purpose of learning about the general linear model is twofold. First, it helps us to understand the unifying principals behind all analyses for a continuous dependent variable. Second, it allows us to create analyses that are tailored to the research questions that are most relevant to us. In other words, understanding the general linear model means that we are not restricted to a few study designs for which there are established analyses. Instead, we can use indicator and interaction variables that best reflect our interest.

In the next chapter, we will look at nonparametric methods for multivariable data sets.

CHAPTER 11
Ordinal Dependent Variable

As for previous chapters about ordinal dependent variables, we expect to find methods in Chapter 11 that we would use as nonparametric analyses in the circumstance in which we are concerned about some of the assumptions made by a method in Chapter 10 (i.e., a method designed for a continuous dependent variable). With that expectation, we look to Chapter 11 for methods that are parallel to those just discussed in Chapter 10. In Chapter 10, we learned about multiple regression and correlation analyses for continuous independent variables, analysis of variance for nominal independent variables, and analysis of covariance for a mixture of continuous and nominal independent variables. A look at Flowchart 9 quickly reveals that few of those analyses have nonparametric parallels.

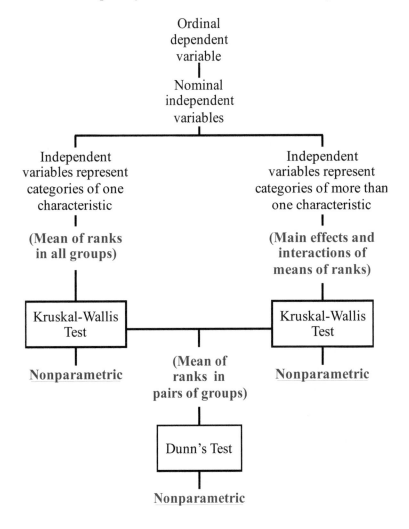

Flowchart 9 Flowchart showing multivariable analysis of an ordinal dependent variable. The point estimate that is most often used to describe the dependent variable is in color. The common name of the statistical test is enclosed in a box. The standard distribution that is used to test hypotheses and calculate confidence intervals is in color and underlined.

When we discussed bivariable analysis of an ordinal dependent variable (Chapter 8), we found that there is no nonparametric parallel to regression analysis. The reason for this is that a slope cannot be estimated for an ordinal dependent variable.[1] In multivariable analysis, this inability implies that we cannot have nonparametric parallels to multiple regression, multiple correlation,[2] or analysis of covariance. That leaves nonparametric parallels only to analysis of variance and posterior testing; statistical methods in which all of the independent variables represent nominal data.

Nonparametric Analysis of Variance

The **Kruskal-Wallis test** is the nonparametric method that is used to perform one-way and factorial analyses of variance without assuming that the sampling distribution is a Gaussian distribution. To perform this test by hand, we begin by assigning relative ranks to the dependent variable values. This is done in the same way in which we assigned ranks to dependent variable values in preparation for a bivariable nonparametric parallel to Student's *t* test: the Mann-Whitney test or the Wilcoxon Rank Sum test (illustrated in Example 8-5). Specifically, all of the dependent variable values are ranked in order of their numeric magnitude without regard to which group those values belong.

To calculate the Kruskal-Wallis test statistic (usually symbolized by *H*) by hand can be tedious, especially if there are tied ranks.[3] Instead, it is much easier to make this calculation with the aid of a computer. This can be done, even if the computer program you use does not have a procedure specifically for the Kruskal-Wallis test. In that case, the computer program's procedure for analysis of variance for continuous dependent variable values can be used to calculate the Kruskal-Wallis test statistic. The way that this is done is to change the dependent variable values to ranks and use the computer to perform an analysis of variance as we would for dependent variable values on a continuous scale. Then, we test the null hypothesis that the mean of the ranks[4] are the same for all the groups in the population (i.e., the nonparametric parallel to the omnibus null hypothesis that the means for all of the groups are equal to the same value) by calculating the Kruskal-Wallis test statistic from the results of the analysis of variance. The Kruskal-Wallis test statistic is calculated from those results as illustrated in Equation{11.1}.[5]

---

[1]A slope (or regression coefficient) tells us how much the numeric magnitude of the dependent variable changes for each one-unit change in the independent variable. On an ordinal scale, we cannot tell how far apart values are. Thus, an ordinal dependent variable precludes us from determining how much the dependent variable changes and, as a result, makes estimation of the slope (or regression coefficient) impossible.

[2]In multivariable analysis, the correlation coefficient tells us about the strength of the association between the dependent variable and all of the independent variables taken together. The way in which all the independent variables are represented is through the multiple regression equation. If regression coefficients cannot be estimated, the independent variables cannot be combined for multiple correlation analysis. Thus, we have bivariable correlation analysis on an ordinal scale, but we do not have multivariable correlation analysis on an ordinal scale.

[3]Recall from Chapter 5 that "tied ranks" refers to the average rank given to all dependent variable values that are equal to each other on the continuous scale.

[4] The mean of the ranks corresponds to the median on the continuous scale.

[5]This is also the way in which we calculated the test statistic for the chi-square test for trend using the REG

$$H = \frac{\text{Model Sum of Squares}}{\text{Total Mean Square}} \qquad \{11.1\}$$

where

$$H \quad = \quad \text{Kruskal-Wallis test statistic}$$

To test the null hypothesis that the mean rank for each of the groups of dependent variable values are the same in the population, we can compare the value calculated in Equation {11.1} to a value in a table of Kruskal-Wallis test statistics (such as Table B.9) or, if the data set consists of more dependent variable values than found in such a table, the Kruskal-Wallis test statistic can be interpreted as a chi-square value with the same number of degrees of freedom as the model degrees of freedom in analysis of variance.[6] This is illustrated in the next example.

Example 11-1   In Example 10-7, we compared serum cholesterol levels among persons in four geographic regions of the United States: Northeast (NE), Northwest (NW), Southeast (SE), and Southwest (SW). In that example, one-way analysis of variance was used to test the null hypothesis that the means for all four groups of dependent variable values are equal to the same value in the population. Now, let us perform a Kruskal-Wallis test to test the nonparametric equivalent to that null hypothesis.

First, we need to convert those data to an ordinal scale. We do that by ranking the dependent variable values from lowest to highest without regard to which group they belong. The data are from Example 10-6 and appear in the following table, along with their ranks.

NE	Rank	NW	Rank	SE	Rank	SW	Rank
197	13.5	194	7.5	220	34	206	25
183	1	185	2	202	21	196	10.5
190	5.5	186	3.5	212	28	195	9
212	28	212	28	221	35	222	36
223	37	209	26	227	39	228	40
202	21	194	7.5	224	38	205	24
201	18.5	186	3.5	197	13.5	197	13.5
202	21	196	10.5	201	18.5	203	23
197	13.5	190	5.5	198	16	199	17
213	30	218	31.5	218	31.5	219	33

procedure in Chapter 9.

[6]Recall from Chapter 10 that the model degrees of freedom are equal to the number of nominal independent variables that are needed to specify the groups of continuous dependent variable values in an analysis of variance.

Next, we use those ranks as the dependent variable values in SAS's ANOVA procedure.

```
                          The ANOVA Procedure

                       Class Level Information

                Class            Levels    Values
                REGION              4       NE NW SE SW

Dependent Variable: RANK_CHOL

                              Sum of
Source             DF         Squares      Mean Square    F Value    Pr > F
Model               3       1208.250000     402.750000      3.53     0.0244
Error              36       4109.750000     114.159722
Corrected Total 39          5318.000000

            R-Square      Coeff Var      Root MSE     RANK_CHOL Mean
            0.227200      52.11978       10.68456        20.50000

Source             DF        Anova SS      Mean Square    F Value    Pr > F
REGION              3       1208.250000     402.750000      3.53     0.0244
```

We cannot use the P-values in this output. Instead, we use the model sum of squares and the total mean square in Equation {11.1} to calculate the Kruskal-Wallis test statistic. Since SAS does not provide the total mean square, we need to calculate it by dividing the total sum of squares by the total degrees of freedom.

$$H = \frac{\text{Model Sum of Squares}}{\text{Total Mean Square}} = \frac{1,208.25}{\dfrac{5,318}{39}} = 8.861$$

To test the null hypothesis that the mean of the ranks of serum cholesterol levels is the same in the four geographic regions in the population, we compare the calculated test statistic (8.861) to the critical value in Table B.9.

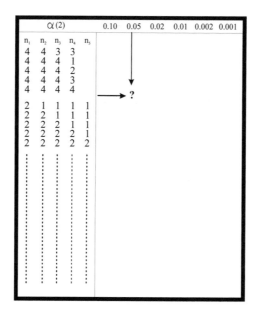

To find a critical value in Table B.9, we look for the same number of groups and the same number of observations in each of the groups in the leftmost columns of the table. In this case, we have four groups of dependent variable values and ten observations in each group. A sample of this size is not listed in Table B.9 (the largest sample with four groups has four observations in each group)..

If the sample is larger than the samples' sizes considered in Table B.9, we compare the calculated statistic (8.861) to a chi-square value in Table B.7 with 3 degrees of freedom (equal to the number of groups minus one). That critical value is equal to 7.815. Since the calculated value (8.861) is greater than the critical value (7.815), we reject the null hypothesis.

For a one-way ANOVA, we also can use SAS's NPAR1WAY procedure to perform the Kruskal-Wallis test. The next example shows the result of using this procedure.

Example 11-2   In Example 11-1, we used the ANOVA procedure to perform a Kruskal-Wallis test. Now, let us analyze those same data using the NPAR1WAY procedure.

The following is the output we obtain when we analyze the data in Example 11-1 using the NPAR1WAY procedure.

```
                        The NPAR1WAY Procedure

            Wilcoxon Scores (Rank Sums) for Variable CHOLESTEROL
                       Classified by Variable REGION

                        Sum of      Expected      Std Dev         Mean
        REGION    N     Scores      Under HO      Under HO       Score
        -----------------------------------------------------------------
        NE        10    189.00       205.0       31.979561       18.900
        NW        10    125.50       205.0       31.979561       12.550
        SE        10    274.50       205.0       31.979561       27.450
        SW        10    231.00       205.0       31.979561       23.100

                     Average scores were used for ties.

                          Kruskal-Wallis Test

                    Chi-Square          8.8608
                    DF                       3
                    Pr > Chi-Square     0.0312
```

The *P*-value for the test of the null hypothesis that the distribution of serum cholesterol levels is the same in the four geographic regions in the population is 0.0312. This *P*-value is the same as the *P*-value we obtain using the ANOVA procedure and Equation {11.1} in Example 11-1. We know this is the case because the chi-square values in the two examples are the same. This *P*-value allows us to reject the null hypothesis and conclude that the distribution of serum cholesterol levels is not the same in all of the geographic regions.

The NPAR1WAY procedure, as its name suggests, can only perform one-way analyses. If the nominal independent variables represent more than one characteristic, we should use a method of analysis that takes this factorial design into account. As suggested earlier, the Kruskal-Wallis test can be extended to factorial designs. To do this, we convert the data to ranks and use those ranks as the dependent variable in the ANOVA procedure.

In factorial analysis of variance, we can test hypotheses about main effects and interactions as well as the omnibus null hypothesis (that the means of the ranks of all the groups are equal to the same value in the population). The nonparametric equivalent to factorial analysis of variance tests null hypotheses about main effects by calculating the Kruskal-Wallis test statistic as shown in Equation {11.2} and tests the null hypothesis that there is no interaction by calculating the Kruskal-Wallis test statistic as shown in Equation {11.3}.

$$H = \frac{\text{Main Effect Sum of Squares}}{\text{Total Mean Square}} \qquad \{11.2\}$$

$$H = \frac{\text{Interaction Sum of Squares}}{\text{Total Mean Square}}$$ {11.3}

The next example demonstrates how we can perform a factorial Kruskal-Wallis test using SAS.

Example 11-3   For this example, let us use the same data set we considered in the two previous examples, but now thinking of geographic region as having two characteristics: north versus south and east versus west. With this factorial design in mind, let us use the Kruskal-Wallis test to test hypotheses about the two main effects and the interaction.

To begin, we need to convert serum cholesterol levels to ranks. This is done without regard to in which group we find the dependent variable value. Thus, the ranks are the same as those given in Example 11-1.

Next, we use those ranks as the dependent variable in the ANOVA procedure and specify two factors represented by the nominal independent variables. The following SAS output results from that analysis:

```
                        The ANOVA Procedure

                     Class Level Information

                Class       Levels    Values
                NS             2       NORTH SOUTH
                EW             2       EAST WEST

Dependent Variable: RANK_CHOL
                                Sum of
Source                  DF      Squares     Mean Square   F Value   Pr > F
Model                    3    1208.250000    402.750000      3.53   0.0244
Error                   36    4109.750000    114.159722
Corrected Total         39    5318.000000

              R-Square    Coeff Var    Root MSE    RANK_CHOL Mean
              0.227200    52.11978     10.68456       20.50000

Source                  DF      Anova SS    Mean Square   F Value   Pr > F
NS                       1     912.0250000   912.0250000      7.99   0.0076
EW                       1     286.2250000   286.2250000      2.51   0.1221
NS*EW                    1      10.0000000    10.0000000      0.09   0.7690
```

Now, let us begin testing hypotheses about interaction and main effects. We learned in Chapter 10 that we need to test the null hypothesis that there is no interaction before we can look at the main effects. Testing for no interaction uses Equation {11.3}.

$$H = \frac{\text{Interaction Sum of Squares}}{\text{Total Mean Square}} = \frac{10}{\dfrac{5,318}{39}} = 0.073$$

To interpret this test statistic, we compare it to a chi-square with the same degrees of freedom we would use to interpret the F-ratio for the interaction. In this case, there is one degree of freedom and the corresponding chi-square value from Table B.7 is equal to 3.814. Since the calculated value (0.073) is less than the tabled value (3.814), we fail to reject the null hypothesis that there is no interaction. This allows us to go on to interpret the main effects.

Next, let us test the north versus south main effect (NS). We do that by using Equation{11.2}.

$$H = \frac{\text{NS}}{\text{Total Mean Square}} = \frac{912.025}{\dfrac{5,318}{39}} = 6.688$$

To interpret this test statistic, we compare it to a chi-square with the same degrees of freedom we would use to interpret the F-ratio for this main effect. In this case, there is one degree of freedom and the corresponding chi-square value from Table B.7 is equal to 3.814. Since the calculated value (6.688) is greater than the tabled value (3.814), we reject the null hypothesis that there is no difference in the distribution of serum cholesterol values between the north and south.

Finally, we test the east versus west main effect (EW). We do that by using Equation {11.2}.

$$H = \frac{\text{EW}}{\text{Total Mean Square}} = \frac{286.225}{\dfrac{5,318}{39}} = 2.099$$

To interpret this test statistic, we compare it to a chi-square with the same degrees of freedom we would use to interpret the F-ratio for this main effect. In this case, there is one degree of freedom and the corresponding chi-square value from Table B.7 is equal to 3.814. Since the calculated value (2.099) is less than the tabled value (3.814), we fail to reject the null hypothesis that there is no difference in the distribution of serum cholesterol values between the east and west.

Posterior Testing

After performing an ANOVA, we do not know which groups are different (unless there are only two groups). To determine which are different, we need to perform a posterior test. The most commonly used posterior test for ordinal dependent variables is called **Dunn's test**. It is similar to the Student-Neuman-Keuls test, introduced in Chapter 10 as a posterior test for continuous dependent variables. An important property of both the Student-Neuman-Keuls test and Dunn's test is that they decrease the chance of making at least one type I error[7] when making pair-wise comparisons without greatly decreasing our ability to reject false null hypotheses (i.e., decreasing statistical power).[8]

The key to maintaining statistical power in both posterior tests is to follow a protocol in selecting the order in which groups are compared. The protocol is the same for both the Student-Neuman-Keuls test and Dunn's test. To begin, we arrange the groups according to the numeric magnitude of the means of their ranks.[9] Then, the two most extreme groups are compared by testing the hypothesis that the mean ranks are the same in the two groups. If we are unable to reject that null hypothesis, then we stop making comparisons and fail to reject _all_ of the pair-wise null hypotheses. If, on the other hand, we reject this null hypothesis, we can compare the lowest group to the next to the highest group and the highest group to the next to the lowest groups. This continues until we have either rejected, or failed to reject all pair-wise null hypotheses. This was illustrated for the Student-Neuman-Keuls test in Example 10.12.

We will take a look at an example of how to perform Dunn's shortly, but first we need see how Dunn's test statistic is calculated. That calculation is in Equation {11.4}.

$$Q = \frac{(\bar{Y}_{rank_1} - \bar{Y}_{rank_2}) - (\mu_{rank_1} - \mu_{rank_2})}{\sqrt{\dfrac{TMS}{n_1} + \dfrac{TMS}{n_2}}} \qquad \{11.4\}$$

where

Q = Dunn's test statistic

$\bar{Y}_{rank_i}$ = observed mean of the ranks in group i

---

[7] Recall from Chapter 3 that a type I error occurs when we reject a true null hypothesis.

[8] This is contrasted to poorer posterior tests, like using Bonferroni's "correction" to control the chance of making a type I error. Those tests control the chance of making at least one type I error, but they do that in a way that greatly decreases statistical power.

[9] The mean of the ranks is the same as the median when there is not the same rank being shared by more than one observation. When there are shared ranks (i.e., "tied" ranks), there are different ways in which we can define the median. The mean of the ranks is one of them.

μ_{rank_i} = population's mean of the ranks in group i

TMS = total mean square from an analysis of variance performed on the ranks of dependent variable values

n_i = number of observations in group i

To interpret the result of using Equation{11.4}, we compare the calculated value to a corresponding value in Table B.10. To find the tabled value, we need to specify k, the number of groups involved in the comparison. This number is equal to 2 plus the groups that are between those being compared. This is easier to see in an example.

Example 11-4   In Example 11-1 we used the ANOVA procedure to perform the Kruskal-Wallis test on serum cholesterol levels in persons from 4 geographic regions. In that example, we were able to reject the null hypothesis that the distributions of serum cholesterol levels are the same for all 4 geographic regions. Now, let us make pair-wise comparisons among the 4 groups using Dunn's test.

To begin, we need to calculate the mean ranks for each of the groups.[10] That calculation is summarized in the following table:

NE	Rank	NW	Rank	SE	Rank	SW	Rank
197	13.5	194	7.5	220	34	206	25
183	1	185	2	202	21	196	10.5
190	5.5	186	3.5	212	28	195	9
212	28	212	28	221	35	222	36
223	37	209	26	227	39	228	40
202	21	194	7.5	224	38	205	24
201	18.5	186	3.5	197	13.5	197	13.5
202	21	196	10.5	201	18.5	203	23
197	13.5	190	5.5	198	16	199	17
213	30	218	31.5	218	31.5	219	33
MEAN	18.90		12.55		27.45		23.10

Then we organize these means of ranks in order of their numeric magnitude:

REGION	NW	NE	SW	SE
MEAN	12.55	18.90	23.10	27.45

---

[10] For a one-way Kruskal-Wallis test using the NPAR1WAY procedure, the means of the ranks are listed in the table in the column labeled "Mean Score" (Example 11-2).

Now, we begin by testing the null hypothesis that the distribution of serum cholesterol levels is the same in the northwest (the lowest mean) as in the southwest (the highest mean). Using, Equation{11.4}, we get:

$$Q = \frac{(\overline{Y}_{\text{rank}_{\text{NW}}} - \overline{Y}_{\text{rank}_{\text{SE}}}) - (\mu_{\text{rank}_{\text{NW}}} - \mu_{\text{rank}_{\text{SE}}})}{\sqrt{\dfrac{\text{TMS}}{n_{\text{NW}}} + \dfrac{\text{TMS}}{n_{\text{SE}}}}} = \frac{(12.55 - 27.45) - 0}{\sqrt{\dfrac{5,318}{39}{10} + \dfrac{5,318}{39}{10}}} = -2.853$$

Next, we compare this calculated value (its absolute value) to a value from Table B.10 that corresponds to an α of 0.05 and k equal to 4 (k is equal to 4 since there are two groups (NE and SW) between the northwest and the southeast.

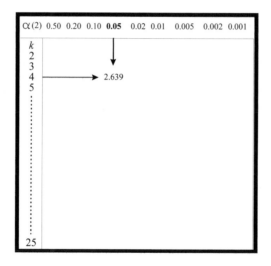

Our calculated value (-2.853) is larger (in absolute value) than the value from Table B.10 (2.639) that corresponds to an α of 0.05 and k equal to 4. Thus, we can reject the null hypothesis that the distribution of serum cholesterol levels among persons from the northwest is the same as the distribution of serum cholesterol levels among persons from the southeast.

Also, rejection of this null hypothesis permits us to make comparisons between groups in which the mean ranks is not as far apart as northwest and southeast. The groups that we can compare now are the northwest to the southwest and the northeast to the southeast. First, let us test the null hypothesis that the distribution of serum cholesterol levels in the northwest is the same as that distribution in the southwest.[11] Using Equation {11.4}, we get:

$$Q = \frac{(\overline{Y}_{\text{rank}_{\text{NW}}} - \overline{Y}_{\text{rank}_{\text{SW}}}) - (\mu_{\text{rank}_{\text{NW}}} - \mu_{\text{rank}_{\text{SW}}})}{\sqrt{\dfrac{\text{TMS}}{n_{\text{NW}}} + \dfrac{\text{TMS}}{n_{\text{SW}}}}} = \frac{(12.55 - 23.10) - 0}{\sqrt{\dfrac{5,318}{39}{10} + \dfrac{5,318}{39}{10}}} = -2.020$$

We compare this calculated value to a value from Table B.10. In this case, k is equal to 3, since there is only one group between the two being compared. This tabled value is equal to 2.394. Since our calculated value (-2.020) is less (in absolute value) than the value from Table B.10 (2.394), we fail to reject the null hypothesis that the distribution of serum cholesterol levels among persons from the northwest is the same as the distribution of serum cholesterol levels among persons from the southwest. Following the protocol for comparing groups, this also implies that we fail to reject null hypotheses for any pairs of groups bracketed by the ones we just compared. Specifically, we fail to reject the null hypothesis that the distribution of serum cholesterol levels among persons from the northwest is the same as the distribution of serum cholesterol levels among persons from the northeast and we fail to reject the null hypothesis that the distribution of serum cholesterol levels among persons from the northeast is the same as the distribution of serum cholesterol levels among persons from the southwest. A convenient way to keep track of these results is to underline the groups that are not statistically different. Thus, the results so far are:

REGION	NW	NE	SW	SE
MEAN	12.55	18.90	23.10	27.45

Even though we failed to reject the null hypothesis that the distribution of serum cholesterol levels among persons from the northwest is the same as the distribution of serum cholesterol levels among persons from the southwest, we are still able to compare the northeast to the southeast, since they are not connected by the line we just drew. Using Equation {11.4} we get:

$$Q = \frac{(\overline{Y}_{\text{rank}_{\text{NE}}} - \overline{Y}_{\text{rank}_{\text{SE}}}) - (\mu_{\text{rank}_{\text{NE}}} - \mu_{\text{rank}_{\text{SE}}})}{\sqrt{\dfrac{\text{TMS}}{n_{\text{NE}}} + \dfrac{\text{TMS}}{n_{\text{SE}}}}} = \frac{(18.90 - 27.45) - 0}{\sqrt{\dfrac{5,318}{39}{10} + \dfrac{5,318}{39}{10}}} = -0.804$$

---

[11] Which of the two pairs of means we compare first is arbitrary, since both comparisons can be made regardless of the result from either of the comparisons.

Since there is one group between the two we just compared, we compare our calculated value (-0.804) to 2.639. This calculated value is less than the value from Table B.10, so we fail to reject the null hypothesis that the distribution of serum cholesterol levels among persons from the northeast is the same as the distribution of serum cholesterol levels among persons from the southeast. Following the protocol, this implies that we also fail to reject the null hypothesis that the distribution of serum cholesterol levels among persons from the northeast is the same as the distribution of serum cholesterol levels among persons from the southwest and the null hypothesis that the distribution of serum cholesterol levels among persons from the southwest is the same as the distribution of serum cholesterol levels among persons from the southeast. To illustrate this result, we add a second line to the list of mean ranks.

REGION	NW	NE	SW	SE
MEAN	12.55	18.90	23.10	27.45

We interpret that table by saying that any groups connected by a line are not statistically different from each other. In other words, the only statistical difference we observed is between the northwest and the southeast.

In the next chapter, we will look at methods for a nominal dependent variable when there is more than one independent variable.

CHAPTER 12
Nominal Dependent Variable

In clinical and epidemiologic research, nominal dependent variables are often used to represent the outcome of interest. Thus, chapters of this text that address nominal dependent variables are of particular interest to clinicians and epidemiologists. Also, research that involves human subjects, by necessity, entails control for extraneous characteristics as part of data analysis. Both of these requirements are addressed in this chapter, which discusses multivariable analysis of nominal dependent variables.

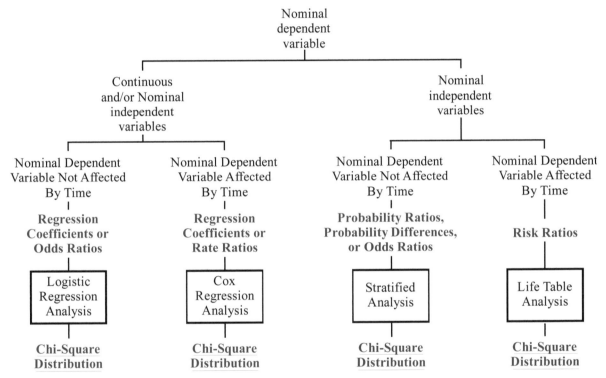

Flowchart 10 Flowchart showing multivariable analysis of a nominal dependent variable. The point estimate that is most often used to describe the dependent variable is in color. The common name of the statistical test is enclosed in a box. The standard distribution that is used to test hypotheses and calculate confidence intervals is in color and underlined.

Flowchart 10 outlines the methods that are most commonly used to analyze multivariable data sets with nominal dependent variables. They are divided into two groups. The first of these groups includes two types of regression analysis. They can be used regardless of the type of data (either continuous or nominal) represented by the independent variables.[1] Thus, these methods are broadly applicable. Their disadvantage is that they involve calculations

---

[1]In Chapter 10, we learned how to include nominal independent variables in regression equations by using indicator variables and interactions. This led us to the principle of the "general linear model" which asserts that all methods of analyzing continuous dependent variables can be represented as regression equations. The same is approximately true for nominal dependent variables, but since the methods for nominal dependent variables are not identical, we refer to them with the principle of the "generalized" linear model.

that are so complex that it is virtually impossible to do them by hand. This is not an issue when we are using a computer to analyze these data, but it does make it a "black box" for which the process is difficult to visualize.

The methods in the second group are not as broadly applicable, since they are restricted to nominal independent variables (or continuous independent variables converted to a nominal scale). Their advantage, however, is that they can be done by hand making it easier to understand how they work. As a result, they play an important role in analysis of health research data, even though the same data can be analyzed using regression analyses.

CONTINUOUS AND/OR NOMINAL INDEPENDENT VARIABLES

Maximum Likelihood Estimation

The reason that multivariable regression analysis for nominal dependent variables presents a challenge is that it uses a method of estimation that is substantially different from anything we have discussed so far. All other analyses that we have considered are based on what is called the method of "**least squares**." As described in Chapter 7, the goal in the method of least squares is to select estimates that minimize the squared differences between observed and estimated values of the dependent variable (Equation {7.3}). Thus, it is a mathematic representation of the method we would use to draw a line to fit a set of points in a scatter plot. Specifically, we draw the line to minimize the difference between the points (that represent the observed values) and the line (that represents the estimated values). The mathematical representation of this process results in formulae we can use to estimate means, slopes, regression coefficients, correlation coefficients, probabilities, rates, and all of the other estimates we have encountered so far.

The method of least squares could be used to estimate regression coefficients for multivariable analysis of nominal dependent variables as well, but, when there is a least one continuous independent variable, these estimates do not come as close to the true values (i.e., the values in the population) as do estimates based on the method of **maximum likelihood**. In maximum likelihood estimation, estimates are selected to maximize the likelihood (i.e., the conditional probability) of observing the sample's data if the population's regression coefficients were equal to the sample's estimates. This probability is illustrated in Equation{12.1}.

$$p(\text{sample's data}|\beta = b) \qquad \qquad \{12.1\}$$

where

$$\beta \quad = \quad \text{population's regression coefficient(s)}$$

$$b \quad = \quad \text{Sample's estimate(s) of regression coefficient(s)}$$

So, the idea with the method of maximum likelihood is to select estimates that maximize the probability of getting a sample like the one we got, assuming that the sample's estimates are, in fact, equal to the population's parameters. This is an iterative process that involves making guesses about the value of the population's parameter and comparing the likelihood of each guess until the one with the highest likelihood is found. As a simple example, suppose that we have a sample of 10 persons, two of whom have a particular disease. From that sample, we want to estimate the prevalence of the disease in the population. The first step in the method of maximum likelihood is to make a guess about the prevalence. Some guesses for this sample are in the first column of Table 12-1. Then, the likelihood of obtaining the sample for each guess is calculated. The likelihoods for this example are in the second column of Table 12-1.[2]

Guess	Likelihood
0.1	0.194
0.2	0.302
0.3	0.233
0.4	0.121
0.5	0.044
0.6	0.011
0.7	0.001
0.8	<0.001
0.9	<0.001

Table 12-1. Likelihood of observing 2 out of 10 persons with a particular disease if the prevalence of the disease is equal to the estimate.

Finally, the maximum likelihood estimate of the prevalence is selected as the guess with the highest likelihood. Since the estimate of 0.2 has the highest likelihood in Table 12-1, it is the maximum likelihood estimate of the prevalence.[3]

If you think that this sounds like a lot of work, you are right! It is much easier to use Equation {6.3} as we did in Chapter 6.

$$\text{Prevalence} = \frac{\text{Number of persons with the disease at time } t}{\text{Total number of persons}} = \frac{2}{10} = 0.2 \qquad \{12.2\}$$

Using a formula to calculate an estimate gives us the least squares estimate. In this example, the maximum likelihood estimate and the least squares estimate are equal to the same value. When we have a nominal dependent variable and there are no continuous independent variables, maximum likelihood estimates are equal to the same value as least squares estimates. In that case, using the formula makes sense. When the dependent variable is nominal and at least one independent variable is continuous however, the two methods do not result in the same estimate. Further, the maximum likelihood estimate is the better estimate in that situation. Then, it makes sense to use the method of maximum likelihood,

---

[2]These likelihoods were calculated using the binomial distribution.

[3]This is the maximum likelihood estimate to the nearest tenth. In practice, we would make more guesses with smaller differences between them, to see if a higher likelihood could be obtained.

as long as we have a computer to make the guesses and search for the one with the highest likelihood of producing the sample's observations.

To interpret the results of analyses that use the method of maximum likelihood (like the regression analyses that appear in the Flowchart 10), understanding the difference between least squares and maximum likelihood estimation prepares us to encounter new types of information when interpreting the results of these analyses. In regression analyses that use least squares estimates (like those described in Chapter 7 and 10), we compare mean squares representing the explained and unexplained variation in dependent variable values in an *F*-ratio. In analyses that use maximum likelihood estimates, we compare likelihoods for full (including all of the independent variables) and reduced (excluding at least one of the independent variables) models in a **likelihood ratio** (Equation{12.3}).

$$LR = \frac{p(\text{sample's data}|\beta = b \text{ for reduced model})}{p(\text{sample's data}|\beta = b \text{ for full model})} \qquad \{12.3\}$$

where

$$LR \quad = \quad \text{likelihood ratio}$$

Before we interpret a likelihood ratio, it is changed into a chi-square value with the number of degrees of freedom equal to the difference in the number of independent variables between the full and reduced models. We will see an example in which we interpret these chi-square values, but first let us take a closer look at one type of regression analysis for a nominal dependent variable.

Logistic Regression Analysis

In Chapter 9, we looked at a regression analysis for a nominal dependent variable called a test for trend (Equation {9.1}). This regression analysis uses a straight line to estimate the probability of an event based on a value of a continuous independent variable (Figure 9-1). One problem with using a straight line to estimate probabilities is that a straight line continues forever, theoretically extending from -∞ to +∞. Probabilities, on the other hand, are restricted to the interval between zero and one. A solution to this problem is to use a curve, instead of a straight line, to estimate probabilities. One such curve is a **sigmoid curve** (Figure 12-1). This curve approaches, but never quite reaches zero or one.

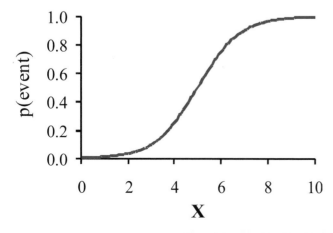

Figure 12-1   Sigmoid curve used to represent the relationship between a nominal dependent variable and a continuous independent variable. The sigmoid curve prevents estimates of the probability of an event from being less than zero or greater than one.

A convenient way to create a sigmoid curve is by using a **transformation**. A transformation is a mathematical change in the dependent variable. In clinical and epidemiologic research, the most common transformation used to create a sigmoid curve is the **logit transformation**. A regression equation that uses the logit transformation is called a **logistic regression**.

   In the logit transformation, we divide the probability of the event by its complement and take the natural logarithm of that fraction. Equation {12.4} illustrates a regression equation that uses the logit transformation.

$$\ln \frac{\theta}{1-\theta} = \alpha + \beta_1 \cdot X_1 + \beta_2 \cdot X_2 + ... + \beta_k \cdot X_k \qquad \{12.4\}$$

where

$\ln$	=	natural log scale (base e)
θ	=	probability of the event represented by the nominal dependent variable in the population
α	=	intercept of the regression equation in the population
β_i	=	regression coefficient for the ith (out of k) independent variable in the population
X_i	=	value of the ith (out of k) independent variable

When we use a transformation for the dependent variable, we perform all of the analyses on the transformed scale, and then we change the results of the analyses back to the original scale for interpretation. Equation {12.5} illustrates how we can change the logistic regression equation back to its original scale.

$$\theta \stackrel{\wedge}{=} p = \frac{1}{1 + e^{-[a + b_1 \cdot X_1 + b_2 \cdot X_2 + ... + b_k \cdot X_k]}} \qquad \{12.5\}$$

where

θ	=	probability of the event represented by the nominal dependent variable in the population
p	=	sample's estimate of the probability of the event represented by the nominal dependent variable
e	=	base of the natural log scale
a	=	sample's estimate of the intercept of the regression equation
b_i	=	sample's estimate of the regression coefficient for the ith (out of k) independent variable

$$X_i \quad = \quad \text{value of the i}^{\text{th}} \text{ (out of } k\text{) independent variable}$$

In logistic regression analysis, we usually change the log scale back to a linear scale, but we leave the probability of the event divided by its complement. This fraction is really the odds of the event, as shown algebraically in Equation{12.6}.[4]

$$\frac{\theta}{1-\theta} \triangleq \frac{p}{1-p} = \frac{\dfrac{\text{events}}{\text{observations}}}{1-\dfrac{\text{events}}{\text{observations}}} = \frac{\dfrac{\text{events}}{\text{observations}}}{\dfrac{\text{observations}}{\text{observations}} - \dfrac{\text{events}}{\text{observations}}} \qquad \{12.6\}$$

$$= \frac{\text{events}}{\text{observations} - \text{events}} = \frac{\text{events}}{\text{nonevents}} = \text{odds}$$

The advantage of leaving the dependent variable as the odds of the event is that the antilog of each regression coefficient can be interpreted as an odds ratio comparing a one unit difference in the value of that independent variable.[5] This is illustrated algebraically in Equation{12.7}.

$$OR = \frac{e^{\ln\frac{\theta}{1-\theta}}}{e^{\ln\frac{\theta}{1-\theta}}} = \frac{e^{\alpha+\beta_1\cdot(X_1+1)+\beta_2\cdot X_2+\dots+\beta_k X_k}}{e^{\alpha+\beta_1\cdot X_1+\beta_2\cdot X_2+\dots+\beta_k X_k}} = \frac{\cancel{e^{\alpha}}\cdot e^{\beta_1\cdot(X_1+1)}\cdot\cancel{e^{\beta_2\cdot X_2}}\cdot\dots\cdot\cancel{e^{\beta_k X_k}}}{\cancel{e^{\alpha}}\cdot e^{\beta_1\cdot X_1}\cdot\cancel{e^{\beta_2\cdot X_2}}\cdot\dots\cdot\cancel{e^{\beta_k X_k}}} \qquad \{12.7\}$$

$$= \frac{e^{\beta_1\cdot(X_1+1)}}{e^{\beta_1\cdot X_1}} = e^{\beta_1} \triangleq \widehat{OR} = e^{b_1}$$

In SAS, we can use the LOGISTIC procedure to perform logistic regression analysis. In the next example, we will see output from this procedure and learn how to interpret it.

Example 12-1   In Examples 9-1 through 9-4, we considered data from a study in which we were interested in the probability that an infection is cured at different doses of an antibiotic. In this study, we randomly assigned 120 persons to one of seven doses of the antibiotic. Suppose that we obtained the following data:

---

[4]Compare to Equation {9.7}.

[5]We could also undo the odds part of the logit transformation to interpret regression coefficients as estimators of the probability ratio of the event, but these estimates require that a value be assigned to each independent variable, rather than to only one independent variable at a time.

Dose (X)	Number Observed (n)	Number Cured (a)
1	60	3
5	10	4
10	10	3
15	10	7
20	10	6
25	10	8
30	10	9

This is a bivariable data set (since there is only one independent variable), but we can use it to see how to interpret the results of logistic regression analysis.

If we were to analyze these data using SAS's LOGISTIC procedure, we would obtain the following output:

```
                       The LOGISTIC Procedure

                         Model Information

          Data Set                    WORK.EX12_1
          Response Variable           CURE
          Number of Response Levels   2
          Number of Observations      14
          Frequency Variable          FREQ
          Sum of Frequencies          120
          Model                       binary logit
          Optimization Technique      Fisher's scoring

                         Response Profile

              Ordered                        Total
              Value      CURE              Frequency
                1        YES                      40
                2        NO                       80

          Probability modeled is CURE='YES'.

                      Model Convergence Status

          Convergence criterion (GCONV=1E-8) satisfied.
```

```
                         Model Fit Statistics

                                              Intercept
                                  Intercept       and
                    Criterion       Only      Covariates
                    AIC            154.763      102.551
                    SC             157.551      108.126
                    -2 Log L       152.763       98.551


              Testing Global Null Hypothesis: BETA=0

         Test                 Chi-Square      DF      Pr > ChiSq
         Likelihood Ratio       54.2127        1        <.0001
         Score                  51.2639        1        <.0001
         Wald                   34.7614        1        <.0001


              Analysis of Maximum Likelihood Estimates

                                   Standard        Wald
    Parameter    DF    Estimate     Error     Chi-Square    Pr > ChiSq
    Intercept     1     -2.4478     0.4006      37.3378       <.0001
    DOSE          1      0.1647     0.0279      34.7614       <.0001


                         Odds Ratio Estimates

                          Point          95% Wald
         Effect         Estimate     Confidence Limits
         DOSE             1.179       1.116      1.245


   Association of Predicted Probabilities and Observed Responses

              Percent Concordant    83.5    Somers' D    0.759
              Percent Discordant     7.6    Gamma        0.834
              Percent Tied           8.9    Tau-a        0.340
              Pairs                 3200    c            0.880
```

When interpreting output from the LOGISTIC procedure, it is a good idea to begin by taking a look at the statement below the "Response Profile" table in the first part of the output to make sure SAS understands which value of the dependent variable represents the event. Here SAS tells us that the event is CURE='YES.' This implies that positive regression coefficients are associated with an increase in the odds of being cured.

As in linear and multiple regression analyses for a continuous dependent variable, logistic regression considers two kinds of hypotheses. One kind addresses all of the independent variables taken as a group. This is the test of the omnibus null hypothesis: that the entire collection of independent variables does not help estimate values of the dependent variable. Here, *P*-values addressing the omnibus null hypothesis are in the table labeled "Testing Global Null Hypothesis." There are three *P*-values in this table, each of which is based on a different normal approximation. The methods in the first and last rows of that table are the most commonly used. The first one is based on the likelihood ratio for which the full model includes all of the independent variables and the reduced model has none of the independent variables. The last one (labeled "Wald") is based on standard error approximations for each regression coefficient.[6] In this case, all three *P*-values are <0.0001. Since these are less than 0.05, we can reject the omnibus null hypothesis. If some, but not all, of those *P*-values are not all less than 0.05, we have to make a choice. We recommend using the likelihood ratio test (in the first row of the table).

The other kind of null hypothesis, in linear and multiple regression, considers the relationship between the dependent variable, and one independent variable while controlling for all of the other independent variables. Specifically, this null hypothesis states that the regression coefficient for the corresponding independent variable is equal to zero in the population. *P*-values for these hypothesis tests are in the table labeled "Analysis of Maximum Likelihood Estimates." In this case, there is only one independent variable and it has a *P*-value (<0.0001) less than 0.05, so we reject this null hypothesis.[7]

Estimates in logistic regression analysis include an intercept and a regression coefficient for each independent variable. They are listed in the same table as the *P*-values for the individual independent variables. Here, the estimate of the intercept is -2.3462 and the regression coefficient for DOSE is 0.1602. Thus, the logistic regression equation is:

$$\ln \frac{\theta}{1-\theta} \triangleq \ln \frac{p}{1-p} = a + b \cdot \text{DOSE} = -2.3462 + (0.1602 \cdot \text{DOSE})$$

One of the ways in which we can use this regression equation is to estimate the probability of cure corresponding to a specific dose. These estimates are calculated using Equation{12.5}. The following figure graphically displays these estimates (colored line) and compares them to estimates made in Chapter 9 assuming a linear relationship (black line) between dose and the probability of cure (from Figure 9-1).

---

[6]This method is the most like the one used to test the omnibus null hypothesis in multiple regression analysis.

[7]Notice that the χ^2 value and the *P*-value here are the same as for the "Wald" method of testing the omnibus null hypothesis. This is parallel to what we observed in linear regression analysis for a continuous dependent variable in Chapter 7.

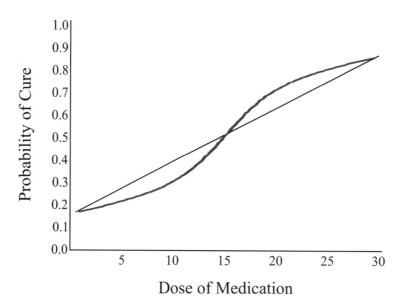

Notice that the estimated values from the logistic regression analysis form a sigmoid curve. In this case, however, there is little difference between the sigmoid curve and the straight line. This is because the observed probabilities of cure are not close to zero or one. The closer the probabilities are to these two extremes, the greater will be the distinction between the sigmoid curve and the straight line.

Another way to interpret the result of logistic regression analysis is to use the regression coefficient as an exponent of e (base of natural logarithms). As shown in Equation{12.7}, this gives us an estimate of the odds ratio for a one-unit change in the independent variable. SAS does this calculation for us. The odds ratio and its 95% confidence interval are listed in the table titled, "Odds Ratio Estimates." In this analysis, the odds ratio estimate is equal to 1.174. This implies that the odds of being cured increases by 17.4% for a one mg increase in dose.

The odds ratio in Example 12-1 (1.174) is very close to one, suggesting that the odds of being cured does not change much as the dose changes. This odds ratio, however, is for a one-unit change in the independent variable. For continuous independent variables, odds ratios with other intervals separating the numerator and denominator make more sense. Equation{12.8} illustrates how odds ratios for other intervals of values of a continuous independent variable.[8]

$$OR_\Delta = \frac{e^{\alpha+\beta_1\cdot(X_1+\Delta)+\beta_2\cdot X_2+...+\beta_k X_k}}{e^{\alpha+\beta_1\cdot X_1+\beta_2\cdot X_2+...+\beta_k X_k}} = \frac{e^{\beta_1\cdot(X_1+\Delta)}}{e^{\beta_1\cdot X_1}} = e^{\beta_1\cdot\Delta} \triangleq e^{b_1\cdot\Delta} \qquad \{12.8\}$$

[8]An equivalent way to do this is by taking the odds ratio for a one unit change in a continuous independent variable to the Δth power (OR^Δ).

where

$$\Delta \quad = \quad \text{interval of independent variable values compared in an odds ratio}$$

The choice of the interval can be somewhat arbitrary. When an interval is not suggested by the study's design or the nature of the event, an interval equal to about ¼ of the range[9] of values included in the sample is commonly used. In the next example, we will calculate an odds ratio for a larger interval of values for DOSE.

Example 12-2 In Example 12-1, we estimated an odds ratio of 1.174 for change in odds of cure for a one-unit (i.e., 1 mg) increase in the dose of a medication. Let us calculate an odds ratio for a larger change in dose.

In this study, doses were assigned in 5 mg increments, so it makes sense to calculate an odds ratio for that same 5 mg difference. To calculate this odds ratio, we use Equation{12.8}:

$$OR_{\Delta=5} \triangleq e^{b_1 \cdot \Delta} = e^{0.1602 \cdot 5} = e^{0.801} = 2.228$$

This odds ratio (2.228) gives us a different impression about how the odds of cure changes as dose is changed. It implies that the odds of cure more than doubles when the dose is increased by 5 mg.

If the independent variable is a zero/one indicator variable, the antilog of its regression coefficient (i.e., e^b) is equal to the odds ratio comparing persons with the characteristic (i.e., when the indicator variable is equal to one) to persons without the characteristic (i.e., when the indicator variable is equal to zero). Thus, we use Equation{12.7}. For minus one/plus one indicator variables (see Tables 10-4 and 10-5), this same odds ratio is calculated by taking the antilog of two times the regression coefficient (Equation{12.9}).

$$OR = \frac{e^{\alpha+\beta_1\cdot(+1)+\beta_2\cdot X_2+\dots+\beta_k X_k}}{e^{\alpha+\beta_1\cdot(-1)+\beta_2\cdot X_2+\dots+\beta_k X_k}} = \frac{e^{\beta_1\cdot(+1)}}{e^{\beta_1\cdot(-1)}} = e^{\beta_1\cdot 2} \tag{12.9}$$

When using SAS's REG procedure, the programmer has to create indicator and interaction variables. The LOGISTIC procedure, on the other hand, can create these variables for us. In doing this, SAS uses minus one/plus one (rather than 0/1) indicator variables. The next example illustrates this feature of the LOGISTIC procedure.

---

[9]In other words, the interval is equal to one quartile.

Example 12-3   In Example 12-1, we analyzed data from a study in which we randomly assigned 120 persons to one of seven doses of an antibiotic. In that analysis we were interested in the probability that an infection was cured for different doses of the antibiotic. Now, suppose that we are also interested in the relationship between the probability of cure and gender, so we randomize an equal number of men and women to each of the doses of antibiotic. When we analyze these data using the LOGISTIC procedure, we obtain the following output:

```
                        The LOGISTIC Procedure

                          Model Information

              Data Set                  WORK.EX12_3
              Response Variable         CURE
              Number of Response Levels 2
              Number of Observations    25
              Frequency Variable        FREQ
              Sum of Frequencies        120
              Model                     binary logit
              Optimization Technique    Fisher's scoring


                          Response Profile

              Ordered                        Total
              Value      CURE              Frequency
                1        YES                      40
                2        NO                       80


          Probability modeled is CURE='YES'.

                    Class Level Information
                                        Design
                                       Variables
              Class     Value              1
              GENDER    FEMALE             1
                        MALE              -1


                   Model Convergence Status
        Convergence criterion (GCONV=1E-8) satisfied.
```

```
                        Model Fit Statistics

                                        Intercept
                         Intercept         and
        Criterion          Only        Covariates
        AIC               154.763         93.606
        SC                157.551        101.969
        -2 Log L          152.763         87.606


            Testing Global Null Hypothesis: BETA=0

        Test              Chi-Square     DF     Pr > ChiSq
        Likelihood Ratio    65.1573       2       <.0001
        Score               57.1687       2       <.0001
        Wald                32.8347       2       <.0001


            Analysis of Maximum Likelihood Estimates

                                    Standard        Wald
Parameter           DF   Estimate     Error     Chi-Square   Pr > ChiSq
Intercept            1    -2.6808     0.4600      33.9565       <.0001
GENDER   FEMALE      1     0.9069     0.3145       8.3159       0.0039
DOSE                 1     0.1835     0.0320      32.8057       <.0001


                    Odds Ratio Estimates

                            Point         95% Wald
       Effect             Estimate    Confidence Limits
       GENDER FEMALE vs MALE  6.133     1.788    21.042
       DOSE                   1.201     1.128     1.279


    Association of Predicted Probabilities and Observed Responses

         Percent Concordant   87.7   Somers' D   0.795
         Percent Discordant    8.2   Gamma       0.829
         Percent Tied          4.1   Tau-a       0.356
         Pairs                3200   c           0.898
```

Let us interpret that output.

This dataset consists of a nominal dependent variable (CURE) and two independent variables: DOSE (a continuous independent variable) and GENDER (a nominal independent variable). In the table titled "Class Level Information," we can see that SAS has assigned a value of +1 to women and -1 to men.

The results of testing the omnibus hypothesis (i.e., that the combination of dose and gender do not help estimate the probability of cure) appear in the table titled "Testing Global Null Hypothesis: BETA=0." This omnibus null hypothesis is rejected, since the P-values are less than 0.05.[10]

The relationships between each of the independent variables and the probability of cure (controlling for the other independent variable) are in the table titled "Analysis of Maximum Likelihood Estimates." This table lists the estimates of the intercept and each of the regressions coefficients in the leftmost column. From that information, we know that the logistic regression equation is:

$$\ln\frac{p}{1-p} = -2.6808 + (0.9069 \cdot \text{GENDER}) + (0.1835 \cdot \text{DOSE})$$

The same table lists (in the rightmost column) the P-values for tests of the null hypothesis that the corresponding parameter (listed in the leftmost column) is equal to zero in the population. We are able to reject this null hypothesis for the regression coefficients for both gender ($P=0.0039$) and dose ($P<0.0001$).

To interpret these regression coefficients, we usually calculate an odds ratio. Since the indicator variable is equal to -1 or +1, we need to use Equation {12.9} to calculate it. SAS uses this same equation in its calculation of the odds ratio for gender (6.133) in the table titled "Odds Ratio Estimates." Since SAS assigned to this indicator variable a value of plus one for women and minus one for men, this odds ratio compares the odds of being cured for women to the odds of being cured for men.[11] The odds ratio of 6.133 tells us that women have six times the odds of being cured compared to men. The table also tells us that the odds ratio for a one mg increase in dose is equal to 1.201 when controlling for gender.

In Example 12-3, we included an indicator variable generated by SAS in a logistic regression analysis. In the next example, we will have SAS include an interaction between dose and gender. By including an interaction, we imply that we are interested in determining if the relationship between dose and the odds of cure is different for the two genders.[12] If this is the case, we need to calculate separate odds ratios for men and women. Equation {12.10} shows how to calculate an odds ratio when the independent variable is included in an interaction.

$$OR_\Delta = \frac{e^{\ln\frac{\theta}{1-\theta}}}{e^{\ln\frac{\theta}{1-\theta}}} = \frac{e^{\alpha+\beta_1\cdot(X_1+\Delta)+\beta_2\cdot X_2+\beta_3\cdot(X_1+\Delta)\cdot X_2}}{e^{\alpha+\beta_1\cdot(X_1)+\beta_2\cdot X_2+\beta_3\cdot(X_1)\cdot X_2}} = \frac{\cancel{e^\alpha}\cdot e^{\beta_1\cdot(X_1+\Delta)}\cdot \cancel{e^{\beta_2\cdot X_2}}\cdot e^{\beta_3\cdot(X_1+\Delta)\cdot X_2}}{\cancel{e^\alpha}\cdot e^{\beta_1\cdot X_1}\cdot \cancel{e^{\beta_2\cdot X_2}}\cdot e^{\beta_3\cdot(X_1)\cdot X_2}} \quad \{12.10\}$$

$$= \frac{e^{\beta_1\cdot(X_1+\Delta)}\cdot e^{\beta_3\cdot(X_1+\Delta)\cdot X_2}}{e^{\beta_1\cdot X_1}\cdot e^{\beta_3\cdot X_1\cdot X_2}} = e^{(\beta_1\cdot\Delta)+(\beta_3\cdot\Delta\cdot X_2)} \triangleq \widehat{OR}_\Delta = e^{(b_1\cdot\Delta)+(b_3\cdot\Delta\cdot X_2)}$$

---

[10]In this text, we recommend focusing on the first P-value, which is based directly on likelihood ratios.

[11]See Tables 10-4 and 10-5 to recall how we interpret a plus one/minus one indicator variable.

[12]Equivalently, an odds ratio comparing the two genders will be different according to the dose of the antibiotic if there is an interaction.

where

OR_Δ = population's odds ratio comparing two values of X_1 that differ by Δ

θ = probability of the event represented by the nominal dependent variable in the population

α = intercept of the logistic regression equation in the population

β_1, β_2 = regression coefficients for X_1 and X_2 in the population

β_3 = regression coefficient for the interaction between X_1 and X_2 in the population

Δ = difference in values of X_1 compared in the odds ratio

$\widehat{OR}$ = sample's estimate of the odds ratio comparing two values of X_1

b_1 = sample's estimate of the regression coefficient for X_1

b_3 = sample's estimate of the regression coefficient for the interaction between X_1 and X_2

X_2 = value of X_2 for which the difference in values of X_1 are compared in the odds ratio

The next example demonstrates how we can calculate an estimate for an odds ratio when the logistic regression equation includes an interaction.

Example 12-4   In Example 12-3, we had SAS create an indicator variable for gender. Now, we have SAS add an interaction between gender and dose and obtain the following output:

```
                    The LOGISTIC Procedure

                      Model Information

          Data Set                     WORK.EX12_4
          Response Variable            CURE
          Number of Response Levels    2
          Number of Observations       25
          Frequency Variable           FREQ
          Sum of Frequencies           120
          Model                        binary logit
          Optimization Technique       Fisher's scoring
```

```
                          Response Profile

              Ordered                         Total
              Value      CURE             Frequency
                 1       YES                     40
                 2       NO                      80


           Probability modeled is CURE='YES'.

                  Class Level Information
                                            Design
                                          Variables
              Class     Value                   1
              GENDER    FEMALE                   1
                        MALE                    -1


                  Model Convergence Status
        Convergence criterion (GCONV=1E-8) satisfied.

                   Model Fit Statistics
                                          Intercept
                             Intercept       and
            Criterion          Only       Covariates
            AIC               154.763        92.770
            SC                157.551       103.920
            -2 Log L          152.763        84.770


          Testing Global Null Hypothesis: BETA=0

        Test               Chi-Square     DF     Pr > ChiSq
        Likelihood Ratio      67.9930      3       <.0001
        Score                 59.2922      3       <.0001
        Wald                  31.3960      3       <.0001


           Analysis of Maximum Likelihood Estimates

                                     Standard       Wald
        Parameter         DF   Estimate    Error   Chi-Square   Pr > ChiSq
        Intercept          1    -2.5631   0.4347     34.7740      <.0001
        GENDER     FEMALE   1     0.3436   0.4347      0.6249      0.4292
        DOSE               1     0.1968   0.0358     30.1266      <.0001
        DOSE*GENDER FEMALE  1     0.0569   0.0358      2.5163      0.1127
```

Let us interpret that output.

___

In the table titled, "Analysis of Maximum Likelihood Estimates," we can see that the interaction between dose and gender occurs in the list of variables. Now, the logistic regression equation is:

$$\ln\frac{p}{1-p} = -2.5631 + (0.3436 \cdot \text{GENDER}) + (0.1968 \cdot \text{DOSE}) + (0.0569 \cdot \text{GENDER} \cdot \text{DOSE})$$

We interpret the interaction in this logistic regression equation just as we did in analysis of covariance (Chapter 10). Namely, the interaction tells us about the difference in slopes between the two genders. For men, the logistic regression equation is:

$$\ln\frac{p}{1-p} = -2.5631 + (0.3436 \cdot [-1]) + (0.1968 \cdot \text{DOSE}) + (0.0569 \cdot [-1] \cdot \text{DOSE})$$
$$= -2.9067 + (0.1399 \cdot \text{DOSE})$$

and for women it is:

$$\ln\frac{p}{1-p} = -2.5631 + (0.3436 \cdot [+1]) + (0.1968 \cdot \text{DOSE}) + (0.0569 \cdot [+1] \cdot \text{DOSE})$$
$$= -2.2195 + (0.2537 \cdot \text{DOSE})$$

Because SAS uses a minus one/plus one indicator variable, the numeric magnitude of the regression coefficient for the interaction tells us how the slopes of the two genders differ from the average of their slopes, rather than how different the slopes are from each other. Even so, the P-value testing the null hypothesis that the regression coefficient for the interaction is equal to zero in the population also tests the null hypothesis that the slopes for men and women are equal to the same value in the population. The P-value is equal to 0.1127. Since it is greater than 0.05, we fail to reject this null hypothesis. In other words, there is not a statistically significant difference between the slopes for the two genders.

In Example 12-3, there was a table in the output (titled "Odds Ratio Estimates") that gave us odds ratios estimates for each of the independent variables. That table is missing here. Because SAS generated the interaction for us, it knows that odds ratios for the variables involved in the interaction cannot be estimated unless a value for the other independent variable(s) is specified.[13] SAS does not know what values are of interest to us, so it calculates none of the odds ratios estimates. As a result, we need to calculate odds ratio estimates by hand.

Equation {12.10} shows us how to calculate an odds ratio for an independent variable that is involved in an interaction. Let us use that equation to calculate the odds ratio comparing men and women who receive a dose of 10 mg:

---

[13]This is true even though the interaction is not statistically significant. We considered removing the interaction term from the regression equation when it is not statistically significant in the Chapter 10 discussion of ANCOVA. We could consider doing that here as well.

$$OR_{\text{DOSE}=10} \triangleq \widehat{OR}_{\text{DOSE}=10} = e^{(b_1 \cdot \Delta)+(b_3 \cdot \Delta \cdot X_2)} = e^{(0.3436 \cdot 1)+(0.0569 \cdot 1 \cdot 10)} = e^{0.9126} = 2.49$$

Now, let us use that equation again to calculate the odds ratio comparing men and women who receive a dose of 20 mg:

$$OR_{\text{DOSE}=10} \triangleq \widehat{OR}_{\text{DOSE}=10} = e^{(b_1 \cdot \Delta)+(b_3 \cdot \Delta \cdot X_2)} = e^{(0.3436 \cdot 1)+(0.0569 \cdot 1 \cdot 20)} = e^{1.4816} = 4.40$$

These two odds ratio estimates are different, but the difference is not statistically significant. We can tell that this is true because the *P*-value for the null hypothesis that the coefficient for the interaction is equal to zero in the population (0.1127) is greater than 0.05. In this case, the interaction might be removed from the logistic regression equation so that a single odds ratio can be estimated to compare men and women regardless of the dose. This odds ratio is the one estimated in Example 12-3 (6.133).

_____

Cox Regression Analysis

Logistic regression analysis is appropriate only when the nominal dependent variable is not affected by time.[14] If it is affected by time, we need to use a method of analysis that takes into account the different periods of time over which we looked for the event. **Cox regression**[15] analysis is the most commonly used regression analysis in this case.

The dependent variable in Cox regression is the rate (i.e., incidence) at which events occur.[16] Rates can have values from zero to +∞. To keep estimates of the rate from being less than zero, a logarithmic transformation is used. Equation {12.11} displays the Cox regression equation.

$$\ln(\text{rate}) = \alpha_t + \beta_1 X_1 + \beta_2 X_2 + ... + \beta_k X_k \qquad \{12.11\}$$

where

$\ln(\text{rate})$ = natural log of the rate at which the event occurs in the population

α_t = function of time

β_i = regression coefficient for the ith (out of *k*) independent variable in the population

_____

[14]Recall from Chapter 6 that a nominal dependent variable is affected by time if: (1) the longer we look for events, the more events we observe and (2) we look longer for events for some people than for others.

[15]Cox regression is also called "proportional hazards" regression.

[16]See Chapter 6 for a discussion of the difference between a rate and a probability.

$$X_i \quad = \quad \text{value of the i}^{\text{th}} \text{ (out of } k\text{) independent variable}$$

$$b_i \quad = \quad \text{sample's estimate of the regression coefficient for the i}^{\text{th}} \text{ (out of } k\text{) independent variable}$$

For the most part, Equation {12.11} looks like other regression equations we have encountered. For instance, each of the independent variables is multiplied by a regression coefficient and, then, added together. However, there is one important difference. The intercept of other regression equations is a constant. In Cox regression analysis, what appears to be the intercept is really a function of time. This is how this analysis can take into account the different periods of time that persons were followed while looking for the event represented by the dependent variable.

When interpreting the result of Cox regression analysis, we usually take the regression coefficient as an exponent of e, the base of the natural logarithm scale. The result is the ratio of the rates corresponding to a one-unit difference in the value of the independent variable as shown algebraically in Equation {12.12}.

$$RR = \frac{e^{\ln(\text{rate})}}{e^{\ln(\text{rate})}} = \frac{e^{\alpha_t + \beta_1 \cdot (X_1 + 1) + \beta_2 \cdot X_2 + \ldots + \beta_k \cdot X_k}}{e^{\alpha_t + \beta_1 \cdot (X_1) + \beta_2 \cdot X_2 + \ldots + \beta_k \cdot X_k}} = \frac{\cancel{e^{\alpha_t}} \cdot e^{\beta_1 \cdot (X_1 + 1)} \cdot \cancel{e^{\beta_2 \cdot X_2}} \cdot \ldots \cdot \cancel{e^{\beta_k \cdot X_k}}}{\cancel{e^{\alpha_t}} \cdot e^{\beta_1 \cdot X_1} \cdot \cancel{e^{\beta_2 \cdot X_2}} \cdot \ldots \cdot \cancel{e^{\beta_k \cdot X_k}}}$$

$$= \frac{e^{\beta_1 \cdot (X_1 + 1)}}{e^{\beta_1 \cdot X_1}} = e^{\beta_1} \triangleq \widehat{RR} = e^{b_1}$$

{12.12}

where

$$RR \quad = \quad \text{population's rate ratio comparing a one-unit difference in the value of } X_1$$

$$\ln(\text{rate}) \quad = \quad \text{natural log of the rate at which the event occurs in the population}$$

$$\alpha_t \quad = \quad \text{function of time}$$

$$\beta_i \quad = \quad \text{regression coefficient for the i}^{\text{th}} \text{ (out of } k\text{) independent variable in the population}$$

$$X_i \quad = \quad \text{value of the i}^{\text{th}} \text{ (out of } k\text{) independent variable}$$

$$\widehat{RR} \quad = \quad \text{sample's estimate of the rate ratio comparing a one-unit difference in the value of } X_1$$

$$b_i \quad = \quad \text{sample's estimate of the regression coefficient for the i}^{\text{th}} \text{ (out of } k\text{) independent variable}$$

In SAS, the PHREG procedure is used to perform Cox regression analysis. In the next example, we will look at the output from this procedure when it is used to analyze a bivariable data set.

Example 12-5   Suppose that we are interested in exposure to an industrial solvent and development of peripheral neuropathy. To study the association between this exposure and disease, we identify 60 persons at the time they began working for the industry that uses the solvent and follow each for as long as they worked for the company. Of these 60 persons, 36 had jobs in which they were directly exposed to the solvent and 24 had jobs in which they were not exposed to the solvent. Imagine that 25 of the exposed persons and 9 of the unexposed persons developed neuropathy while working for the industry.

If we were to use SAS's FREQ procedure to analyze these data, we would get the following output:

```
                          The FREQ Procedure

                   Table of EXPOSURE by NEUROPATHY

            EXPOSURE       NEUROPATHY

            Frequency
            Percent
            Row Pct
            Col Pct    YES       NO            Total
            YES              25        11         36
                          41.67     18.33      60.00
                          69.44     30.56
                          73.53     42.31
            NO                9        15         24
                          15.00     25.00      40.00
                          37.50     62.50
                          26.47     57.69
            Total            34        26         60
                          56.67     43.33     100.00



         Estimates of the Common Relative Risk (Row1/Row2)


    Type of Study    Method              Value    95% Confidence Limits


    Case-Control     Mantel-Haenszel    3.7879     1.2749      11.2543
     (Odds Ratio)    Logit              3.7879     1.2749      11.2543
    Cohort           Mantel-Haenszel    1.8519     1.0577       3.2423
     (Col1 Risk)     Logit              1.8519     1.0577       3.2423
    Cohort           Mantel-Haenszel    0.4889     0.2732       0.8748
     (Col2 Risk)     Logit              0.4889     0.2732       0.8748
```

Examining this output leads us to conclude (incorrectly) that there is an association between exposure and development of neuropathy. The risk ratio[17] is equal to 1.8519 and its 95% confidence interval (1.0577 to 3.2423) does not include one (the null value)[18]. This implies that the risks of neuropathy are significantly different between persons who were exposed and persons who were not exposed to the solvent.

Before drawing this conclusion, however, we need to consider if development of neuropathy is dependent on time. In Chapter 6, we learned that a nominal dependent variable is considered to be affected by time if: (1) the longer we look for events, the more we find and (2) we look for the event longer for some persons than we do for other persons.

For these data, the first criterion is satisfied, since the longer we follow someone; the more likely it is that we will see them develop neuropathy. The second criterion is satisfied, as well. This is true here, because persons were followed for as long as they worked for the company. We can assume that this length of time is different for different individuals.[19] Thus, the second criterion is satisfied and we conclude that this is a nominal dependent variable that is affected by time.

When we have a nominal dependent variable affected by time, we need to use a method of analysis that takes time into account. Cox regression is such a method.

In our dataset, we have one nominal independent variable; exposure. As in other types of regression analysis, a nominal independent variable needs to be represented with an indicator variable. Unlike the LOGISTIC procedure, the PHREG procedure does not create these indicator variables for us. This means that the programmer needs to create indicator variables. The following output is the result of analyzing these data using SAS's PHREG procedure with an indicator called EXPOSE which is equal to one if the person is exposed and equal zero if the person is not exposed:

```
                         The PHREG Procedure
                         Model Information

                 Data Set              WORK.COXREG
                 Dependent Variable    TIME
                 Censoring Variable    NEURO
                 Censoring Value(s)    0
                 Ties Handling         BRESLOW

         Summary of the Number of Event and Censored Values
                                                   Percent
              Total      Event    Censored    Censored
               60         34         26        43.33
```

---

[17]Use of the risk ratio assumes that everyone was followed for the same period of time.

[18]See Chapter 9 for an explanation of how to select the appropriate risk ratio on output from the FREQ procedure.

[19]One way to determine to what degree the second criterion is satisfied is to compare the mean follow-up times for the two groups. In our example, the mean follow-up time for unexposed persons is 15 years and the mean follow-up time for exposed persons is 26 years. This is a substantial difference.

```
                               Convergence Status
                    Convergence criterion (GCONV=1E-8) satisfied.

                             Model Fit Statistics

                                    Without             With
                    Criterion      Covariates        Covariates
                    -2 LOG L        219.464            219.282
                    AIC             219.464            221.282
                    SBC             219.464            222.809

                    Testing Global Null Hypothesis: BETA=0

             Test                 Chi-Square       DF      Pr > ChiSq
             Likelihood Ratio        0.1818          1        0.6698
             Score                   0.1863          1        0.6660
             Wald                    0.1859          1        0.6663

                    Analysis of Maximum Likelihood Estimates

                 Parameter   Standard                        Hazard  95% Hazard Ratio
     Variable DF  Estimate     Error  Chi-Square  Pr > ChiSq  Ratio  Confidence Limits
     EXPOSE    1  -0.17661   0.40957     0.1859      0.6663    0.838   0.376      1.870
```

Let us interpret this output.

The first thing we notice is that the Cox regression output looks quite a bit like logistic regression output. This is because both methods use the maximum likelihood approach to make estimates of the regression coefficients. There are a few differences, however. For instance, in the table titled "Summary of the Number of Event and Censored Values," we are told that here are 34 events and 26 "censored" observations. We learned in Chapter 6 that a censored observation refers to an individual who did not have the event over the length of time that they were followed. This implies that we do not know whether or not they would have had the event if we had continued to follow them.

One part of the output from the PHREG procedure that is familiar is the table titled, "Testing Global Null Hypothesis: BETA=0." It is from this table that we get information about the omnibus null hypothesis. If this were a multivariable data set, the omnibus hypothesis would be that the entire collection of independent variables does not help estimate the rate at which persons develop neuropathy. In this example, we have only one independent variable, which is an indicator of exposure.[20] The *P*-values in this table are greater than 0.05, so we fail to reject this null hypothesis.

The final table in the output is titled "Analysis of Maximum Likelihood Estimates." It

---

[20]We learned in Chapter 7 that, in bivariable regression analysis, the test of the omnibus null hypothesis is the same as the test of the null hypothesis that the slope is equal to zero in the population.

is in this table that we find estimates of the regression coefficients and the result of testing the null hypothesis that each regression coefficient is equal to zero in the population. Since this is a bivariable data set, we draw the same conclusion that we did when testing the omnibus null hypothesis. Namely, we fail to reject the null hypothesis that the regression coefficient for the indicator of exposure is equal to zero in the population, because the *P*-value (0.6663) is greater than 0.05.

Let us take a moment to consider this result and compare it to the conclusion we drew when we used the FREQ procedure to estimate the risk ratio. The risk ratio indicated a statistically significant association between exposure and neuropathy. The rate ratio indicates no statistically significant association between exposure and neuropathy. Which conclusion is correct? The correction conclusion comes from the Cox regression analysis, since this analysis takes into account the fact that the members of the exposed group were followed, on the average, 11 years longer than members of the unexposed group. This difference in time of follow-up explains the greater number of events among persons in the exposed group.

There are two features of this last table in PHREG output that are different from what we are used to seeing in regression analyses. First, there is no estimate of the intercept. This is because the "intercept" in Cox regression analysis is a function of time instead of equal to a single value. Second, the last columns of that table report a "hazard ratio" and its 95% confidence interval. What SAS is calling a hazard ratio is really the rate ratio for a one-unit change in that particular independent variable. In output from the LOGISTIC procedure, the odds ratios appear in a separate table, but in the PHREG procedure, the rate ratios (i.e., "hazard ratios") are included in the same table as the estimates of the regression coefficients.

In logistic regression analysis, SAS calculates an odds ratio for a one-unit change in the value of continuous independent variables. This usually gives us an odds ratio that is very close to one, even though it might be statistically significant. The same is true in Cox regression analysis. When an independent variable represents continuous data, we often calculate a rate ratio for a larger change in the value of this variable. Equation {12.13} shows how this is done (compare to Equation{12.8}).

$$RR_\Delta = \frac{e^{\ln(\text{rate})}}{e^{\ln(\text{rate})}} = \frac{e^{\alpha_t + \beta_1 \cdot (X_1 + \Delta) + \beta_2 \cdot X_2 + ... + \beta_k \cdot X_k}}{e^{\alpha_t + \beta_1 \cdot (X_1) + \beta_2 \cdot X_2 + ... + \beta_k \cdot X_k}} = \frac{e^{\beta_1 \cdot (X_1 + \Delta)}}{e^{\beta_1 \cdot X_1}} = e^{\beta_1 \cdot \Delta} \triangleq \widehat{RR}_\Delta = e^{b_1 \cdot \Delta} \quad \{12.13\}$$

where

$$\Delta \quad = \quad \text{interval of independent variable values compared in a rate ratio}$$

In the next example, we will see how to use this calculation when interpreting output from the PHREG procedure.

Example 12-6   In Example 12-5, we were interested in exposure to an industrial solvent and development of peripheral neuropathy. Now, suppose that we want to control for differences in fasting blood glucose between the exposure groups (diabetes can cause peripheral neuropathy). The following output is obtained when we add blood glucose as a continuous independent variable:

```
                          The PHREG Procedure
                          Model Information

             Data Set                   WORK.COXREG
             Dependent Variable         TIME
             Censoring Variable         NEURO
             Censoring Value(s)         0
             Ties Handling              BRESLOW


        Summary of the Number of Event and Censored Values

                                               Percent
              Total      Event    Censored     Censored
               60         34         26         43.33


                        Convergence Status

         Convergence criterion (GCONV=1E-8) satisfied.


                       Model Fit Statistics

                           Without          With
             Criterion    Covariates      Covariates
             -2 LOG L       219.464         207.432
             AIC            219.464         211.432
             SBC            219.464         214.485


            Testing Global Null Hypothesis: BETA=0

        Test              Chi-Square     DF     Pr > ChiSq
        Likelihood Ratio     12.0318      2        0.0024
        Score                11.2637      2        0.0036
        Wald                 10.6338      2        0.0049


            Analysis of Maximum Likelihood Estimates

             Parameter   Standard                               Hazard    95% Hazard Ratio
Variable  DF   Estimate    Error   Chi-Square  Pr > ChiSq       Ratio     Confidence Limits
EXPOSE    1    -0.42734   0.42431    1.0143       0.3139         0.652      0.284     1.498
GLUCOSE   1     0.04091   0.01263   10.4993       0.0012         1.042      1.016     1.068
```

Let us interpret this output.

Now, we have two independent variables listed in the table titled "Analysis of Maximum Likelihood Estimates." Of these, the indicator of exposure is not statistically significant (P = 0.3139) but the continuous independent variable, GLUCOSE is statistically significant (P = 0.0012). The rate ratio (i.e., "hazard ratio") comparing a one-unit change in glucose is 1.042, which is very close to the null value (one). One reason for this is that the difference in fasting blood glucose being compared in this rate ratio is very small. To better assess the relationship between the rate of developing peripheral neuropathy and blood glucose, let us calculate the rate ratio for a 10-unit change in blood glucose. To do this, we use Equation{12.13}:

$$\widehat{RR}_{\Delta=10} = e^{b_1 \cdot \Delta} = e^{0.04091 \cdot 10} = 1.51$$

Thus, we estimate that the rate at which new cases of peripheral neuropathy occur increases by 51% for a 10 mg/dL increase in fasting blood glucose.

In Example 12-6, the analysis included an indicator variable and a continuous independent variable, but no interaction between these two variables. If Cox regression equation includes an interaction, the rate ratios calculated by the PHREG procedure are incorrect.[21] In this case, we need to calculate rate ratio estimates by hand. Equation {12.14} shows this calculation:[22]

$$RR_\Delta = \frac{e^{\ln(\text{rate})}}{e^{\ln(\text{rate})}} = \frac{e^{\alpha_t + \beta_1 \cdot (X_1 + \Delta) + \beta_2 \cdot X_2 + \beta_3 \cdot (X_1 + \Delta) \cdot X_2}}{e^{\alpha_t + \beta_1 \cdot (X_1) + \beta_2 \cdot X_2 + \beta_3 \cdot (X_1) \cdot X_2}} = \frac{\cancel{e^{\alpha_t}} \cdot e^{\beta_1 \cdot (X_1 + \Delta)} \cdot \cancel{e^{\beta_2 \cdot X_2}} \cdot e^{\beta_3 \cdot (X_1 + \Delta) \cdot X_2}}{\cancel{e^{\alpha_t}} \cdot e^{\beta_1 \cdot X_1} \cdot \cancel{e^{\beta_2 \cdot X_2}} \cdot e^{\beta_3 \cdot (X_1) \cdot X_2}}$$

$$= \frac{e^{\beta_1 \cdot (X_1 + \Delta)} \cdot e^{\beta_3 \cdot (X_1 + \Delta) \cdot X_2}}{e^{\beta_1 \cdot X_1} \cdot e^{\beta_3 \cdot X_1 \cdot X_2}} = e^{(\beta_1 \cdot \Delta) + (\beta_3 \cdot \Delta \cdot X_2)} \triangleq \widehat{RR}_\Delta = e^{(b_1 \cdot \Delta) + (b_3 \cdot \Delta \cdot X_2)} \qquad \{12.14\}$$

In the next example, we will see how to interpret the result of Cox regression analysis when the regression equation includes an interaction.

---

[21]In the LOGISTIC procedure, SAS knows when interactions occur in the regression equation and does not provide estimates of the odds ratios for the variables involved in an interaction. The PHREG procedure does not recognize interactions. As a result, SAS will estimate rate ratios for the interactions as well as the variables involved in them.

[22] Compare to Equation {12.10})

Example 12-7   In Example 12-6, we were interested in exposure to an industrial solvent and development of peripheral neuropathy while controlling for blood glucose level. Now, suppose that we add an interaction between exposure and blood glucose. The following output is obtained when we do this:

```
                          The PHREG Procedure
                          Model Information

                Data Set               WORK.COXREG
                Dependent Variable     TIME
                Censoring Variable     NEURO
                Censoring Value(s)     0
                Ties Handling          BRESLOW


         Summary of the Number of Event and Censored Values


                                              Percent
                Total      Event   Censored   Censored
                  60         34        26       43.33


                        Convergence Status
            Convergence criterion (GCONV=1E-8) satisfied.


                        Model Fit Statistics

                              Without          With
                Criterion    Covariates     Covariates
                -2 LOG L       219.464        204.274
                AIC            219.464        210.274
                SBC            219.464        214.853


                Testing Global Null Hypothesis: BETA=0

           Test              Chi-Square      DF     Pr > ChiSq
           Likelihood Ratio    15.1903         3       0.0017
           Score               15.1872         3       0.0017
           Wald                13.8026         3       0.0032


                Analysis of Maximum Likelihood Estimates

                  Parameter Standard                  Hazard    95% Hazard Ratio
Variable    DF   Estimate    Error Chi-Square Pr > ChiSq  Ratio  Confidence Limits
EXPOSE       1    5.01225  3.37314   2.2080     0.1373   150.242   0.202  111689.4
GLUCOSE      1    0.08503  0.03067   7.6854     0.0056     1.089   1.025     1.156
EXP_GLUCOSE  1   -0.05426  0.03265   2.7621     0.0965     0.947   0.888     1.010
```

Let us interpret this output.

Since exposure and glucose are involved in an interaction, we cannot interpret the rate ratio estimates for these variables provided by SAS. Instead, we need to use Equation{12.14}. The fact that the equation includes this interaction implies that we need to calculate separate estimates of the rate ratio corresponding to a 10 mg/dL change in blood glucose for each exposure category. For unexposed persons, this estimate is:

$$\widehat{RR}_{\Delta=10} = e^{(b_2 \cdot \Delta)+(b_3 \cdot \Delta \cdot X_2)} = e^{(0.08503 \cdot 10)+(-0.05426 \cdot 10 \cdot 0)} = 2.34$$

For exposed persons, this estimate is:

$$\widehat{RR}_{\Delta=10} = e^{(b_2 \cdot \Delta)+(b_3 \cdot \Delta \cdot X_2)} = e^{(0.08503 \cdot 10)+(-0.05426 \cdot 10 \cdot 1)} = 1.36$$

Even though these rate ratio estimates are equal to different values for exposed and unexposed persons, the difference is not statistically significant. We know that this is the case, since the P-value for the interaction (0.0965) is greater than 0.05.

NOMINAL INDEPENDENT VARIABLES

When independent variables represent nominal data, they separate dependent variable values into groups. When this occurs in multivariable analysis of a nominal dependent variable, we select one of the independent variables to be compared directly to the dependent variable. Then, all of the remaining independent variables are assumed to represent characteristics for which we would like to control.

Stratified Analysis

If the nominal dependent variable is not affected by time and all of the independent variables are nominal, we can use **stratified analysis** to analyze our data. The idea in stratified analysis is to select one of the nominal independent variables to be compared to the nominal dependent variable in 2 × 2 tables. Then, the rest of the nominal independent variables are used to separate the data into groups (i.e., **strata**) within each of which we compare the dependent variable and the selected independent variable. This separation of the data into strata eliminates confounding by these variables. The next example demonstrates how this works.

Example 12-8   Suppose that we are interested in the relationship between exposure to a particular food additive and development of diabetes. Further, suppose that we are concerned that gender might be a confounder because women are at higher risk for diabetes and are more likely to consume food with the additive than are men. In other words, we want to control for the potential confounding effect of gender. In stratified analysis, we can control for gender by separating the data into two gender strata. Imagine that the following frequencies were observed:

MEN   **Diabetes**

		Yes	No	
		Yes	No	
Exposure	Yes	30	30	60
	No	30	30	60
		60	60	120

WOMEN   **Diabetes**

		Yes	No	
		Yes	No	
Exposure	Yes	100	10	110
	No	10	1	11
		110	11	121

There are a number of ways in which we could summarize the relationship between exposure and the risk of diabetes in each of these strata (i.e., **strata-specific estimates**), but with each we would see the same thing for these data. For example, the following are odds ratios comparing exposure to the occurrence of diabetes for each of the gender strata (using Equation {9.8}).

$$\widehat{OR}_{\text{MEN}} = \frac{a \cdot d}{b \cdot c} = \frac{30 \cdot 30}{30 \cdot 30} = 1.00$$

$$\widehat{OR}_{\text{WOMEN}} = \frac{a \cdot d}{b \cdot c} = \frac{100 \cdot 1}{10 \cdot 10} = 1.00$$

With odds ratios equal to one, there is no apparent association between exposure and risk of diabetes in either of the two genders. If we had not divided the data into these two strata, however, we would have a different impression. Combining the data across the two strata we get the following:[23]

---

[23]We are doing this to illustrate what would happen if we combined the data over strata. In practice, combining the data is not an appropriate response to observation of similar strata-specific estimates.

BOTH GENDERS

Diabetes

		Yes	No	
Exposure	Yes	130	40	170
	No	40	31	71
		107	71	241

$$\widehat{OR} = \frac{a \cdot d}{b \cdot c} = \frac{130 \cdot 31}{40 \cdot 40} = 2.52$$

Now, it appears that there is a relatively strong relationship between exposure and diabetes.[24] This result, however, reflects the relationship between gender and diabetes (women are at higher risk of diabetes) and between gender and exposure (women are more often exposed), rather than a relationship between exposure and diabetes. By stratifying the data according to gender, we are able to control for its effect.

When using stratified analysis, we sometimes see that the relationship between the dependent and independent variable used to construct the 2 × 2 tables is essentially the same regardless of which stratum is considered. This was true in Example 12-8. In that example, regardless of whether we are thinking about men or women, there is no association between exposure and risk of diabetes. When these strata-specific estimates are similar across strata, we do not need to report separate measures of association for each stratum. Instead, we would like to have a single measure of association that represents all strata. We call that single measure of association a **summary estimate**.

We might be tempted at this point to combine all of the data into a single 2 × 2 table and calculate an estimate from this 2 × 2 table to serve as the summary estimate. Resist that temptation! To combine the data would be to remove control of confounding. Example 12-8 shows what can happen when control of confounders is removed; we can get a biased view of the association between the two variables. Instead of combining data across strata, we calculate a summary estimate by combining the strata-specific estimates.

There are two ways in which we commonly combine the strata-specific estimates to obtain a summary estimate. One way is to calculate a weighted average[25] of the strata-specific estimates using the precision of each estimate as the weight. The result is called a **precision-based estimate**. The other way is to separately combine the numerators and the

---

[24]This observation of an association suggested by the combined data, even when there is no association in either of the strata is sometimes called "Simpson's paradox."

[25]See Equation 7.25 for a description of a weighted average.

denominators of a ratio measure of association across strata and, then divide the sum of the numerators by the sum of the denominators. The result is called a **Mantel-Haenszel estimate**.

Of the two types of summary estimates, the Mantel-Haenszel estimates are the easier to calculate by hand. Further, the two types of estimates are usually very close in value. So, if they are to be calculated by hand, we recommend using the Mantel-Haenszel estimates. Equations {12.15} and {12.16} illustrate Mantel-Haenszel summary estimates of the odds ratio and risk ratio.

$$OR \triangleq \overline{OR} = \frac{\sum_{i=1}^{k} a_i \cdot d_i \Big/ n_i}{\sum_{i=1}^{k} b_i \cdot c_i \Big/ n_i} \qquad \{12.15\}$$

$$RR \triangleq \overline{RR} = \frac{\sum_{i=1}^{k} a_i \cdot (c_i + d_i) \Big/ n_i}{\sum_{i=1}^{k} c_i \cdot (a_i + b_i) \Big/ n_i} \qquad \{12.16\}$$

where

$\overline{OR}$ = summary estimate of the odds ratio

$\overline{RR}$ = summary estimate of the risk ratio

a_i, b_i, c_i, d_i = observed frequencies in the 2×2 table in the ith stratum of k strata[26]

n_i = number of observations in the ith stratum of k strata

In the next example, we will take a look at calculation of Mantel-Haenszel summary estimates of the odds ratio and risk ratio.

Example 12-9   Suppose that we are interested in the relationship between long-term steroid therapy and the risk of developing cataracts. To study this relationship, we identify 116 persons initiating this therapy and 100 persons initiating an alternative therapy. Then, we follow persons in both groups for 5 years to observe the development of cataracts. In analyzing these observations, we want to control for the effect of gender, since women are more likely to be exposed to steroid therapy and are greater risk of developing cataracts.

---

[26]See Tables 9-1 and 9-2 to see how the cell frequencies are assigned to a 2×2 table for cohort and case-control studies, respectively.

Suppose that we observe the following results:[27]

WOMEN

Cataracts

		Yes	No	
Therapy	Yes	31	49	80
	No	13	37	50
		44	86	130

$$OR \triangleq \widehat{OR} = \frac{a \cdot d}{b \cdot c} = \frac{31 \cdot 37}{49 \cdot 13} = 1.80$$

$$\frac{\theta_1}{\theta_2} \triangleq \frac{p_1}{p_2} = \frac{\dfrac{a}{a+b}}{\dfrac{c}{c+d}} = \frac{\dfrac{31}{31+49}}{\dfrac{13}{13+37}} = 1.49$$

MEN

Cataracts

		Yes	No	
Therapy	Yes	13	23	36
	No	9	41	50
		22	64	86

$$OR \triangleq \widehat{OR} = \frac{a \cdot d}{b \cdot c} = \frac{13 \cdot 41}{23 \cdot 9} = 2.57$$

$$\frac{\theta_1}{\theta_2} \triangleq \frac{p_1}{p_2} = \frac{\dfrac{a}{a+b}}{\dfrac{c}{c+d}} = \frac{\dfrac{13}{13+23}}{\dfrac{9}{9+41}} = 2.01$$

Let us calculate the Mantel-Haenszel summary estimates of the odds ratio and risk ratio

[27]Strata-specific estimates of the odds ratio and risk ratio are calculated using Equations {9.8} and {9.6} respectively.

from these data.

To calculate the summary estimate of the odds ratio, we use Equation{12.15}.

$$OR \triangleq \overline{OR} = \frac{\sum_{i=1}^{k} a_i \cdot d_i / n_i}{\sum_{i=1}^{k} b_i \cdot c_i / n_i} = \frac{31 \cdot 37/130 + 13 \cdot 41/86}{49 \cdot 13/130 + 23 \cdot 9/86} = 2.06$$

If we are willing to assume that the odds ratio comparing the odds of developing diabetes between exposed and unexposed persons is the same for women and men, then we do not have to provide separate estimates for the two genders. Instead, we estimate that the odds ratio is equal to 2.06 regardless of gender.

To calculate the summary estimate of the risk ratio, we use Equation{12.16}.

$$RR \triangleq \overline{RR} = \frac{\sum_{i=1}^{k} a_i \cdot (c_i + d_i) / n_i}{\sum_{i=1}^{k} c_i \cdot (a_i + b_i) / n_i} = \frac{\left[31 \cdot (13+37)/130\right] + \left[13 \cdot (9+41)/86\right]}{\left[13 \cdot (31+49)/130\right] + \left[9 \cdot (13+23)/86\right]} = 1.66$$

If we are willing to assume that the risk ratio comparing the risk of developing diabetes between exposed and unexposed persons is the same for women and men, then we do not have to provide separate estimates for the two genders. Instead, we estimate that the risk ratio is equal to 1.66 regardless of gender.

Soon, we will take a look at output from stratified analysis using SAS, but first we need to think about how to decide whether or not a summary estimate makes sense. If, in the population, there are different strengths of association in each of the strata, we do not want to provide a single estimate.[28] Instead, we want to provide strata-specific estimates if those values are different in the population.

In Example 12-8, the strata-specific estimates are both equal to one. In that case, we would certainly use the same estimate (i.e., 1.00) for both genders. In practice, however, we cannot expect to see strata-specific estimates all exactly equal to each other when we take random samples, even if they are equal to the same value in the population. Instead, we expect to see some differences among those estimates due to the role of chance in selecting the sample. In Example 12-9, for instance, the strata-specific estimates are close, but not

---

[28]Epidemiologists refer to different strengths of association in different strata as **effect modification**. This is the same as what statisticians call an interaction.

identical between men and women. The question is: Are they close enough to assume they are estimating the same odds ratio and risk ratio in the population?

To answer this question, we need a method to compare the strata-specific estimates that can take this role of chance into account. Most often, we make this decision by testing the null hypothesis that the strata-specific measures of association are equal to the same value in the population. This is called a **test of homogeneity**. If we are able to reject this null hypothesis, we conclude that there are different associations in each stratum in the population. In that case, we do not want to use a summary estimate. Instead, we report the strata-specific estimates. If we fail to reject this null hypothesis, on the other hand, we conclude that a summary estimate makes sense. In that case, we report one estimate that applies to all of the strata.

Now, let us take a look at an example that uses SAS's FREQ procedure to perform a stratified analysis.

Example 12-10 In Example 12-9 we looked at the results of a study in which we examined the relationship between long-term steroid therapy and the risk of developing cataracts while controlling for the potential confounding effects of gender. If we were to analyze the data from Example 12-9 using the FREQ procedure, we would observe the following output:

```
                          The FREQ Procedure

                     Table 1 of THERAPY by CATARACTS
                     Controlling for GENDER=FEMALE


                   THERAPY        CATARACTS

          Frequency
          Percent
          Row Pct
          Col Pct     YES        NO            Total
          YES              31         49          80
                       23.85      37.69       61.54
                       38.75      61.25
                       70.45      56.98

          NO               13         37          50
                       10.00      28.46       38.46
                       26.00      74.00
                       29.55      43.02

          Total            44         86         130
                       33.85      66.15      100.00
```

```
              Statistics for Table 1 of THERAPY by CATARACTS
                     Controlling for GENDER=FEMALE

              Estimates of the Relative Risk (Row1/Row2)

     Type of Study                Value       95% Confidence Limits

     Case-Control (Odds Ratio)    1.8006      0.8290        3.9110
     Cohort (Col1 Risk)           1.4904      0.8661        2.5645
     Cohort (Col2 Risk)           0.8277      0.6514        1.0517

                     Sample Size = 130
```

```
                    Table 2 of THERAPY by CATARACTS
                     Controlling for GENDER=MALE

              THERAPY        CATARACTS

              Frequency
              Percent
              Row Pct
              Col Pct    YES        NO            Total
              YES           13         23            36
                         15.12      26.74         41.86
                         36.11      63.89
                         59.09      35.94
              NO             9         41            50
                         10.47      47.67         58.14
                         18.00      82.00
                         40.91      64.06
              Total         22         64            86
                         25.58      74.42        100.00


              Statistics for Table 2 of THERAPY by CATARACTS
                     Controlling for GENDER=MALE

              Estimates of the Relative Risk (Row1/Row2)

     Type of Study                Value       95% Confidence Limits

     Case-Control (Odds Ratio)    2.5749      0.9553        6.9399
     Cohort (Col1 Risk)           2.0062      0.9629        4.1798
     Cohort (Col2 Risk)           0.7791      0.5901        1.0286

                     Sample Size = 86
```

```
...........................................................................
:          Summary Statistics for THERAPY by CATARACTS                    :
:                    Controlling for GENDER                                :
:                                                                          :
:        Cochran-Mantel-Haenszel Statistics (Based on Table Scores)        :
:                                                                          :
:      Statistic   Alternative Hypothesis    DF     Value     Prob         :
:     ─────────────────────────────────────────────────────────────       :
:         1        Nonzero Correlation        1     5.4220   0.0199        :
:                                                                          :
:           Estimates of the Common Relative Risk (Row1/Row2)              :
:                                                                          :
:     Type of Study    Method              Value    95% Confidence Limits  :
:    ──────────────────────────────────────────────────────────────       :
:     Case-Control     Mantel-Haenszel     2.0557   1.1152      3.7892     :
:       (Odds Ratio)   Logit               2.0625   1.1196      3.7994     :
:                                                                          :
:     Cohort           Mantel-Haenszel     1.6555   1.0712      2.5585     :
:       (Col1 Risk)    Logit               1.6555   1.0700      2.5612     :
:                                                                          :
:     Cohort           Mantel-Haenszel     0.8068   0.6730      0.9673     :
:       (Col2 Risk)    Logit               0.8066   0.6728      0.9671     :
:                                                                          :
:                                                                          :
:                     Breslow-Day Test for                                 :
:                  Homogeneity of the Odds Ratios                          :
:                ──────────────────────────────────                       :
:                  Chi-Square              0.3106                          :
:                  DF                           1                          :
:                  Pr > ChiSq             0.5773                           :
:                                                                          :
...........................................................................
```

Let us interpret this output.

In the first two pages of this output, SAS has given us information about each stratum (i.e., for men and for women). This information includes a 2 × 2 table for each stratum as well as point and interval estimates for the odds ratio and the probability ratio (in this case, the risk ratio). We interpret these results the same way we did in bivariable analysis (see Example 9-12). For women, the risk ratio estimate is equal to 1.4904 and the limits of the 95% confidence interval are 0.8661 and 2.5645. Since this confidence interval includes one, we cannot reject the null hypothesis that the risk ratio is equal to one for women in the population. For men, the risk ratio estimate is equal to 2.0062 and the limits of the 95% confidence interval are 0.9629 and 4.1798. As with women, this confidence interval includes one, so we cannot reject the null hypothesis that the risk ratio is equal to one for men in the population.

    This part of stratified analysis is like bivariable analysis, except that we are controlling for differences between genders by looking at one gender at a time. The third page of the output is where we consider calculating a single estimate of the risk ratio that can be applied to both genders. The strata-specific estimates (1.49 and 2.01) are not equal to the same value, but the difference might be due only to chance. To decide, we go to the bottom of the last page of the output, where we are given the results of a test of homogeneity.[29] To interpret these results, we look at the P-value (in the line labeled "Pr > ChiSq"). Since this P-value (0.5773) is greater than 0.05, we fail to reject the null hypothesis that the risk ratios are equal to the same value for men and women. We take this to imply that it makes sense to calculate a summary estimate.

The summary estimates for the odds ratio and risk ratio are presented in the table titled "Estimates of the Common Relative Risk (Row1/Row2)." There are two summary estimates and confidence intervals for each of these measures of association. These two estimates and their confidence intervals were equal to the same value in bivariable analysis.[30] They are not the same in multivariable analysis. This is because they provide the results of the two different ways in which we can calculate a summary estimate. The precision-based estimates are the ones labeled as "Logit" in the "Methods" column of this table. The Mantel-Haenszel estimates are labeled as such in this same column.

There are a couple of things we can see by examining those estimates. First, we can see that the Mantel-Haenszel estimates calculated by SAS are the same as the estimates we calculated by hand in Example 12-9. More important, we can see that there is very little difference between the estimates. So, it does not matter which method we use to calculate summary estimates; we will get just about the same result.

The summary estimates for the odds ratio are equal to about 2.06 and the summary estimates of the risk ratio are equal to about 1.66.[31] The confidence intervals for both the odds ratio and the risk ratio exclude the null value (one). This implies that we are able to reject the null hypotheses that the odds ratio and the risk ratio are equal to one in the population. So, we conclude that exposed persons have a higher risk of diabetes and that this difference in risk is similar between men and women.

In this example, we were able to test the null hypotheses that the odds ratio and the risk ratio are equal to one in the population by noticing that the 95% confidence intervals do not include one. Another way in which we could test that null hypothesis is by using the **Mantel-Haenszel test**. We first encountered this test in Chapter 9, where it was an option for 2 × 2 table analysis (Equation {9.19}). This test also can be used to test two or more 2 × 2 tables. Equation {12.17} illustrates how this chi-square statistic can be used to test the

---

[29]This test compares the odds ratios, rather than the risk ratios. Under most circumstances, however, homogeneity of the odds ratio suggests homogeneity of the risk ratio.

[30]We can verify that by looking at the strata-specific results.

[31]Recall from Chapter 9 that the risk ratio can be found in one of the rows labeled "Cohort." Which row we use depends on which column of the 2 × 2 table corresponds to the event. Here, the event is developing cataracts, which is represented by column 1. So, the risk ratio estimate is in the middle row of this table.

null hypotheses that the risk ratio and odds ratio are equal to one and the hypothesis that the risk difference is equal to zero in the population.[32]

$$\chi^2_{1df} = \frac{\left(\sum_{i=1}^{k} a_i - \sum_{i=1}^{k} E(a_i)\right)^2}{\sum_{i=1}^{k} \frac{(a_i+b_i)\cdot(c_i+d_i)\cdot(a_i+c_i)\cdot(b_i+d_i)}{n_i^2\cdot(n_i-1)}}$$ {12.17}

where

χ^2_{1df}	=	chi-square statistic with one degree of freedom
a_i	=	observed frequency in the upper left-hand cell of the 2 × 2 table in the ith stratum of k strata
$E(a_i)$	=	expected frequency for the upper left-hand cell of the 2 × 2 table in the ith stratum of k strata (from Equation 9-13)
(a_i+b_i), (c_i+d_i), (a_i+c_i), (b_i+d_i)	=	marginal frequencies from the 2 × 2 table in the ith stratum of k strata
n_i	=	total number of observations in the 2 × 2 table in the ith stratum of k strata

In the next example, we see how the Mantel-Haenszel test is performed in stratified analysis.

Example 12-11 In Example 12-10 we looked at the results of a study in which we examined the relationship between long-term steroid therapy and the risk of developing cataracts while controlling for the potential confounding effects of gender. In that example, we used confidence intervals for the odds ratio and the risk ratio to test the null hypotheses that the odds ratio and the risk ratio are equal to one in the population. Now, let us test those null hypotheses using the Mantel-Haenszel test.

The formula for calculation of the Mantel-Haenszel chi-square statistic is in Equation {12.17}. In that equation, there are three quantities that are added up over each of the strata. Two of them are in the numerator of that equation. They are the observed number of persons in the "a" cell of the 2 × 2 table and the expected number of observations in that cell if the null hypotheses were true (from Equation {9.13}). The third quantity is the denominator of the equation. To see from where these values come, let us take another look at the strata-specific 2 × 2 tables.

---

[32]Recall from Chapter 9 that these three null hypotheses are always true together or false together. Thus, we do not need separate hypothesis tests for each estimate.

WOMEN   **Cataracts**

		Yes	No	
Therapy	Yes	31	49	80
	No	13	37	50
		44	86	130

$$a_{\female} = 31$$

$$E(a_{\female}) = \frac{(a_{\female} + b_{\female}) \cdot (a_{\female} \cdot c_{\female})}{n_{\female}} = \frac{80 \cdot 44}{130} = 27.08$$

$$\frac{(a_{\female} + b_{\female}) \cdot (c_{\female} + d_{\female}) \cdot (a_{\female} + c_{\female}) \cdot (b_{\female} + d_{\female})}{n_{\female}^2 \cdot (n_{\female} - 1)} = \frac{80 \cdot 50 \cdot 44 \cdot 86}{130^2 \cdot 129} = 6.94$$

MEN   **Cataracts**

		Yes	No	
Therapy	Yes	13	23	36
	No	9	41	50
		22	64	86

$$a_{\male} = 13$$

$$E(a_{\male}) = \frac{(a_{\male} + b_{\male}) \cdot (a_{\male} \cdot c_{\male})}{n_{\male}} = \frac{36 \cdot 22}{86} = 9.21$$

$$\frac{(a_{\male} + b_{\male}) \cdot (c_{\male} + d_{\male}) \cdot (a_{\male} + c_{\male}) \cdot (b_{\male} + d_{\male})}{n_{\male}^2 \cdot (n_{\male} - 1)} = \frac{36 \cdot 50 \cdot 22 \cdot 64}{86^2 \cdot 85} = 4.03$$

Then, we combine those strata-specific values in Equation {12.17}

$$\chi^2_{1df} = \frac{\left(\sum_{i=1}^{k} a_i - \sum_{i=1}^{k} E(a_i)\right)^2}{\sum_{i=1}^{k} \frac{(a_i + b_i) \cdot (c_i + d_i) \cdot (a_i + c_i) \cdot (b_i + d_i)}{n_i^2 \cdot (n_i - 1)}} = \frac{\left((31+13) - (27.08 + 9.21)\right)^2}{6.94 + 4.03} = 5.42$$

To test the null hypotheses, we compare this calculated value (5.42) to a critical value from Table B.7 that corresponds to one degree of freedom and an α of 0.05 (3.841). Since the calculated value is greater than the critical value (i.e., 5.42>3.841), we reject the null hypotheses that the odds ratio and the risk ratio are equal to one in the population.

The results of the Mantel-Haenszel test are also provided by SAS in the FREQ procedure (see Example 12-10). They are on the last page of the SAS output in the table titled "Cochran-Mantel-Haenszel Statistics (Based on Table Scores)." The P-value is equal to 0.0199. Since this P-value is less than 0.05, we reject the null hypotheses that the odds ratio and the risk ratio are equal to one in the population.

Relationship between Stratified Analysis and Logistic Regression

In Chapter 10 ("Multivariable Analysis of a Continuous Dependent Variable"), we learned about the principle of the general linear model. This principle unifies all of the analyses we have discussed for continuous dependent variables by allowing all of those analyses to be expressed as regression equations. We have a similar concept that applies to nominal dependent variables. It is called the principle of the **generalized linear model**. The reason for this new name is to reflect the fact that we can get very similar, rather than exact, results by expressing analyses for a nominal dependent variable as regression analyses. The reason that these are not exactly the same is because most of the methods we use to analyze nominal dependent variables are normal approximations. Different approximations give slightly different results.

As an example of the generalized linear model, let us consider logistic regression and stratified analysis. Both methods are appropriate for a nominal dependent variable not affected by time. The distinction is that all of the independent variables in stratified analysis are nominal.[33] The next example demonstrates the effect of using logistic regression to perform a stratified analysis.

---

[33]To continue this comparison, we can think of stratified analysis for a nominal dependent variable being similar to factorial ANOVA for a continuous dependent variable. The categories of one "factor" in stratified analysis are used to separate dependent variable values into two groups within each stratum. Categories of the other "factor" are used to separate the data into strata. The "main effect" of the first factor in stratified analysis is represented by the summary estimate. This summary estimate makes sense only if there is homogeneity among strata. This is the same as having no interaction in factorial ANOVA.

Example 12-12 Suppose that we are interested in the relationship between a particular exposure and a disease, but we are concerned about the potential confounding effect of age. To analyze our data, we decide to use stratified analysis. To create age strata, we divide the data into three age groups: (1) less than 40 years, (2) 40 to 49 years, and (3) 50 or more years. Analyzing these data using the FREQ procedure, suppose that we get the following results:

```
                 Table 1 of EXPOSURE by DISEASE
               Controlling for AGEGROUP=Less than 40

           EXPOSURE       DISEASE

       Frequency
       Percent
       Row Pct
       Col Pct   YES         NO              Total
       YES             2          10           12
                    3.08       15.38        18.46
                   16.67       83.33
                   20.00       18.18
       NO              8          45           53
                   12.31       69.23        81.54
                   15.09       84.91
                   80.00       81.82
       Total          10          55           65
                   15.38       84.62       100.00


           Statistics for Table 1 of EXPOSURE by DISEASE
               Controlling for AGEGROUP=Less than 40


           Estimates of the Relative Risk (Row1/Row2)

    Type of Study                 Value       95% Confidence Limits

    Case-Control (Odds Ratio)     1.1250      0.2067        6.1228
    Cohort (Col1 Risk)            1.1042      0.2677        4.5551
    Cohort (Col2 Risk)            0.9815      0.7438        1.2952

                    Sample Size = 65
```

```
                    Table 2 of EXPOSURE by DISEASE
                   Controlling for AGEGROUP=40 to 49


             EXPOSURE      DISEASE

        Frequency
        Percent
        Row Pct
        Col Pct    YES        NO            Total
        YES           4         28            32
                   7.02      49.12         56.14
                  12.50      87.50
                  57.14      56.00

        NO            3         22            25
                   5.26      38.60         43.86
                  12.00      88.00
                  42.86      44.00

        Total         7         50            57
                  12.28      87.72        100.00


          Statistics for Table 2 of EXPOSURE by DISEASE
                Controlling for AGEGROUP=40 to 49


           Estimates of the Relative Risk (Row1/Row2)


   Type of Study                 Value      95% Confidence Limits

   Case-Control (Odds Ratio)     1.0476      0.2120      5.1770
   Cohort (Col1 Risk)            1.0417      0.2562      4.2350
   Cohort (Col2 Risk)            0.9943      0.8180      1.2086

                    Sample Size = 57
```

```
                    Table 3 of EXPOSURE by DISEASE
                    Controlling for AGEGROUP=50 or more

               EXPOSURE        DISEASE

          Frequency
          Percent
          Row Pct
          Col Pct     YES         NO            Total
          YES              32          24           56
                        41.03       30.77        71.79
                        57.14       42.86
                        86.49       58.54
          NO                5          17           22
                         6.41       21.79        28.21
                        22.73       77.27
                        13.51       41.46
          Total            37          41           78
                        47.44       52.56       100.00


            Statistics for Table 3 of EXPOSURE by DISEASE
                    Controlling for AGEGROUP=50 or more

            Estimates of the Relative Risk (Row1/Row2)


    Type of Study                  Value      95% Confidence Limits

    Case-Control (Odds Ratio)     4.5333       1.4661      14.0179
    Cohort (Col1 Risk)            2.5143       1.1261       5.6136
    Cohort (Col2 Risk)            0.5546       0.3801       0.8093

                      Sample Size = 78
```

```
........................................................................................
:            Summary Statistics for EXPOSURE by DISEASE                                 :
:                      Controlling for AGEGROUP                                         :
:                                                                                       :
:         Cochran-Mantel-Haenszel Statistics (Based on Table Scores)                    :
:                                                                                       :
:       Statistic    Alternative Hypothesis    DF      Value     Prob                   :
:       ----------------------------------------------------------------                :
:           1        Nonzero Correlation         1     4.6958    0.0302                  :
:                                                                                       :
:              Estimates of the Common Relative Risk (Row1/Row2)                        :
:                                                                                       :
:      Type of Study      Method            Value      95% Confidence Limits            :
:      --------------------------------------------------------------------             :
:      Case-Control       Mantel-Haenszel   2.3340      1.0812        5.0384             :
:        (Odds Ratio)     Logit             2.2630      1.0069        5.0861             :
:                                                                                       :
:      Cohort             Mantel-Haenszel   1.8384      0.9952        3.3959             :
:        (Col1 Risk)      Logit             1.7976      0.9618        3.3599             :
:                                                                                       :
:      Cohort             Mantel-Haenszel   0.8278      0.7056        0.9711             :
:        (Col2 Risk)      Logit             0.9069      0.7829        1.0505             :
:                                                                                       :
:                                                                                       :
:                          Breslow-Day Test for                                         :
:                    Homogeneity of the Odds Ratios                                      :
:                    -----------------------------                                      :
:                    Chi-Square              3.0911                                     :
:                    DF                           2                                      :
:                    Pr > ChiSq              0.2132                                     :
:                                                                                       :
:                    Total Sample Size = 200                                            :
........................................................................................
```

From this output, we see that the *P*-value from the test of homogeneity (0.2132) is greater than 0.05. This implies that it makes sense to interpret a summary estimate. For the odds ratio, the summary estimate (using the Mantel-Haenszel method) is 2.33.[34] Using the Mantel-Haenszel test to test the null hypothesis that this odds ratio is equal to one in the population is equal to 0.0302. Since this is less than 0.05, we reject that null hypothesis

Now, let us use logistic regression analysis to represent this stratified analysis. To do this, we will have SAS create indicator variables to represent the three strata. The following output shows the result of this analysis:

---

[34]We are focusing on the odds ratio because we want to compare stratified analysis to logistic regression analysis, which is usually interpreted using odds ratios.

```
                        The LOGISTIC Procedure
                          Model Information

           Data Set                    WORK.EX12_10
           Response Variable           DISEASE
           Number of Response Levels   2
           Number of Observations      200
           Model                       binary logit
           Optimization Technique      Fisher's scoring


                          Response Profile

               Ordered                        Total
                 Value     DISEASE          Frequency
                   1       YES                     54
                   2       NO                     146


          Probability modeled is DISEASE='YES'.


                     Class Level Information
                                           Design
                                          Variables
             Class      Value              1      2
             EXPOSURE   YES                1
                        NO                -1
             AGEGROUP   50 or more         1      0
                        40 to 49           0      1
                        Less than 40      -1     -1


                  Model Convergence Status
         Convergence criterion (GCONV=1E-8) satisfied.


                     Model Fit Statistics

                                         Intercept
                            Intercept        and
            Criterion         Only        Covariates
            AIC              235.304        209.442
            SC               238.602        222.636
            -2 Log L         233.304        201.442


         Testing Global Null Hypothesis: BETA=0

      Test              Chi-Square      DF     Pr > ChiSq
      Likelihood Ratio    31.8610        3        <.0001
      Score               31.3448        3        <.0001
      Wald                27.6760        3        <.0001
```

```
.....................................................................
:               Analysis of Maximum Likelihood Estimates             :
:                                                                    :
:                                  Standard        Wald              :
:  Parameter              DF    Estimate    Error   Chi-Square   Pr > ChiSq :
:  Intercept               1     -1.2847   0.1965    42.7626     <.0001  :
:  EXPOSURE   YES           1      0.4226   0.1961     4.6453     0.0311  :
:  AGEGROUP  50 or more     1      0.9897   0.2442    16.4286     <.0001  :
:  AGEGROUP  40 to 49       1     -0.7976   0.3093     6.6523     0.0099  :
:                                                                    :
:                        Odds Ratio Estimates                        :
:                                        Point        95% Wald       :
:    Effect                            Estimate    Confidence Limits  :
:    EXPOSURE YES vs NO                  2.329      1.080     5.023   :
:    AGEGROUP 50 or more  vs Less than 40  3.260      1.337     7.952   :
:    AGEGROUP 40 to 49    vs Less than 40  0.546      0.182     1.640   :
:                                                                    :
:   Association of Predicted Probabilities and Observed Responses    :
:                                                                    :
:          Percent Concordant    64.2    Somers' D    0.463         :
:          Percent Discordant    17.9    Gamma        0.564         :
:          Percent Tied          17.9    Tau-a        0.184         :
:          Pairs                 7884    c            0.732         :
.....................................................................
```

Let us compare the results from stratified analysis to the results from logistic regression analysis.

In this example, we analyzed these data two ways. First, we used stratified analysis with strata defined by three age groups. In that analysis, the summary estimate of the odds ratio comparing the odds of disease between exposed and unexposed persons was 2.3340 and 2.2630 using the Mantel-Haenszel and logit methods respectively.

Second, we used logistic regression analysis using indicator variables to represent the three age groups. From logistic regression, the estimate of the odds ratio comparing the odds of disease between exposed and unexposed persons was equal to 2.329. This is very close, but not exactly equal to the summary estimates from stratified analysis.

The same is true for confidence intervals and for the test of the null hypothesis that the odds ratio is equal to one in the population. In stratified analysis the 95% confidence intervals were 1.0812 to 5.0384 and 1.0069 to 5.0861 for the two methods. In logistic regression analysis, the 95% confidence interval is 1.080 to 5.023. This is very close, but not exactly equal to the result of stratified analysis. The same is true for the P-values. For the null hypothesis that the odds ratio is equal to one in the population, the P-value in stratified analysis is equal to 0.0302. In logistic regression, the corresponding P-value is equal to 0.0311.

In Example 12-12, we controlled for age by defining age groups. When we do that, there still is variation in age among persons in each age group.[35] All we have done is to reduce the variability of this continuous confounder, not eliminate it. The result is that we have not completely controlled for the confounding effect of age. The potential result of incomplete control of a confounder is illustrated in the next example.

Example 12-13 In Example 12-12, we performed a logistic regression analysis in which age was represented by two indicator variables to separate the three age groups. Now, suppose that we perform another logistic regression analysis, but including age as a continuous independent variable. Doing that produces the following output.

```
                    The LOGISTIC Procedure

                      Model Information

           Data Set                    WORK.EX12_10
           Response Variable           DISEASE
           Number of Response Levels   2
           Number of Observations      200
           Model                       binary logit
           Optimization Technique      Fisher's scoring

                      Response Profile
              Ordered                      Total
              Value     DISEASE         Frequency
                 1      YES                    54
                 2      NO                    146

           Probability modeled is DISEASE='YES'.

                   Class Level Information

                                        Design
                                       Variables
              Class      Value             1
              EXPOSURE   YES               1
                         NO               -1

                 Model Convergence Status

        Convergence criterion (GCONV=1E-8) satisfied.
```

---

[35]Recall from Chapter 10 that the way which multivariable analysis controls confounding is by eliminating variation in the independent variable that is correlated with other independent variables before looking at the association between that independent variable and the dependent variable.

```
                         Model Fit Statistics

                                              Intercept
                                  Intercept       and
               Criterion           Only       Covariates
                  AIC              235.304      211.855
                  SC               238.602      221.750
                 -2 Log L          233.304      205.855

             Testing Global Null Hypothesis: BETA=0

          Test                Chi-Square    DF      Pr > ChiSq
          Likelihood Ratio       27.4483     2        <.0001
          Score                  25.5678     2        <.0001
          Wald                   22.5191     2        <.0001

             Analysis of Maximum Likelihood Estimates

                                   Standard       Wald
     Parameter      DF   Estimate    Error    Chi-Square   Pr > ChiSq
     Intercept       1   -3.9691     0.8376     22.4555      <.0001
     EXPOSURE  YES    1    0.2165     0.1975      1.2016      0.2730
     AGE             1    0.0615     0.0168     13.3905      0.0003

                      Odds Ratio Estimates

                            Point        95% Wald
         Effect           Estimate    Confidence Limits
         EXPOSURE YES vs NO  1.542      0.711      3.344
         AGE                 1.063      1.029      1.099

    Association of Predicted Probabilities and Observed Responses

          Percent Concordant    72.8    Somers' D    0.471
          Percent Discordant    25.7    Gamma        0.478
          Percent Tied           1.5    Tau-a        0.187
          Pairs                 7884    c            0.735
```

Let us compare this output (including age as a continuous independent variable) to the logistic regression output in Example 12-12 (including age as two indicator variables).

To consider how well we have controlled for age as a confounder, what we want to do is to compare the apparent relationship between exposure (another independent variable) and disease (the dependent variable). If there is confounding, we will see an apparent relationship between exposure and disease, even though such a relationship does not exist.

In Example 12-12, the odds ratio comparing the odds of disease between exposed and unexposed persons was equal to 2.329 and was statistically significant (*P*-value = 0.0311).

These are the results from controlling for age by defining three age groups. In the current example, however, the odds ratio comparing the odds of disease between exposed and unexposed persons is equal to 1.542 and is not statistically significant (*P*-value = 0.2730). The difference between the two analyses is that age is only partially controlled by defining age groups. In this circumstance, we say that there is **residual confounding** of the relationship between exposure and disease by age.

Life Table Analysis

When the nominal dependent variable is affected by time, we can take the differences in the length of follow-up into account by estimating rates. Another option is to consider time a confounder and stratify the data by time periods. Then, we are able to estimate risks instead of rates. The method we use to do this is called **life table analysis**.[36] Life table analysis shares an important property with stratified analysis. For both, we can perform the analyses by hand and, as a result, see what is happening in the analysis.

In Chapter 6, we saw how staggered admission can lead to a nominal dependent variable being affected by time (see Figure 6-2). In life table analysis, we measure time differently for each person followed. Time begins for each person when we begin following that person. This is called **study-relative time**. Figure 12-2 shows how study-relative time compares to calendar-relative time.

Calendar-Relative Time

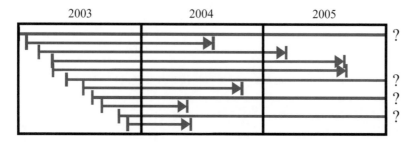

Study-Relative Time

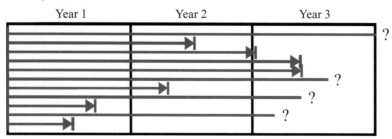

Figure 12-2 **Staggered admission of 11 subjects during the first year of a 3-year study.** Symbols used are: ⊢ indicates the time at which the individual entered the study (and consequently, the time at which follow-up began), ▶ indicates follow-up ending because of occurrence of the event of interest, and ? indicates end of follow-up without the event (because the study was concluded). The upper figure shows follow-up according to calendar-relative time. The lower figure shows follow-up according to study-relative time. Study-relative time starts at zero for each subject when their follow-up begins, regardless of the date in calendar time.

---

[36]This comes from the fact that life tables were originally used with death as the event. These methods, however, can be used for any event for which a risk can be calculated.

Life table analysis stratifies observations according to study-relative time. Since time is continuous, this is tantamount to representing time with one or more nominal independent variables. If we are doing the calculations by hand, we usually use only a few intervals for time. For the data in Figure 12-2, for instance, we would probably stratify time by year, creating three time strata. In each of these strata, we have two life tables, each specified by a particular value of the nominal independent variable that we want to compare to dependent variable values (e.g., exposure in a cohort study). Table 12-1 illustrates the usual format for each life table.

Table 12-1 Format of a life table applied to data observed in Figure 12-2. Each time period represents one year in study-relative time. In the "Persons" column is the number of persons without the event at the beginning of the time period. In the "Events" column is the number of persons who had the event during the time period. In the "Withdrawals" column is the number of persons for whom follow-up ended during the time period, but who did not have the event (i.e., censored observations). The probabilities in the last two columns are discussed below.

Time Period	Persons	Events	Withdrawals	Probability of No Event	Cumulative Probability
1	11	2	0	0.82	0.82
2	9	3	0	0.67	0.55
3	6	2	4	0.33	0.18

There are two probabilities that are calculated as part of life table analysis. The first is the probability of the event not occurring during that time period given that the person went through each of the previous time periods without the event occurring.[37] Equation {12.18} shows how this probability can be calculated.

$$p(\overline{event}_{t_i} | \overline{event}_{t<i}) = 1 - \frac{a_{t_i}}{n_{t_i}} \qquad \{12.18\}$$

where

$\overline{event}_{t_i}$ =   not having the event during the ith time period

$\overline{event}_{t<i}$ =   not having the event prior to the ith time period

a_{t_i} =   number of events during the ith time period

---

[37]Notice that this is a conditional probability in which not having the event during the current time period is the conditional event and not having the event in previous time periods is the conditioning event. Conditional probabilities are discussed in Chapter 1.

n_{t_i} = number of persons without the event at the beginning of the ith time period

The second probability in the life table is the probability of not having the event during the current time period and all previous time periods, thus it is called a **cumulative probability**. This probability is calculated by multiplying the probabilities in Equation {12.18} for the current and all pervious time periods.[38] This calculation is illustrated in Equation {12.19}.

$$ p(\overline{event}_{t_i} \text{ and } \overline{event}_{t_{<i}}) = \prod_{k=1}^{i} p(\overline{event}_{t_k} | \overline{event}_{t_{k-1}}) \qquad \{12.19\} $$

where

$\overline{event}_{t_i}$ = not having the event during the ith (out of k) time period

$\overline{event}_{t_{<i}}$ = not having the event prior to the ith (out of k) time period

$\prod_{k=1}^{i}$ = product with k going from 1 (the first time period) to i (the time period for which the probability is being calculated)

The next example illustrates these calculations.

Example 12-14 Suppose that we conduct a cohort study of persons in a particular industry. In this study, we select 80 persons who are beginning to work in an area in which they will be exposed to a byproduct of the manufacturing process and another 80 persons who are beginning to work in areas without this exposure. These persons are recruited over a 4-year period (i.e., by staggered admission). At the end of each year of follow-up, we examine those persons and determine who has evidence of liver damage. Imagine that we make the following observations:

Year of Follow-up*	Exposed			Unexposed		
	Persons	Events	Withdrawals	Persons	Events	Withdrawals
1	80	0	20	80	0	20
2	60	4	16	60	2	18
3	40	11	9	40	1	19
4	20	10	10	20	3	17

*Study-relative time

Let us create life tables for these two groups.

---

[38]This is the probability of the intersection of the probabilities of remaining event-free in all of the time periods up to and including the current time period. We learned in Chapter 1 that we use the multiplication rule to find the intersection of events.

For the exposed group, the probabilities of not having evidence of liver damage in each period, (given that there was no evidence of liver damage in previous periods) are calculated using Equation{12.18}.

$$p(\overline{event}_{t=1}) = 1 - \frac{a_{t=1}}{n_{t=1}} = 1 - \frac{0}{80} = 1 - 0 = 1.000$$

$$p(\overline{event}_{t=2}|\overline{event}_{t=1}) = 1 - \frac{a_{t=2}}{n_{t=2}} = 1 - \frac{4}{60} = 1 - 0.067 = 0.933$$

$$p(\overline{event}_{t=3}|\overline{event}_{t=1 \text{ and } 2}) = 1 - \frac{a_{t=3}}{n_{t=3}} = 1 - \frac{11}{40} = 1 - 0.275 = 0.725$$

$$p(\overline{event}_{t=4}|\overline{event}_{t=1, 2, \text{ and } 3}) = 1 - \frac{a_{t=4}}{n_{t=4}} = 1 - \frac{10}{20} = 1 - 0.500 = 0.500$$

These probabilities go in the fifth column of the life table and they are used to calculate the cumulative probabilities using Equation{12.19}.

$$p(\overline{event}_{t=2} \text{ and } \overline{event}_{t=1}) = p(\overline{event}_{t=2}|\overline{event}_{t=1}) \cdot p(\overline{event}_{t=1}) = 0.933 \cdot 1.000 = 0.933$$

$$p(\overline{event}_{t=3} \text{ and } \overline{event}_{t=2} \text{ and } \overline{event}_{t=1}) =$$
$$p(\overline{event}_{t=3}|\overline{event}_{t=1 \text{ and } 2}) = p(\overline{event}_{t=2}|\overline{event}_{t=1}) \cdot p(\overline{event}_{t=1}) = 0.725 \cdot 0.933 \cdot 1.000 = 0.677$$

$$p(\overline{event}_{t=4} \text{ and } \overline{event}_{t=3} \text{ and } \overline{event}_{t=2} \text{ and } \overline{event}_{t=1}) =$$
$$p(\overline{event}_{t=4}|\overline{event}_{t=1, 2, \text{ and } 4}) \cdot p(\overline{event}_{t=3}|\overline{event}_{t=1 \text{ and } 2}) \cdot p(\overline{event}_{t=2}|\overline{event}_{t=1}) \cdot p(\overline{event}_{t=1})$$
$$= 0.500 \cdot 0.725 \cdot 0.933 \cdot 1.000 = 0.338$$

Then, we organize these values in a life table for exposed persons.

Time Period	Exposed Persons	Events	Withdrawals	Probability of No Event	Cumulative Probability
1	80	0	20	1.000	1.000
2	60	4	16	0.933	0.933
3	40	11	9	0.725	0.677
4	20	10	10	0.500	0.338

We create a life table for unexposed persons in the same way. First, we calculate the probabilities of not having evidence of liver damage in each period, (given that there was no evidence of liver damage in previous periods) using Equation{12.18}.

$$p(\overline{event}_{t=1}) = 1 - \frac{a_{t=1}}{n_{t=1}} = 1 - \frac{0}{80} = 1 - 0 = 1.000$$

$$p(\overline{event}_{t=2} | \overline{event}_{t=1}) = 1 - \frac{a_{t=2}}{n_{t=2}} = 1 - \frac{2}{60} = 1 - 0.033 = 0.967$$

$$p(\overline{event}_{t=3} | \overline{event}_{t=1 \text{ and } 2}) = 1 - \frac{a_{t=3}}{n_{t=3}} = 1 - \frac{1}{40} = 1 - 0.025 = 0.975$$

$$p(\overline{event}_{t=4} | \overline{event}_{t=1, 2, \text{ and } 3}) = 1 - \frac{a_{t=4}}{n_{t=4}} = 1 - \frac{3}{20} = 1 - 0.150 = 0.850$$

Then, we calculate the cumulative probabilities using Equation{12.19}.

$$p(\overline{event}_{t=2} \text{ and } \overline{event}_{t=1}) = p(\overline{event}_{t=2} | \overline{event}_{t=1}) \cdot p(\overline{event}_{t=1}) = 0.967 \cdot 1.000 = 0.967$$

$$p(\overline{event}_{t=3} \text{ and } \overline{event}_{t=2} \text{ and } \overline{event}_{t=1}) =$$
$$p(\overline{event}_{t=3} | \overline{event}_{t=1 \text{ and } 2}) = p(\overline{event}_{t=2} | \overline{event}_{t=1}) \cdot p(\overline{event}_{t=1}) = 0.975 \cdot 0.967 \cdot 1.000 = 0.942$$

$$p(\overline{event}_{t=4} \text{ and } \overline{event}_{t=3} \text{ and } \overline{event}_{t=2} \text{ and } \overline{event}_{t=1}) =$$
$$p(\overline{event}_{t=4} | \overline{event}_{t=1, 2, \text{ and } 4}) \cdot p(\overline{event}_{t=3} | \overline{event}_{t=1 \text{ and } 2}) \cdot p(\overline{event}_{t=2} | \overline{event}_{t=1}) \cdot p(\overline{event}_{t=1}) =$$
$$0.850 \cdot 0.975 \cdot 0.967 \cdot 1.000 = 0.801$$

Finally, we organize those values in a life table for unexposed persons.

Time Period	Unexposed Persons	Events	Withdrawals	Probability of No Event	Cumulative Probability
1	80	0	20	1.000	1.000
2	60	2	18	0.967	0.967
3	40	1	19	0.975	0.942
4	20	3	17	0.850	0.801

Life tables are usually summarized by calculating risks. Risks are the complement of the cumulative probability of not experiencing the event. They can be calculated for each time period in the life table. Equation {12.20} illustrates that calculation.

$$\text{Risk}_i = 1 - p(\overline{event}_{t=i} \text{ and } \overline{event}_{t=i-1} \text{ and } ... \text{ and } \overline{event}_{t=1}) \qquad \{12.20\}$$

where

$$\text{Risk}_i = \text{risk of having the event up to and including the } i^{th} \text{ time period}$$

$$\overline{event}_{t=i} = \text{not having the event during the } i^{th} \text{ time period}$$

The next example shows how these risks are calculated and compared.

Example 12-15 In Example 12-14, we constructed life tables from data collected in a cohort study of the risk of liver damage related to exposure to a byproduct of a manufacturing process. Let us calculate risk estimates and compare them between exposed and unexposed persons.

First, we calculate risk estimates using Equation {12.20}. For example, the cumulative probability of avoiding liver damage over the entire 4-year period of follow-up for exposed persons was estimated in Example 12-14 to be 0.338. Thus, the 4-year risk of liver damage for exposed persons is:

$$\text{Risk}_{4-year} = 1 - p(\overline{event}_{t=4} \text{ and } \overline{event}_{t=3} \text{ and } \overline{event}_{t=2} \text{ and } \overline{event}_{t=1}) = 1 - 0.338 = 0.662$$

The 4-year risk for unexposed persons is calculated as:

$$\text{Risk}_{4-year} = 1 - p(\overline{event}_{t=4} \text{ and } \overline{event}_{t=3} \text{ and } \overline{event}_{t=2} \text{ and } \overline{event}_{t=1}) = 1 - 0.801 = 0.199$$

To compare risks between exposed and unexposed, we usually compared them as a ratio.[39] The following table summarizes the risks and their ratios for these data.

Risk Period	Exposed		Unexposed		Risk Ratio
	Cumulative Probability	Risk	Cumulative Probability	Risk	
1	1.000	0	1.000	0	--
2	0.933	0.067	0.967	0.033	2.00
3	0.677	0.323	0.942	0.058	5.57
4	0.338	0.662	0.801	0.199	3.33

Thus, the exposed group has twice the risk of liver disease after 2 years, 5.57 times the risk after 3 years and 3.33 times the risk after 4 years.

---

[39]See Chapter 9 for a discussion of the distinction in interpretation between probability differences and probability ratios.

So far, we have calculated probabilities by assuming that the persons who withdrew from the study[40] did so at the end of the time period. This assumption is reflected by the fact that all of the persons who withdrew are included in the denominator of Equation{12.18}. When we make this assumption, the type of life table analysis we are using is called the **Kaplan-Meier** method.[41] This is the most commonly used type of life table analysis.

Another, more realistic, assumption that we could make about the persons who withdrew is that their follow-up ended sometime during the time period. If we do not know when they withdrew, we can assume that there was a uniform rate of withdrawal over the study period. For example, if 52 persons withdrew during a 1-year time period, we could assume that, on the average, one person withdrew each week. This implies that the mean length of follow-up among withdrawals is equal to half of the time period (e.g., 26 weeks). This is the same as saying that persons who withdrew were at risk for the event, on the average, for half of the time of persons who did not withdraw.[42] To put this in a form that can be used in life table analysis, we assume that this is the same as having half of the number of persons who withdrew at risk for the entire time period. With this assumption about persons who withdraw from follow-up, we are using what is called the **actuarial** method of life table analysis.[43] Equation {12.21} shows how this affects calculation of the probability of avoiding the event (compare to Equation{12.18}).

$$p(\overline{event}_{t=i} | \overline{event}_{t<i}) = 1 - \frac{a_{t=i}}{n_{t=i} - \frac{w_{t=i}}{2}}$$ {12.21}

where

$\overline{event}_{t=i}$ = not having the event during the ith time period

$\overline{event}_{t<i}$ = not having the event prior to the ith time period

$a_{t=i}$ = number of events during the ith time period

$n_{t=i}$ = number of persons without the event at the beginning of the ith time period

$w_{t=i}$ = number of withdrawals during the ith time period

---

[40]We learned in Chapter 6 that "withdrawals" include persons who are not followed any further for any reason, including termination of the study.

[41]This is also called the product-limit method, usually by statisticians rather than health researchers.

[42]In calculation of risks, we do not make an adjustment for the time that each person who had the event was followed. If we were calculating follow-up time (e.g., to estimate incidence), however, we would make the same adjustment. This is discussed in Chapter 6.

[43]This is also called the Cutler-Ederer method.

The next example shows how the actuarial method affects risk estimates in life table analysis.

Example 12-16 In Example 12-14, we constructed life tables using the Kaplan-Meier method. Now, let us reconstruct the life table for exposed persons using the actuarial method.

Instead of using Equation {12.18}, we use Equation {12.21} to calculate the probabilities of not having evidence of liver damage in each period, given that there was no evidence of liver damage in previous periods.

$$p(\overline{event}_{t=1})=1-\frac{a_{t=1}}{n_{t=1}-\frac{w_{t=1}}{2}}=1-\frac{0}{80-\frac{20}{2}}=1-0=1.000$$

$$p(\overline{event}_{t=2}|\overline{event}_{t=1})=1-\frac{a_{t=2}}{n_{t=2}-\frac{w_{t=2}}{2}}=1-\frac{4}{60-\frac{16}{2}}=1-0.077=0.923$$

$$p(\overline{event}_{t=3}|\overline{event}_{t=1 \text{ and } 2})=1-\frac{a_{t=3}}{n_{t=3}-\frac{w_{t=3}}{2}}=1-\frac{11}{40-\frac{9}{2}}=1-0.310=0.690$$

$$p(\overline{event}_{t=4}|\overline{event}_{t=1, 2, \text{ and } 3})=1-\frac{a_{t=4}}{n_{t=4}-\frac{w_{t=4}}{2}}=1-\frac{10}{20-\frac{10}{2}}=1-0.667=0.333$$

Then we use Equation {12.19} to calculate the cumulative probabilities:

$$p(\overline{event}_{t=2} \text{ and } \overline{event}_{t=1}) = p(\overline{event}_{t=2}|\overline{event}_{t=1}) \cdot p(\overline{event}_{t=1})=0.923 \cdot 1.000=0.923$$

$$p(\overline{event}_{t=3} \text{ and } \overline{event}_{t=2} \text{ and } \overline{event}_{t=1}) =$$
$$p(\overline{event}_{t=3}|\overline{event}_{t=1 \text{ and } 2})=p(\overline{event}_{t=2}|\overline{event}_{t=1}) \cdot p(\overline{event}_{t=1})=0.690 \cdot 0.923 \cdot 1.000=0.637$$

$$p(\overline{event}_{t=4} \text{ and } \overline{event}_{t=3} \text{ and } \overline{event}_{t=2} \text{ and } \overline{event}_{t=1}) =$$
$$p(\overline{event}_{t=4}|\overline{event}_{t=1, 2, \text{ and } 4}) \cdot p(\overline{event}_{t=3}|\overline{event}_{t=1 \text{ and } 2}) \cdot p(\overline{event}_{t=2}|\overline{event}_{t=1}) \cdot p(\overline{event}_{t=1})$$
$$= 0.333 \cdot 0.690 \cdot 0.923 \cdot 1.000 = 0.212$$

Thus, the life table for exposed persons is:

Time Period	Persons	Exposed Events	Withdrawals	Probability of No Event	Cumulative Probability
1	80	0	20	1.000	1.000
2	60	4	16	0.923	0.923
3	40	11	29	0.690	0.637
4	20	10	30	0.333	0.212

To see the effect of using the actuarial method on risk estimates, let us use Equation {12.20} to estimate the 4-year risk of liver damage.

$$\text{Risk}_{4-year} = 1 - p(\overline{event}_{t=4} \text{ and } \overline{event}_{t=3} \text{ and } \overline{event}_{t=2} \text{ and } \overline{event}_{t=1}) = 1 - 0.212 = 0.788$$

The Kaplan-Meier estimate of this risk was found in Example 12-15 to be 0.662. This is lower than the actuarial estimate (0.788). The actuarial estimate of risk will always be higher than the Kaplan-Meier estimate when there are withdrawals during the risk period.

The difference between these two methods of calculating risk becomes less as the length of the time period between examinations becomes shorter. If we know exactly when a person had the event or withdrew, the Kaplan-Meier method and the actuarial method would yield the same risk estimate.

Often, the results of life table analysis are summarized graphically in what is called a **survival curve**. This name is a little misleading, since it suggests a curved line. Rather, survival curves are usually "staircase" plots in which the cumulative probability of avoiding the event is changed for each time period. Figure 12-3 shows survival curves for the life tables in Example 12-14.

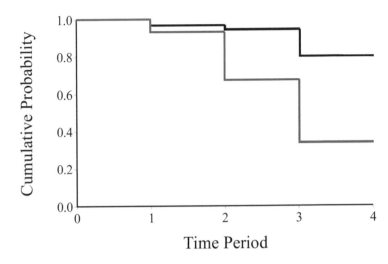

Figure 12-3 Survival curves for the cumulative probability of avoiding liver damage among persons who were exposed (colored line) or unexposed (black line) to a manufacturing byproduct. These cumulative probabilities were calculated in Example 12-14.

The survival curves in Figure 12-3 suggest that, as the length of follow-up increases, the differences in the risk of liver damage between the two exposure groups becomes greater. This is a common observation in survival curves. It is important to keep in mind, however, that the number of persons contributing to probability estimates decreases as the length of follow-up increases. This is because, as time goes on, fewer persons are followed, either because they have had the event or they have withdrawn from follow-up. Fewer persons contributing to probability estimates results in less precise estimates. So, we need to be cautious about over-interpretation of differences seen during the later time periods.

To take chance into account in life table analysis, we usually test the null hypothesis that the cumulative probabilities are the same in the groups being compared. The most common method we used to test this null hypothesis is a normal approximation called the **log-rank test**. Actually, this is not a new test, just a new name. In Chapter 9, we learned about the Mantel-Haenszel test that can be used for 2×2 table analyses (see Equation {9.19}). Earlier in this chapter, we learned that the Mantel-Haenszel test is also used in stratified analysis (see Equation {12.17}). The log-rank test is really just the Mantel-Haenszel test applied to data stratified by time period. The next example shows how we can conduct the log-rank test to test the null hypothesis that the risk ratio is equal to one in the population.

Example 12-17 In Example 12-14, we constructed life tables for a group of persons who were exposed to a byproduct of a manufacturing process and another group of persons who were not exposed, comparing their risks of developing liver damage. In Example 12-15, we estimated the 4-year risk ratio to be equal to 3.33. Now, let us test the null hypothesis that the risk ratio in the population is equal to one.

First, we need to rearrange the data so that they are organized into strata that represent the four time periods:

YEAR 1

Liver Damage

		Yes	No	
Exposure	Yes	0	80	80
	No	0	80	80
		0	160	160

YEAR 2

Liver Damage

		Yes	No	
Exposure	Yes	4	56	60
	No	2	58	60
		6	114	120

YEAR 3

Liver Damage

		Yes	No	
Exposure	Yes	11	29	40
	No	1	39	40
		12	68	80

YEAR 4

Liver Damage

		Yes	No	
Exposure	Yes	10	10	20
	No	3	17	20
		13	27	40

To test this null hypothesis by hand, we use Equation{12.17}:

$$\chi_{1df}^2 = \frac{\left(\sum_{i=1}^{k} a_i - \sum_{i=1}^{k} E(a_i)\right)^2}{\sum_{i=1}^{k} \dfrac{(a_i+b_i)\cdot(c_i+d_i)\cdot(a_i+c_i)\cdot(b_i+d_i)}{n_i^2\cdot(n_i-1)}}$$

$$= \frac{\left((0+4+11+10)-(\dfrac{0\cdot80}{160}+\dfrac{6\cdot60}{120}+\dfrac{12\cdot40}{80}+\dfrac{13\cdot20}{40})\right)^2}{\dfrac{80\cdot80\cdot0\cdot160}{160^2\cdot(160-1)}+\dfrac{60\cdot60\cdot6\cdot114}{120^2\cdot(120-1)}+\dfrac{40\cdot40\cdot12\cdot68}{80^2\cdot(80-1)}+\dfrac{20\cdot20\cdot13\cdot27}{40^2\cdot(40-1)}} = 14.40$$

The result of this calculation (14.40) is compared to a chi-square value with one degree of freedom that corresponds to an α of 0.05. We learn from Table B.7 that the critical value is 3.841. Since the calculated value (14.4) is greater than the critical value (3.841), we reject the null hypothesis that the ratio of 4-year risks is equal to one in the population.

SAS can do life table analyses in its LIFETEST procedure. The next example shows output from the LIFETEST procedure.

Example 12-18 In Example 12-14, we examined the risk of liver damage from a cohort study of persons in a particular industry using a Kaplan-Meier life table analysis. Let us analyze those same data using the LIFETEST procedure.

The first part of the output from the LIFETEST procedure shows the life tables, but it does that by having each person listed as a row headed by the time that the person either had the event or withdrew from the study. So, in the data from Example 12-14, there are 80 rows in each table to account for the 80 persons in each group. You can distinguish between persons who had the event (which SAS calls "Failures") and persons who withdrew from the study by noticing an asterisk in the "time" column for persons who withdrew or an increase in the number in the column labeled "Number Failed" for persons who had the event. The first table is for the exposed persons.

```
                        The LIFETEST Procedure
                     Stratum 1: GROUP = exposed
                     Product-Limit Survival Estimates
```

time	Survival	Failure	Survival Standard Error	Number Failed	Number Left
0.00000	1.0000	0	0	0	80
1.00000*	.	.	.	0	79
1.00000*	.	.	.	0	78
1.00000*	.	.	.	0	77
1.00000*	.	.	.	0	76
1.00000*	.	.	.	0	75
1.00000*	.	.	.	0	74
1.00000*	.	.	.	0	73
1.00000*	.	.	.	0	72
1.00000*	.	.	.	0	71
1.00000*	.	.	.	0	70
1.00000*	.	.	.	0	69
1.00000*	.	.	.	0	68
1.00000*	.	.	.	0	67
1.00000*	.	.	.	0	66
1.00000*	.	.	.	0	65
1.00000*	.	.	.	0	64
1.00000*	.	.	.	0	63
1.00000*	.	.	.	0	62
1.00000*	.	.	.	0	61
1.00000*	.	.	.	0	60
2.00000	.	.	.	1	59
2.00000	.	.	.	2	58
2.00000	.	.	.	3	57
2.00000	0.9333	0.0667	0.0322	4	56
2.00000*	.	.	.	4	55
2.00000*	.	.	.	4	54
2.00000*	.	.	.	4	53
2.00000*	.	.	.	4	52
2.00000*	.	.	.	4	51
2.00000*	.	.	.	4	50
2.00000*	.	.	.	4	49
2.00000*	.	.	.	4	48
2.00000*	.	.	.	4	47
2.00000*	.	.	.	4	46
2.00000*	.	.	.	4	45
2.00000*	.	.	.	4	44
2.00000*	.	.	.	4	43
2.00000*	.	.	.	4	42
2.00000*	.	.	.	4	41
2.00000*	.	.	.	4	40
3.00000	.	.	.	5	39
3.00000	.	.	.	6	38
3.00000	.	.	.	7	37
3.00000	.	.	.	8	36

3.00000	.	.	.	9	35
3.00000	.	.	.	10	34
3.00000	.	.	.	11	33
3.00000	.	.	.	12	32
3.00000	.	.	.	13	31
3.00000	.	.	.	14	30
3.00000	0.6767	0.3233	0.0699	15	29
3.00000*	.	.	.	15	28
3.00000*	.	.	.	15	27
3.00000*	.	.	.	15	26
3.00000*	.	.	.	15	25
3.00000*	.	.	.	15	24
3.00000*	.	.	.	15	23
3.00000*	.	.	.	15	22
3.00000*	.	.	.	15	21
3.00000*	.	.	.	15	20
4.00000	.	.	.	16	19
4.00000	.	.	.	17	18
4.00000	.	.	.	18	17
4.00000	.	.	.	19	16
4.00000	.	.	.	20	15
4.00000	.	.	.	21	14
4.00000	.	.	.	22	13
4.00000	.	.	.	23	12
4.00000	.	.	.	24	11
4.00000	0.3383	0.6617	0.0833	25	10
4.00000*	.	.	.	25	9
4.00000*	.	.	.	25	8
4.00000*	.	.	.	25	7
4.00000*	.	.	.	25	6
4.00000*	.	.	.	25	5
4.00000*	.	.	.	25	4
4.00000*	.	.	.	25	3
4.00000*	.	.	.	25	2
4.00000*	.	.	.	25	1
4.00000*	.	.	.	25	0

NOTE: The marked survival times are censored observations.

Summary Statistics for Time Variable time

Quartile Estimates

	Point	95% Confidence Interval	
Percent	Estimate	[Lower	Upper)
75	.	4.00000	.
50	4.00000	4.00000	.
25	3.00000	3.00000	4.00000

Mean	Standard Error
3.61000	0.08796

The second table is for the unexposed persons.

```
                      Stratum 2: GROUP = unexpose

                   Product-Limit Survival Estimates

                                 Survival
                                 Standard     Number      Number
    time      Survival   Failure   Error      Failed       Left
  0.00000      1.0000       0         0          0          80
  1.00000*       .          .         .          0          79
  1.00000*       .          .         .          0          78
  1.00000*       .          .         .          0          77
  1.00000*       .          .         .          0          76
  1.00000*       .          .         .          0          75
  1.00000*       .          .         .          0          74
  1.00000*       .          .         .          0          73
  1.00000*       .          .         .          0          72
  1.00000*       .          .         .          0          71
  1.00000*       .          .         .          0          70
  1.00000*       .          .         .          0          69
  1.00000*       .          .         .          0          68
  1.00000*       .          .         .          0          67
  1.00000*       .          .         .          0          66
  1.00000*       .          .         .          0          65
  1.00000*       .          .         .          0          64
  1.00000*       .          .         .          0          63
  1.00000*       .          .         .          0          62
  1.00000*       .          .         .          0          61
  1.00000*       .          .         .          0          60
  2.00000        .          .         .          1          59
  2.00000      0.9667     0.0333    0.0232       2          58
  2.00000*       .          .         .          2          57
  2.00000*       .          .         .          2          56
  2.00000*       .          .         .          2          55
  2.00000*       .          .         .          2          54
  2.00000*       .          .         .          2          53
  2.00000*       .          .         .          2          52
  2.00000*       .          .         .          2          51
  2.00000*       .          .         .          2          50
  2.00000*       .          .         .          2          49
  2.00000*       .          .         .          2          48
  2.00000*       .          .         .          2          47
  2.00000*       .          .         .          2          46
  2.00000*       .          .         .          2          45
  2.00000*       .          .         .          2          44
  2.00000*       .          .         .          2          43
  2.00000*       .          .         .          2          42
  2.00000*       .          .         .          2          41
  2.00000*       .          .         .          2          40
  3.00000      0.9425     0.0575    0.0329       3          39
  3.00000*       .          .         .          3          38
  3.00000*       .          .         .          3          37
  3.00000*       .          .         .          3          36
```

3.00000*	.	.	.	3	35
3.00000*	.	.	.	3	34
3.00000*	.	.	.	3	33
3.00000*	.	.	.	3	32
3.00000*	.	.	.	3	31
3.00000*	.	.	.	3	30
3.00000*	.	.	.	3	29
3.00000*	.	.	.	3	28
3.00000*	.	.	.	3	27
3.00000*	.	.	.	3	26
3.00000*	.	.	.	3	25
3.00000*	.	.	.	3	24
3.00000*	.	.	.	3	23
3.00000*	.	.	.	3	22
3.00000*	.	.	.	3	21
3.00000*	.	.	.	3	20
4.00000	.	.	.	4	19
4.00000	.	.	.	5	18
4.00000	0.8011	0.1989	0.0803	6	17
4.00000*	.	.	.	6	16
4.00000*	.	.	.	6	15
4.00000*	.	.	.	6	14
4.00000*	.	.	.	6	13
4.00000*	.	.	.	6	12
4.00000*	.	.	.	6	11
4.00000*	.	.	.	6	10
4.00000*	.	.	.	6	9
4.00000*	.	.	.	6	8
4.00000*	.	.	.	6	7
4.00000*	.	.	.	6	6
4.00000*	.	.	.	6	5
4.00000*	.	.	.	6	4
4.00000*	.	.	.	6	3
4.00000*	.	.	.	6	2
4.00000*	.	.	.	6	1
4.00000*	.	.	.	6	0

NOTE: The marked survival times are censored observations.

Summary Statistics for Time Variable time

Quartile Estimates

	Point	95% Confidence Interval	
Percent	Estimate	[Lower	Upper)
75	.	.	.
50	.	.	.
25	.	4.00000	.

Mean	Standard Error
3.90917	0.05654

At the end of each life table, SAS provides some information about time. For instance, it tells us the average time the persons in that table were followed. After the tables, SAS summarizes the tables by telling us about how many persons there were in each table and how many of those persons had the event ("Failed") and how many withdrew ("Censored"). That is followed by the results of testing the null hypothesis that there are equal risks in the two groups in the population.

```
            Summary of the Number of Censored and Uncensored Values


                                                         Percent
   Stratum   GROUP       Total  Failed   Censored       Censored
         1   exposed        80      25         55          68.75
         2   unexpose       80       6         74          92.50
         -----------------------------------------------------------
      Total                160      31        129          80.63

   Testing Homogeneity of Survival Curves for time over Strata

                            Rank Statistics

                 GROUP      Log-Rank     Wilcoxon
                 exposed      9.5000       660.00
                 unexpose    -9.5000      -660.00

        Covariance Matrix for the Log-Rank Statistics

                 GROUP        exposed       unexpose
                 exposed      6.26925       -6.26925
                 unexpose    -6.26925        6.26925

        Covariance Matrix for the Wilcoxon Statistics

                 GROUP        exposed       unexpose
                 exposed      40819.0       -40819.0
                 unexpose    -40819.0        40819.0

             Test of Equality over Strata

                                              Pr >
            Test      Chi-Square    DF      Chi-Square
            Log-Rank     14.3957     1         0.0001
            Wilcoxon     10.6715     1         0.0011
            -2Log(LR)    12.5128     1         0.0004
```

SAS provides the results of three hypothesis tests.[44] Each of these tests is a normal approximation. The one labeled "Log-Rank" is the Mantel-Haenszel test we performed in

---

[44]These are the same three tests we saw testing the omnibus null hypothesis in the LOGISTIC and PHREG procedures, even though the estimates in life table analysis use the least squares method of estimation.

Example 12-17 (compare the Chi-square values). It has a *P*-value of 0.0001. Since this is less than 0.05, we can reject the null hypothesis and conclude that the risks of liver damage are different between the two groups in the population.

_____

This concludes our discussion of the most commonly used statistical methods in health research.

APPENDIX A
Flowcharts

Chapters 4 through 12 are structured to reflect the thinking process of statisticians when choosing a statistical method to analyze a particular set of data. At the beginning of each of those chapters, the methods discussed in that chapter appear in a flowchart that summarizes statisticians' thinking process. In this appendix, we have brought those flowcharts together so that they are easier to use. As explained in the introduction to Part Two, you should start by using the master flowchart (designated as Flowchart 1 in the text) that appears below. Following the steps in this flowchart will lead to the chapter of the text that discusses the types of statistical methods that might be used to analyze a particular set of data. The flowcharts following the master flowchart in this appendix are labeled according to the chapter in which they are discussed. Examining these flowcharts will reveal the most commonly used statistical methods to analyze your data.

In each of the subsequent flowcharts, the estimate that is most often used to describe the dependent variable is in color, the common name of the statistical test is enclosed in a box, the standard distribution (or approach) that is used to test hypotheses and/or calculate confidence intervals is in color and underlined.

MASTER FLOWCHART

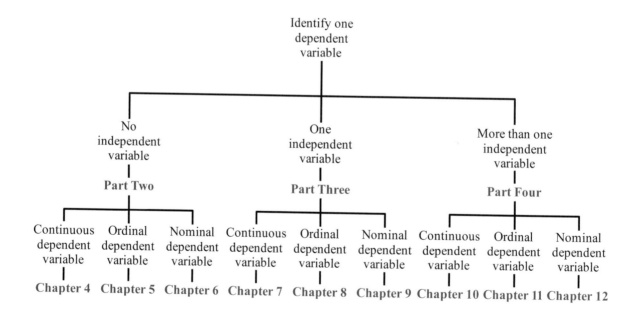

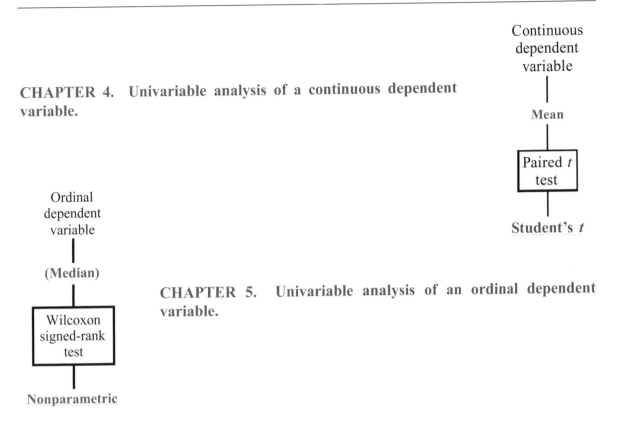

CHAPTER 4. Univariable analysis of a continuous dependent variable.

CHAPTER 5. Univariable analysis of an ordinal dependent variable.

CHAPTER 6. Univariable analysis of a nominal dependent variable.

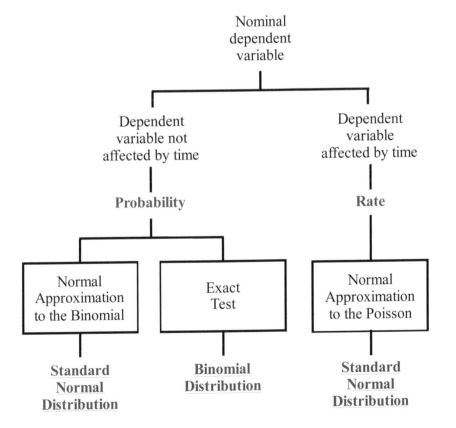

CHAPTER 7. Bivariable analysis of a continuous dependent variable.

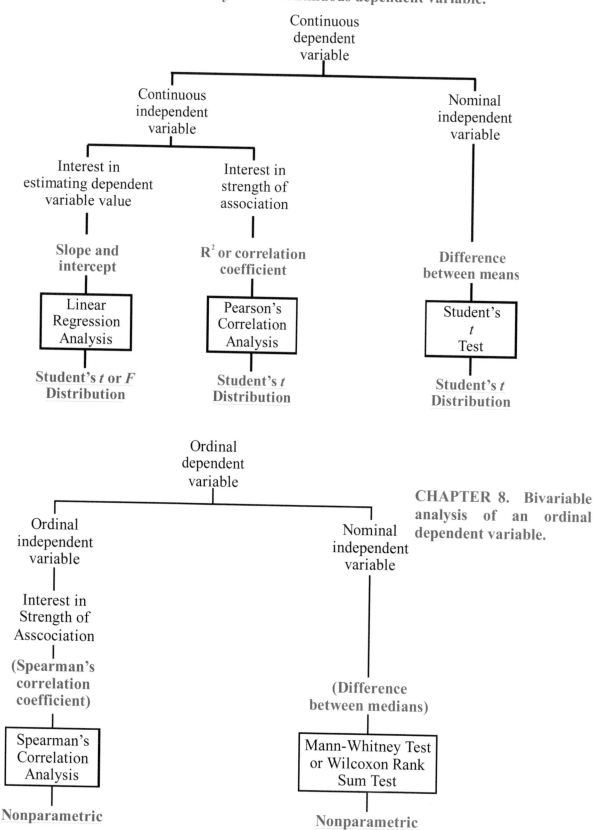

CHAPTER 9. Bivariable analysis of a nominal dependent variable.

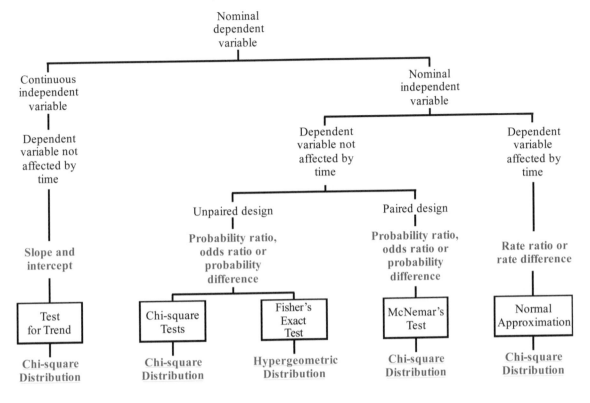

CHAPTER 10. Multivariable analysis of a continuous dependent variable.

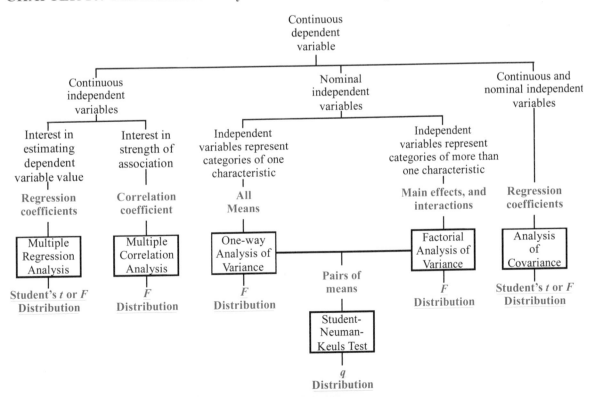

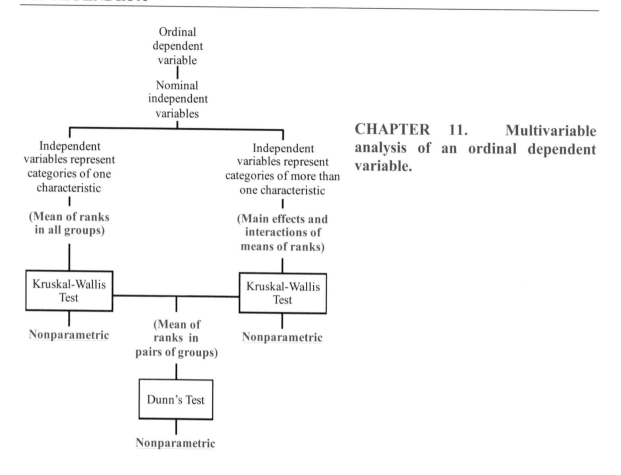

CHAPTER 11. Multivariable analysis of an ordinal dependent variable.

CHAPTER 12. Multivariable analysis of a nominal dependent variable.

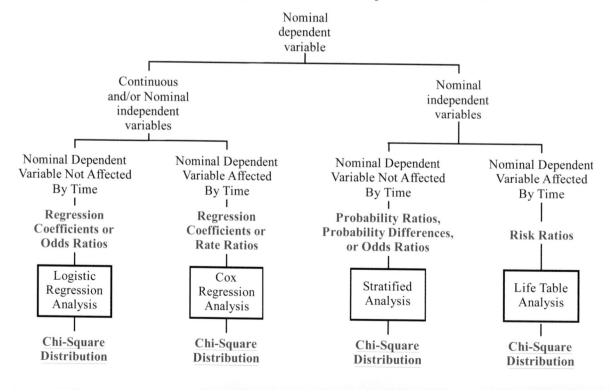

APPENDIX B

Statistical Tables

Table B.1 Area in one tail of the standard normal distribution*

z	0	1	2	3	4	5	6	7	8	9
0.0	0.5000	0.4960	0.4920	0.4880	0.4840	0.4801	0.4761	0.4721	0.4681	0.4641
0.1	0.4602	0.4562	0.4522	0.4483	0.4443	0.4404	0.4364	0.4325	0.4286	0.4247
0.2	0.4207	0.4168	0.4129	0.4090	0.4052	0.4013	0.3974	0.3936	0.3897	0.3859
0.3	0.3821	0.3783	0.3745	0.3707	0.3669	0.3632	0.3594	0.3557	0.3520	0.3483
0.4	0.3446	0.3409	0.3372	0.3336	0.3300	0.3264	0.3228	0.3192	0.3156	0.3121
0.5	0.3085	0.3050	0.3015	0.2981	0.2946	0.2912	0.2877	0.2843	0.2810	0.2776
0.6	0.2743	0.2709	0.2676	0.2643	0.2611	0.2578	0.2546	0.2514	0.2483	0.2451
0.7	0.2420	0.2389	0.2358	0.2327	0.2297	0.2266	0.2236	0.2207	0.2177	0.2148
0.8	0.2119	0.2090	0.2061	0.2033	0.2005	0.1977	0.1949	0.1922	0.1894	0.1867
0.9	0.1841	0.1814	0.1788	0.1762	0.1736	0.1711	0.1685	0.1660	0.1635	0.1611
1.0	0.1587	0.1562	0.1539	0.1515	0.1492	0.1469	0.1446	0.1423	0.1401	0.1379
1.1	0.1357	0.1335	0.1314	0.1292	0.1271	0.1251	0.1230	0.1210	0.1190	0.1170
1.2	0.1151	0.1131	0.1112	0.1093	0.1075	0.1056	0.1038	0.1020	0.1003	0.0985
1.3	0.0968	0.0951	0.0934	0.0918	0.0901	0.0885	0.0869	0.0853	0.0838	0.0823
1.4	0.0808	0.0793	0.0778	0.0764	0.0749	0.0735	0.0721	0.0708	0.0694	0.0681
1.5	0.0668	0.0655	0.0643	0.0630	0.0618	0.0606	0.0594	0.0582	0.0571	0.0559
1.6	0.0548	0.0537	0.0526	0.0516	0.0505	0.0495	0.0485	0.0475	0.0465	0.0455
1.7	0.0446	0.0436	0.0427	0.0418	0.0409	0.0401	0.0392	0.0384	0.0375	0.0367
1.8	0.0359	0.0351	0.0344	0.0336	0.0329	0.0322	0.0314	0.0307	0.0301	0.0294
1.9	0.0287	0.0281	0.0274	0.0268	0.0262	0.0256	0.0250	0.0244	0.0239	0.0233
2.0	0.0228	0.0222	0.0217	0.0212	0.0207	0.0202	0.0197	0.0192	0.0188	0.0183
2.1	0.0179	0.0174	0.0170	0.0166	0.0162	0.0158	0.0154	0.0150	0.0146	0.0143
2.2	0.0139	0.0136	0.0132	0.0129	0.0125	0.0122	0.0119	0.0116	0.0113	0.0110
2.3	0.0107	0.0104	0.0102	0.0099	0.0096	0.0094	0.0091	0.0089	0.0087	0.0084
2.4	0.0082	0.0080	0.0078	0.0075	0.0073	0.0071	0.0069	0.0068	0.0066	0.0064
2.5	0.0062	0.0060	0.0059	0.0057	0.0055	0.0054	0.0052	0.0051	0.0049	0.0048
2.6	0.0047	0.0045	0.0044	0.0043	0.0041	0.0040	0.0039	0.0038	0.0037	0.0036
2.7	0.0035	0.0034	0.0033	0.0032	0.0031	0.0030	0.0029	0.0028	0.0027	0.0026
2.8	0.0026	0.0025	0.0024	0.0023	0.0023	0.0022	0.0021	0.0021	0.0020	0.0019
2.9	0.0019	0.0018	0.0018	0.0017	0.0016	0.0016	0.0015	0.0015	0.0014	0.0014
3.0	0.0013	0.0013	0.0013	0.0012	0.0012	0.0011	0.0011	0.0011	0.0010	0.0010
3.1	0.0010	0.0009	0.0009	0.0009	0.0008	0.0008	0.0008	0.0008	0.0007	0.0007
3.2	0.0007	0.0007	0.0006	0.0006	0.0006	0.0006	0.0006	0.0005	0.0005	0.0005
3.3	0.0005	0.0005	0.0005	0.0004	0.0004	0.0004	0.0004	0.0004	0.0004	0.0003
3.4	0.0003	0.0003	0.0003	0.0003	0.0003	0.0003	0.0003	0.0003	0.0003	0.0002
3.5	0.0002	0.0002	0.0002	0.0002	0.0002	0.0002	0.0002	0.0002	0.0002	0.0002
3.6	0.0002	0.0002	0.0001	0.0001	0.0001	0.0001	0.0001	0.0001	0.0001	0.0001
3.7	0.0001	0.0001	0.0001	0.0001	0.0001	0.0001	0.0001	0.0001	0.0001	0.0001
3.8	0.0001	0.0001	0.0001	0.0001	0.0001	0.0001	0.0001	0.0001	0.0001	0.0001

*To determine the area in one tail of the standard normal distribution, calculate a standard normal deviate (z) to two decimal places. Find the first two digits of that deviate (units and tenths) in the left-hand column. Find the third digit (hundredths) in the top row. The corresponding area is at the intersection of that column and that row.

Table B.2 Critical values of Student's *t* distribution*

$\alpha(2)$	0.50	0.20	0.10	0.05	0.02	0.01	0.005	0.002	0.001
$\alpha(1)$	0.25	0.10	0.05	0.025	0.01	0.005	0.0025	0.001	0.0005
df									
1	1.000	3.078	6.314	12.71	31.82	63.66	127.3	318.3	636.6
2	0.816	1.886	2.920	4.303	6.965	9.925	14.09	22.33	31.60
3	0.765	1.638	2.353	3.182	4.541	5.841	7.453	10.22	12.92
4	0.741	1.533	2.132	2.776	3.747	4.604	5.598	7.173	8.610
5	0.727	1.476	2.015	2.571	3.365	4.032	4.773	5.893	6.869
6	0.718	1.440	1.943	2.447	3.143	3.707	4.317	5.208	5.959
7	0.711	1.415	1.895	2.365	2.998	3.499	4.029	4.785	5.408
8	0.706	1.397	1.860	2.306	2.896	3.355	3.833	4.501	5.041
9	0.703	1.383	1.833	2.262	2.821	3.250	3.690	4.297	4.781
10	0.700	1.372	1.812	2.228	2.764	3.169	3.581	4.144	4.587
11	0.697	1.363	1.796	2.201	2.718	3.106	3.497	4.025	4.437
12	0.695	1.356	1.782	2.179	2.681	3.055	3.428	3.930	4.318
13	0.694	1.350	1.771	2.160	2.650	3.012	3.372	3.852	4.221
14	0.692	1.345	1.761	2.145	2.624	2.977	3.326	3.787	4.140
15	0.691	1.341	1.753	2.131	2.602	2.947	3.286	3.733	4.073
16	0.690	1.337	1.746	2.120	2.583	2.921	3.252	3.686	4.015
17	0.689	1.333	1.740	2.110	2.567	2.898	3.222	3.646	3.965
18	0.688	1.330	1.734	2.101	2.552	2.878	3.197	3.610	3.922
19	0.688	1.328	1.729	2.093	2.539	2.861	3.174	3.579	3.883
20	0.687	1.325	1.725	2.086	2.528	2.845	3.153	3.552	3.850
22	0.686	1.321	1.717	2.074	2.508	2.819	3.119	3.505	3.792
24	0.685	1.318	1.711	2.064	2.492	2.797	3.091	3.467	3.745
26	0.684	1.315	1.706	2.056	2.479	2.779	3.067	3.435	3.707
28	0.683	1.313	1.701	2.048	2.467	2.763	3.047	3.408	3.674
30	0.683	1.310	1.697	2.042	2.457	2.750	3.030	3.385	3.646
32	0.682	1.309	1.694	2.037	2.449	2.738	3.015	3.365	3.622
34	0.682	1.307	1.691	2.032	2.441	2.728	3.002	3.348	3.601
36	0.681	1.306	1.688	2.028	2.434	2.719	2.990	3.333	3.582
38	0.681	1.304	1.686	2.024	2.429	2.712	2.980	3.319	3.566
40	0.681	1.303	1.684	2.021	2.423	2.704	2.971	3.307	3.551
45	0.680	1.301	1.679	2.014	2.412	2.690	2.952	3.281	3.520
50	0.679	1.299	1.676	2.009	2.403	2.678	2.937	3.261	3.496
55	0.679	1.297	1.674	2.004	2.396	2.668	2.925	3.245	3.477
60	0.679	1.296	1.671	2.000	2.390	2.660	2.915	3.232	3.460
65	0.678	1.295	1.669	1.997	2.385	2.654	2.906	3.221	3.447
70	0.678	1.294	1.667	1.994	2.381	2.648	2.899	3.211	3.435
75	0.678	1.293	1.665	1.992	2.377	2.643	2.893	3.203	3.425
80	0.678	1.292	1.664	1.990	2.374	2.639	2.887	3.195	3.416
85	0.677	1.291	1.663	1.988	2.371	2.635	2.882	3.189	3.409
90	0.677	1.291	1.662	1.987	2.368	2.632	2.878	3.183	3.402
100	0.677	1.290	1.660	1.984	2.364	2.626	2.871	3.174	3.390
150	0.676	1.287	1.655	1.976	2.351	2.609	2.849	3.145	3.357
200	0.676	1.286	1.653	1.972	2.345	2.601	2.839	3.131	3.340
500	0.675	1.283	1.648	1.965	2.334	2.586	2.820	3.107	3.310
∞	0.674	1.282	1.645	1.960	2.326	2.576	2.807	3.090	3.290

*To locate Student's *t*-value, find the degrees of freedom in the leftmost column and the appropriate α at the top of the table ($\alpha(2)$ indicates a two-tailed value and $\alpha(1)$ indicates a one-tailed value). The number in the body of the table where this row and column intersect is Student's *t*-value from a distribution with that number of degrees of freedom and that corresponds to an area equal to α.

Table B.3 Critical values of Wilcoxon's T statistic*

$\alpha(2)$ $\alpha(1)$	0.50 0.25	0.20 0.10	0.10 0.05	0.05 0.025	0.02 0.01	0.01 0.005	0.005 0.0025	0.001 0.0005
n								
4	2	0						
5	4	2	0					
6	6	3	2	0				
7	9	5	3	2	0			
8	12	8	5	3	1	0		
9	16	10	8	5	3	1	0	
10	20	14	10	8	5	3	1	
11	24	17	13	10	7	5	3	0
12	29	21	17	13	9	7	5	1
13	35	26	21	17	12	9	7	2
14	40	31	25	21	15	12	9	4
15	47	36	30	25	19	15	12	6
16	54	42	35	29	23	19	15	8
17	61	48	41	34	27	23	19	11
18	69	55	47	40	32	27	23	14
19	77	62	53	46	37	32	27	18
20	86	69	60	52	43	37	32	21
21	95	77	67	58	49	42	37	25
22	104	86	75	65	55	48	42	30
23	114	94	83	73	62	54	48	35
24	125	104	91	81	69	61	54	40
25	136	113	100	89	76	68	60	45
26	148	124	110	98	84	75	67	51
27	160	134	119	107	92	83	74	57
28	172	145	130	116	101	91	82	64
29	185	157	140	126	110	100	90	71
30	198	169	151	137	120	109	98	78
32	226	194	175	159	140	128	116	94
34	257	221	200	182	162	148	136	111
36	289	250	227	208	185	171	157	130
38	323	281	256	235	211	194	180	150
40	358	313	286	264	238	220	204	172
42	396	348	319	294	266	247	230	195
44	436	384	353	327	296	276	258	220
46	477	422	389	361	328	307	287	246
48	521	462	426	396	362	339	318	274
50	566	503	466	434	397	373	350	304
55	688	615	573	536	493	465	438	385
60	822	739	690	648	600	567	537	476
65	968	875	820	772	718	681	647	577
70	1126	1022	960	907	846	805	767	689
75	1296	1181	1112	1053	986	940	898	811
80	1478	1351	1276	1211	1136	1086	1039	943
85	1672	1533	1451	1380	1298	1242	1191	1086
90	1878	1727	1638	1560	1471	1410	1355	1240
95	2097	1933	1836	1752	1655	1589	1529	1404
100	2327	2151	2045	1955	1850	1779	1714	1578

*To locate Wilcoxon's T value, find the sample's size in the leftmost column and the appropriate α at the top of the table ($\alpha(2)$ indicates a two-tailed value and $\alpha(1)$ indicates a one-tailed value). A calculated T value is statistically significant (i.e., the null hypothesis can be rejected) if it is equal to or less than the value in the table.

Table B.4 Critical values of the *F* distribution*

				Numerator df = 1					
α(↓)	0.25	0.10	0.05	0.025	0.01	0.005	0.0025	0.001	0.0005
Denom df									
1	5.83	39.9	161.	648.	4050.	16200.	64800.	$4 \cdot 10^5$	$2 \cdot 10^6$
2	2.57	8.53	18.5	38.5	98.5	199.	399.	999.0	2000.
3	2.02	5.54	10.1	17.4	34.1	55.6	89.6	167.	267.
4	1.81	4.54	7.71	12.2	21.2	31.3	45.7	74.1	106.
5	1.69	4.06	6.61	10.0	16.3	22.8	31.4	47.2	63.6
6	1.62	3.78	5.99	8.81	13.7	18.6	24.8	35.5	46.1
7	1.57	3.59	5.59	8.07	12.2	16.2	21.1	29.2	37.0
8	1.54	3.46	5.32	7.57	11.3	14.7	18.8	25.4	31.6
9	1.51	3.36	5.12	7.21	10.6	13.6	17.2	22.9	28.0
10	1.49	3.29	4.96	6.94	10.0	12.8	16.0	21.0	25.5
11	1.47	3.23	4.84	6.72	9.65	12.2	15.2	19.7	23.7
12	1.46	3.18	4.75	6.55	9.33	11.8	14.5	18.6	22.2
13	1.45	3.14	4.67	6.41	9.07	11.4	13.9	17.8	21.1
14	1.44	3.10	4.60	6.30	8.86	11.1	13.5	17.1	20.2
15	1.43	3.07	4.54	6.20	8.68	10.8	13.1	16.6	19.5
16	1.42	3.05	4.49	6.12	8.53	10.6	12.8	16.1	18.9
17	1.42	3.03	4.45	6.04	8.40	10.4	12.6	15.7	18.4
18	1.41	3.01	4.41	5.98	8.29	10.2	12.3	15.4	17.9
19	1.41	2.99	4.38	5.92	8.18	10.1	12.1	15.1	17.5
20	1.40	2.97	4.35	5.87	8.10	9.94	11.9	14.8	17.2
21	1.40	2.96	4.32	5.83	8.02	9.83	11.8	14.6	16.9
22	1.40	2.95	4.30	5.79	7.95	9.73	11.6	14.4	16.6
23	1.39	2.94	4.28	5.75	7.88	9.63	11.5	14.2	16.4
24	1.39	2.93	4.26	5.72	7.82	9.55	11.4	14.0	16.2
25	1.39	2.92	4.24	5.69	7.77	9.48	11.3	13.9	16.0
26	1.38	2.91	4.23	5.66	7.72	9.41	11.2	13.7	15.8
27	1.38	2.90	4.21	5.63	7.68	9.34	11.1	13.6	15.6
28	1.38	2.89	4.20	5.61	7.64	9.28	11.0	13.5	15.5
29	1.38	2.89	4.18	5.59	7.60	9.23	11.0	13.4	15.3
30	1.38	2.88	4.17	5.57	7.56	9.18	10.9	13.3	15.2
35	1.37	2.85	4.12	5.48	7.42	8.98	10.6	12.9	14.7
40	1.36	2.84	4.08	5.42	7.31	8.83	10.4	12.6	14.4
45	1.36	2.82	4.06	5.38	7.23	8.71	10.3	12.4	14.1
50	1.35	2.81	4.03	5.34	7.17	8.63	10.1	12.2	13.9
60	1.35	2.79	4.00	5.29	7.08	8.49	9.96	12.0	13.5
70	1.35	2.78	3.98	5.25	7.01	8.40	9.84	11.8	13.3
80	1.34	2.77	3.96	5.22	6.96	8.33	9.75	11.7	13.2
90	1.34	2.76	3.95	5.20	6.93	8.28	9.68	11.6	13.0
100	1.34	2.76	3.94	5.18	6.90	8.24	9.62	11.5	12.9
200	1.33	2.73	3.89	5.10	6.76	8.06	9.38	11.2	12.5
500	1.33	2.72	3.86	5.05	6.69	7.95	9.23	11.0	12.3
∞	1.32	2.71	3.84	5.02	6.64	7.88	9.14	10.8	12.1

*To locate an *F* value, first find the table that is headed by the degrees of freedom in the numerator of your *F* ratio. Then, find the degrees of freedom in the denominator of your *F* ratio in the leftmost column. Finally, find the appropriate α at the top of the table. The number in the body of the table where this row and column intersect is the *F* statistic from a distribution with those numerator and denominator degrees of freedom and that corresponds to an area of α in one tail of the *F* distribution.

Table B.4 *Continued*

	Numerator df = 2								
α(⌐)	0.25	0.10	0.05	0.025	0.01	0.005	0.0025	0.001	0.0005
Denom df									
1	7.50	49.5	200.	800.	5000.	20000.	80000.	$5 \cdot 10^5$	$2 \cdot 10^6$
2	3.00	9.00	19.0	39.0	99.0	199.	399.	999.	2000.
3	2.28	5.46	9.55	16.0	30.8	49.8	79.0	149.	237.
4	2.00	4.32	6.94	10.6	18.0	26.3	38.0	61.2	87.4
5	1.85	3.78	5.79	8.43	13.3	18.3	25.0	37.1	49.8
6	1.76	3.46	5.14	7.26	10.9	14.5	19.1	27.0	34.8
7	1.70	3.26	4.74	6.54	9.55	12.4	15.9	21.7	27.2
8	1.66	3.11	4.46	6.06	8.65	11.0	13.9	18.5	22.7
9	1.62	3.01	4.26	5.71	8.02	10.1	12.5	16.4	19.9
10	1.60	2.92	4.10	5.46	7.56	9.43	11.6	14.9	17.9
11	1.58	2.86	3.98	5.26	7.21	8.91	10.8	13.8	16.4
12	1.56	2.81	3.89	5.10	6.93	8.51	10.3	13.0	15.3
13	1.55	2.76	3.81	4.97	6.70	8.19	9.84	12.3	14.4
14	1.53	2.73	3.74	4.86	6.51	7.92	9.47	11.8	13.7
15	1.52	2.70	3.68	4.77	6.36	7.70	9.17	11.3	13.2
16	1.51	2.67	3.63	4.69	6.23	7.51	8.92	11.0	12.7
17	1.51	2.64	3.59	4.62	6.11	7.35	8.70	10.7	12.3
18	1.50	2.62	3.55	4.56	6.01	7.21	8.51	10.4	11.9
19	1.49	2.61	3.52	4.51	5.93	7.09	8,35	10.2	11.6
20	1.49	2.59	3.49	4.46	5.85	6.99	8.21	9.95	11.4
21	1.48	2.57	3.47	4.42	5.78	6.89	8.08	9.77	11.2
22	1.48	2.56	3.44	4.38	5.72	6.81	7.96	9.61	11.0
23	1.47	2.55	3.42	4.35	5.66	6.73	7.86	9.47	10.8
24	1.47	2.54	3.40	4.32	5.61	6.66	7.77	9.34	10.6
25	1.47	2.53	3.39	4.29	5.57	6.60	7.69	9.22	10.5
26	1.46	2.52	3.37	4.27	5.53	6.54	7.61	9.12	10.3
27	1.46	2.51	3.35	4.24	5.49	6.49	7.54	9.02	10.2
28	1.46	2.50	3.34	4.22	5.45	6.44	7.48	8.93	10.1
29	1.45	2.50	3.33	4.20	5.42	6.40	7.42	8.85	9.99
30	1.45	2.49	3.32	4.18	5.39	6.35	7.36	8.77	9.90
35	1.44	2.46	3.27	4.11	5.27	6.19	7.14	8.47	9.52
40	1.44	2.44	3.23	4.05	5.18	6.07	6.99	8.25	9.25
45	1.43	2.42	3.20	4.01	5.11	5.97	6.86	8.09	9.04
50	1.43	2.41	3.18	3.97	5.06	5.90	6.77	7.96	8.88
60	1.42	2.39	3.15	3.93	4.98	5.79	6.63	7.77	8.65
70	1.41	2.38	3.13	3.89	4.92	5.72	6.53	7.64	8.49
80	1.41	2.37	3.11	3.86	4.88	5.67	6.46	7.54	8.37
90	1.41	2.36	3.10	3.84	4.85	5.62	6.41	7.47	8.28
100	1.41	2.36	3.09	3.83	4.82	5.59	6.37	7.41	8.21
200	1.40	2.33	3.04	3.76	4.71	5.44	6.17	7.15	7.90
500	1.39	2.31	3.01	3.72	4.65	5.35	6.06	7.00	7.72
∞	1.39	2.30	3.00	3.69	4.61	5.30	5.99	6.91	7.60

Table B.4 *Continued*

	Numerator df = 3								
$\alpha(\ |\ )$	0.25	0.10	0.05	0.025	0.01	0.005	0.0025	0.001	0.0005
Denom df									
1	8.20	53.6	216.	864.	5400.	21600.	86500.	$5 \cdot 10^5$	$2 \cdot 10^6$
2	3.15	9.16	19.2	39.2	99.2	199.	399.	999.	2000.
3	2.36	5.39	9.28	15.4	29.5	47.5	76.1	141.	225.
4	2.05	4.19	6.59	9.98	16.7	24.3	35.0	56.2	80.1
5	1.88	3.62	5.41	7.76	12.1	16.5	22.4	33.2	44.4
6	1.78	3.29	4.76	6.60	9.78	12.9	16.9	23.7	30.5
7	1.72	3.07	4.35	5.89	8.45	10.9	13.8	18.8	23.5
8	1.67	2.92	4.07	5.42	7.59	9.60	12.0	15.8	19.4
9	1.63	2.81	3.86	5.08	6.99	8.72	10.7	13.9	16.8
10	1.60	2.73	3.71	4.83	6.55	8.08	9.83	12.6	15.0
11	1.58	2.66	3.59	4.63	6.22	7.60	9.17	11.6	13.7
12	1.56	2.61	3.49	4.47	5.95	7.23	8.65	10.8	12.7
13	1.55	2.56	3.41	4.35	5.74	6.93	8.24	10.2	11.9
14	1.53	2.52	3.34	4.24	5.56	6.68	7.91	9.73	11.3
15	1.52	2.49	3.29	4.15	5.42	6.48	7.63	9.34	10.8
16	1.51	2.46	3.24	4.08	5.29	6.30	7.40	9.01	10.3
17	1.50	2.44	3.20	4.01	5.19	6.16	7.21	8.73	9.99
18	1.49	2.42	3.16	3.95	5.09	6.03	7.04	8.49	9.69
19	1.49	2.40	3.13	3.90	5.01	5.92	6.89	8.28	9.42
20	1.48	2.38	3.10	3.86	4.94	5.82	6.76	8.10	9.20
21	1.48	2.36	3.07	3.82	4.87	5.73	6.64	7.94	8.99
22	1.47	2.35	3.05	3.78	4.82	5.65	6.54	7.80	8.82
23	1.47	2.34	3.03	3.75	4.76	5.58	6.45	7.67	8.66
24	1.46	2.33	3.01	3.72	4.72	5.52	6.36	7.55	8.51
25	1.46	2.32	2.99	3.69	4.68	5.46	6.29	7.45	8.39
26	1.45	2.31	2.98	3.67	4.64	5.41	6.22	7.36	8.27
27	1.45	2.30	2.96	3.65	4.60	5.36	6.16	7.27	8.16
28	1.45	2.29	2.95	3.63	4.57	5.32	6.10	7.19	8.07
29	1.45	2.28	2.93	3.61	4.54	5.28	6.05	7.12	7.98
30	1.44	2.28	2.92	3.59	4.51	5.24	6.00	7.05	7.89
35	1.43	2.25	2.87	3.52	4.40	5.09	5.80	6.79	7.56
40	1.42	2.23	2.84	3.46	4.31	4.98	5.66	6.59	7.33
45	1.42	2.21	2.81	3.42	4.25	4.89	5.55	6.45	7.15
50	1.41	2.20	2.79	3.39	4.20	4.83	5.47	6.34	7.01
60	1.41	2.18	2.76	3.34	4.13	4.73	5.34	6.17	6.81
70	1.40	2.16	2.74	3.31	4.07	4.66	5.26	6.06	6.67
80	1.40	2.15	2.72	3.28	4.04	4.61	5.19	5.97	6.57
90	1.39	2.15	2.71	3.26	4.01	4.57	5.14	5.91	6.49
100	1.39	2.14	2.70	3.25	3.98	4.54	5.11	5.86	6.43
200	1.38	2.11	2.65	3.18	3.88	4.41	4.94	5.63	6.16
500	1.37	2.09	2.62	3.14	3.82	4.33	4.84	5.51	6.01
∞	1.37	2.08	2.62	3.12	3.78	4.28	4.77	5.42	5.91

Table B.4 *Continued*

					Numerator df = 4				
$\alpha(1)$	0.25	0.10	0.05	0.025	0.01	0.005	0.0025	0.001	0.0005
Denom df									
1	8.58	55.8	225.	900.	5620.	22500.	90000.	$6 \cdot 10^5$	$2 \cdot 10^6$
2	3.23	9.24	19.2	39.2	99.2	199.	399.	999.	2000.
3	2.39	5.34	9.12	15.1	28.7	46.2	73.9	137.	218.
4	2.06	4.11	6.39	9.60	16.0	23.2	33.3	53.4	76.1
5	1.89	3.52	5.19	7.39	11.4	15.6	21.0	31.1	41.5
6	1.79	3.18	4.53	6.23	9.15	12.0	15.7	21.9	28.1
7	1.72	2.96	4.12	5.52	7.85	10.1	12.7	17.2	21.4
8	1.66	2.81	3.84	5.05	7.01	8.81	10.9	14.4	17.6
9	1.63	2.69	3.63	4.72	6.42	7.96	9.74	12.6	15.1
10	1.59	2.61	3.48	4.47	5.99	7.34	8.89	11.3	13.4
11	1.57	2.54	3.36	4.28	5.67	6.88	8.25	10.3	12.2
12	1.55	2.48	3.26	4.12	5.41	6.52	7.76	9.63	11.2
13	1.53	2.43	3.18	4.00	5.21	6.23	7.37	9.07	10.5
14	1.52	2.39	3.11	3.89	5.04	6.00	7.06	8.62	9.95
15	1.51	2.36	3.06	3.80	4.89	5.80	6.80	8.25	9.48
16	1.50	2.33	3.01	3.73	4.77	5.64	6.58	7.94	9.08
17	1.49	2.31	2.96	3.66	4.67	5.50	6.39	7.68	8.75
18	1.48	2.29	2.93	3.61	4.58	5.37	6.23	7.46	8.47
19	1.47	2.27	2.90	3.56	4.50	5.27	6.09	7.27	8.23
20	1.47	2.25	2.87	3.51	4.43	5.17	5.97	7.10	8.02
21	1.46	2.23	2.84	3.48	4.37	5.09	5.86	6.95	7.83
22	1.45	2.22	2.82	3.44	4.31	5.02	5.76	6.81	7.67
23	1.45	2.21	2.80	3.41	4.26	4.95	5.67	6.70	7.52
24	1.44	2.19	2.78	3.38	4.22	4.89	5.60	6.59	7.39
25	1.44	2.18	2.76	3.35	4.18	4.84	5.53	6.49	7.27
26	1.44	2.17	2.74	3.33	4.14	4.79	5.46	6.41	7.16
27	1.43	2.17	2.73	3.31	4.11	4.74	5.40	6.33	7.06
28	1.43	2.16	2.71	3.29	4.07	4.70	5.35	6.25	6.97
29	1.43	2.15	2.70	3.27	4.04	4.66	5.30	6.19	6.89
30	1.42	2.14	2.69	3.25	4.02	4.62	5.25	6.12	6.82
35	1.41	2.11	2.64	3.18	3.91	4.48	5.07	5.88	6.51
40	1.40	2.09	2.61	3.13	3.83	4.37	4.93	5.70	6.30
45	1.40	2.07	2.58	3.09	3.77	4.29	4.83	5.56	6.13
50	1.39	2.06	2.56	3.05	3.72	4.23	4.75	5.46	6.01
60	1.38	2.04	2.53	3.01	3.65	4.14	4.64	5.31	5.82
70	1.38	2.03	2.50	2.97	3.60	4.08	4.56	5.20	5.70
80	1.38	2.02	2.49	2.95	3.56	4.03	4.50	5.12	5.60
90	1.37	2,01	2.47	2.93	3.53	3.99	4.45	5.06	5.53
100	1.37	2.00	2.46	2.92	3.51	3.96	4.42	5.02	5.48
200	1.36	1.97	2.42	2.85	3.41	3.84	4.26	4.81	5.23
500	1.35	1.96	2.39	2.81	3.36	3.76	4.17	4.69	5.09
∞	1.35	1.94	2.37	2.79	3.32	3.72	4.11	4.62	5.00

Table B.4 *Continued*

α(1)	0.25	0.10	0.05	0.025	0.01	0.005	0.0025	0.001	0.0005
					Numerator df = 5				
Denom df									
1	8.82	57.2	230.	922.	5760.	23100.	92200.	$6 \cdot 10^5$	$2 \cdot 10^6$
2	3.28	9.29	19.3	39.3	99.3	199.	399.	999.	2000.
3	2.41	5.31	9.01	14.9	28.2	45.4	72.6	135.	214.
4	2.07	4.05	6.26	9.36	15.5	22.5	32.3	51.7	73.6
5	1.89	3.45	5.05	7.15	11.0	14.9	20.2	29.8	39.7
6	1.79	3.11	4.39	5.99	8.75	11.5	14.9	20.8	26.6
7	1.71	2.88	3.97	5.29	7.46	9.52	12.0	16.2	20.2
8	1.66	2.73	3.69	4.82	6.63	8.30	10.3	13.5	16.4
9	1.62	2.61	3.48	4.48	6.06	7.47	9.12	11.7	14.1
10	1.59	2.52	3.33	4.24	5.64	6.87	8.29	10.5	12.4
11	1.56	2.45	3.20	4.04	5.32	6.42	7.67	9.58	11.2
12	1.54	2.39	3.11	3.89	5.06	6.07	7.20	8.89	10.4
13	1.52	2.35	3.03	3.77	4.86	5.79	6.82	8.35	9.66
14	1.51	2.31	2.96	3.66	4.69	5.56	6.51	7.92	9.11
15	1.49	2.27	2.90	3.58	4.56	5.37	6.26	7.57	8.66
16	1.48	2.24	2.85	3.50	4.44	5.21	6.05	7.27	8.29
17	1.47	2.22	2.81	3.44	4.34	5.07	5.87	7.02	7.98
18	1.46	2.20	2.77	3.38	4.25	4.96	5.72	6.81	7.71
19	1.46	2.18	2.74	3.33	4.17	4.85	5.58	6.62	7.48
20	1.45	2.16	2.71	3.29	4.10	4.76	5.46	6.46	7.27
21	1.44	2.14	2.68	3.25	4.04	4.68	5.36	6.32	7.10
22	1.44	2.13	2.66	3.22	3.99	4.61	5.26	6.19	6.94
23	1.43	2.11	2.64	3.18	3.94	4.54	5.18	6.08	6.80
24	1.43	2.10	2.62	3.15	3.90	4.49	5.11	5.98	6.68
25	1.42	2.09	2.60	3.13	3.85	4.43	5.04	5.89	6.56
26	1.42	2.08	2.59	3.10	3.82	4.38	4.98	5.80	6.46
27	1.42	2.07	2.57	3.08	3.78	4.34	4.92	5.73	7.37
28	1.41	2.06	2.56	3.06	3.75	4.30	4.87	5.66	6.28
29	1.41	2.06	2.55	3.04	3.73	4.26	4.82	5.59	6.21
30	1.41	2.05	2.53	3.03	3.70	4.23	4.78	5.53	6.13
35	1.40	2.02	2.49	2.96	3.59	4.09	4.60	5.30	5.85
40	1.39	2.00	2.45	2.90	3.51	3.99	4.47	5.13	5.64
45	1.38	1.98	2.42	2.86	3.45	3.91	4.37	5.00	5.49
50	1.37	1.97	2.40	2.83	3.41	3.85	4.30	4.90	5.37
60	1.37	1.95	2.37	2.79	3.34	3.76	4.19	4.76	5.20
70	1.36	1.93	2.35	2.75	3.29	3.70	4.11	4.66	5.08
80	1.36	1.92	2.33	2.73	3.26	3.65	4.05	4.58	4.99
90	1.35	1.91	2.32	2.71	3.23	3.62	4.01	4.53	4.92
100	1.35	1.91	2.31	2.70	3.21	3.59	3.97	4.48	4.87
200	1.34	1.88	2.26	2.63	3.11	3.47	3.82	4.29	4.64
500	1.33	1.86	2.23	2.59	3.05	3.40	3.73	4.18	4.51
∞	1.33	1.85	2.22	2.57	3.02	3.35	3.68	4.10	4.42

Table B.4 *Continued*

				Numerator df = 6					
α(l)	0.25	0.10	0.05	0.025	0.01	0.005	0.0025	0.001	0.0005
Denom df									
1	8.98	58.2	234.	937.	5860.	23400.	93700.	$6 \cdot 10^5$	$2 \cdot 10^6$
2	3.31	9.33	19.3	39.3	99.3	199.	399.	999.	2000.
3	2.42	5.28	8.94	14.7	27.9	44.8	71.7	133.	211.9
4	2.08	4.01	6.16	9.20	15.2	22.0	31.5	50.5	71.9
5	1.89	3.40	4.95	6.98	10.7	14.5	19.6	28.8	38.5
6	1.78	3.05	4.28	5.82	8.47	11.1	14.4	20.0	25.6
7	1.71	2.83	3.87	5.12	7.19	9.16	11.5	15.5	19.3
8	1.65	2.67	3.58	4.65	6.37	7.95	9.83	12.9	15.7
9	1.61	2.55	3.37	4.32	5.80	7.13	8.68	11.1	13.3
10	1.58	2.46	3.22	4.07	5.39	6.54	7.87	9.93	11.7
11	1.55	2.39	3.09	3.88	5.07	6.10	7.27	9.05	10.6
12	1.53	2.33	3.00	3.73	4.82	5.76	6.80	8.38	9.74
13	1.51	2.28	2.92	3.60	4.62	5.48	6.44	7.86	9.07
14	1.50	2.24	2.85	3.50	4.46	5.26	6.14	7.44	8.53
15	1.48	2.21	2.79	3.41	4.32	5.07	5.89	7.09	8.10
16	1.47	2.18	2.74	3.34	4.20	4.91	5.68	6.80	7.74
17	1.46	2.15	2.70	3.28	4.10	4.78	5.51	6.56	7.43
18	1.45	2.13	2.66	3.22	4.01	4.66	5.36	6.35	7.18
19	1.44	2.11	2.63	3.17	3.94	4.56	5.23	6.18	6.95
20	1.44	2.09	2.60	3.13	3.87	4.47	5.11	6.02	6.76
21	1.43	2.08	2.57	3.09	3.81	4.39	5.01	5.88	6.59
22	1.42	2.06	2.55	3.05	3.76	4.32	4.92	5.76	6.44
23	1.42	2.05	2.53	3.02	3.71	4.26	4.84	5.65	6.30
24	1.41	2.04	2.51	2.99	3.67	4.20	4.76	5.55	6.18
25	1.41	2.02	2.49	2.97	3.63	4.15	4.70	5.46	6.07
26	1.41	2.01	2.47	2.94	3.59	4.10	4.64	5.38	5.98
27	1.40	2.00	2.46	2.92	3.56	4.06	4.58	5.31	5.89
28	1.40	2.00	2.45	2.90	3.53	4.02	4.53	5.24	5.80
29	1.40	1.99	2.43	2.88	3.50	3.98	4.48	5.18	5.73
30	1.39	1.98	2.42	2.87	3.47	3.95	4.44	5.12	5.66
35	1.38	1.95	2.37	2.80	3.37	3.81	4.27	4.89	5.39
40	1.37	1.93	2.34	2.74	3.29	3.71	4.14	4.73	5.19
45	1.36	1.91	2.31	2.70	3.23	3.64	4.05	4.61	5.04
50	1.36	1.90	2.29	2.67	3.19	3.58	3.98	4.51	4.93
60	1.35	1.87	2.25	2.63	3.12	3.49	3.87	4.37	4.76
70	1.34	1.86	2.23	2.59	3.07	3.43	3.79	4.28	4.64
80	1.34	1.85	2.21	2.57	3.04	3.39	3.74	4.20	4.56
90	1.33	1.84	2.20	2.55	3.01	3.35	3.70	4.15	4.50
100	1.33	1.83	2.19	2.54	2.99	3.33	3.66	4.11	4.45
200	1.32	1.80	2.14	2.47	2.89	3.21	3.52	3.92	4.22
500	1.31	1.79	2.12	2.43	2.84	3.14	3.43	3.81	4.10
∞	1.31	1.77	2.10	2.41	2.80	3.09	3.37	3.74	4.02

Table B.4 *Continued*

				Numerator df = 7					
α(⎮)	0.25	0.10	0.05	0.025	0.01	0.005	0.0025	0.001	0.0005
Denom df									
1	9.10	58.9	237.	948.	5930.	23700.	94900.	$6 \cdot 10^5$	$2 \cdot 10^6$
2	3.34	9.35	19.4	39.4	99.4	199.	399.	999.	2000.
3	2.43	5.27	8.89	14.6	27.7	44.4	71.0	132.	209.
4	2.08	3.98	6.09	9.07	15.0	21.6	31.0	49.7	70.7
5	1.89	3.37	4.88	6.85	10.5	14.2	19.1	28.2	37.6
6	1.78	3.01	4.21	5.70	8.26	10.8	14.0	19.5	24.9
7	1.70	2.78	3.79	4.99	6.99	8.89	11.2	15.0	18.7
8	1.64	2.62	3.50	4.53	6.18	7.69	9.49	12.4	15.1
9	1.60	2.51	3.29	4.20	5.61	6.88	8.36	10.7	12.8
10	1.57	2.41	3.14	3.95	5.20	6.30	7.56	9.52	11.2
11	1.54	2.34	3.01	3.76	4.89	5.86	6.97	8.66	10.1
12	1.52	2.28	2.91	3.61	4.64	5.52	6.51	8.00	9.28
13	1.50	2.23	2.83	3.48	4.44	5.25	6.15	7.49	8.63
14	1.49	2.19	2.76	3.38	4.28	5.03	5.86	7.08	8.11
15	1.47	2.16	2.71	3.29	4.14	4.85	5.62	6.74	7.68
16	1.46	2.13	2.66	3.22	4.03	4.69	5.41	6.46	7.33
17	1.45	2.10	2.61	3.16	3.93	4.56	5.24	6.22	7.04
18	1.44	2.08	2.58	3.10	3.84	4.44	5.09	6.02	6.78
19	1.43	2.06	2.54	3.05	3.77	4.34	4.96	5.85	6.57
20	1.43	2.04	2.51	3.01	3.70	4.26	4.85	5.69	6.38
21	1.42	2.02	2.49	2.97	3.64	4.18	4.75	5.56	6.21
22	1.41	2.01	2.46	2.93	3.59	4.11	4.66	5.44	6.07
23	1.41	1.99	2.44	2.90	3.54	4.05	4.58	5.33	5.94
24	1.40	1.98	2.42	2.87	3.50	3.99	4.51	5.23	5.82
25	1.40	1.97	2.40	2.85	3.46	3.94	4.44	5.15	5.71
26	1.39	1.96	2.39	2.82	3.42	3.89	4.38	5.07	5.62
27	1.39	1.95	2.37	2.80	3.39	3.85	4.33	5.00	5.53
28	1.39	1.94	2.36	2.78	3.36	3.81	4.28	4.93	5.45
29	1.38	1.93	2.35	2.76	3.33	3.77	4.24	4.87	5.38
30	1.38	1.93	2.33	2.75	3.30	3.74	4.19	4.82	5.31
35	1.37	1.90	2.29	2.68	3.20	3.61	4.02	4.59	5.04
40	1.36	1.87	2.25	2.62	3.12	3.51	3.90	4.44	4.85
45	1.35	1.85	2.22	2.58	3.07	3.43	3.81	4.32	4.71
50	1.34	1.84	2.20	2.55	3.02	3.38	3.74	4.22	4.60
60	1.33	1.82	2.17	2.51	2.95	3.29	3.63	4.09	4.44
70	1.33	1.80	2.14	2.47	2.91	3.23	3.56	3.99	4.32
80	1.32	1.79	2.13	2.45	2.87	3.19	3.50	3.92	4.24
90	1.32	1.78	2.11	2.43	2.84	3.15	3.46	3.87	4.18
100	1.32	1.78	2.10	2.42	2.82	3.13	3.43	3.83	4.13
200	1.30	1.75	2.06	2.35	2.73	3.01	3.29	3.65	3.92
500	1.30	1.73	2.03	2.31	2.68	2.94	3.20	3.54	3.80
∞	1.29	1.72	2.01	2.29	2.64	2.90	3.15	3.47	3.72

Table B.4 *Continued*

				Numerator df = 8					
$\alpha(1)$	0.25	0.10	0.05	0.025	0.01	0.005	0.0025	0.001	0.0005
Denom df									
1	9.19	59.4	239.	957.	5980.	23900.	95700.	$6\cdot10^5$	$2\cdot10^6$
2	3.35	9.37	19.4	39.4	99.4	199.	399.	999.	2000.
3	2.44	5.25	8.85	14.5	27.5	44.1	70.5	131.	208.
4	2.08	3.95	6.04	8.98	14.8	21.4	30.6	49.0	69.7
5	1.89	3.34	4.82	6.76	10.3	14.0	18.8	27.6	36.9
6	1.78	2.98	4.15	5.60	8.10	10.6	13.7	19.0	24.3
7	1.70	2.75	3.73	4.90	6.84	8.68	10.9	14.6	18.2
8	1.64	2.59	3.44	4.43	6.03	7.50	9.24	12.0	14.6
9	1.60	2.47	3.23	4.10	5.47	6.69	8.12	10.4	12.4
10	1.56	2.38	3.07	3.85	5.06	6.12	7.33	9.20	10.9
11	1.53	2.30	2.95	3.66	4.74	5.68	6.74	8.35	9.76
12	1.51	2.24	2.85	3.51	4.50	5.35	6.29	7.71	8.94
13	1.49	2.20	2.77	3.39	4.30	5.08	5.93	7.21	8.29
14	1.48	2.15	2.70	3.29	4.14	4.86	5.64	6.80	7.78
15	1.46	2.12	2.64	3.20	4.00	4.67	5.40	6.47	7.37
16	1.45	2.09	2.59	3.12	3.89	4.52	5.20	6.19	7.02
17	1.44	2.06	2.55	3.06	3.79	4.39	5.03	5.96	6.73
18	1.43	2.04	2.51	3.01	3.71	4.28	4.89	5.76	6.48
19	1.42	2.02	2.48	2.96	3.63	4.18	4.76	5.59	6.27
20	1.42	2.00	2.45	2.91	3.56	4.09	4.65	5.44	6.09
21	1.41	1.98	2.42	2.87	3.51	4.01	4.55	5.31	5.92
22	1.40	1.97	2.40	2.84	3.45	3.94	4.46	5.19	5.78
23	1.40	1.95	2.37	2.81	3.41	3.88	4.38	5.09	5.65
24	1.39	1.94	2.36	2.78	3.36	3.83	4.31	4.99	5.54
25	1.39	1.93	2.34	2.75	3.32	3.78	4.25	4.91	5.43
26	1.38	1.92	2.32	2.73	3.29	3.73	4.19	4.83	5.34
27	1.38	1.91	2.31	2.71	3.26	3.69	4.14	4.76	5.25
28	1.38	1.90	2.29	2.69	3.23	3.65	4.09	4.69	5.18
29	1.37	1.89	2.28	2.67	3.20	3.61	4.04	4.64	5.11
30	1.37	1.88	2.27	2.65	3.17	3.58	4.00	4.58	5.04
35	1.36	1.85	2.22	2.58	3.07	3.45	3.83	4.36	4.78
40	1.35	1.83	2.18	2.53	2.99	3.35	3.71	4.21	4.59
45	1.34	1.81	2.15	2.49	2.94	3.28	3.62	4.09	4.45
50	1.33	1.80	2.13	2.46	2.89	3.22	3.55	4.00	4.34
60	1.32	1.77	2.10	2.41	2.82	3.13	3.45	3.86	4.19
70	1.32	1.76	2.07	2.38	2.78	3.08	3.37	3.77	4.08
80	1.31	1.75	2.06	2.35	2.74	3.03	3.32	3.70	4.00
90	1.31	1.74	2.04	2.34	2.72	3.00	3.28	3.65	3.94
100	1.30	1.73	2.03	2.32	2.69	2.97	3.25	3.61	3.89
200	1.29	1.70	1.98	2.26	2.60	2.86	3.11	3.43	3.68
500	1.28	1.68	1.96	2.22	2.55	2.79	3.03	3.33	3.56
∞	1.28	1.67	1.94	2.19	2.51	2.74	2.97	3.27	3.48

Table B.4 *Continued*

					Numerator df = 9				
$\alpha(\,\mid\,)$	0.25	0.10	0.05	0.025	0.01	0.005	0.0025	0.001	0.0005
Denom df									
1	9.26	59.9	241.	963.	6020.	24100.	96400.	$6 \cdot 10^5$	$2 \cdot 10^6$
2	3.37	9.38	19.4	39.4	99.4	199.	399.	999.	2000.
3	2.44	5.24	8.81	14.5	27.3	43.9	70.1	130.	207.
4	2.08	3.94	6.00	8.90	14.7	21.1	30.3	48.5	69.0
5	1.89	3.32	4.77	6.68	10.2	13.8	18.5	27.2	36.3
6	1.77	2.96	4.10	5.52	7.98	10.4	13.4	18.7	23.9
7	1.69	2.72	3.68	4.82	6.72	8.51	10.7	14.3	17.8
8	1.63	2.56	3.39	4.36	5.91	7.34	9.03	11.8	14.3
9	1.59	2.44	3.18	4.03	5.35	6.54	7.92	10.1	12.1
10	1.56	2.35	3.02	3.78	4.94	5.97	7.14	8.96	10.6
11	1.53	2.27	2.90	3.59	4.63	5.54	6.56	8.12	9.48
12	1.51	2.21	2.80	3.44	4.39	5.20	6.11	7.48	8.66
13	1.49	2.16	2.71	3.31	4.19	4.94	5.76	6.98	8.03
14	1.47	2.12	2.65	3.21	4.03	4.72	5.47	6.58	7.52
15	1.46	2.09	2.59	3.12	3.89	4.54	5.23	6.26	7.11
16	1.44	2.06	2.54	3.05	3.78	4.38	5.04	5.98	6.77
17	1.43	2.03	2.49	2.98	3.68	4.25	4.87	5.75	6.49
18	1.42	2.02	2.46	2.93	3.60	4.14	4.72	5.56	6.24
19	1.41	1.98	2.42	2.88	3.52	4.04	4.60	5.39	6.03
20	1.41	1.96	2.39	2.84	3.46	3.96	4.49	5.24	5.85
21	1.40	1.95	2.37	2.80	3.40	3.88	4.39	5.11	5.69
22	1.39	1.93	2.34	2.76	3.35	3.81	4.30	4.99	5.55
23	1.39	1.92	2.32	2.73	3.30	3.75	4.22	4.89	5.43
24	1.38	1.91	2.30	2.70	3.26	3.69	4.15	4.80	5.31
25	1.38	1.89	2.28	2.68	3.22	3.64	4.09	4.71	5.21
26	1.37	1.88	2.27	2.65	3.18	3.60	4.03	4.64	5.12
27	1.37	1.87	2.25	2.63	3.15	3.56	3.98	4.57	5.04
28	1.37	1.87	2.24	2.61	3.12	3.52	3.93	4.50	4.96
29	1.36	1.86	2.22	2.59	3.09	3.48	3.89	4.45	4.89
30	1.36	1.85	2.21	2.57	3.07	3.45	3.85	4.39	4.82
35	1.35	1.82	2.16	2.50	2.96	3.32	3.68	4.18	4.57
40	1.34	1.79	2.12	2.45	2.89	3.22	3.56	4.02	4.38
45	1.33	1.77	2.10	2.41	2.83	3.15	3.47	3.91	4.25
50	1.32	1.76	2.07	2.38	2.78	3.09	3.40	3.82	4.14
60	1.31	1.74	2.04	2.33	2.72	3.01	3.30	3.69	3.98
70	1.31	1.72	2.02	2.30	2.67	2.95	3.23	3.60	3.88
80	1.30	1.71	2.00	2.28	2.64	2.91	3.17	3.53	3.80
90	1.30	1.70	1.99	2.26	2.61	2.87	3.13	3.48	3.74
100	1.29	1.69	1.97	2.24	2.59	2.85	3.10	3.44	3.69
200	1.28	1.66	1.93	2.18	2.50	2.73	2.96	3.26	3.49
500	1.27	1.64	1.90	2.14	2.44	2.66	2.88	3.16	3.37
∞	1.27	1.63	1.88	2.11	2.41	2.62	2.83	3.10	3.30

Table B.4 *Continued*

	Numerator df = 10								
$\alpha(1)$	0.25	0.10	0.05	0.025	0.01	0.005	0.0025	0.001	0.0005
Denom df									
1	9.32	60.2	242.	969.	6060.	24200.	96900.	$6 \cdot 10^5$	$2 \cdot 10^6$
2	3.38	9.39	19.4	39.4	99.4	199.	399.	999.	2000.
3	2.44	5.23	8.79	14.4	27.2	43.7	69.8	129.	206.
4	2.08	3.92	5.96	8.84	14.5	21.0	30.0	48.1	68.3
5	1.89	3.30	4.74	6.62	10.1	13.6	18.3	26.9	35.9
6	1.77	2.94	4.06	5.46	7.87	10.3	13.2	18.4	23.5
7	1.69	2.70	3.64	4.76	6.62	8.38	10.5	14.1	17.5
8	1.63	2.54	3.35	4.30	5.81	7.21	8.87	11.5	14.0
9	1.59	2.42	3.14	3.96	5.26	6.42	7.77	9.89	11.8
10	1.55	2.32	2.98	3.72	4.85	5.85	6.99	8.75	10.3
11	1.52	2.25	2.85	3.53	4.54	5.42	6.41	7.92	9.24
12	1.50	2.19	2.75	3.37	4.30	5.09	5.97	7.29	8.43
13	1.48	2.14	2.67	3.25	4.10	4.82	5.62	6.80	7.81
14	1.46	2.10	2.60	3.15	3.94	4.60	5.33	6.40	7.31
15	1.45	2.06	2.54	3.06	3.80	4.42	5.10	6.08	6.91
16	1.44	2.03	2.49	2.99	3.69	4.27	4.90	5.81	6.57
17	1.43	2.00	2.45	2.92	3.59	4.14	4.73	5.58	6.29
18	1.42	1.98	2.41	2.87	3.51	4.03	4.59	5.39	6.05
19	1.41	1.96	2.38	2.82	3.43	3.93	4.46	5.22	5.81
20	1.40	1.94	2.35	2.77	3.37	3.85	4.35	5.08	5.66
21	1.39	1.92	2.32	2.73	3.31	3.77	4.26	4.95	5.50
22	1.39	1.90	2.30	2.70	3.26	3.70	4.17	4.83	5.36
23	1.38	1.89	2.27	2.67	3.21	3.64	4.09	4.73	5.24
24	1.38	1.88	2.25	2.64	3.17	3.59	4.03	4.64	5.13
25	1.37	1.87	2.24	2.61	3.13	3.54	3.96	4.56	5.03
26	1.37	1.86	2.22	2.59	3.09	3.49	3.91	4.48	4.94
27	1.36	1.85	2.20	2.57	3.06	3.45	3.85	4.41	4.86
28	1.36	1.84	2.19	2.55	3.03	3.41	3.81	4.35	4.78
29	1.35	1.83	2.18	2.53	3.00	3.38	3.76	4.29	4.71
30	1.35	1.82	2.16	2.51	2.98	3.34	3.72	4.24	4.65
35	1.34	1.79	2.11	2.44	2.88	3.21	3.56	4.03	4.39
40	1.33	1.76	2.08	2.39	2.80	3.12	3.44	3.87	4.21
45	1.32	1.74	2.05	2.35	2.74	3.04	3.35	3.76	4.08
50	1.31	1.73	2.03	2.32	2.70	2.99	3.28	3.67	3.97
60	1.30	1.71	1.99	2.27	2.63	2.90	3.18	3.54	3.82
70	1.30	1.69	1.97	2.24	2.59	2.85	3.11	3.45	3.71
80	1.29	1.68	1.95	2.21	2.55	2.80	3.05	3.39	3.64
90	1.29	1.67	1.94	2.19	2.52	2.77	3.01	3.34	3.58
100	1.28	1.66	1.93	2.18	2.50	2.74	2.98	3.30	3.53
200	1.27	1.63	1.88	2.11	2.41	2.63	2.84	3.12	3.33
500	1.26	1.61	1.85	2.07	2.36	2.56	2.76	3.02	3.22
∞	1.25	1.60	1.83	2.05	2.32	2.52	2.71	2.96	3.14

Table B.4 *Continued*

					Numerator df = 12				
$\alpha(\mid)$	0.25	0.10	0.05	0.025	0.01	0.005	0.0025	0.001	0.0005
Denom df									
1	9.41	60.7	244.	977.	6110.	24400.	97700.	$6 \cdot 10^5$	$2 \cdot 10^6$
2	3.39	9.41	19.4	39.4	99.4	199.	399.	999.	2000.
3	2.45	5.22	8.74	14.3	27.1	43.4	69.3	128.	204.
4	2.08	3.90	5.91	8.75	14.4	20.7	29.7	47.4	67.4
5	1.89	3.27	4.68	6.52	9.89	13.4	18.0	26.4	35.2
6	1.77	2.90	4.00	5.37	7.72	10.0	12.9	18.0	23.0
7	1.68	2.67	3.57	4.67	6.47	8.18	10.3	13.7	17.0
8	1.62	2.50	3.28	4.20	5.67	7.01	8.61	11.2	13.6
9	1.58	2.38	3.07	3.87	5.11	6.23	7.52	9.57	11.4
10	1.54	2.28	2.91	3.62	4.71	5.66	6.75	8.45	9.94
11	1.51	2.21	2.79	3.43	4.40	5.24	6.18	7.63	8.88
12	1.49	2.15	2.69	3.28	4.16	4.91	5.74	7.00	8.09
13	1.47	2.10	2.60	3.15	3.96	4.64	5.40	6.52	7.48
14	1.45	2.05	2.53	3.05	3.80	4.43	5.12	6.13	6.99
15	1.44	2.02	2.48	2.96	3.67	4.25	4.88	5.81	6.59
16	1.43	1.99	2.42	2.89	3.55	4.10	4.69	5.55	6.26
17	1.41	1.96	2.38	2.82	3.46	3.97	4.52	5.32	5.98
18	1.40	1.93	2.34	2.77	3.37	3.86	4.38	5.13	5.75
19	1.40	1.91	2.31	2.72	3.30	3.76	4.26	4.97	5.55
20	1.39	1.89	2.28	2.68	3.23	3.68	4.15	4.82	5.37
21	1.38	1.87	2.25	2.64	3.17	3.60	4.06	4.70	5.21
22	1.37	1.86	2.23	2.60	3.12	3.54	3.97	4.58	5.08
23	1.37	1.84	2.20	2.57	3.07	3.47	3.89	4.48	4.96
24	1.36	1.83	2.18	2.54	3.03	3.42	3.83	4.39	4.85
25	1.36	1.82	2.16	2.51	2.99	3.37	3.76	4.31	4.75
26	1.35	1.81	2.15	2.49	2.96	3.33	3.71	4.24	4.66
27	1.35	1.80	2.13	2.47	2.93	3.28	3.66	4.17	4.58
28	1.34	1.79	2.12	2.45	2.90	3.25	3.61	4.11	4.51
29	1.34	1.78	2.10	2.43	2.87	3.21	3.56	4.05	4.44
30	1.34	1.77	2.09	2.41	2.84	3.18	3.52	4.00	4.38
35	1.32	1.74	2.04	2.34	2.74	3.05	3.36	3.79	4.13
40	1.31	1.71	2.00	2.29	2.66	2.95	3.25	3.64	3.95
45	1.30	1.70	1.97	2.25	2.61	2.88	3.16	3.53	3.82
50	1.30	1.68	1.95	2.22	2.56	2.82	3.09	3.44	3.71
60	1.29	1.66	1.92	2.17	2.50	2.74	2.99	3.32	3.57
70	1.28	1.64	1.89	2.14	2.45	2.68	2.92	3.23	3.46
80	1.27	1.63	1.88	2.11	2.42	2.64	2.87	3.16	3.39
90	1.27	1.62	1.86	2.09	2.39	2.61	2.83	3.11	3.33
100	1.27	1.61	1.85	2.08	2.37	2.58	2.80	3.07	3.28
200	1.25	1.58	1.80	2.01	2.27	2.47	2.66	2.90	3.09
500	1.24	1.56	1.77	1.97	2.22	2.40	2.58	2.81	2.97
∞	1.24	1.55	1.75	1.94	2.18	2.36	2.53	2.74	2.90

Table B.4 *Continued*

				Numerator df = 14					
$\alpha(1)$	0.25	0.10	0.05	0.025	0.01	0.005	0.0025	0.001	0.0005
Denom df									
1	9.47	61.1	245.	983.	6140.	24600.	98300.	$6 \cdot 10^5$	$2 \cdot 10^6$
2	3.41	9.42	19.4	39.4	99.4	199.	399.	999.	2000.
3	2.45	5.20	8.71	14.3	26.9	43.2	69.0	128.	203.
4	2.08	3.88	5.87	8.68	14.2	20.5	29.4	46.9	66.8
5	1.89	3.25	4.64	6.46	9.77	13.2	17.8	26.1	34.7
6	1.76	2.88	3.96	5.30	7.60	9.88	12.7	17.7	22.6
7	1.68	2.64	3.53	4.60	6.36	8.03	10.1	13.4	16.6
8	1.62	2.48	3.24	4.13	5.56	6.87	8.43	10.9	13.3
9	1.57	2.35	3.03	3.80	5.01	6.09	7.35	9.33	11.1
10	1.54	2.26	2.86	3.55	4.60	5.53	6.58	8.22	9.67
11	1.51	2.18	2.74	3.36	4.29	5.10	6.02	7.41	8.62
12	1.48	2.12	2.64	3.21	4.05	4.77	5.58	6.79	7.84
13	1.46	2.07	2.55	3.08	3.86	4.51	5.24	6.31	7.23
14	1.44	2.02	2.48	2.98	3.70	4.30	4.96	5.93	6.75
15	1.43	1.99	2.42	2.89	3.56	4.12	4.73	5.62	6.36
16	1.42	1.95	2.37	2.82	3.45	3.97	4.54	5.35	6.03
17	1.41	1.93	2.33	2.75	3.35	3.84	4.37	5.13	5.76
18	1.40	1.90	2.29	2.70	3.27	3.73	4.23	4.94	5.53
19	1.39	1.88	2.26	2.65	3.19	3.64	4.11	4.78	5.33
20	1.38	1.86	2.22	2.60	3.13	3.55	4.00	4.64	5.15
21	1.37	1.84	2.20	2.56	3.07	3.48	3.91	4.51	5.00
22	1.36	1.83	2.17	2.53	3.02	3.41	3.82	4.40	4.87
23	1.36	1.81	2.15	2.50	2.97	3.35	3.75	4.30	4.75
24	1.35	1.80	2.13	2.47	2.93	3.30	3.68	4.21	4.64
25	1.35	1.79	2.11	2.44	2.89	3.25	3.62	4.13	4.54
26	1.34	1.77	2.09	2.42	2.86	3.20	3.56	4.06	4.46
27	1.34	1.76	2.08	2.39	2.82	3.16	3.51	3.99	4.38
28	1.33	1.75	2.06	2.37	2.79	3.12	3.46	3.93	4.30
29	1.33	1.75	2.05	2.36	2.77	3.09	3.42	3.88	4.24
30	1.33	1.74	2.04	2.34	2.74	3.06	3.38	3.82	4.18
35	1.31	1.70	1.99	2.27	2.64	2.93	3.22	3.62	3.93
40	1.30	1.68	1.95	2.21	2.56	2.83	3.10	3.47	3.76
45	1.29	1.66	1.92	2.17	2.51	2.76	3.02	3.36	3.63
50	1.28	1.64	1.89	2.14	2.46	2.70	2.95	3.27	3.52
60	1.27	1.62	1.86	2.09	2.39	2.62	2.85	3.15	3.38
70	1.27	1.60	1.84	2.06	2.35	2.56	2.78	3.06	3.28
80	1.26	1.59	1.82	2.03	2.31	2.52	2.73	3.00	3.20
90	1.26	1.58	1.80	2.02	2.29	2.49	2.69	2.95	3.14
100	1.25	1.57	1.79	2.00	2.27	2.46	2.65	2.91	3.10
200	1.24	1.54	1.74	1.93	2.17	2.35	2.52	2.74	2.91
500	1.23	1.52	1.71	1.89	2.12	2.28	2.44	2.64	2.79
∞	1.22	1.50	1.69	1.87	2.08	2.24	2.39	2.58	2.72

Table B.4 *Continued*

				Numerator df = 16					
α(|)	0.25	0.10	0.05	0.025	0.01	0.005	0.0025	0.001	0.0005
Denom df									
1	9.52	61.3	246.	987.	6170.	24700.	98700.	$6 \cdot 10^5$	$2 \cdot 10^6$
2	3.41	9.43	19.4	39.4	99.4	199.	399.	999.	2000.
3	2.46	5.20	8.69	14.2	26.8	43.0	68.7	127.	202.
4	2.08	3.86	5.84	8.63	14.2	20.4	29.2	46.6	66.2
5	1.88	3.23	4.60	6.40	9.68	13.1	17.6	25.8	34.3
6	1.76	2.86	3.92	5.24	7.52	9.76	12.6	17.4	22.3
7	1.68	2.62	3.49	4.54	6.28	7.91	9.91	13.2	16.4
8	1.62	2.45	3.20	4.08	5.48	6.76	8.29	10.8	13.0
9	1.57	2.33	2.99	3.74	4.92	5.98	7.21	9.15	10.9
10	1.53	2.23	2.83	3.50	4.52	5.42	6.45	8.05	9.46
11	1.50	2.16	2.70	3.30	4.21	5.00	5.89	7.24	8.43
12	1.48	2.09	2.60	3.15	3.97	4.67	5.46	6.63	7.65
13	1.46	2.04	2.51	3.03	3.78	4.41	5.11	6.16	7.05
14	1.44	2.00	2.44	2.92	3.62	4.20	4.84	5.78	6.57
15	1.42	1.96	2.38	2.84	3.49	4.02	4.61	5.46	6.18
16	1.41	1.93	2.33	2.76	3.37	3.87	4.42	5.20	5.86
17	1.40	1.90	2.29	2.70	3.27	3.75	4.25	4.99	5.59
18	1.39	1.87	2.25	2.64	3.19	3.64	4.11	4.80	5.36
19	1.38	1.85	2.21	2.59	3.12	3.54	3.99	4.64	5.16
20	1.37	1.83	2.18	2.55	3.05	3.46	3.89	4.49	4.99
21	1.36	1.81	2.16	2.51	2.99	3.38	3.79	4.37	4.84
22	1.36	1.80	2.13	2.47	2.94	3.31	3.71	4.26	4.71
23	1.35	1.78	2.11	2.44	2.89	3.25	3.63	4.16	4.59
24	1.34	1.77	2.09	2.41	2.85	3.20	3.56	4.07	4.48
25	1.34	1.76	2.07	2.38	2.81	3.15	3.50	3.99	4.39
26	1.33	1.75	2.05	2.36	2.78	3.11	3.45	3.92	4.30
27	1.33	1.74	2.04	2.34	2.75	3.07	3.40	3.86	4.22
28	1.32	1.73	2.02	2.32	2.72	3.03	3.35	3.80	4.15
29	1.32	1.72	2.01	2.30	2.69	2.99	3.31	3.74	4.08
30	1.32	1.71	1.99	2.28	2.66	2.96	3.27	3.69	4.02
35	1.30	1.67	1.94	2.21	2.56	2.83	3.11	3.48	3.78
40	1.29	1.65	1.90	2.15	2.48	2.74	2.99	3.34	3.61
45	1.28	1.63	1.87	2.11	2.43	2.66	2.90	3.23	3.48
50	1.27	1.61	1.85	2.08	2.38	2.61	2.84	3.14	3.38
60	1.26	1.59	1.82	2.03	2.31	2.53	2.74	3.02	3.23
70	1.26	1.57	1.79	2.00	2.27	2.47	2.67	2.93	3.13
80	1.25	1.56	1.77	1.97	2.23	2.43	2.62	2.87	3.06
90	1.25	1.55	1.76	1.95	2.21	2.39	2.58	2.82	3.00
100	1.24	1.54	1.75	1.94	2.19	2.37	2.55	2.78	2.96
200	1.23	1.51	1.69	1.87	2.09	2.25	2.41	2.61	2.76
500	1.22	1.49	1.66	1.83	2.04	2.19	2.33	2.52	2.65
∞	1.21	1.47	1.64	1.80	2.00	2.14	2.28	2.45	2.58

Table B.4 *Continued*

	Numerator df = 18								
α (1)	0.25	0.10	0.05	0.025	0.01	0.005	0.0025	0.001	0.0005
Denom df									
1	9.55	61.6	247.	990.	6190.	24800.	99100.	$6 \cdot 10^5$	$2 \cdot 10^6$
2	3.42	9.44	19.4	39.4	99.4	199.	399.	999.	2000.
3	2.46	5.19	8.67	14.2	26.8	42.9	68.5	127.	202.
4	2.08	3.85	5.82	8.59	14.1	20.3	29.0	46.3	65.8
5	1.88	3.22	4.58	6.36	9.61	13.0	17.4	25.6	34.0
6	1.76	2.85	3.90	5.20	7.45	9.66	12.4	17.3	22.0
7	1.67	2.61	3.47	4.50	6.21	7.83	9.79	13.1	16.2
8	1.61	2.44	3.17	4.03	5.41	6.68	8.18	10.6	12.8
9	1.56	2.31	2.96	3.70	4.86	5.90	7.11	9.01	10.7
10	1.53	2.22	2.80	3.45	4.46	5.34	6.35	7.91	9.30
11	1.50	2.14	2.67	3.26	4.15	4.92	5.79	7.11	8.27
12	1.47	2.08	2.57	3.11	3.91	4.59	5.36	6.51	7.50
13	1.45	2.02	2.48	2.98	3.72	4.33	5.02	6.03	6.90
14	1.43	1.98	2.41	2.88	3.56	4.12	4.74	5.66	6.43
15	1.42	1.94	2.35	2.79	3.42	3.95	4.51	5.35	6.04
16	1.40	1.91	2.30	2.72	3.31	3.80	4.32	5.09	5.72
17	1.39	1.88	2.26	2.65	3.21	3.67	4.16	4.87	5.45
18	1.38	1.85	2.22	2.60	3.13	3.56	4.02	4.68	5.23
19	1.37	1.83	2.18	2.55	3.05	3.46	3.90	4.52	5.03
20	1.36	1.81	2.15	2.50	2.99	3.38	3.79	4.38	4.86
21	1.36	1.79	2.12	2.46	2.93	3.31	3.70	4.26	4.71
22	1.35	1.78	2.10	2.43	2.88	3.24	3.62	4.15	4.58
23	1.34	1.76	2.08	2.39	2.83	3.18	3.54	4.05	4.46
24	1.34	1.75	2.05	2.36	2.79	3.12	3.47	3.96	4.35
25	1.33	1.74	2.04	2.34	2.75	3.08	3.41	3.88	4.26
26	1.33	1.72	2.02	2.31	2.72	3.03	3.36	3.81	4.17
27	1.32	1.71	2.00	2.29	2.68	2.99	3.31	3.75	4.10
28	1.32	1.70	1.99	2.27	2.65	2.95	3.26	3.69	4.02
29	1.31	1.69	1.97	2.25	2.63	2.92	3.22	3.63	3.96
30	1.31	1.69	1.96	2.23	2.60	2.89	3.18	3.58	3.90
35	1.29	1.65	1.91	2.16	2.50	2.76	3.02	3.38	3.66
40	1.28	1.62	1.87	2.11	2.42	2.66	2.90	3.23	3.49
45	1.27	1.60	1.84	2.07	2.36	2.59	2.82	3.12	3.36
50	1.27	1.59	1.81	2.03	2.32	2.53	2.75	3.04	3.26
60	1.26	1.56	1.78	1.98	2.25	2.45	2.65	2.91	3.11
70	1.25	1.55	1.75	1.95	2.20	2.39	2.58	2.83	3.01
80	1.24	1.53	1.73	1.92	2.17	2.35	2.53	2.76	2.94
90	1.24	1.52	1.72	1.91	2.14	2.32	2.49	2.71	2.88
100	1.23	1.52	1.71	1.89	2.12	2.29	2.46	2.68	2.84
200	1.22	1.48	1.66	1.82	2.03	2.18	2.32	2.51	2.65
500	1.21	1.46	1.62	1.78	1.97	2.11	2.24	2.41	2.54
∞	1.20	1.44	1.60	1.75	1.93	2.06	2.19	2.35	2.47

Table B.4 *Continued*

	Numerator df = 20								
$\alpha(1)$	0.25	0.10	0.05	0.025	0.01	0.005	0.0025	0.001	0.0005
Denom df									
1	9.58	61.7	248.	993.	6210.	24800.	99300.	$6 \cdot 10^5$	$2 \cdot 10^6$
2	3.43	9.44	19.4	39.4	99.4	199.	399.	999.	2000.
3	2.46	5.18	8.66	14.2	26.7	42.8	68.3	126.	201.
4	2.08	3.84	5.80	8.56	14.0	20.2	28.9	46.1	65.5
5	1.88	3.21	4.56	6.33	9.55	12.9	17.3	25.4	33.8
6	1.76	2.84	3.87	5.17	7.40	9.59	12.3	17.1	21.8
7	1.67	2.59	3.44	4.47	6.16	7.75	9.70	12.9	16.0
8	1.61	2.42	3.15	4.00	5.36	6.61	8.09	10.5	12.7
9	1.56	2.30	2.94	3.67	4.81	5.83	7.02	8.90	10.6
10	1.52	2.20	2.77	3.42	4.41	5.27	6.27	7.80	9.17
11	1.49	2.12	2.65	3.23	4.10	4.86	5.71	7.01	8.14
12	1.47	2.06	2.54	3.07	3.86	4.53	5.28	6.40	7.37
13	1.45	2.01	2.46	2.95	3.66	4.27	4.94	5.93	6.78
14	1.43	1.96	2.39	2.84	3.51	4.06	4.66	5.56	6.31
15	1.41	1.92	2.33	2.76	3.37	3.88	4.44	5.25	5.93
16	1.40	1.89	2.28	2.68	3.26	3.73	4.25	4.99	5.61
17	1.39	1.86	2.23	2.62	3.16	3.61	4.09	4.78	5.34
18	1.38	1.84	2.19	2.56	3.08	3.50	3.95	4.59	5.12
19	1.37	1.81	2.16	2.51	3.00	3.40	3.83	4.43	4.92
20	1.36	1.79	2.12	2.46	2.94	3.32	3.72	4.29	4.75
21	1.35	1.78	2.10	2.42	2.88	3.24	3.63	4.17	4.60
22	1.34	1.76	2.07	2.39	2.83	3.18	3.54	4.06	4.47
23	1.34	1.74	2.05	2.36	2.78	3.12	3.47	3.96	4.36
24	1.33	1.73	2.03	2.33	2.74	3.06	3.40	3.87	4.25
25	1.33	1.72	2.01	2.30	2.70	3.01	3.34	3.79	4.16
26	1.32	1.71	1.99	2.28	2.66	2.97	3.28	3.72	4.07
27	1.32	1.70	1.97	2.25	2.63	2.93	3.23	3.66	3.99
28	1.31	1.69	1.96	2.23	2.60	2.89	3.19	3.60	3.92
29	1.31	1.68	1.94	2.21	2.57	2.86	3.14	3.54	3.86
30	1.30	1.67	1.93	2.20	2.55	2.82	3.11	3.49	3.80
35	1.29	1.63	1.88	2.12	2.44	2.69	2.95	3.29	3.56
40	1.28	1.61	1.84	2.07	2.37	2.60	2.83	3.14	3.39
45	1.27	1.58	1.81	2.03	2.31	2.53	2.74	3.04	3.26
50	1.26	1.57	1.78	1.99	2.27	2.47	2.68	2.95	3.16
60	1.25	1.54	1.75	1.94	2.20	2.39	2.58	2.83	3.02
70	1.24	1.53	1.72	1.91	2.15	2.33	2.51	2.74	2.92
80	1.23	1.51	1.70	1.88	2.12	2.29	2.46	2.68	2.85
90	1.23	1.50	1.69	1.86	2.09	2.25	2.42	2.63	2.79
100	1.23	1.49	1.68	1.85	2.07	2.23	2.38	2.59	2.75
200	1.21	1.46	1.62	1.78	1.97	2.11	2.25	2.42	2.56
500	1.20	1.44	1.59	1.74	1.92	2.04	2.17	2.33	2.45
∞	1.19	1.42	1.57	1.71	1.88	2.00	2.12	2.27	2.37

Table B.4 *Continued*

				Numerator df $= \infty$					
$\alpha(1)$	0.25	0.10	0.05	0.025	0.01	0.005	0.0025	0.001	0.0005
Denom df									
1	9.85	63.3	254.	1020.	6370.	25500.	$1 \cdot 10^5$	$6 \cdot 10^5$	$3 \cdot 10^6$
2	3.48	9.49	19.5	39.5	99.5	199.	399.	999..	2000.
3	2.47	5.13	8.53	13.9	26.1	41.8	66.8	123.	196.
4	2.08	3.76	5.63	8.26	13.5	19.3	27.6	44.0	62.6
5	1.87	3.11	4.37	6.02	9.02	12.1	16.3	23.8	31.6
6	1.74	2.72	3.67	4.85	6.88	8.88	11.4	15.7	20.0
7	1.65	2.47	3.23	4.14	5.65	7.08	8.81	11.7	14.4
8	1.58	2.29	2.93	3.67	4.86	5.95	7.25	9.33	11.3
9	1.53	2.16	2.71	3.33	4.31	5.19	6.21	7.81	9.26
10	1.48	2.06	2.54	3.08	3.91	4.64	5.47	6.76	7.91
11	1.45	1.97	2.40	2.88	3.60	4.23	4.93	6.00	6.93
12	1.42	1.90	2.30	2.72	3.36	3.90	4.51	5.42	6.20
13	1.40	1.85	2.21	2.60	3.17	3.65	4.18	4.97	5.64
14	1.38	1.80	2.13	2.49	3.00	3.44	3.91	4.60	5.19
15	1.36	1.76	2.07	2.40	2.87	3.26	3.69	4.31	4.83
16	1.34	1.72	2.01	2.32	2.75	3.11	3.50	4.06	4.52
17	1.33	1.69	1.96	2.25	2.65	2.98	3.34	3.85	4.27
18	1.32	1.66	1.92	2.19	2.57	2.87	3.20	3.67	4.05
19	1.30	1.63	1.88	2.13	2.49	2.78	3.08	3.51	3.87
20	1.29	1.61	1.84	2.09	2.42	2.69	2.97	3.38	3.71
21	1.28	1.59	1.81	2.04	2.36	2.61	2.88	3.26	3.56
22	1.28	1.57	1.78	2.00	2.31	2.55	2.80	3.15	3.43
23	1.27	1.55	1.76	1.97	2.26	2.48	2.72	3.05	3.32
24	1.26	1.53	1.73	1.94	2.21	2.43	2.65	2.97	3.22
25	1.25	1.52	1.71	1.91	2.17	2.38	2.59	2.89	3.13
26	1.25	1.50	1.69	1.88	2.13	2.33	2.54	2.82	3.05
27	1.24	1.49	1.67	1.85	2.10	2.29	2.48	2.75	2.97
28	1.24	1.48	1.65	1.83	2.06	2.25	2.44	2.69	2.90
29	1.23	1.47	1.64	1.81	2.03	2.21	2.39	2.64	2.84
30	1.23	1.46	1.62	1.79	2.01	2.18	2.35	2.59	2.78
35	1.20	1.41	1.56	1.70	1.89	2.04	2.18	2.38	2.54
40	1.19	1.38	1.51	1.64	1.80	1.93	2.06	2.23	2.37
45	1.18	1.35	1.47	1.59	1.74	1.85	1.97	2.12	2.23
50	1.16	1.33	1.44	1.55	1.68	1.79	1.89	2.03	2.13
60	1.15	1.29	1.39	1.48	1.60	1.69	1.78	1.89	1.98
70	1.13	1.27	1.35	1.44	1.54	1.62	1.69	1.79	1.87
80	1.12	1.24	1.32	1.40	1.49	1.56	1.63	1.72	1.79
90	1.12	1.23	1.30	1.37	1.46	1.52	1.58	1.66	1.72
100	1.11	1.21	1.28	1.35	1.43	1.49	1.54	1.62	1.67
200	1.07	1.14	1.19	1.23	1.28	1.31	1.35	1.39	1.42
500	1.05	1.09	1.11	1.14	1.16	1.18	1.20	1.23	1.24
∞	1.00	1.00	1.00	1.00	1.00	1.00	1.00	1.00	1.00

Table B.5 Critical values of Spearman's correlation coefficient*

$\alpha(2)$ $\alpha(1)$	0.50 0.25	0.20 0.10	0.10 0.05	0.05 0.025	0.02 0.01	0.01 0.005	0.005 0.0025	0.002 0.001	0.001 0.0005
n									
4	0.600	1.000	1.000						
5	0.500	0.800	0.900	1.000	1.000				
6	0.371	0.657	0.829	0.886	0.943	1.000	1.000		
7	0.321	0.571	0.714	0.786	0.893	0.929	0.964	1.000	1.000
8	0.310	0.524	0.643	0.738	0.833	0.881	0.905	0.952	0.976
9	0.267	0.483	0.600	0.700	0.783	0.833	0.867	0.917	0.933
10	0.248	0.455	0.564	0.648	0.745	0.794	0.830	0.879	0.903
11	0.236	0.427	0.536	0.618	0.709	0.755	0.800	0.845	0.873
12	0.217	0.406	0.503	0.587	0.678	0.727	0.769	0.818	0.846
13	0.209	0.385	0.484	0.560	0.648	0.703	0.747	0.791	0.824
14	0.200	0.367	0.464	0.538	0.626	0.679	0.723	0.771	0.802
15	0.189	0.354	0.446	0.521	0.604	0.654	0.700	0.750	0.779
16	0.182	0.341	0.429	0.503	0.582	0.635	0.679	0.729	0.762
17	0.176	0.328	0.414	0.485	0.566	0.615	0.662	0.713	0.748
18	0.170	0.317	0.401	0.472	0.550	0.600	0.643	0.695	0.728
19	0.165	0.309	0.391	0.460	0.535	0.584	0.628	0.677	0.712
20	0.161	0.299	0.380	0.447	0.520	0.570	0.612	0.662	0.696
21	0.156	0.292	0.370	0.435	0.508	0.556	0.599	0.648	0.681
22	0.152	0.284	0.361	0.425	0.496	0.544	0.586	0.634	0.667
23	0.148	0.278	0.353	0.415	0.486	0.532	0.573	0.622	0.654
24	0.144	0.271	0.344	0.406	0.476	0.521	0.562	0.610	0.642
25	0.142	0.265	0.337	0.398	0.466	0.511	0.551	0.598	0.630
26	0.138	0.259	0.331	0.390	0.457	0.501	0.541	0.587	0.619
27	0.136	0.255	0.324	0.382	0.448	0.491	0.531	0.577	0.608
28	0.133	0.250	0.317	0.375	0.440	0.483	0.522	0.567	0.598
29	0.130	0.245	0.312	0.368	0.433	0.475	0.513	0.558	0.589
30	0.128	0.240	0.306	0.362	0.425	0.467	0.504	0.549	0.580
35	0.118	0.222	0.283	0.335	0.394	0.433	0.468	0.510	0.539
40	0.110	0.207	0.264	0.313	0.368	0.405	0.439	0.479	0.507
45	0.103	0.194	0.248	0.294	0.347	0.382	0.414	0.453	0.479
50	0.097	0.184	0.235	0.279	0.329	0.363	0.393	0.430	0.456
55	0.093	0.175	0.224	0.266	0.314	0.346	0.375	0.411	0.435
60	0.089	0.168	0.214	0.255	0.300	0.331	0.360	0.394	0.418
65	0.085	0.161	0.206	0.244	0.289	0.318	0.346	0.379	0.402
70	0.082	0.155	0.198	0.235	0.278	0.307	0.333	0.365	0.388
75	0.079	0.150	0.191	0.227	0.269	0.297	0.322	0.353	0.375
80	0.076	0.145	0.185	0.220	0.260	0.287	0.312	0.342	0.363
85	0.074	0.140	0.180	0.213	0.252	0.279	0.303	0.332	0.353
90	0.072	0.136	0.174	0.207	0.245	0.271	0.294	0.323	0.343
95	0.070	0.133	0.170	0.202	0.239	0.264	0.287	0.314	0.334
100	0.068	0.129	0.165	0.197	0.233	0.257	0.279	0.307	0.326

*To find Spearman's correlation coefficient that is associated with a certain chance of making a type I error, find the column corresponding with that value of α at the top of table ($\alpha(2)$ indicates a two-tailed value and $\alpha(1)$ indicates a one-tailed value) and the row corresponding to the sample's size in the leftmost column. The value in the body of the table where that column and row intersect is the absolute value of Spearman's correlation coefficient that is expected to occur in α of the samples when Spearman's correlation coefficient is equal to zero in the population.

Table B.6 Critical values of the Mann-Whitney U statistic*

$\alpha(2)$		0.20	0.10	0.05	0.02	0.01	0.005	0.002	0.001
$\alpha(1)$		0.10	0.05	0.025	0.01	0.005	0.0025	0.001	0.0005
n_s	n_L								
1	1	--	--	--	--	--	--	--	--
	2	--	--	--	--	--	--	--	--
	3	--	--	--	--	--	--	--	--
	4	--	--	--	--	--	--	--	--
	5	--	--	--	--	--	--	--	--
	6	--	--	--	--	--	--	--	--
	7	--	--	--	--	--	--	--	--
	8	--	--	--	--	--	--	--	--
	9	9	--	--	--	--	--	--	--
	10	10	--	--	--	--	--	--	--
	12	12	--	--	--	--	--	--	--
	14	14	--	--	--	--	--	--	--
	16	16	--	--	--	--	--	--	--
	18	18	--	--	--	--	--	--	--
	20	19	20	--	--	--	--	--	--
	22	21	22	--	--	--	--	--	--
	24	23	24	--	--	--	--	--	--
	26	25	26	--	--	--	--	--	--
	28	27	28	--	--	--	--	--	--
	30	28	30	--	--	--	--	--	--
	32	30	32	--	--	--	--	--	--
	34	32	34	--	--	--	--	--	--
	36	34	36	--	--	--	--	--	--
	38	36	38	--	--	--	--	--	--
1	40	37	39	40	--	--	--	--	--
2	2	--	--	--	--	--	--	--	--
	3	6	--	--	--	--	--	--	--
	4	8	--	--	--	--	--	--	--
	5	9	10	--	--	--	--	--	--
	6	11	12	--	--	--	--	--	--
	7	10	14	--	--	--	--	--	--
	8	14	15	16	--	--	--	--	--
	9	16	17	18	--	--	--	--	--
	10	17	19	20	--	--	--	--	--
	12	20	22	23	--	--	--	--	--
	14	23	25	27	28	--	--	--	--
	16	27	29	31	32	--	--	--	--
	18	30	32	34	36	--	--	--	--
	20	33	36	38	39	40	--	--	--
	22	36	39	41	43	44	--	--	--
	24	39	42	45	47	48	--	--	--
	26	42	46	48	51	52	--	--	--
	28	45	49	52	54	55	56	--	--
	30	48	53	55	58	59	60	--	--
	32	51	56	59	62	63	64	--	--
	34	55	59	63	65	67	68	--	--
	36	58	63	66	69	71	72	--	--
	38	61	66	70	73	75	76	--	--
	40	64	69	73	77	78	79	--	--

*To find a Mann-Whitney U statistic that is associated with a certain chance of making a type I error, find the column corresponding with that value of α at the top of table ($\alpha(2)$ indicates a two-tailed value and $\alpha(1)$ indicates a one-tailed value) and the row corresponding to the sample's size in the leftmost column. The value in the body of the table where that column and row intersect is the value of the Mann-Whitney U statistic that is expected to occur in α of the samples when there is no association between the groups in the population.

Table B.6 *Continued*

nS	nL	α(2) 0.20 / α(1) 0.10	0.10 / 0.05	0.05 / 0.025	0.02 / 0.01	0.01 / 0.005	0.005 / 0.0025	0.002 / 0.001	0.001 / 0.0005
2	32	51	56	59	62	63	64	--	--
	34	55	59	63	65	67	68	--	--
	36	58	63	66	69	71	72	--	--
	38	61	66	70	73	75	76	--	--
	40	64	69	73	77	78	79	--	--
3	3	8	9	--	--	--	--	--	--
	4	11	12	--	--	--	--	--	--
	5	13	14	15	--	--	--	--	--
	6	15	16	17	--	--	--	--	--
	7	15	19	20	21	--	--	--	--
	8	19	21	22	24	--	--	--	--
	9	22	23	25	26	27	--	--	--
	10	24	26	27	29	30	--	--	--
	12	28	31	32	34	35	36	--	--
	14	32	35	37	40	41	42	--	--
	16	37	40	42	45	46	47	--	--
	18	41	45	47	50	52	53	54	--
	20	45	49	52	55	57	58	60	--
	22	50	54	57	60	62	64	65	66
	24	54	59	62	66	68	69	71	72
	26	58	63	67	71	73	75	77	78
	28	63	68	72	76	79	80	82	83
	30	67	73	77	81	84	86	88	89
	32	71	77	82	87	89	91	94	95
	34	76	82	87	92	95	97	99	101
	36	80	87	92	97	100	103	105	106
	38	84	91	97	102	105	108	111	112
3	40	89	96	102	107	111	114	116	118
4	4	13	15	16	--	--	--	--	--
	5	16	18	19	20	--	--	--	--
	6	19	21	22	23	24	--	--	--
	7	20	24	25	27	28	--	--	--
	8	25	27	28	30	31	32	--	--
	9	27	30	32	33	35	36	--	--
	10	30	33	35	37	38	39	40	--
	12	36	39	41	43	45	46	48	--
	14	41	45	47	50	52	53	55	56
	16	47	50	53	57	59	60	62	63
	18	52	56	60	63	66	67	69	71
	20	58	62	66	70	72	75	77	78
	22	63	68	72	77	79	82	84	85
	24	69	74	79	83	86	89	91	93
	26	74	80	85	90	93	96	98	100
	28	80	86	91	96	100	103	106	108
4	30	85	92	97	103	107	110	113	115

Table B.6 *Continued*

n_S	n_L	α(2) 0.20 / α(1) 0.10	0.10 / 0.05	0.05 / 0.025	0.02 / 0.01	0.01 / 0.005	0.005 / 0.0025	0.002 / 0.001	0.001 / 0.0005
4	32	91	98	104	110	114	117	120	122
	34	96	104	110	116	120	124	127	130
	36	102	110	116	123	127	131	135	137
	38	107	116	122	130	134	138	142	144
4	40	113	121	129	136	141	145	149	152
5	5	20	21	23	24	25	--	--	--
	6	23	25	27	28	29	30	--	--
	7	24	29	30	32	34	35	--	--
	8	30	32	34	36	38	39	40	--
	9	33	36	38	40	42	43	44	45
	10	37	39	42	44	46	47	49	50
	12	43	47	49	52	54	56	58	59
	14	50	54	57	60	63	64	67	68
	16	57	61	65	68	71	73	75	77
	18	63	68	72	76	79	81	84	86
	20	70	75	80	84	87	90	93	95
	22	77	82	97	92	96	98	102	104
	24	84	90	95	100	104	107	110	113
	26	90	97	102	108	112	115	119	121
	28	97	104	110	116	120	124	128	130
	30	104	111	117	124	128	132	136	139
	32	110	118	125	132	137	141	145	148
	34	117	125	132	140	145	149	154	157
	36	124	132	140	148	153	158	163	166
	38	130	140	147	156	161	166	171	175
5	40	137	147	155	164	169	174	180	184
6	6	27	29	31	33	34	35	--	--
	7	29	34	36	38	39	40	42	--
	8	35	38	40	44	49	50	52	53
	9	39	42	44	47	49	50	52	53
	10	43	46	49	52	54	55	57	58
	12	51	55	58	61	63	65	68	69
	14	59	63	67	71	73	75	78	79
	16	67	71	75	80	83	85	88	90
	18	74	80	84	89	92	95	98	100
	20	82	88	93	98	102	105	108	111
	22	90	96	102	108	111	115	119	121
	24	98	105	111	117	121	125	129	132
	26	106	113	119	126	131	134	139	142
	28	114	122	128	135	140	144	149	152
6	30	122	130	137	145	150	154	159	163

Table B.6 *Continued*

α(2)	0.20	0.10	0.05	0.02	0.01	0.005	0.002	0.001
α(1)	0.10	0.05	0.025	0.01	0.005	0.0025	0.001	0.0005

n_S	n_L								
6	32	129	138	146	154	159	164	169	173
	34	137	147	154	163	169	174	179	183
	36	145	155	163	172	178	184	190	194
	38	153	163	172	182	188	193	200	204
6	40	161	172	181	191	197	203	210	214
7	7	36	38	41	43	45	46	48	49
	8	40	43	46	49	50	52	54	55
	9	45	48	51	54	56	58	60	61
	10	49	53	56	59	61	63	65	67
	12	58	63	66	70	72	75	77	79
	14	67	72	76	81	83	86	89	91
	16	76	82	86	91	94	97	101	103
	18	85	91	96	102	105	108	112	115
	20	94	101	106	112	116	120	124	126
	22	103	110	116	123	127	131	135	138
	24	112	120	126	133	138	142	147	150
	26	121	129	136	144	149	153	158	162
	28	130	139	146	154	160	164	170	174
	30	139	149	156	165	170	176	181	185
	32	148	158	166	175	181	187	193	197
	34	157	168	176	186	192	198	204	209
	36	166	177	186	196	203	209	216	221
	38	175	187	196	207	214	220	227	232
7	40	184	196	206	217	225	231	239	244
8	8	45	49	51	55	57	58	60	62
	9	50	54	57	61	63	65	67	68
	10	56	60	63	67	69	71	74	75
	12	66	70	74	79	81	84	87	89
	14	76	81	86	90	94	96	100	102
	16	86	92	97	102	106	109	113	115
	18	96	103	108	114	118	122	126	129
	20	106	113	119	126	130	134	139	142
	22	117	124	131	138	142	147	152	155
	24	127	135	142	150	155	159	165	168
	26	137	146	153	161	167	172	177	181
	28	147	156	164	173	179	184	190	195
	30	157	167	175	185	191	197	203	208
	32	167	178	187	197	203	209	216	221
	34	177	188	198	208	215	222	229	234
	36	188	199	209	220	228	234	242	247
	38	198	210	220	232	240	247	255	260
8	40	208	221	231	244	252	259	268	273

Table B.6 *Continued*

$\alpha(2)$		0.20	0.10	0.05	0.02	0.01	0.005	0.002	0.001
$\alpha(1)$		0.10	0.05	0.025	0.01	0.005	0.0025	0.001	0.0005
n_S	n_L								
9	9	56	60	64	67	70	72	74	76
	10	62	66	70	74	77	79	82	83
	12	73	78	82	87	90	93	96	98
	14	85	90	95	100	104	107	111	113
	16	96	102	107	113	117	121	125	128
	18	107	114	120	126	131	135	139	142
	20	118	126	132	140	144	149	154	157
	22	130	138	145	153	158	162	168	172
	24	141	150	157	166	171	176	182	186
	26	152	162	170	179	185	190	196	201
	28	164	174	182	192	198	204	211	215
	30	175	185	194	205	212	218	225	230
	32	186	197	207	218	225	231	239	244
	34	197	209	219	231	238	245	253	259
	36	209	221	232	244	252	259	267	273
	38	220	233	244	257	265	273	282	288
9	40	231	245	257	270	279	286	296	302
10	10	68	73	77	81	84	87	90	92
	12	81	86	91	96	99	102	106	108
	14	93	99	104	110	114	117	121	124
	16	106	112	118	124	129	133	137	140
	18	118	125	132	139	143	148	153	156
	20	130	138	145	153	158	163	168	172
	22	143	152	159	167	173	178	184	188
	24	155	165	173	182	188	193	200	204
	26	168	178	186	196	202	208	215	220
	28	180	191	200	210	217	223	231	236
	30	192	204	213	224	232	238	246	252
	32	205	217	227	239	246	253	262	267
	34	217	230	241	253	261	268	277	283
	36	229	243	254	267	276	284	293	299
	38	242	256	268	281	290	299	308	315
10	40	254	269	281	296	305	314	324	331

Table B.7 Critical values of the chi-square distribution*

α(1)	0.50	0.25	0.10	0.05	0.025	0.01	0.005	0.001
df								
1	0.455	1.323	2.706	3.841	5.024	6.635	7.879	10.828
2	1.386	2.773	4.605	5.991	7.378	9.210	10.597	13.816
3	2.366	4.108	6.251	7.815	9.348	11.345	12.838	16.266
4	3.357	5.385	7.779	9.488	11.143	13.277	14.860	18.467
5	4.351	6.626	9.236	11.070	12.833	15.086	16.750	20.515
6	5.348	7.841	10.645	12.592	14.449	16.812	18.548	22.458
7	6.346	9.037	12.017	14.067	16.013	18.475	20.278	24.322
8	7.344	10.219	13.362	15.507	17.535	20.090	21.955	26.124
9	8.343	11.389	14.684	16.919	19.023	21.666	23.589	27.877
10	9.342	12.549	15.987	18.307	20.483	23.209	25.188	29.588
11	10.341	13.701	17.275	19.675	21.920	24.725	26.757	31.264
12	11.340	14.845	18.549	21.026	23.337	26.217	28.300	32.909
13	12.340	15.984	19.812	22.362	24.736	27.688	29.819	34.528
14	13.339	17.117	21.064	23.685	26.119	29.141	31.319	36.123
15	14.339	18.245	22.307	24.996	27.488	30.578	32.801	37.697
16	15.338	19.369	23.542	26.296	28.845	32.000	34.267	39.252
17	16.338	20.489	24.769	27.587	30.191	33.409	35.718	40.790
18	17.338	21.605	25.989	28.869	31.526	34.805	37.156	42.312
19	18.338	22.718	27.204	30.144	32.852	36.191	38.582	43.820
20	19.337	23.828	28.412	31.410	34.170	37.566	39.997	45.315
21	20.337	24.935	29.615	32.671	35.479	38.932	41.401	46.797
22	21.337	26.039	30.813	33.924	36.781	40.289	42.796	48.268
23	22.337	27.141	32.007	35.172	38.076	41.638	44.181	49.728
24	23.337	28.241	33.196	36.415	39.364	42.980	45.559	51.179
25	24.337	29.339	34.382	37.652	40.646	44.314	46.928	52.620
26	25.336	30.435	35.563	38.885	41.923	45.642	48.290	54.052
27	26.336	31.528	36.741	40.113	43.195	46.963	49.645	55.476
28	27.336	32.620	37.916	41.337	44.461	48.278	50.993	56.892
29	28.336	33.711	39.087	42.557	45.722	49.588	52.336	58.301
30	29.336	34.800	40.256	43.773	46.979	50.892	53.672	59.703
35	34.336	40.223	46.059	49.802	53.203	57.342	60.275	66.619
40	39.335	45.616	51.805	55.758	59.342	63.691	66.766	73.402
45	44.335	50.985	57.505	61.656	65.410	69.957	73.166	80.077
50	49.335	56.334	63.167	67.505	71.420	76.154	79.490	86.661
55	54.335	61.665	68.796	73.311	77.380	82.292	85.749	93.168
60	59.335	66.981	74.397	79.082	83.298	88.379	91.952	99.607
65	64.335	72.285	79.973	84.821	89.177	94.422	98.105	105.99
70	69.334	77.577	85.527	90.531	95.023	100.43	104.22	112.32
75	74.334	82.858	91.061	96.217	100.84	106.39	110.29	118.60
80	79.334	88.130	96.578	101.88	106.63	112.33	116.32	124.84
85	84.334	93.394	102.08	107.52	112.39	118.24	122.33	131.04
90	89.334	98.650	107.57	113.15	118.14	124.12	128.30	137.21
95	94.334	103.90	113.04	118.75	123.86	129.97	134.25	143.34
100	99.334	109.14	118.50	124.34	129.56	135.81	140.17	149.45

*To locate a chi-square value, find the degrees of freedom in the leftmost column and the appropriate α at the top of the table (only one-tailed α are appropriate in the chi-square distribution). The number in the body of the table where this row and column intersect is the value from the chi-square distribution with that number of degrees of freedom and that corresponds to an area equal to α in the upper tail.

Table B.8 Critical values of the q distribution*

				$\alpha(2) = 0.10$					
k	2	3	4	5	6	7	8	9	10
df									
1	8.929	13.44	16.36	18.49	20.15	21.51	22.64	23.62	24.48
2	4.130	5.733	6.773	7.538	8.139	8.633	9.049	9.409	9.725
3	3.328	4.467	5.199	5.738	6.162	6.511	6.806	7.062	7.287
4	3.015	3.976	4.586	5.035	5.388	5.679	5.926	6.139	6.327
5	2.850	3.717	4.264	4.664	4.979	5.238	5.458	5.648	5.816
6	2.748	3.559	4.065	4.435	4.726	4.966	5.168	5.344	5.499
7	2.680	3.451	3.931	4.280	4.555	4.780	4.972	5.137	5.283
8	2.630	3.374	3.843	4.169	4.431	4.646	4.829	4.987	5.126
9	2.592	3.316	3.761	4.084	4.337	4.545	4.721	4.873	5.007
10	2.563	3.270	3.704	4.018	4.264	4.465	4.636	4.783	4.913
11	2.540	3.234	3.658	3.965	4.205	4.401	4.568	4.711	4.838
12	2.521	3.204	3.621	3.922	4.156	4.349	4.511	4.652	4.776
13	2.505	3.179	3.589	3.885	4.116	4.305	4.464	4.602	4.724
14	2.491	3.158	3.563	3.854	4.081	4.267	4.424	4.560	4.680
15	2.479	3.140	3.540	3.828	4.052	4.235	4.390	4.524	4.641
16	2.469	3.124	3.520	3.804	4.026	4.207	4.360	4.492	4.608
17	2.460	3.110	3.503	3.784	4.004	4.183	4.334	4.464	4.579
18	2.452	3.098	3.488	3.767	30984	4.161	4.311	4.440	4.554
19	2.455	3.087	3.474	3.751	3.966	4.142	4.290	4.418	4.531
20	2.439	3.078	3.462	3.736	3.950	4.124	4.271	4.398	4.510
30	2.400	3.017	3.648	3.648	3.851	4.016	4.155	4.275	4.381
40	2.381	2.988	3.349	3.605	3.803	3.963	4.099	4.215	4.317
50	2.372	2.974	3.584	3.584	3.586	3.937	4.071	4.185	4.286
60	2.363	2.959	3.562	3.562	3.562	3.911	4.042	4.155	4.254
∞	2.326	2.902	3.478	3.478	3.478	3.808	4.931	4.037	4.129

k	11	12	13	14	15	16	17	18	19
df									
1	25.24	25.92	26.54	27.10	27.62	28.10	28.54	28.96	29.35
2	10.01	10.26	10.49	10.70	10.89	11.07	11.24	11.39	11.54
3	7.487	7.667	7.832	7.982	8.120	8.249	8.368	8.479	8.584
4	6.495	6.645	6.783	6.909	7.025	7.133	7.233	7.327	7.414
5	5.966	6.101	6.223	6.336	6.440	6.536	6.626	6.710	6.789
6	5.637	5.762	5.875	5.979	6.075	6.164	6.247	6.325	6.398
7	5.413	5.530	5.637	5.735	5.826	5.910	5.988	6.061	6.130
8	5.250	5.362	5.464	5.558	5.644	5.274	5.799	5.869	5.935
9	5.127	5.234	5.333	5.423	5.506	5.583	5.655	5.723	5.786
10	5.029	5.134	5.229	5.317	5.397	5.472	5.542	5.607	5.668
11	4.951	5.053	5.146	5.231	5.309	5.382	5.450	5.514	5.573
12	4.886	4.986	5.077	5.160	5.236	5.308	5.374	5.436	4.495
13	4.832	4.930	5.019	5.100	5.176	5.245	5.311	5.372	5.429
14	4.786	4.882	4.970	5.050	5.124	5.192	5.256	5.316	5.373
15	4.746	4.841	4.927	5.006	5.079	5.147	5.209	5.269	5.324
16	4.712	4.805	4.890	4.968	5.040	5.107	5.169	5.227	5.282
17	4.682	4.774	4.858	4.935	5.005	5.071	5.133	5.190	5.244
18	4.655	4.746	4.829	4.905	4.975	5.040	5.101	5.158	5.211
19	4.631	4.721	4.803	4.879	4.948	5.012	5.073	5.129	5.182
20	4.609	4.699	4.780	4.855	4.924	4.987	5.047	5.103	5.155
30	4.474	4.559	4.635	4.706	4.770	4.830	4.866	4.939	4.988
40	4.408	4.490	4.564	4.632	4.695	4.752	4.807	4.857	4.905
50	4.375	4.456	4.519	4.595	4.657	4.714	4.767	4.816	4.863
60	4.342	4.421	4.493	4.558	4.619	4.675	4.727	4.775	4.821
∞	4.211	4.285	4.351	4.412	4.468	4.519	4.568	4.612	4.654

*To find a value of q, first locate the table headed by the appropriate value of α. Then, find the degrees of freedom in the leftmost column and the number of means involved in the comparison (k) in the top row of the table. Where this row and column intersect is the value of q corresponding to an area of α in the q distribution with that number of degrees of freedom and k means.

Table B.8 *Continued*

					$\alpha(2) = 0.05$				
k	2	3	4	5	6	7	8	9	10
df									
1	17.97	26.98	32.82	37.08	40.17	43.12	45.40	47.36	49.07
2	6.085	8.331	9.798	10.88	11.74	12.44	13.03	13.54	13.99
3	4.501	5.910	6.825	7.502	8.037	8.478	8.853	9.177	9.462
4	3.927	5.040	5.757	6.287	6.707	7.053	7.347	7.602	7.826
5	3.635	4.602	5.218	5.673	6.033	6.330	6.582	6.802	6.995
6	3.461	4.339	4.896	5.305	5.628	5.895	6.122	6.319	6.493
7	3.344	4.165	4.681	5.060	5.359	5.606	5.815	5.998	6.158
8	3.261	4.041	4.529	4.886	5.167	5.399	5.597	5.767	5.918
9	3.199	3.949	4.415	4.756	5.024	5.244	5.432	5.595	5.739
10	3.151	3.877	4.327	4.654	5.912	5.124	5.305	5.461	5.599
11	3.133	3.820	4.256	4.574	4.823	5.028	5.202	5.353	5.487
12	3.082	3.773	4.199	4.508	4.751	4.950	5.119	5.265	5.395
13	3.055	3.735	4.151	4.453	4.690	4.885	5.049	5.192	5.318
14	3.033	3.702	4.111	4.407	4.639	4.829	4.990	5.131	5.254
15	3.014	3.674	4.076	4.367	4.595	4.782	4.940	5.077	5.198
16	2.998	3.649	4.046	4.333	4.557	4.741	4.897	5.031	5.150
17	2.984	3.628	4.020	4.303	4.524	4.705	4.858	4.991	5.108
18	2.971	3.609	3.997	4.277	4.495	4.673	4.824	4.956	5.071
19	2.960	3.593	3.977	4.253	4.469	4.645	4.794	4.924	5.038
20	2.950	3.578	3.958	4.232	4.445	4.620	4.768	4.896	5.008
30	2.888	3.486	3.845	4.102	4.302	4.464	4.602	4.720	4.824
40	2.858	3.442	3.791	4.039	4.232	4.389	4.521	4.635	4.735
50	2.844	4.423	3.764	4.008	4.196	4.352	4.481	4.593	4.691
60	2.829	3.399	3.399	3.977	4.163	4.314	4.441	4.550	4.646
∞	2.772	3.314	3.633	3.858	4.030	4.170	4.286	4.387	4.474

k	11	12	13	14	15	16	17	18	19
df									
1	50.59	51.96	53.20	54.33	55.36	56.32	57.22	58.04	58.83
2	14.39	14.75	15.08	15.38	15.65	15.91	16.14	16.37	16.57
3	9.717	9.946	10.15	10.35	10.53	10.69	10.84	10.98	11.11
4	8.027	8.208	8.373	8.525	8.664	8.794	8.914	9.028	9.134
5	7.168	7.324	7.466	7.596	7.717	7.828	7.932	8.030	8.122
6	6.649	6.789	6.917	7.034	7.143	7.244	7.338	7.426	7.508
7	6.302	6.431	6.550	6.658	6.759	6.852	6.939	7.020	7.097
8	6.054	6.175	6.287	6.389	6.483	6.571	6.653	6.729	6.802
9	5.867	5.983	6.089	6.186	6.276	6.359	6.437	6.510	6.579
10	5.722	5.833	5.935	6.028	6.114	6.194	6.269	6.339	6.405
11	5.605	5.713	5.811	5.901	6.984	6.062	6.134	6.202	6.265
12	5.511	5.615	5.710	5.798	5.878	5.953	6.023	6.089	6.151
13	5.431	5.533	5.625	5.711	5.789	5.862	5.931	5.995	6.055
14	5.364	5.463	5.554	5.637	5.714	5.786	5.852	5.915	5.974
15	5.306	5.404	5.493	5.574	5.649	5.720	5.785	5.846	5.904
16	5.256	5.352	5.439	5.520	5.593	5.662	5.727	5.786	5.843
17	5.212	5.307	5.392	5.471	5.544	5.612	5.675	5.734	5.790
18	5.174	5.267	5.352	5.429	5.501	5.568	5.630	5.688	5.743
19	5.140	5.231	5.315	5.391	5.462	5.528	5.589	5.647	5.701
20	5.108	5.199	5.282	5.357	5.427	5.493	5.553	5.610	5.663
30	4.917	5.001	5.077	5.147	5.211	5.271	5.327	5.379	5.429
40	4.824	4.904	4.977	5.044	5.106	5.163	5.216	5.266	5.313
50	4.778	4.856	4.928	4.993	5.054	5.110	5.162	5.210	5.256
60	4.732	4.808	4.878	4.942	5.001	5.056	5.107	5.154	5.199
∞	4.552	4.622	4.685	4.743	4.796	4.845	4.891	4.934	4.974

Table B.8 *Continued*

				α(2) = 0.01					
k	2	3	4	5	6	7	8	9	10
df									
1	90.03	135.0	164.3	185.6	202.2	215.8	227.2	237.0	245.6
2	14.04	19.02	22.29	24.72	26.63	28.20	29.53	30.68	31.69
3	8.261	10.62	12.17	13.33	14.24	15.00	15.64	16.20	16.69
4	6.512	8.120	9.173	9.958	10.58	11.10	11.55	11.93	12.27
5	5.702	6.976	7.804	8.421	8.913	9.321	9.669	9.972	10.24
6	5.243	6.331	7.033	7.556	7.973	8.318	8.613	8.869	9.097
7	4.949	5.919	6.543	7.005	7.373	7.679	7.939	8.166	8.368
8	4.746	5.635	6.204	6.625	6.960	7.237	7.474	7.681	7.863
9	4.596	5.428	5.957	6.348	6.658	6.915	7.134	7.325	7.495
10	4.482	5.270	5.769	6.163	6.428	6.669	6.875	7.055	7.213
11	4.392	5.146	5.621	5.970	6.247	6.476	6.672	6.842	6.992
12	4.320	5.046	5.502	5.836	6.101	6.321	6.507	6.670	6.814
13	4.260	4.964	5.404	5.727	5.981	6.192	6.372	6.528	6.667
14	4.210	4.895	5.322	5.634	5.881	6.085	6.258	6.409	6.543
15	4.168	4.836	5.252	5.556	5.796	5.994	6.162	6.309	6.439
16	4.131	4.786	5.192	5.489	5.722	5.915	6.079	6.022	6.349
17	4.099	4.742	5.140	5.430	5.659	5.847	6.007	6.147	6.270
18	4.071	4.703	5.094	5.379	5.603	5.788	5.944	6.081	6.201
19	4.046	4.670	5.054	5.334	5.554	5.735	5.889	6.022	6.141
20	4.024	4.639	5.018	5.294	5.510	5.688	5.839	5.970	6.087
30	3.889	4.455	4.799	5.048	5.242	5.401	5.536	5.653	5.756
40	3.825	4.367	4.696	4.931	5.114	5.265	5.392	5.502	5.559
50	3.794	4.325	4.645	4.874	5.014	5.198	5.322	5.429	5.503
60	3.762	4.282	4.595	4.818	4.991	5.133	5.253	5.356	5.447
∞	3.643	4.120	4.403	4.603	4.757	4.882	4.987	5.078	5.157

k	11	12	13	14	15	16	17	18	19
df									
1	253.2	260.0	266.2	271.8	277.0	281.8	286.3	290.4	294.3
2	32.59	33.40	34.13	34.81	35.43	36.00	36.53	37.03	37.50
3	17.13	17.53	17.89	18.22	18.52	18.81	19.07	19.32	19.55
4	12.57	12.84	13.09	13.32	13.53	13.73	13.91	14.08	14.24
5	10.48	10.70	10.89	11.08	11.24	11.40	11.55	11.68	11.81
6	9.301	9.485	9.653	9.808	9.951	10.08	10.21	10.32	10.43
7	8.548	8.711	8.860	8.997	9.124	9.242	9.353	9.456	9.554
8	8.027	8.176	8.312	8.436	8.552	8.659	8.760	8.854	8.943
9	7.647	7.784	7.910	8.025	8.132	8.232	8.325	8.412	8.495
10	7.356	7.485	7.603	7.712	7.812	7.906	7.993	8.076	8.153
11	7.128	7.250	7.362	7.465	7.560	7.649	7.732	7.809	7.883
12	6.943	7.060	7.167	7.265	7.356	7.441	7.520	7.594	7.665
13	6.791	6.903	7.006	7.101	7.188	7.269	7.345	7.417	7.485
14	6.664	6.772	6.871	6.962	7.047	7.126	7.199	7.268	7.333
15	6.555	6.660	6.757	6.845	6.927	7.003	7.074	7.142	7.204
16	6.462	6.564	6.658	6.744	6.823	6.898	6.967	7.032	7.093
17	6.381	6.480	6.572	6.656	6.734	6.806	6.873	6.937	6.997
18	6.310	6.407	6.497	6.579	6.655	6.725	6.792	6.854	6.912
19	6.247	6.342	6.430	6.510	6.585	6.654	6.719	6.780	6.837
20	6.191	6.285	6.371	6.450	6.523	6.591	6.654	6.714	6.771
30	5.849	5.932	6.008	6.078	6.143	6.203	6.259	6.311	6.361
40	5.686	5.764	5.835	5.900	5.961	6.017	6.069	6.119	6.165
50	5.607	5.682	5.751	5.814	5.873	5.927	5.978	6.025	6.060
60	5.528	5.601	5.667	5.728	5.785	5.837	5.886	6.931	5.974
∞	5.227	5.290	5.348	5.400	5.448	5.493	5.535	5.611	5.611

Table B.8 *Continued*

α(2) = 0.001

k	2	3	4	5	6	7	8	9	10
df									
1	900.3	1351.	1643.	1856.	2022.	2158.	2272.	2370.	2455.
2	44.69	60.42	70.77	78.43	84.49	89.46	93067	97.30	100.5
3	18.28	23.32	26.65	29.13	31.11	32.74	34.12	35.33	36.39
4	12.18	14.99	16.84	18.23	19.34	20.26	21.04	21.73	22.33
5	9.714	11.67	12.96	13.93	14.71	15.35	15.90	16.38	16.81
6	8.427	9.960	10.97	11.72	12.32	12.83	13.26	13.63	13.97
7	7.648	8.930	9.763	10.40	10.90	11.32	11.68	11.99	12.27
8	7.130	8.250	8.978	9.522	9.958	10.32	10.64	10.91	11.15
9	6.762	7.768	8.419	8.906	9.295	9.619	9.897	10.14	10.36
10	6.487	7.411	8.006	8.450	8.804	9.099	9.352	9.573	9.769
11	6.275	7.136	7.687	8.098	8.426	8.699	8.933	9.138	9.319
12	6.106	6.917	7.436	7.821	8.127	8.383	8.601	8.793	8.962
13	5.970	6.740	7.231	7.595	7.885	8.126	8.333	8.513	8.673
14	5.856	6.594	7.062	7.409	7.685	7.195	8.110	8.282	8.434
15	5.760	6.470	6.290	7.252	7.517	7.736	7.925	8.088	8.234
16	5.678	6.365	6.799	7.119	7.374	7.585	7.766	7.923	8.063
17	5.608	6.275	6.695	7.005	7.250	7.454	7.629	7.781	7.916
18	5.546	6.196	6.604	6.905	7.143	7.341	7.510	7.657	7.788
19	5.492	6.127	6.525	6.817	7.049	7.242	7.405	7.549	7.676
20	5.444	6.065	6.454	6.740	6.966	7.154	7.313	7.453	7.577
30	5.156	5.698	6.033	6.278	6.470	6.628	6.763	6.880	6.984
40	5.022	5.528	5.838	6.063	6.240	6.386	6.509	6.616	6.711
50	4.958	5.447	5.746	5.902	6.131	6.271	6.389	6.491	6.581
60	4.894	5.365	5.653	5.860	6.022	6.155	6.268	6.366	6.451
∞	4.654	5.063	5.309	5.619	5.619	5.730	5.823	5.093	5.973

k	11	12	13	14	15	16	17	18	19
df									
1	2532.	2600.	2662.	2718.	2770.	28.18	2863.	2904.	2943.
2	103.3	105.9	108.2	110.4	112.3	114.2	115.9	117.4	118.9
3	37.34	38.20	38.98	39.69	40.35	40.97	41.54	42.07	42.58
4	22.87	23.36	23.81	24.21	24.59	24.94	25.27	25.58	25.87
5	17.18	17.53	17.85	18.13	18.41	18.66	18.89	19.10	19.31
6	14.27	14.54	14.79	15.01	15.22	15.42	15.60	15.78	15.94
7	12.52	12.74	12.95	13.14	13.32	13.48	13.64	13.78	13.92
8	11.36	11.56	11.74	11.91	12.06	12.21	12.34	12.47	12.59
9	10.55	10.73	10.89	11.03	11.08	11.30	11.42	11.54	11.64
10	9.946	10.11	10.25	10.39	10.52	10.64	10.75	10.85	10.95
11	9.482	9.630	9.766	9.892	10.01	10.12	10.22	10.31	10.41
12	9.115	9.254	9.381	9.489	9.606	9.707	9.802	9.891	9.975
13	8.817	8.948	9.068	9.178	9.281	9.376	9.466	9.550	9.629
14	8.571	8.696	8.809	8.914	9.012	9.103	9.188	9.267	9.343
15	8.365	8.483	8.592	8.693	8.786	8.872	8.954	9.030	9.102
16	8.189	8.303	8.407	8.504	8.593	8.676	8.755	8.828	8.897
17	8.037	8.148	8.248	8.342	8.427	8.508	8.583	8.654	8.720
18	7.906	8.012	8.110	8.199	8.283	8.361	8.434	8.502	8.567
19	7.790	7.893	7.988	8.075	8.156	8.232	8.303	8.369	8.432
20	7.688	7.788	7.880	7.966	8.044	8.118	8.186	8.251	8.312
30	7.077	7.162	7.239	7.310	7.375	7.437	7.494	7.548	7.599
40	6.796	6.872	6.942	7.007	7.067	7.122	7.174	7.223	7.269
50	6.762	6.735	6.802	6.864	6.871	6.973	7.023	7.069	7.113
60	6.528	6.598	6.661	6.720	6.774	6.824	6.871	6.914	6.965
∞	6.036	6.092	6.144	6.191	6.234	6.274	6.312	6.347	6.380

Table B.9 Critical values of Kruskal-Wallis H statistics*

n_1	n_2	n_3	n_4	n_5	$\alpha(2)$ 0.10	0.05	0.02	0.01	0.005	0.002	0.001
2	2	2			4.571						
3	2	1			4.286						
3	2	2			4.500	4.714					
3	3	1			4.571	5.143					
3	3	2			4.556	5.361	6.250				
3	3	3			4.622	5.600	6.489	(7.200)	7.200		
4	2	1			4.500						
4	2	2			4.458	5.333	6.000				
4	3	1			4.056	5.208					
4	3	2			4.511	5.444	6.144	6.444	7.000		
4	3	3			4.709	5.791	6.564	6.745	7.318	8.018	
4	4	1			4.167	4.967	(6.667)	6.667			
4	4	2			4.555	5.455	6.600	7.036	7.282	7.855	
4	4	3			4.545	5.598	6.712	7.144	7.598	8.227	8.909
4	4	4			4.654	5.692	6.962	7.654	8.000	8.654	9.269
5	2	1			4.200	5.000					
5	2	2			4.373	5.160	6.000	6.533			
5	3	1			4.018	4.960	6.044				
5	3	2			4.651	5.251	6.124	6.909	7.182		
5	3	3			4.533	5.648	6.533	7.079	7.636	8.048	8.727
5	4	1			3.987	4.985	6.431	6.955	7.364		
5	4	2			4.541	5.273	6.505	7.205	7.573	8.114	8.591
5	4	3			4.549	5.656	6.676	7.445	7.927	8.481	8.795
5	4	4			4.619	5.657	6.953	7.760	8.189	8.868	9.168
5	5	1			4.109	5.127	6.145	7.309	8.182		
5	5	2			4.623	5.338	6.446	7.338	8.131	6.446	7.338
5	5	3			4.545	5.705	6.866	7.578	8.316	8.809	9.521
5	5	4			4.523	5.666	7.000	7.823	8.523	9.163	9.606
5	5	5			4.940	5.780	7.220	8.000	8.780	9.620	9.920
6	1	1			------						
6	2	1			4.200	4.822					
6	2	2			4.545	5.345	6.182	6.982			
6	3	1			3.909	4.855	6.236				
6	3	2			4.682	5.348	6.227	6.970	7.515	8.182	
6	3	3			4.538	5.615	6.590	7.410	7.872	8.628	9.346
6	4	1			4.038	4.947	6.174	7.106	7.614		
6	4	2			4.494	5.340	6.571	7.340	7.846	8.494	8.827
6	4	3			4.604	5.610	6.725	7.500	8.033	8.918	9.170
6	4	4			4.595	5.681	6.900	7.795	8.381	9.167	9.861
6	5	1			4.128	4.990	6.138	7.182	8.077	8.515	

*To find a value of H, find the numbers of observations in each of the groups of dependent variable values in the leftmost column. It does not matter which group is considered group 1, etc.. Where this row and column intersect is the value of H that is expected to occur in α of the samples when there are differences between the groups in the population.

Table B.9 *Continued*

n₁	n₂	n₃	n₄	n₅	0.10	0.05	0.02	0.01	0.005	0.002	0.001
				α(2)							
6	5	2			4.596	5.338	6.585	7.376	8.196	8.967	9.189
6	5	3			4.535	5.602	6.829	7.590	8.314	9.150	9.669
6	5	4			4.522	5.661	7.018	7.936	8.643	9.458	9.960
6	5	5			4.547	5.729	7.110	8.028	8.859	9.771	10.271
6	6	1			4.000	4.945	6.286	7.121	8.165	9.077	9.692
6	6	2			4.438	5.410	6.667	7.467	8.210	9.219	9.752
6	6	3			4.558	5.625	6.900	7.725	8.458	9.458	10.150
6	6	4			4.548	5.724	7.107	8.000	8.754	9.662	10.342
6	6	5			4.542	5.765	7.152	8.124	8.987	9.948	10.524
6	6	6			4.643	5.801	7.240	8.222	9.170	10.187	10.889
7	7	7			4.594	5.819	7.332	8.378	9.373	10.516	11.310
8	8	8			4.595	5.805	7.355	8.465	9.495	10.805	11.705
2	2	1	1		-----						
2	2	2	1		5.357	5.679					
2	2	2	2		5.667	6.167	(6.667)	6.667			
3	1	1	1		-----						
3	2	1	1		5.143						
3	2	2	1		5.556	5.833	6.500				
3	2	2	2		5.644	6.333	6.978	7.133	7.533		
3	3	1	1		5.333	6.333					
3	3	2	1		5.689	6.244	6.689	7.200	7.400		
3	3	2	2		5.745	6.527	7.182	7.636	7.873	8.018	8.455
3	3	3	1		5.655	6.600	7.109	7.400	8.055	8.345	
3	3	3	2		5.879	6.727	7.636	8.105	8.379	8.803	9.030
3	3	3	3		6.026	7.000	7.872	8.538	8.897	9.462	9.513
4	1	1	1		-----						
4	2	1	1		5.250	5.833					
4	2	2	1		5.533	6.133	6.667	7.000			
4	2	2	2		5.755	6.545	7.091	7.391	7.964	8.291	
4	3	1	1		5.067	6.178	6.711	7.067			
4	3	2	1		5.591	6.309	7.018	7.455	7.773	8.182	
4	3	2	2		5.750	6.621	7.530	7.871	8.273	8.689	8.909
4	3	3	1		5.689	6.545	7.485	7.758	8.212	8.697	9.182
4	3	3	2		5.872	6.795	7.763	8.333	8.718	9.167	8.455
4	3	3	3		6.016	6.984	7.995	8.659	9.253	9.709	10.016
4	4	1	1		5.182	5.945	7.091	7.909	7.909		
4	4	2	1		5.568	6.386	7.364	7.886	8.341	8.591	8.909
4	4	2	2		5.808	6.731	7.750	8.346	8.692	9.269	9.462
4	4	3	1		5.692	6.635	7.660	8.231	8.583	9.038	9.327
4	4	3	2		5.901	6.874	7.951	8.621	9.165	9.615	9.945

Table B.9 *Continued*

n_1	n_2	n_3	n_4	n_5	0.10	0.05	0.02	0.01	0.005	0.002	0.001
				$\alpha(2)$							
4	4	3	3		6.019	7.038	8.181	8.876	9.495	10.105	10.467
4	4	4	1		5.564	6.725	7.879	8.588	9.000	9.478	9.758
4	4	4	2		5.914	6.957	8.157	8.871	9.486	10.043	10.429
4	4	4	3		6.042	7.142	8.350	9.075	9.742	10.542	10.929
4	4	4	4		6.088	7.235	8.515	9.287	9.971	10.809	11.338
2	1	1	1	1	-----						
2	2	1	1	1	5.786						
2	2	2	1	1	6.250	6.750					
2	2	2	2	1	6.600	7.133	(7.533)	7.533			
2	2	2	2	2	6.982	7.418	8.073	8.291	(8.727)	8.727	
3	1	1	1	1	-----						
3	2	1	1	1	6.139	6.583					
3	2	2	1	1	6.511	6.800	7.400	7.600			
3	2	2	2	1	6.709	7.309	7.836	8.127	8.327	8.618	
3	2	2	2	2	6.955	7.682	8.303	8.682	8.985	9.273	9.364
3	3	1	1	1	6.311	7.111	7.467				
3	3	2	1	1	6.600	7.200	7.892	8.073	8.345		
3	3	2	2	1	6.788	7.591	8.258	8.576	8.924	9.167	9.303
3	3	2	2	2	7.026	7.910	8.667	9.115	9.474	9.769	10.026
3	3	3	1	1	6.788	7.576	8.242	8.424	8.848	(9.455)	9.455
3	3	3	2	1	6.910	7.769	8.590	9.051	9.410	9.769	9.974
3	3	3	2	2	7.121	8.044	9.011	9.505	9.890	10.330	10.637
3	3	3	3	1	7.077	8.000	8.879	9.451	9.846	10.286	10.549
3	3	3	3	2	7.210	8.200	9.267	9.876	10.333	10.838	11.171
3	3	3	3	3	7.333	8.333	9.467	10.200	10.733	10.267	11.667

Table B.10 Critical values of Dunn's Q statistics*

$\alpha(2)$	0.50	0.20	0.10	0.05	0.02	0.01	0.005	0.002	0.001
k									
2	0.674	1.282	1.645	1.960	2.327	2.576	2.807	3.091	3.291
3	1.383	1.834	2.128	2.394	2.713	2.936	3.144	3.403	3.588
4	1.732	2.128	2.394	2.639	2.936	3.144	3.342	3.588	3.765
5	1.960	2.327	2.576	2.807	3.091	3.291	3.481	3.719	3.891
6	2.128	2.475	2.713	2.936	3.209	3.403	3.588	3.820	3.988
7	2.261	2.593	2.823	3.038	3.304	3.494	3.675	3.902	4.067
8	2.369	2.690	2.914	3.124	3.384	3.570	3.748	3.972	4.134
9	2.461	2.773	2.992	3.197	3.453	3.635	3.810	4.031	4.191
10	2.540	2.845	3.059	3.261	3.512	3.692	3.865	4.083	4.241
11	2.609	2.908	3.119	3.317	3.565	3.743	3.914	4.129	4.286
12	2.671	2.965	3.172	3.368	3.613	3.789	3.957	4.171	4.326
13	2.726	3.016	3.220	3.414	3.656	3.830	3.997	4.209	4.363
14	2.777	3.062	3.264	3.456	3.695	3.868	4.034	4.244	4.397
15	2.823	3.105	3.304	3.494	3.731	3.902	4.067	4.276	4.428
16	2.866	3.144	3.342	3.529	3.765	3.935	4.098	4.305	4.456
17	2.905	3.181	3.376	3.562	3.796	3.965	4.127	4.333	4.483
18	2.942	3.215	3.409	3.593	3.825	3.993	4.154	4.359	4.508
19	2.976	3.246	3.439	3.622	3.852	4.019	4.179	4.383	4.532
20	3.008	3.276	3.467	3.649	3.878	4.044	4.203	4.406	4.554
21	3.038	3.304	3.494	3.675	3.902	4.067	4.226	4.428	4.575
22	3.067	3.331	3.519	3.699	3.925	4.089	4.247	4.448	4.595
23	3.094	3.356	3.543	3.722	3.947	4.110	4.268	4.468	4.614
24	3.120	3.380	3.566	3.744	3.968	4.130	4.287	4.486	4.632
25	3.144	3.403	3.588	3.765	3.988	4.149	4.305	4.504	4.649

*To find a value of Q, find the number of means of ranks in the comparison interval in the leftmost column, then locate the desired α value in the top row of the table. Where this column and row intersect is the value of Q that is expected to occur in α of the samples from a population in which there is no association between the groups.

Table B.11 Ranks associated with the limits of a confidence interval for the median.*

	90% Interval		95% Interval		99% Interval	
n	Lower	Upper	Lower	Upper	Lower	Upper
7	1	7	-	-	-	-
8	1	8	1	8	-	-
9	2	8	1	9	-	-
10	2	9	1	10	-	-
11	2	10	2	10	1	11
12	3	10	2	11	1	12
13	3	11	2	12	1	13
14	3	12	3	12	2	13
15	4	12	3	13	2	14
16	4	13	4	13	2	15
17	5	13	4	14	3	15
18	5	14	4	15	3	16
19	5	15	5	15	3	17
20	6	15	5	16	4	17
21	6	16	6	16	4	18
22	7	16	6	17	4	19
23	7	17	6	18	5	19
24	7	18	7	18	5	20
25	8	18	7	19	6	20
26	8	19	8	19	6	21
27	9	19	8	20	6	22
28	9	20	8	21	7	22
29	10	20	9	21	7	23
30	10	21	9	22	7	24
31	10	22	10	22	8	24
32	11	22	10	23	8	25
33	11	23	10	24	9	25
34	12	23	11	24	9	26
35	12	24	11	25	9	27
36	13	24	12	25	10	27
37	13	25	12	26	10	28
38	13	26	12	27	11	28
39	14	26	13	27	11	29
40	14	27	13	28	11	30

*To determine a confidence interval for a median, rank the data according to numeric magnitude. Then, locate the sample's size in the left-most column and the level of confidence in the top row. Where those two intersect, you will find the ranks of the data that correspond to the lower and upper limits of the confidence interval.

APPENDIX C
Standard Distributions

Standard distributions are used to take chance into account for estimation of parameters of distributions of continuous and nominal dependent variables. These standard distributions belong to two families: the Gaussian family and the binomial family.

Gaussian Family

The distributions of the Gaussian family are derived from the standard normal (z) distribution. Other members of the family arise from the addition of parameters to the standard normal distribution. There are two parameters that are called degrees of freedom. The first (df_1) represents the amount of information the sample contains to estimate the variance. The second (df_2) represents the number of independent variables. Another parameter (k) represents the number of means involved in a hypothesis test. Three of the distributions are symmetric around zero (z, t, and q) and two are asymmetric with zero as the lower limit of possible values (F and χ^2). Standard distributions in the Gaussian family are used either for continuous dependent variables or for nominal dependent variables when a normal approximation is used to take chance into account. The distributions to the right of the broken line are for continuous dependent variables and the distributions to the left of the broken line are for nominal dependent variables.

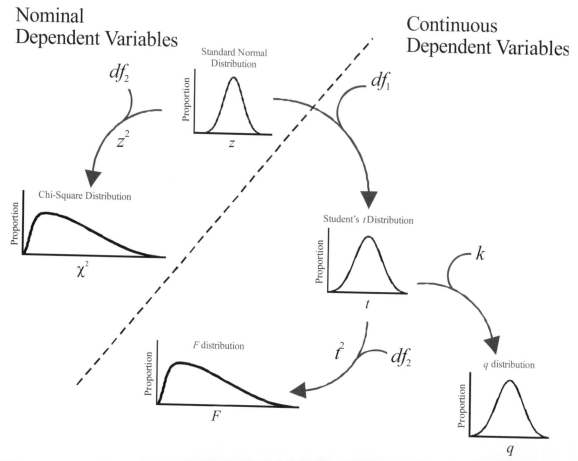

Binomial Family

The distributions of the binomial family are discrete distributions derived from the binomial distribution. These are the sampling distributions we used when we are conducting exact tests or calculating exact confidence intervals for a nominal dependent variable. We encountered three members of this family. The binomial and Poisson distributions are for univariable samples and the hypergeometric distribution is for a bivariable sample. The Poisson distribution represents what happens to the binomial distribution as the number of events (a) approaches zero and the number of observations (n) approaches infinity. The parameter of the Poisson distribution is equal to the number of events. The hypergeometric represents two binomial distributions combined. The parameter of the hypergeometric distribution is any value that describes a 2×2 table with a given set of marginal frequencies.

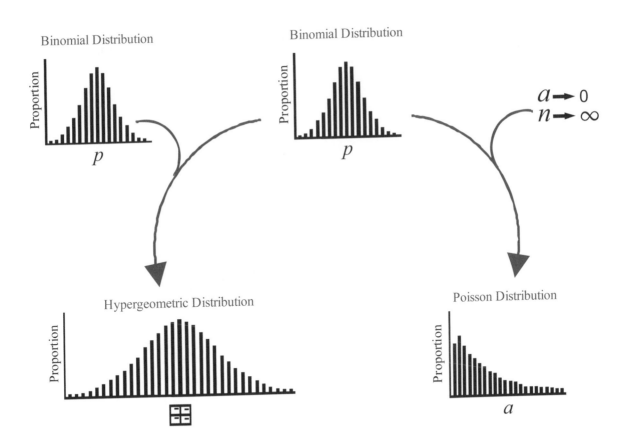

Index